Beginning JSP, JSF and Tomcat

Java Web Development

D0890724

Giulio Zambon

Apress®

Beginning JSP, JSF and Tomcat

ISBN-13 (pbk): 978-1-4302-4623-7

ISBN-13 (electronic): 978-1-4302-4624-4

President and Publisher: Paul Manning
Lead Editor: Steve Anglin
Developmental Editor: Douglas Pundick, Ralph Moore
Technical Reviewer: Boris Minkin, Manuel Joran Elera
Editorial Board: Steve Anglin, Ewan Buckingham, Gary Cornell, Louise Corrigan, Morgan Ertel, Jonathan Gennick, Jonathan Hassell, Robert Hutchinson, Michelle Lowman, James Markham, Matthew Moodie, Jeff Olson, Jeffrey Pepper, Douglas Pundick, Ben Renow-Clarke, Dominic Shakeshaft, Gwenan Spearing, Matt Wade, Tom Welsh
Coordinating Editors: Katie Sullivan
Copy Editor: Michael Sandlin
Compositor: Bytheway Publishing Services
Indexer: SPi Global
Artist: SPi Global
Cover Designer: Anna Ishchenko

Distributed to the book trade worldwide by Springer Science+Business Media New York, 233 Spring Street, 6th Floor, New York, NY 10013. Phone 1-800-SPRINGER, fax (201) 348-4505, e-mail orders-ny@springer-sbm.com, or visit www.springeronline.com.

For information on translations, please e-mail rights@apress.com, or visit www.apress.com.

Apress and friends of ED books may be purchased in bulk for academic, corporate, or promotional use. eBook versions and licenses are also available for most titles. For more information, reference our Special Bulk Sales–eBook Licensing web page at www.apress.com/bulk-sales.

Any source code or other supplementary materials referenced by the author in this text is available to readers at www.apress.com. For detailed information about how to locate your book's source code, go to www.apress.com/source-code.

Contents at a Glance

Contents

About the Author

Giulio Zambon's first love was physics, but he decided to dedicate himself to software development more than 30 years ago: back when computers were still made of transistors and core memories, programs were punched on cards, and Fortran only had arithmetic IFs. Over the years, he learned a dozen computer languages and worked with all sorts of operating systems. His specific interests were in telecom and real-time systems, and he managed several projects to their successful completion.

In 2001 Giulio founded his own company offering computer telephony integration (CTI) services, and he used JSP and Tomcat exclusively to develop the web side of the service platform. Back in Australia after many years in Europe, he now dedicates himself to writing software to generate and solve numeric puzzles. His web site, http://zambon.com.au/, is written in JSP on his dedicated server, which, unsurprisingly, runs Tomcat!

About the Technical Reviewers

Boris Minkin is a senior technical architect at a major financial corporation. He has more than 20 years of experience working in various areas of information technology and financial services. Boris obtained his master's degree in information systems at Stevens Institute of Technology, New Jersey. His professional interests are in Internet technology, service-oriented architecture, enterprise application architecture, multi-platform distributed applications, cloud, distributed caching, Java, grid, and high performance computing. You can contact Boris at bm@panix.com.

Manuel Jordan Elera is an autodidactic developer and researcher who enjoys learning new technologies for his own experiments and creating new integrations. Manuel won the 2010 Springy Award-Community Champion. In his limited free time, he reads the Bible and composes music on his guitar. Manuel is a senior member in the Spring Community Forums known as dr_pompeii and a technical reviewer for important books about Spring Source projects, all published by Apress. Read more and contact him through his blog at http://manueljordan.wordpress.com and follow him on his Twitter account, @dr_pompei.

CHAPTER 1

Introducing JSP and Tomcat

Interactivity is what makes the Web really useful. By interacting with a remote server, you can find the information you need, keep in touch with your friends, or purchase something online. And every time you type something into a web form, an application "out there" interprets your request and prepares a web page to respond.

To understand JSP, you first need to have a clear idea of what happens when you ask your browser to view a web page, either by typing a URL into the address field of your browser or by clicking on a hyperlink. Figure 1-1 shows you how it works.

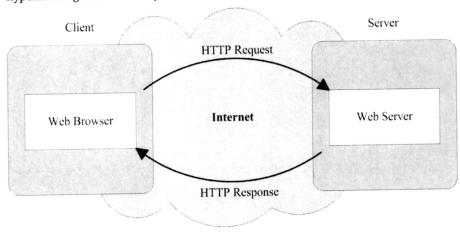

Figure 1-1. Viewing a plain HTML page

The following steps show what happens when you request your browser to view a static web page:

1. When you type an address such as `http://www.website.com/path/whatever.html` into the address field, your browser first resolves `www.website.com` (i.e., the name of the web server) into the corresponding Internet Protocol (IP) address, usually by asking the Domain Name Server provided by your Internet Service Provider (ISP). Then your browser sends an HTTP request to the newly found IP address to receive the content of the file identified by `/path/whatever.html`.

2. In reply, the web server sends an HTTP response containing a plain-text HTML page. Images and other non-textual components, such as sound and video clips, only appear in the page as references.

3. Your browser receives the response, interprets the HTML code contained in the page, requests the non-textual components from the server, and displays the lot.

JavaServer Pages (JSP) is a technology that helps you create such dynamically generated pages by converting script files into executable Java modules; JavaServer Faces (JSF) is a package that facilitates interactivity with the page viewers; and Tomcat is an application that can execute your code and act as a web server for your dynamic pages.

Everything you need to develop JSP/JSF web applications is available for free download from the Internet; but to install all the necessary packages and tools and obtain an integrated development environment, you need to proceed with care. There is nothing more annoying than having to deal with incorrectly installed software. When something doesn't work, the problem will always be difficult to find.

In this chapter, I'll introduce you to Java servlets and JSP, and I'll show you how they work together within Tomcat to generate dynamic web pages. But, first of all, I will guide you through the installation of Java and Tomcat: there wouldn't be much point in looking at code you can't execute on your PC, would there?

You'll have to install more packages as you progress. Do these installations correctly, and you will never need to second guess yourself. In total, you will need at least 300MB of disk space for Java and Tomcat alone and twice as much space to install the Eclipse development environment.

To run all the examples contained in this book, I used a PC with a 2.6GHz AMD Athlon 64x2 (nothing fancy, nowadays) with 1GB of memory and running Windows Vista SP2. Before performing any installation, I reformatted the hard disk and re-installed the OS from the original DVD. **I don't suggest for a moment that you do the same!** I did it for two opposite but equally important reasons: first, I didn't want existing stuff to interfere with the latest packages needed for web development; second, I didn't want to rely on anything already installed. I wanted to be sure to give you the full list of what you need.

At the time of this writing, the latest versions of all the packages you will need to install are:

Java: 1.7.0 update 3 (installation explained in this chapter)
Tomcat web server: 7.0.26 (installation also explained in this chapter)
Eclipse development environment: Indigo 3.7.2 (installation explained in Chapter 2)
MySQL database: 5.5.21.0 (installation explained in Chapter 6)
MySQL Java database connector (JDBC): 5.1.18 (installation also explained in Chapter 6)
JavaServer Faces: 2.1.7 (installation explained in Chapter 7)

I included Eclipse on the list because an integrated development environment is extremely useful for developing software. And MySQL is listed because any non-trivial web application is likely to need handling data.

Of course, after this book is published, there will most likely be newer releases of all the aforementioned packages. Nevertheless, you should be able to adapt my instructions to install the latest versions without any problem.

One last recommendation: to be sure that everything will work correctly, please follow the installation instructions to the letter. It will save you endless headaches.

'Nuff said. Here we go.

Installing Java

Nothing runs without Java, and you need two different Java packages: one is the runtime environment (JRE), which lets you execute Java, and the other is the Java Development Kit (JDK), which lets you compile Java sources into executable classes.

They are downloadable together from Oracle's web site. Here's what you need to do:

1. Go to the URL http://www.oracle.com/technetwork/java/javase/downloads /index.html.

2. Click on the big button marked "Java Download" (the latest version at the time of writing is 7u3). This will take you to the page "Java SE Development Kit 7 Downloads."

3. Select "Accept License Agreement" and then click on the link jdk-7u3-windows-i586.exe.

    The actual link might refer to a version other than "7u3," but you need to download either "Windows x86 (32-bit)" or "Windows x64 (64-bit)," according to type of processor of your PC. Although I am using a 64-bit PC, I have tested all the examples in this book with 32-bit packages because I didn't want to test everything twice.

4. Execute the file.

5. Accept the license agreement when requested and install everything.

At this point, you should have the folder C:\Program Files\Java\ with two subfolders: jdk1.7.0_03 and jre7, or the equivalent folders for the version you have downloaded.

In order to be able to compile Java from the command line, you need to add the JDK path to the PATH environment variable. From the Windows Start menu, select Settings ➤ Control Panel ➤ System. When the System Properties dialog opens, click on the "Advanced system settings" link that you find on the left-hand side and then on the Advanced tab. Finally, to reach the dialog that lets you modify the PATH variable, click on the "Environment Variables" button. You will see the double dialog window shown in Figure 1-2.

Figure 1-2. The Environment Variables double dialog

You might see a PATH variable on the top dialog, but what you need to do is scroll the bottom dialog by clicking on its sidebar until you see a variable named Path. Double-click it (or highlight it and click the "Edit..." button) and insert at the beginning of its value the text "C:\Program Files\Java\jdk1.7.0_03\ bin;", as shown in Figure 1-3.

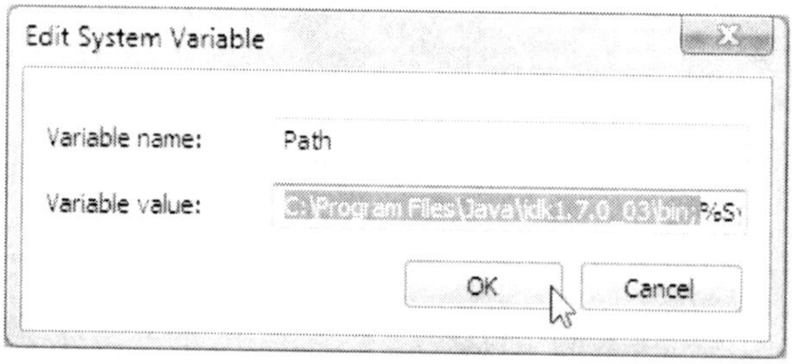

Figure 1-3. Update the Path variable

The semicolon at the end of the text is essential because it separates the new path from the existing ones. Do not insert additional spaces before or after.

Click on the "OK" button to save the changes. Then click this button another couple of times until the system dialog closes.

Java Test

To test the Java installation, you can use the little application shown in Listing 1-1.

Listing 1-1. Exec_http.java

```java
/* Exec_http.java - Launches a web page
 *
 * Usage: Exec_http URL [arg1 [arg2 [...]]]
 * where URL is without "http://"
 *
 */
import java.io.*;
import java.net.*;
class Exec_http {
  public static void main(String[] vargs)
      throws java.net.MalformedURLException ,java.io.IOException
      {
    String  dest = "http://";

    if (vargs.length <= 0) {
      System.out.println("Usage: Exec_http page [args]");
      System.exit(1);
      }
    else {
      dest += vargs[0];
      for (int k = 1; k < vargs.length; k++) {
        dest += ((k == 1) ? "?" : "&") + vargs[k];
        }
      }
    System.out.println(dest);
    URL            url = new URL(dest);
    Object         obj = url.getContent();
    InputStream  resp = (InputStream)obj;
    byte[]         b = new byte[256];
    int            n = resp.read(b);
    while (n != -1) {
      System.out.print(new String(b, 0, n));
      n = resp.read(b);
      }
    }
  }
```

It lets you open a web page from the command line. Note that all the code described in this book is available for download from the Apress web site (http://www.apress.com/9781430246237). You don't need to retype it. You can find the examples in folders with the same names as the corresponding chapters. I will refer to the root directory of the software package associated with this book with the string %SW_HOME%.

Copy the file %SW_HOME%\01 Getting Started\java\Exec_http.java to a work directory. For simplicity, I use the desktop: but in my case, this makes sense because I use the computer exclusively to develop the examples used in this book.

Open a command-line window by clicking the Start button and selecting Programs ➤ Accessories ➤ Command Prompt. Then, after changing to your work directory, type "javac Exec_http.java" to compile the application. It should return the prompt without saying anything. If this happens, it means that you have correctly updated the Path system variable. If you want to know more about what the javac compiler is doing, type –verbose between javac and the name of the file.

You will see a file named Exec_http.class in your work directory.

Now, to run the application, type "java Exec_http" followed by the URL of the page you want to display. Any URL will do, but remember that the command-line accessory doesn't understand HTML. Therefore, if you display any commercial page, you will see a long stream of text filling the window.

To test the application, I placed on one of my web servers a one-line text file. Figure 1-4 shows what happened.

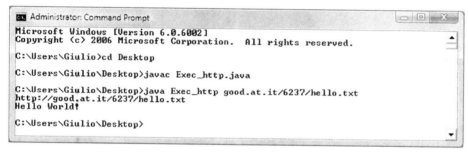

Figure 1-4. Testing Java

You are welcome to use hello.txt for your test. Hopefully, I will remember to keep it online!

Installing Tomcat

This is the Java web server, which is the servlet container that allows you to run JSP. If you have already installed an older version of Tomcat, you should remove it before installing a new version.

Tomcat listens to three communication ports of your PC (8005, 8009, and 8080). Before you install Tomcat, you should check whether some already-installed applications are listening to one or more of those ports. To do so, open a DOS window and type the command netstat /a. It will display a list of active connections in tabular form. The second column of the table will look like this:

```
Local Address
0.0.0.0:135
0.0.0.0:445
0.0.0.0:3306
```

The port numbers are the numbers after the colon. If you see one or more of the ports Tomcat uses, after installing Tomcat, you will have to change the ports it listens to, as explained in Chapter 10. There, you will also learn the purpose of those three ports.

Here's how to install Tomcat 7 correctly:

1. Go to the URL http://tomcat.apache.org/download-70.cgi. Immediately below the second heading ("Quick Navigation"), you will see four links: KEYS, 7.0.26, Browse, and Archives.

2. By clicking on 7.0.26, you will be taken toward the bottom of the same page to a heading with the same version number. Below the version heading, you will

see the subheading "Core". Below that, immediately above the next subheading, you will see three links arranged as follows: 32-bit/64-bit Windows Service Installer (pgp, md5).

3.   Click on 32-bit/64-bit Windows Service Installer to download the file apache-tomcat-7.0.26.exe (8.2 MB).

4.   Before launching the installer file, you have to check its integrity. To do so, you need a small utility to calculate its checksum. There are several freely available on the Internet. I downloaded WinMD5Free from http://www.winmd5.com/, and it worked for me, but this doesn't mean I consider it better than any other similar utility. It just happened to be the first one I saw. The program doesn't require any special installation: just unzip it and launch. When you open the Tomcat installer file, you will see a 32-digit hexadecimal number very much like this: 8ad7d25179168e74e3754391cdb24679.

5.   Go back to the page from which you downloaded the Tomcat installer and click on the md5 link (the third one, and second within the parentheses). This will open a page containing a single line of text, like this: 8ad7d25179168e74e3754391cdb24679 *apache-tomcat-7.0.26.exe

     If the hex string is identical to that calculated by the checksum utility, you know that the version of Tomcat installer you have downloaded has not been corrupted or modified in any way.

6.   Now that you have verified the correctness of the Tomcat installer, launch it.

7.   After you've agreed to the terms of the license, you will then see the dialog shown in Figure 1-5. Click on the plus sign before the Tomcat item and select "Service" and "Native" as shown in the figure before clicking on the "Next >" button.

8.   I chose to install Tomcat in the directory "C:\Program Files\Apache Software Foundation\Tomcat" instead of the default "Tomcat 7.0". This is because sometimes you might like to point to this directory (normally referred to as %CATALINA_HOME%) from within a program, and one day you might replace Tomcat 7.0 with Tomcat 8.0. By calling Tomcat's home directory "Tomcat" you are "safe" for years to come. You can also decide to leave the default. In general, by using the defaults, you are likely to encounter fewer problems, because the default settings of any applications are always tested best!

9.   Next, the Tomcat installer will ask you to specify the connector port and UserID plus password for the administrator login. Leave the port set to 8080, because all the examples in this book refer to port 8080. If you want, you can always change it later to the HTTP standard port (which is 80). As UserID/Password, you might as well use your Windows user name and password. It is not critical.

10. Lastly, you will need to provide the path of a Java Runtime Environment. This is the path you saw when installing Java (see previous section). With the version of Java I installed, the correct path is C:\Program Files\Java\jre7.

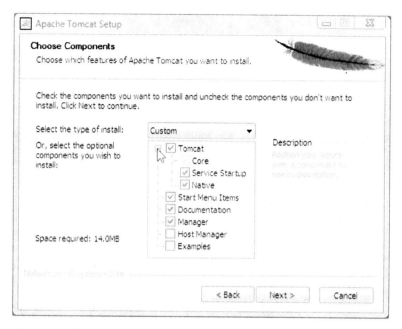

Figure 1-5. Tomcat's Service and Native settings

Tomcat runs as a Windows service. To start it and stop it, you can right-click the Apache Service Manager icon in the notification area of Windows' toolbar and select the corresponding operation. You can also achieve the same result by opening Windows' Services control panel (and right-clicking the Tomcat entry, as shown in Figure 1-6).

Figure 1-6. Stopping and starting Tomcat from the Services control panel

In any case, to go to the Services control panel, click on Windows' Start menu and select Setting ➤ Control Panel ➤ Administrative Tools ➤ Services. You will see dozens of entries, but when you reach the Tomcat services, its status should be "Started".

With Java and Tomcat in place, we can finally begin playing with JSP!

Simple Tomcat Test

To see that Tomcat is working properly, open a browser and type localhost:8080. You should see the page shown in Figure 1-7 (Firefox in the example).

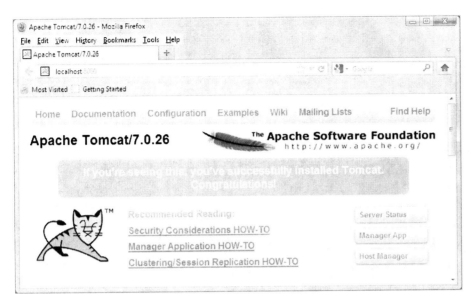

Figure 1-7. *The localhost home page*

Windows might state that it needs to block a startup program that requires permission. To solve this problem, turn off Windows' User Account Control by going into the User Accounts control panel and clicking on "Turn User Account Control on or off". This User Account Control can be a nuisance anyway, because it asked for authorization every time I worked with files in directories considered protected, including all directories in the "Program Files" folder.

At some point after rebooting, if you are running Vista, Windows' Program Compatibility Assistant might display a dialog stating that the Sun Java Scheduler, located at C:\Program Files\Common Files\Java Update\jusched.exe, is incompatible with your version of Windows. To get rid of this problem, you need to select "Run" after clicking on "Start," type in the text field "msconfig" (without double quotes), and hit Enter. Select the "Startup" tab in the dialog, find the entry for the Java updater, and remove it.

What Is JSP?

JSP is a technology that lets you add dynamic content to web pages. In absence of JSP, to update the appearance or the content of plain static HTML pages, you always have to do it by hand. Even if all you want to do is change a date or a picture, you must edit the HTML file and type in your modifications. Nobody is going to do it for you, whereas with JSP, you can make the content dependent on many factors, including the time of the day, the information provided by the user, the user's history of interaction with your web site, and even the user's browser type. This capability is essential to provide online services in which you can tailor each response to the viewer who made the request, depending on the viewer's preferences and requirements. A crucial aspect of providing meaningful online services is for the system to be able to *remember* data associated with the service and its users. That's why databases play an essential role in dynamic web pages. But let's take it one step at a time.

HISTORY

Sun Microsystems introduced JSP in 1999. Developers quickly realized that additional tags would be useful, and the JSP Standard Tag Library (JSTL) was born. JSTL is a collection of custom tag libraries that encapsulates the functionality of many JSP standard applications, thereby eliminating repetitions and making the applications more compact. Together with JSTL also came the JSP Expression Language (EL).

In 2003, with the introduction of JSP 2.0, EL was incorporated into the JSP specification, making it available for custom components and template text, not just for JSTL, as was the case in the previous versions. Additionally, JSP 2.0 made it possible to create custom tag files, thereby perfecting the extendibility of the language.

In parallel to the evolution of JSP, several frameworks to develop web applications became available. In 2004, one of them, JavaServer Faces (JSF), focused on building user interfaces (UIs) and used JSP by default as the underlying scripting language. It provided an API, JSP custom tag libraries, and an expression language.

The Java Community Process (JCP), formed in 1998, released in May 2006 the Java Specification Request (JSR) 245 titled *JavaServer Pages 2.1*, which effectively aligned JSP and JSF technologies. In particular, JSP 2.1 included a Unified EL (UEL) that merged the two versions of EL defined in JSP 2.0 and JSF 1.2 (itself specified as JSR 252). Sun Microsystems includes JSP 2.1 in its Java Platform, Enterprise Edition 5 (Java EE 5), finalized in May 2006 as JSR 244.

The latest version of Java is 7 (specified in JSR 342 and released in July 2011). It includes JSP 2.2, Servlets 3.1 (JSR 340), EL 3.0 (JSR 341), and JSF 2.2 (JSR 344). Version 8 is expected in mid-2013. At the time of this writing, Java 7 is only available as part of the JSE (Java Standard Edition) platform. The latest version of Java released in the JEE (Java Enterprise Edition) platform is 6 (update 32).

The latest version of Tomcat (7.0), supports Servlets 3.0 and JSF 2.1.7.

Viewing a JSP Page

With JSP, the web page doesn't actually exist on the server. As you can see in Figure 1-8, the server creates it fresh when responding to each request.

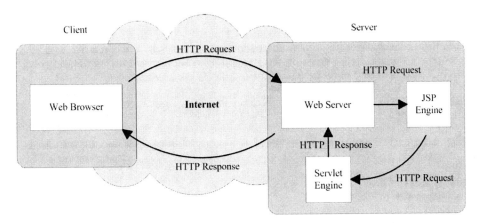

Figure 1-8. Viewing a JSP page

The following steps explain how the web server creates the web page:

1. As with a normal page, your browser sends an HTTP request to the web server. This doesn't change with JSP, although the URL probably ends in `.jsp` instead of `.html` or `.htm`.

2. The web server is not a normal server, but rather a Java server, with the extensions necessary to identify and handle Java servlets. The web server recognizes that the HTTP request is for a JSP page and forwards it to a JSP engine.

3. The JSP engine loads the JSP page from disk and converts it into a Java servlet. From this point on, this servlet is indistinguishable from any other servlet developed directly in Java rather than JSP, although the automatically generated Java code of a JSP servlet is not always easy to read, and you should never modify it by hand.

4. The JSP engine compiles the servlet into an executable class and forwards the original request to another part of the web server called the *servlet engine.* Note that the JSP engine only converts the JSP page to Java and recompiles the servlet if it finds that the JSP page has changed since the last request. This makes the process more efficient than with other scripting languages (such as PHP) and therefore faster.

5. The servlet engine loads the servlet class and executes it. During execution, the servlet produces an output in HTML format, which the servlet engine passes to the web server inside an HTTP response.

6. The web server forwards the HTTP response to your browser.

7. Your web browser handles the dynamically generated HTML page inside the HTTP response exactly as if it were a static page. In fact, static and dynamic web pages are in the same format.

You might ask, "Why do you say that with JSP, the page is created fresh for each request, if the server only converts and compiles the JSP source if you have updated it since the previous request?"

What reaches your browser is the output generated by the servlet (that is, by the converted and compiled JSP page), not the JSP page itself. The same servlet produces different outputs depending on the parameters of the HTTP request and other factors. For example, suppose you're browsing the products offered by an online shop. When you click on the image of a product, your browser generates an HTTP request with the product code as a parameter. As a result, the servlet generates an HTML page with the description of that product. The server doesn't need to recompile the servlet for each product code.

The servlet queries a database containing the details of all the products, obtains the description of the product you're interested in, and formats an HTML page with that data. This is what dynamic HTML is all about!

Plain HTML is not capable of interrogating a database, but Java is, and JSP gives you the means of including snippets of Java inside an HTML page.

Hello World!

A small example of JSP will give you a more practical idea of how JSP works. Let's start once more from HTML. Listing 1-2 shows you a plain HTML page to display "Hello World!" in your browser's window.

Listing 1-2. hello.html

```
<html>
<head><title>Hello World static HTML</title></head>
<body>
Hello World!
</body>
</html>
```

Create the folder %CATALINA_HOME%\webapps\ROOT\tests\ and store in it hello.html. Then type the following URL in your browser to see the web page:

```
http://localhost:8080/tests/hello.html
```

Normally, to ask your browser to check that the syntax of the page conforms to the XHTML standard of the World Wide Web Consortium (W3C), you would have to start the page with the following lines:

```
<?xml version="1.0" encoding="UTF-8"?>
<!DOCTYPE html PUBLIC "-//W3C//DTD XHTML 1.0 Strict//EN"
  "http://www.w3.org/TR/xhtml1/DTD/xhtml1-strict.dtd">
```

You'd also have to replace

```
<html>
```

with

```
<html xmlns="http://www.w3.org/1999/xhtml">
```

However, for this simple example, I prefer to keep the code to what's essential. Figure 1-9 shows you how this page will appear in your browser.

Figure 1-9. "Hello World!" in plain HTML

If you direct your browser to show the page source, not surprisingly, you'll see exactly what's shown in Listing 1-2. To obtain the same result with a JSP page, you only need to insert a JSP directive before the first line, as shown in Listing 1-3, and change the file extension from .html to .jsp.

Listing 1-3. "Hello World!" in a Boring JSP Page

```
<%@page language="java" contentType="text/html"%>
<html>
<head><title>Hello World not-so-dynamic HTML</title></head>
<body>
Hello World!
</body>
</html>
```

Obviously, there isn't much point in using JSP for such a simple page. It only pays to use JSP if you include dynamic content. Check out Listing 1-4 for something more juicy.

Listing 1-4. hello.jsp

```
<%@page language="java" contentType="text/html"%>
<html>
<head><title>Hello World dynamic HTML</title></head>
<body>
Hello World!
<%
  out.println("<br/>Your IP address is " + request.getRemoteAddr());

  String userAgent = request.getHeader("user-agent");
  String browser = "unknown";

  out.print("<br/>and your browser is ");
  if (userAgent != null) {
    if (userAgent.indexOf("MSIE") > -1) {
      browser = "MS Internet Explorer";
      }
    else if (userAgent.indexOf("Firefox") > -1) {
      browser = "Mozilla Firefox";
      }
    else if (userAgent.indexOf("Opera") > -1) {
      browser = "Opera";
      }
    else if (userAgent.indexOf("Chrome") > -1) {
```

```
        browser = "Google Chrome";
        }
    else if (userAgent.indexOf("Safari") > -1) {
        browser = "Apple Safari";
        }
    }
  out.println(browser);
  %>
</body>
</html>
```

As with hello.html, you can view hello.jsp by placing it in Tomcat's ROOT\tests folder.

The code within the <% ... %> pair is a scriptlet written in Java. When Tomcat's JSP engine interprets this module, it creates a Java servlet like that shown in Listing 1-5 (with some indentation and empty lines removed).

Listing 1-5. Java Code from the "Hello World!" JSP Page

```
out.write("\r\n");
out.write("<html>\r\n");
out.write("<head><title>Hello World dynamic HTML</title></head>\r\n");
out.write("<body>\r\n");
out.write("Hello World!\r\n");
out.write('\r');
out.write('\n');
out.println("<br/>Your IP address is " + request.getRemoteAddr());
String userAgent = request.getHeader("user-agent");
String browser = "unknown";
out.print("<br/>and your browser is ");
if (userAgent != null) {
  if (userAgent.indexOf("MSIE") > -1) {
    browser = "MS Internet Explorer";
    }
  else if (userAgent.indexOf("Firefox") > -1) {
    browser = "Mozilla Firefox";
    }
  else if (userAgent.indexOf("Opera") > -1) {
    browser = "Opera";
    }
  else if (userAgent.indexOf("Chrome") > -1) {
    browser = "Google Chrome";
    }
  else if (userAgent.indexOf("Safari") > -1) {
    browser = "Apple Safari";
    }
  }
out.println(browser);
out.write("\r\n");
out.write("</body>\r\n");
out.write("</html>\r\n");
```

As I said before, this servlet executes every time a browser sends a request to the server. However, before the code shown in Listing 1-5 executes, the server binds the variable out to a character stream associated with the content of the HTML response. As a result, everything written to out ends up in the HTML page that you'll see in your browser. As you can see, Tomcat copies the scriptlet in your JSP file into the servlet, and sends everything outside the scriptlet directly to the output. This should clarify how HTML and Java work together in a JSP page.

As the variable out is defined in each servlet, you can use it within any JSP module to insert something into the response (more on variables in Chapter 2).

Another such "global" JSP variable is request (of type HttpServletRequest). The request contains the IP address from which the request was originated—that is, of the remote computer with the browser (remember that this code runs on the server). To extract the address from the request, you only need to execute its method getRemoteAddr(). The request also contains information about the browser. When some browsers send a request, they provide somewhat misleading information, and the format is complex. However, the code in Listing 1-4 shows you how to recognize the most widely used browsers.

If you add to your JSP the line

```
out.println("<br/>" + userAgent);
```

You will see what information is contained in the request. It also tells you whether the browser is running on a Windows system or a Mac.

Figure 1-10 shows the generated page as it appears in a browser.

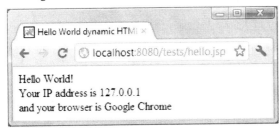

Figure 1-10. *"Hello World!" in JSP with Google Chrome*

Notice that the IP address 127.0.0.1 is consistent with the host localhost. And just in case you want to see that the HTML is indeed dynamic, check out Figure 1-11. Incidentally, the method you use in hello.jsp to identify Internet Explorer is the official one provided by Microsoft.

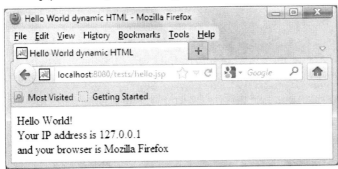

Figure 1-11. *"Hello World!" in JSP with Mozilla Firefox*

Listing the HTML-Request Parameters

With JSP you can generate dynamic web pages. That's settled. But the utility of dynamic pages goes well beyond recognizing what browser the viewer is using or displaying different information on different days. What really matters is to be able to adapt the content of a web page on the basis of who the viewer is and what the viewer wants.

Each HTML request includes a series of parameters, which are usually the results of what the viewer enters into a form before hitting the "Submit" button. Additional parameters can also be part of the URL itself. For example, pages in multilingual websites sometimes have URLs ending with "?lang=en" to tell the server that it should format the requested page in English.

Listing 1-6 shows a simple JSP page that lists all the HTML-request parameters. It is a useful little tool you can use to easily check what your HTML pages actually send to the server.

Listing 1-6. req_params.jsp

```
<%@page language="java" contentType="text/html"%>
<%@page import="java.util.*, java.io.*"%>
<%
  Map       map = request.getParameterMap();
  Object[] keys = map.keySet().toArray();
  %>
<html><head><title>Request Parameters</title></head><body>
  Map size = <%=map.size()%>
  <table border="1">
    <tr><td>Map element</td><td>Par name</td><td>Par value[s]</td></tr>
<%
    for (int k = 0; k < keys.length; k++) {
      String[] pars = request.getParameterValues((String)keys[k]);
      out.print("<tr><td>" + k + "</td><td>'" + keys[k] + "'</td><td>");
      for (int j = 0; j < pars.length; j++) {
        if (j > 0) out.print(", ");
        out.print("'" + pars[j] + "'");
        }
      out.println("</td></tr>");
      }
  %>
  </table>
</body></html>
```

The interesting bits are in the lines I have highlighted in bold. The first one tells you that the parameters are stored in an object of type Map and shows you how to retrieve the list of the parameter names.

The second highlighted line shows you how to insert the value of a Java variable directly into the output (i.e., into the HTML page), by enclosing it between the pair <%= and %>. This is a different from using a scriptlet—in which you can use JSP to build dynamicity into a web page.

The third highlighted line shows how to request the values of each parameter you know the name of. I said "values" instead of "value" because each parameter can appear more than once within the same request. For example, if you view the URL

```
http://localhost:8080/tests/req_params.jsp?a=b&c=d&a=zzz&empty=&empty=&1=22
```

you get what you see in Figure 1-12.

You could have used getParameterNames instead of getParameterMap. To do so, you would have replaced

```
Object[] keys = map.keySet().toArray();
```

with

```
Enumeration enumPar = request.getParameterNames();
```

You would have also changed the loop to get through all parameters, from

```
for (int k = 0; k < keys.length; k++) {
```

to

```
while (enumPar.hasMoreElements()) {
```

And finally, to get the parameter names one by one, you would have used enumPar.nextElement() instead of (String)keys[k]. It wouldn't have made any difference in the example, but with a map, you get the parameter names in alphabetical order, while with the other method, you wouldn't.

Furthermore, a Map object comes with some useful methods. For example, containsValue lets you check whether the map contains a given value.

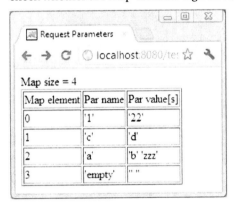

Figure 1-12. Output of req_params.jsp

Notice that the parameter aptly named empty appears twice in the query string, which results in two empty strings in the parameter map. Also, looking at the parameter a, you'll notice that the values are returned in the same order in which they appear in the query string.

Summary

In this chapter, you learned how to install Java and Tomcat and how to check that they work correctly.

After explaining what happens on the server when you click a link in your browser to view a new page, I introduced servlet and JSP technologies and explained what role they play in a web server.

Then, I showed you a simple HTML page and how you can begin to add dynamic content to it with JSP.

Finally, you learned how to use JSP to display the HTTP-request parameters.

Perhaps this was not the most exciting chapter, but you now have in place a basic development and run environment, without which you wouldn't be able to proceed. And you have had your first taste of JSP.

In the next chapter, you'll learn more about JavaServer pages and how you can best structure web applications.

CHAPTER 2

■ ■ ■

JSP Elements

A JSP page is made out of a page template, which consists of HTML code and JSP elements such as *scripting* elements, *directive* elements, and *action* elements. In the previous chapter, after explaining how to install Java and Tomcat, I introduced you to JSP and explained JSP's role within web applications. In this chapter, I'll describe in detail the first two types of JSP elements. For the action elements, refer to Chapter 4.

Introduction

Scripting elements consist of code delimited by particular sequences of characters. The scriptlets, which you encountered in the examples in Chapter 1 and delimited by the pair `<%` and `%>`, are one of the three possible types of scripting elements. The other two are declarations and expressions.

All scripting elements are Java fragments capable of manipulating Java objects, invoking their methods and catching Java exceptions. They can send data to the output, and they execute when the page is requested.

In the `hello.jsp` example of Chapter 1 (Listing 1-4), you saw that `request.getHeader("user-agent")` returns a string that describes the client's web browser, despite the fact that the variable `request` wasn't defined anywhere. It worked because Tomcat defines several *implicit objects*: `application`, `config`, `exception`, `out`, `pageContext`, `request`, `response`, and `session`.

Directive elements are messages to the JSP container (i.e., Tomcat). Their purpose is to provide information on the page itself necessary for its translation. As they have no association with each individual request, directive elements do not output any text to the HTML response.

The first line of the `hello.jsp` example was a directive:

```
<%@page language="java" contentType="text/html"%>
```

Besides page, the other directives available in JSP pages are `include` and `taglib`.

Action elements specify activities that, like the scripting elements, need to be performed when the page is requested, because their purpose is precisely to encapsulate activities that Tomcat performs when handling an HTTP request from a client. Action elements can use, modify, and/or create objects, and they may affect the way data is sent to the output. There are more than a dozen standard actions: `attribute`, `body`, `element`, `fallback`, `forward`, `getProperty`, `include`, `param`, `params`, `plugin`, `setProperty`, `text`, and `useBean`. For example, the following action element includes in a JSP page the output of another page:

```
<jsp:include page="another.jsp"/>
```

In addition to the standard action elements, JSP also provides a mechanism that lets you define custom actions, in which a prefix of your choice replaces the prefix `jsp` of the standard actions. The *tag extension mechanism* lets you create libraries of custom actions, which you can then use in all your applications. Several custom actions became so popular within the programming community that Sun Microsystems (now Oracle) decided to standardize them. The result is JSTL, the JSP Standard Tag Library.

The *Expression Language* (EL) is an additional JSP component that provides easy access to external objects (i.e., Java beans). EL was introduced in JSP 2.0 as an alternative to the scripting elements, but you can also use EL and scripting elements together. I will describe EL in Chapter 4, after explaining the action elements.

In the next sections, I will first go through the scripting elements, because they are easier to understand and you can use them to glue together the rest. Then, I will describe the implicit objects and the directives. To help you find the correct examples in the software package for this chapter, I divided them in folders named according to the section title and the functionality tested (e.g., `request object - authentication`).

Scripting Elements and Java

Scripting elements let you embed Java code in an HTML page.[1] Every Java executable—whether it's a free-standing program running directly within a runtime environment, an applet executing inside a browser, or a servlet executing in a container such as Tomcat—boils down to instantiating classes into objects and executing their methods. This might not be so apparent with JSP, since Tomcat wraps every JSP page into a class of type `Servlet` behind the scenes, but it still applies.

Java methods consist of a sequence of operations to instantiate objects, allocate memory for variables, calculate expressions, perform assignments, or execute other methods.

In this section, I'll summarize the syntax of Java while keeping JSP in mind.

Scriptlets

A scriptlet is a block of Java code enclosed between `<%` and `%>`. For example, this code includes two scriptlets that let you switch an HTML element on or off depending on a condition:

```
<% if (condition) { %>
<p>This is only shown if the condition is satisfied</p>
<%   } %>
```

Expressions

An expression scripting element inserts into the page the result of a Java expression enclosed in the pair `<%=` and `%>`. For example, in the following snippet of code, the expression scripting element inserts the current date into the generated HTML page:

```
<%@page import="java.util.Date"%>
Server date and time: <%=new Date()%>
```

You can use within an expression scripting element any Java expression, provided it results in a value. In practice, it means that every Java expression will do, except the execution of a method of type void. For example, `<%=(condition) ? "yes" : "no"%>` is valid, because it calculates to a string. You would obtain the same output with the scriptlet `<%if (condition) out.print("yes") else out.print("no");%>`.

---

[1] Jeff Friesen, *Beginning Java 7* (Berkeley, CA: Apress, 2012) is the definitive guide to the Java language.

Note that an expression is not a Java statement. Accordingly, it has no semicolon at the end.

Declarations

A declaration scripting element is a Java variable declaration enclosed between `<%!` and `%>`. It results in an instance variable shared by all requests for the same page. See the "Example: Testing Concurrency" section for an example on how you can use it.

Data Types and Variables

Java makes available primitive data types similar to the basic types of C/C++ (see Table 2-1). However, there is one important, if not so apparent, difference. The precision of the numeric types is implementation-dependent in C, but it is guaranteed to be constant across platforms in Java.

Table 2-1. Java Data Types

Name	Class	Description
byte	Byte	1-byte signed integer (-128 to +127)
short	Short	2-byte signed integer (-32,768 to +32,767)
int	Integer	4-byte signed integer (-2,147,483,648 to +2,147,483,647)
long	Long	8-byte signed integer (approximately -10^{19} to $+10^{19}$)
float	Float	32-bit signed floating-point (8-bit exponent, 23-bit precision)
double	Double	64-bit signed floating-point (11-bit exponent, 52-bit precision)
char	Character	16-bit unsigned Unicode
boolean	Boolean	Either true or false

The second column of Table 2-1 gives you the names of the so-called *wrapper classes* that Java makes available for each primitive type. These classes provide some useful static methods to manipulate numbers. For example, `Integer.parseInt(String s, int radix)` interprets a string as a number in the base set by the second argument and returns it as an `int` value (e.g., `Integer.parseInt("12", 16)` and `Integer.parseInt("10010", 2)` both return 18).

In Java, like in C, you can define octal literals by sticking a zero in front of the number, and hexadecimal literals by adding 0x or 0X. For example, both 0123, which means 1×64 + 2×8 + 3×1, and 0x53, which means 5×16 + 3×1, are different ways of representing the decimal number 83. With Java 7, you also have the suffixes 0b and 0B to identify binary literals. This means that you can also write decimal 83 as 0b1010011.

I will be mentioning new features of Java introduced with Java 7 as they become relevant. They are nice, and useful to improve code readability and maintainability, but before embracing them, check that all servers to which you will deploy your applications have been upgraded to Java 7.

Programs in Java can be platform-independent because all platform dependencies are "hidden" inside libraries. The wrapper classes I just mentioned are in the java.lang library, together with dozens of other general classes such as String and Math. You can find the full documentation of the Java 7.0 platform at http://docs.oracle.com/javase/7/docs/, and a description of its classes at http://docs.oracle.com/javase/7/docs/api/.

Here are some examples of how you can declare variables and initialize them:

```
String aString = "abcdxyz";
int k = aString.length();   // k is then set to 7
char c = aString.charAt(4);  // c is set to 'x'
static final NAME = "John Doe";
```

The final keyword in the last example of declarations makes the variable unchangeable. This is how you define constants in Java. The static keyword indicates that a variable is to be shared by all objects within the same application that are instantiated from the class.

The use of static variables in JSP requires some further comment. In JSP, you can declare variables in three ways:

```
<% int k = 0; %>
<%! int k = 0; %>
<%! static int k = 0; %>
```

The first declaration means that a new variable is created for each incoming HTTP client request; the second one means that a new variable is created for each new instance of the servlet; and the third one means that the variable is shared among all instances of the servlet.

Tomcat converts each JSP page into a subclass of the HTTP Servlet class (javax.servlet.http.HttpServlet). Normally, Tomcat instantiates each one of these classes only once and then creates a Java thread for each incoming request. It then executes the same servlet object within each thread. If the application runs on a distributed environment or for high numbers of requests, Tomcat can instantiate the same servlet more than once. Therefore, only the third declaration guarantees that the variable will be shared among all requests.

Tomcat keeps the servlet code buried deep in the folder named work. For example, the servlet generated from webapps\ROOT\tests\a.jsp is in work\Catalina\localhost_\org\apache\jsp\tests\ and is named a_jsp.java.

You're free to name your variables as you like, though your case-sensitive string of characters must begin with a letter, a dollar, or an underscore, and not contain a space. That said, be aware that the following keywords are reserved and will cause a compilation error: abstract, assert, boolean, break, byte, case, catch, char, class, const, continue, default, do, double, else, enum, extends, final, finally, float, for, goto, if, implements, import, instanceof, int, interface, long, native, new, package, private, protected, public, return, short, static, strictfp, super, switch, synchronized, this, throw, throws, transient, try, void, volatile, and while. Whenever possible, use capital letters for constants. It is not necessary, but it makes the code more readable and is a well-established coding practice.

To use special characters within a string, you need to escape them with a backslash, as shown in Table 2-2. With \u followed by up to four hexadecimal digits, you can specify any Unicode character. For example, you can enter the Greek capital letter delta as \u0394.

Table 2-2. Escaped Special Characters

Character	Escaped
backslash	\\
backspace	\b
carriage return	\r
double quote	\"
form feed	\f
line feed	\n
single quote	\'
tab	\t

Objects and Arrays

To create an object of a certain type (i.e., to instantiate a class), use the keyword new, as in the following example:

```
Integer integerVar = new Integer(55);
```

This creates an object of type Integer with value 55.

You can have arrays of any object type or primitive data type, as in the following examples of array declarations:

```
int[] intArray1;
int[] intArray2 = {10, 100, 1000};
String[] stringArray = {"a", "bb"};
```

intArray1 is null; intArray2 is an array of length 3 containing 10, 100, and 1000; and stringArray is an array of length 2 containing the strings "a" and "bb". Although arrays look special, they're actually just objects and treated like that. Therefore, you can initialize them with new. For example, the following line of code declares an integer array with 10 elements, each initialized to zero:

```
int[] array = new int[10];
```

A two-dimensional table is an array in which each element object is itself an array. This is *not* like in C, where a single block of memory contains all elements of multidimensional tables. For example, this line of code represents a table of two rows, but the first row has three elements, while the second one has only two:

```
int[][] table1 = {{11, 12, 13}, {21, 22}};
```

If you define something like this:

```
int[][] table = new int[2][3];
```

you have a table with two rows and three columns, with all elements initialized to zero.

When declaring a table, you can leave the last (innermost) dimension empty. For example, the following declaration results in a table of two rows, but the rows are undefined and remain set to null:

```
int[][] table = new int[2][];
```

Before being able to assign values to the individual elements of such partially defined table, you will have to declare its rows or assign to them already declared monodimensional arrays:

```
table[0] = new int[5];
int[] anArray = {10, 100};
table[1] = anArray;
```

Operators, Assignments, and Comparisons

There are no surprises with the binary operators—that is, the operators that require two operands. They include the expected addition, subtraction, multiplication, division, and modulus (i.e., the remainder of an integer division) operators. When applied to string, the addition operator concatenates them.

Besides the normal assignment operator represented by the equal sign, there is also an assignment operator for each binary operator. For example, the following line of code means that you take the current value of the variable a, add to it b, and store it back into a:

```
a += b;  // same as a = a + b;
```

The most commonly used unary operators (i.e. operators that require a single operand) include the minus sign, which changes the sign of what follows, and the increment and decrement operators:

```
a = -b;
a++;  // same as a += 1;
a--;  // same as a -= 1;
```

You can assign the value of an expression of one type to a variable of another type, but with some restrictions. With numeric types, you can only assign values to variables that are of the same type or "larger." For example, you can assign an int value to a variable of type long, but to assign a long value to an int variable, you'd have to *typecast* (i.e., downcast) the value, as in int iVar = (int)1234567L;. Be careful with that, because you might lose precision when downcasting floating point numbers!

You can assign objects to variables of other types, but only if the type of the variable is a superclass of the class from which you instantiated the object. Similarly to the downcasting of numeric types, you can typecast a value of a superclass into a variable of a subclass type.

Comparison operators are straightforward when applied to primitive data types. You have == to check for equality, != to check for inequality, > to check for "greater than," >= to check for "greater than or equal to," < to check for "less than," and <= to check for "less than or equal to." Nothing surprising there. However, you have to be careful when you make comparisons between objects, as the following example illustrates:

```
String s1 = "abc";
String s2 = "abc";
String s3 = "abcd".substring(0,3);
boolean b1 = (s1 == "abc");  // parentheses not needed but nice!
boolean b2 = (s1 == s2);
boolean b3 = (s1 == s3);
```

As perhaps you expected, b1 and b2 turn out to be true, but b3 is false, although s3 was set to "abc"! The problem is that comparison operators don't look inside the objects. They only check whether the objects are *the same instance* of a class, not whether they hold the same value. Therefore, as long as you shift around the "abc" string, the compiler keeps referring to the same instance of a literal string, and everything behaves as expected. However, when you create a different instance of "abc," the check for equality fails. The lesson to be learned is that if you want to compare the content of objects, you have to use the equals method. In this example, s1.equals(s3) would have returned true.

For objects, you also have the comparison operator instanceof, which isn't available for primitive data types like int. For example, ("abc" instanceof String) calculates to true. Be aware that an object isn't only an instance of the class it was instantiated from, but it's also an instance of all its superclasses up to and including Object, which is the superclass of all classes. It makes sense: a String is also an Object, even if the reverse often is not true.

With && for *logical and,* || for *logical or,* and ! for *logical not,* you can concatenate comparisons to form more complex conditions. For example, ((a1 == a2) && !(b1 || b2)) calculates to true only if a1 equals a2 and both boolean variables b1 and b2 are false.

Selections

The following statement assigns to the string variable s a different string depending on a condition:

```
if (a == 1) {
  s = "yes";
  }
else {
  s = "no";
  }
```

You can omit the else part.

You could have achieved an identical result with a conditional expression and a single assignment:

```
String s = (a== 1) ? "yes" : "no";
```

You could also achieve the same result with the following code:

```
switch(a) {
  case 1:
    s = "yes";
    break;
  default:
    s = "no";
    break;
  }
```

Obviously, the switch statement is only useful when there are more than just two alternatives. For example, instead of having a chain of if/else statements, as in the following example:

```
if (expression == 3) {...}
else if (expression == 10) {...}
else {...}
```

you would gain both in clarity and in concisiveness with:

```
switch (expression) {
  case (3): ... break;
```

25

```
case (10): ... break;
default: ... break;
}
```

At the very least, you'll calculate the expression only once. Note that if you omit a break, execution continues to the following case.

With Java 7, the switch variable can be of type String. Therefore, you can write switches like the following one:

```
String yn;
...
switch (yn) {
  case ("y"): /* handle the yes case */ break;
  case ("n"): /* handle the no case */ break;
  default: /* is something fishy going on? */ break;
}
```

Iterations

This statement repeatedly executes the *statements* with increasing values of k, beginning from *init-value*:

```
for (int k = init-value; k < limit; k++) { statements; }
```

The general format is

```
for (initial-assignment; end-condition; iteration-expression) { statements; }
```

The *initial-assignment* is executed only once, before entering the loop. The *statements* are then repeatedly executed as long as the *end-condition* is satisfied. As the *end-condition* is checked before executing the *statements*, they are not executed at all if the *end-condition* is false from the beginning. The *iteration-expression* is executed at the end of each iteration, before the *end-condition* is checked to see whether the loop should be reentered for a new iteration.

You can omit either the *initial-assignment* or the *iteration-expression*. If you omit both, you should replace the for loop with a while loop. The following two lines are equivalent:

```
while (end-condition) { statements; }
for (;end-condition;) { statements; }
```

The do-while statement is an alternative to the while loop:

```
do { statements; } while (end-condition);
```

The do-while statement checks the *end-condition* at the end of an iteration instead of at the beginning, like the for and while loops do. As a result, the statements inside a do-while loop are always executed at least once, even when the *end-condition* is false from the beginning.

The iteration statements described so far are identical to those of C, but Java also supports a variant of the for loop tailored to make the handling of collections easier. Suppose you need a method that produces a concatenation of a set of strings. It might look like this:

```
String concatenate(Set<String> ss) {
  String conc = "";
  Iterator<String> iter = ss.iterator();
  while (iter.hasNext()) {
    conc += iter.next();
    }
```

```
    return conc;
    }
```

With the Java for-each variant of the for loop, you can drop the definition of the iterator and write clearer code:

```
String concatenate(Set<String> ss) {
    String conc = "";
    for (String s : ss) {
        conc += s;
        }
    return conc;
    }
```

Implicit Objects

The most commonly used implicit objects defined by Tomcat are out and request, followed by application and session. But I will go through them in alphabetical order, for ease of reference.

Whether you create objects within JSP pages or Tomcat implicitly creates them for you, you cannot use them properly unless you know in which scope they are available. There are four possible scopes. In order of increasing generality, they are: *page, request, session,* and *application.* You will learn more about them in the following pages.

In general, if you are not sure what class a particular object instantiates, you can always display its name with the following expression:

```
<%=the_misterious_object.getClass().getName()%>
```

The application Object

The application object is an instance of the class org.apache.catalina.core.ApplicationContextFacade, which Tomcat defines to implement the interface javax.servlet.ServletContext. It provides access to the resources shared within the web application. For example, by adding an attribute (which can be an object of any type) to application, you can ensure that all JSP files that make up your web application have access to it.

Example: Using an Attribute to Enable and Disable Conditional Code

One of the advantages of using JSP is that the web server doesn't need to reinterpret the source file of a page every time a client requests that page. The JSP container translates each JSP page into a Java file and compiles it into a class, but this only happens when you update the JSP source. You might like to be able to switch on or off some particular functionality for debugging or other purposes, without having to edit one or more file and force Tomcat to recompile them when you flip the switch. To achieve this result, you only need to wrap the functionality in question inside a conditional statement, as the following one:

```
if (application.getAttribute("do_it") != null) {
    /* ...place your "switchable" functionality here... */
    }
```

You also need to include two small JSP pages in your application. The first one to set the attribute do_it (see Listing 2-1) and the second one to remove it (see Listing 2-2).

Listing 2-1. do_it.jsp

```
<%@page language="java" contentType="text/html"%>
<html><head><title>Conditional code ON</title></head>
<body>Conditional code
<%
   application.setAttribute("do_it", "");
   if (application.getAttribute("do_it") == null) out.print("not");
   %>
enabled</body></html>
```

Listing 2-2. do_it_not.jsp

```
<%@page language="java" contentType="text/html"%>
<html><head><title>Conditional code OFF</title></head>
<body>Conditional code
<%
   application.removeAttribute("do_it");
   if (application.getAttribute("do_it") == null) out.print("not");
   %>
enabled</body></html>
```

When you want to enable the conditional code, you just type the URL of do_it.jsp in your browser. Until you disable it by typing the URL of do_it_not.jsp or by restarting Tomcat, the conditional code will remain enabled in all pages of your application. Notice that in the example do_it.jsp only sets the attribute do_it to an empty string, but you can also define different values to have a finer selection of code to be activated.

Note that you can use the same mechanism to switch on and off HTML code.

Example: Using an Attribute to Control Logging

You might find it useful to be able to control the logging of some events to a particular file dynamically. To do so, you need to include two JSP files in your application (see Listings 2-3 and 2-4).

Listing 2-3. log_on.jsp

```
<%@page language="java" contentType="text/html"%>
<%@ page import="MyClasses.*"%>
<html><head><title>Switch the log ON</title></head><body>
<%
   MyLog log = (MyLog)application.getAttribute("logFile");
   if (log == null) {
      try {
         log = new MyLog("logs/mylog.log");
         application.setAttribute("logFile", log);
         log.println("Logging enabled");
         out.println("Logging enabled");
         }
      catch (Exception e) {
         out.println(e.getMessage());
         }
```

```
    }
  else {
    log.println("Attempt to enable logging");
    out.println("Logging was already enabled");
    }
  %>
</body></html>
```

Listing 2-4. log_off.jsp

```
<%@page language="java" contentType="text/html"%>
<%@ page import="MyClasses.*"%>
<html><head><title>Switch the log OFF</title></head><body>
<%
  MyLog log = (MyLog)application.getAttribute("logFile");
  if (log != null) {
    log.println("Logging disabled");
    log.close();
    application.removeAttribute("logFile");
    }
  %>
Done.
</body></html>
```

After checking that there is no application attribute named logFile, log_on.jsp instantiates the MyLog class and saves the object as an application attribute named logFile. After that, you can easily make an entry in the log file from any JSP of the same application, as shown in Listing 2-5.

Listing 2-5. check_logging.jsp

```
<%@ page import="MyClasses.*"%>
<%
  MyLog log = (MyLog)application.getAttribute("logFile");
  if (log != null) log.println("This is my entry in the log");
  %>
```

In log_off.jsp, after checking that the logFile attribute exists, you close the log file and remove the attribute. The logging is then disabled in all JSPs of the application, because any attempt to get the logFile attribute returns a null. The only piece of the puzzle that you still need is how to make the MyLog class.

This is also simple:

- Open the folder %CATALINA_HOME%\webapps\ROOT\WEB-INF\.

- If WEB-INF has no subfolder named classes (it shouldn't, if you have a fresh installation of Tomcat), create one.

- Inside the newly created folder, create a folder named MyClasses, and place in it the file MyLog.java shown in Listing 2-6.

- Open a command-line window and compile MyLog.java with javac, as explained in Chapter 1 for Exec_http.java.

- Restart Tomcat.

Listing 2-6. MyLog.java

```java
/* MyLog.java - Implements a log class */
package MyClasses;
import java.util.Date;
import java.text.SimpleDateFormat;
import java.io.FileWriter;
import java.io.PrintWriter;
import java.io.IOException;
public class MyLog {
  private static final SimpleDateFormat TIME_FMT =
                      new SimpleDateFormat("yyyy-MM-dd HH:mm:ss:SSS");
  private static PrintWriter log = null;
  public MyLog(String logpath) throws IOException {
    log = new PrintWriter(new FileWriter(logpath, true));
    }
  public static synchronized void println(String s) {
    log.println(TIME_FMT.format(new java.util.Date()) + " - " + s);
    log.flush();
    }
  public static synchronized void close() {
    log.close();
    }
  }
```

MyLog.java opens your log file in append mode and adds the date and time to your entry before writing it into the file. Notice that the methods are synchronized, so that several pages can log entries at the same time without them getting mixed up. An alternative would have been to make MyLog a subclass of PrintWriter. Then you could have had all the methods of PrintWriter available, and you wouldn't have needed to define a close method within MyLog. However, I wanted to have the methods synchronized, even if this seems like overkill.

If you place all three JSP files in %CATALINA_HOME%\webapps\ROOT\tests\, to test the logging you only need to type in a web browser http://localhost:8080/tests/log_on.jsp followed by check_logging.jsp and log_off.jsp.

In the folder %CATALINA_HOME%\logs\, you will find the file mylog.log containing three lines like the following ones:

```
2012-05-09 16:38:09:000 - Logging enabled
2012-05-09 16:38:12:183 - This is my entry in the log
2012-05-09 16:38:15:583 - Logging disabled
```

Adding classes to the default Tomcat application is not really the way it should be done. For one thing, casually restarting Tomcat aborts all user sessions. In the next chapter, I'll explain how to create separate, self-contained applications. Then, everything will become clearer.

The config Object

The config object is an instance of the org.apache.catalina.core.StandardWrapperFacade class, which Tomcat defines to implement the interface javax.servlet.ServletConfig. Tomcat uses this object to pass information to the servlets.

The following config method is the only one you might ever use; its use is trivial:

```
config.getServletName()
```

The method returns the servlet name, which is the string contained in the <servlet-name> element defined in the WEB-INF\web.xml file. You will learn more about this file later on. The default for <servlet-name> is jsp.

The exception Object

The exception object is an instance of a subclass of Throwable (e.g., java.lang.NullPointerException) and is only available in error pages.

Listing 2-7 shows you two methods to send the stack trace to the output. The first one, using getStackTrace, gives you access to each trace element as an object of type java.lang.StackTraceElement, which you can then analyze with methods such as getClassName, getFileName, getLineNumber, and getMethodName.

Listing 2-7. stack_trace.jsp

```
<%@page language="java" contentType="text/html"%>
<%@page import="java.util.*, java.io.*"%>
<%@page isErrorPage="true"%>
<html><head><title>Print stack trace</title></head><body>
From exception.getStackTrace():<br/>
<pre><%
  StackTraceElement[] trace = exception.getStackTrace();
  for (int k = 0; k < trace.length; k++) {
    out.println(trace[k]);
    }
  %></pre>
Printed with exception.printStackTrace(new PrintWriter(out)):
<pre><%
  exception.printStackTrace(new PrintWriter(out));
  %></pre>
</body></html>
```

Notice the directive <%@page isErrorPage="true"%>, without which the implicit object exception is not defined. If you execute this page as if it were a normal page, you will get a NullPointerException. Listing 2-8 shows a simple example of how you can use an error page.

Listing 2-8. cause_exception.jsp

```
<%@page language="java" contentType="text/html"%>
<%@page errorPage="stack_trace.jsp"%>
<html><head><title>Cause null pointer exception</title></head><body>
<%
  String a = request.getParameter("notThere");
  int len = a.length(); // causes a null pointer exception
  %>
</body></html>
```

Notice the <%@page errorPage="stack_trace.jsp"%> directive, which links the error page of Listing 2-7 to the occurrence of exceptions. To cause a NullPointerException, the page requests a parameter that doesn't exist and then accesses it. If you use try/catch to trap the exception, obviously the error page is not executed.

To see the two pages in action, place them in %CATALINA_HOME%\webapps\ROOT\tests\ folder and type in a browser http://localhost:8080/tests/cause_exception.jsp.

The out Object

You use the out object in JSP as you use the System.out object in Java: to write to the standard output. The standard output for a JSP page is the body of the HTML response sent back to the client. Therefore, the scriptlet <%out.print(*expression*);%> causes the result of the expression to be displayed in the client's browser. You can achieve the same result by simply typing <%=*expression*%>.

Keep in mind that whatever you write in a JSP page outside scriptlets and other JSP elements is sent to the output anyway. Therefore, the following three lines have exactly the same effect on the response:

```
<% out.print("abc"); %>
<%="abc"%>
abc
```

Clearly, it makes no sense to use the first two formats when you need to write literal values. To decide whether to use a scriptlet delimited by <%..%> or an expression delimited by <%=..%>, you should look at the surrounding code and decide what makes it as easy to read as possible.

The most useful methods of the object out are print and println. The only difference between the two is that println appends a newline character to the output. As an argument, both methods accept a string or any other primitive type variable. In the following example, the int value stored in intVar is automatically converted to a string:

```
out.print("a string" + intVar + obj.methodReturningString() + ".");
```

Incidentally, you could use either of the following two methods to do the conversion manually:

```
String s = Integer.toString(intVar);
String s = "" + intVar;
```

Be aware that if you try to print an object or an array by sticking its name into a print statement, you *won't* necessarily see its content in the output. If the object doesn't support a toString() method, you'll see a mysterious string representing the reference to the object.

As I already said, everything within a JSP page that's outside JSP elements is sent to the output, including the newline characters that follow each element. This causes a proliferation of empty lines in the output. For example, this code causes three empty lines in the output:

```
<% first element %>  here is a newline!
<% second element %>  here is a newline!
<% third element %>  here is a newline!
```

To remove the empty lines, you have three options. First, you can "chain" the element delimiters, so that the newlines are *inside* the elements and don't show up in the output:

```
<% first element %><%
  second element %><%
  third element %>  here is a newline!
```

Second, you can put the newlines inside JSP comments (although it will make your code difficult to read):

```
<% first element %><%--
--%><% second element %><%--
--%><% third element %>   here is a newline!
```

Third, you can write the following directive at the beginning of your page:

```
<%@page trimDirectiveWhitespaces="true"%>
```

and this will remove all unnecessary spaces from the output, including the newlines.

Most manuals state that out is an instance of the `javax.servlet.jsp.JspWriter` class, which you can use to write into the response. This is not entirely correct, because `JspWriter` is an abstract class, and as such, it cannot be instantiated. In reality, out is an instance of the nonabstract class `org.apache.jasper.runtime.JspWriterImpl`, which extends `JspWriter`. Tomcat defines `JspWriterImpl` precisely to implement the `JspWriter` methods. For all practical purposes, this is inconsequential to you, but some of you sharp-eyed readers might have thought that I was talking about instantiating an abstract class. It usually pays to be precise.

The `JspWriter` class includes the definition of a handful of fields. You won't need them, but mentioning them gives me the opportunity to give you some useful information.

The `autoFlush` field tells you whether the `JspWriter` is flushed automatically when its buffer fills up or whether an `IOException` is thrown upon overflow. The default for out is `true`, which means that Tomcat will send a partial response to the client if the buffer fills up. You can set it to `false` with the directive `<%@page autoFlush="false"%>`, and you should do so if you expect the client to be an application. Sending the response in "chunks" is perfectly OK when the client is a browser, but an application will probably expect the response in a single block. If you expect the client to be an application and set `autoFlush` to `false`, you should also use `<%@page buffer="size-in-kb"%>`, to ensure that the output buffer is large enough to store your largest response. The field `autoFlush` is protected, but you can obtain its value with the `isAutoFlush` method.

The `bufferSize` field is the size in bytes of the output buffer. The default for out is 8,192 bytes. It's a protected field, but you can obtain its value with the `getBufferSize` method.

There are also three constant integer fields (`DEFAULT_BUFFER`, `NO_BUFFER`, and `UNBOUNDED_BUFFER`, of type `public static final int`), but you can safely ignore them. Just for the record, they're respectively used to test whether the `JspWriter` is buffered (and uses the default buffer size), isn't buffered, or is buffered with an unbounded buffer. Besides the fact that you have no variable or attribute to check against these values, you're in any case well served by the `getBufferSize` method (which returns 0 if the output is not buffered).

You've already seen in several examples that you can use `print` and `println` to write to the output buffer. As an argument, you can use any of the eight primitive data types of Java (`boolean`, `char`, `byte`, `short`, `int`, `long`, `float`, and `double`), an array of characters (`char[]`), an object (`java.lang.Object`), or a string (`java.lang.String`). In practice, you'll usually use a `String` argument, as in the following example:

```
out.print("fun(" + arg + ") = " + fun(arg));
```

Here, `fun(arg)` is executed, and both `arg` and the value returned by `fun(arg)` are automatically converted to strings to be concatenated with the rest.

The `write` method, inherited from `java.io.Writer`, sends a portion of an array of characters or of a string to the output. For example, if `cbuf` is a variable of type `char[]`, `out.write(cbuf, offs, len)` will write a portion of `cbuf`, with `offs` being the offset of the first character and `len` being the number of characters to be copied. You could achieve the same result by extracting a part of the array with the following code and then printing it with `print`:

```
char[] portion = java.util.Arrays.copyOfRange(cbuf, offs, offs+len-1)
```

However, it would be less efficient, because first you would be copying a portion of the original array—an operation you don't need when using write.

You're not likely to use any of the other methods, and you should definitely avoid using close, which closes the output stream. Tomcat closes the stream when it is safe to do so, and you don't want to fiddle with it.

The pageContext Object

Most manuals state that pageContext is an instance of the javax.servlet.jsp.PageContext class to access all objects and attributes of a JSP page. Similar to what I said concerning JspWriter, this is only partly true, because this class, like JspWriter, is also abstract. In reality, pageContext is an instance of the nonabstract class org.apache.jasper.runtime.PageContextImpl, which extends PageContext.

The PageContext class defines several fields, including PAGE_SCOPE, REQUEST_SCOPE, SESSION_SCOPE, and APPLICATION_SCOPE, which identify the four possible scopes. It also supports more than 40 methods, about half of which are inherited from the javax.servlet.jsp.JspContext class.

You have to pay particular attention when using the removeAttribute method, which accepts either one or two arguments. For example, pageContext.removeAttribute("attrName") removes the attribute from *all* scopes, while the following code only removes it from the page scope:

```
pageContext.removeAttribute("attrName", PAGE_SCOPE)
```

The request Object

The request variable gives you access within your JSP page to the HTTP request sent to it by the client. It's an instance of the org.apache.catalina.connector.RequestFacade class, which Tomcat defines to implement the javax.servlet.http.HttpServletRequest and javax.servlet.ServletRequest interfaces.

More on Request Parameters and Client Info

In Chapter 1, you have already seen how to list all the parameters of a request. When accessing individual parameters by name, you should use some caution. Typically, you do it with the following line of code:

```
String myPar = request.getParameter("par-name");
```

And then, you do something with the parameter only if it exists—i.e., if getParameter returns a non-null value:

```
if (par != null) { ...
```

Note that in the request generated by a URL like this:

```
http://localhost:8080/my_page.jsp?aaa&bbb=&ccc=3
```

the parameters aaa and bbb exist but are set to the empty string. Therefore, getParameter does *not* return null for them.

As you already saw in Chapter 1, the request can include more than one value associated with the same parameter. For example, the following URL generates a request with three values for the parameter aaa:

```
http://localhost:8080/my_page.jsp?aaa&aaa=4&aaa=7
```

If you execute getParameter, you only get the first value, which is the empty string in the example. If you want to get them all, you have to use a different method:

```
String[] ppar = request.getParameterValues("par-name");
```

and this returns an array of strings. To check that the parameter has actually been set only once and to something other than the empty string, you might then perform the following test:

```
if (ppar != null  &&  ppar.length == 1  &&  ppar[0].length() > 0) { ...
```

In Chapter 1, you also saw how to determine the type of browser that sent the request. Another useful piece of information you can get about the client is its preferred locale. For example, the following line of code could set the variable clientLocale to the string "en_US":

```
String clientLocale = request.getLocale().toString();
```

But if the viewer were in a country where a language other than English is spoken, you might get other locales (e.g., "de_DE" for German). If you had a multilingual site, the locale would tell you the working language of your user. You could check whether you support it and, if you do, set it as a default for the response.

The getRemoteHost method, which returns the client's host name (or that of its proxy server), could be useful in a similar way, because you could look at the string after the last dot to identify foreign domain names (e.g., it for Italy). Unfortunately, in many cases, the remote address cannot be resolved to a name, and you end up getting only the client's IP address, exactly as if you had called the getRemoteAddress method. Services available on the Internet let you resolve an IP address to the country where the system resides, but you might have to pay for a reliable service.

⬛ **Caution** You cannot mix methods that handle parameters with methods that handle the request content, or methods that access the request content in different ways. For example, if you execute any two of the methods request.getParameter, getReader, and getInputStream when handling a request, the second one you execute will fail.

Example: Listing the Headers

Listing 2-9 shows code that displays the request headers.

Listing 2-9. req_headers.jsp

```
<%@page language="java" contentType="text/html"%>
<%@page import="java.util.*"%>
<html><head><title>Request Headers</title></head><body>
<%
  Enumeration headers = request.getHeaderNames();
  int kh = 0;
  while (headers.hasMoreElements()) {
    String hName = (String)headers.nextElement();
    out.println("------- " + hName);
    Enumeration hValues = request.getHeaders(hName);
```

```
    while (hValues.hasMoreElements()) {
      out.println("<br/>   " + hValues.nextElement());
      }
    out.println("<br/>");
    }
  %>
</body></html>
```

Figures 2-1, 2-2, 2-3, and 2-4 show the request headers generated respectively by Chrome, Firefox, IE, and Opera. Interesting, aren't they?

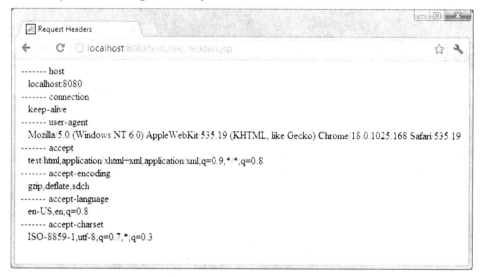

Figure 2-1. Request headers generated by Google Chrome

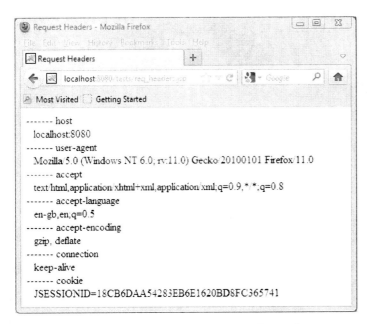

Figure 2-2. *Request headers generated by Mozilla Firefox*

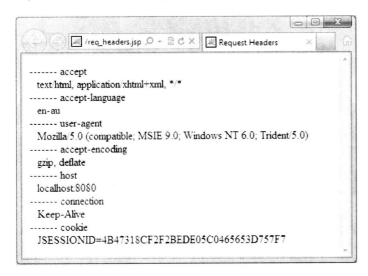

Figure 2-3. *Request headers generated by Microsoft Internet Explorer*

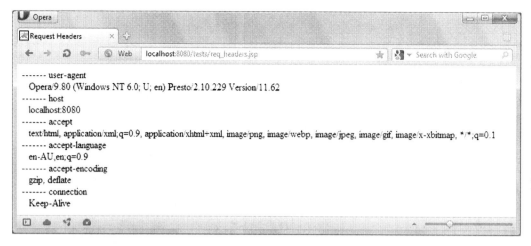

Figure 2-4. Request headers generated by Opera

Example: User Authentication

The browsers can display a user/password dialog to provide a basic authentication mechanism by limiting access to specific folders to particular user *roles*. First, you have to define the users and their roles in the `tomcat-users.xml` file that you find in Tomcat's `conf` folder. Listing 2-10 shows you what you should insert into `tomcat-users.xml` to define a couple of new users and the two roles `canDoThis` and `canDoThat`.

Listing 2-10. tomcat-users.xml Fragment

```
<tomcat-users>
  <role rolename="canDoThis"/>
  <role rolename="canDoThat"/>
  <user username="aBloke" password="whatever" roles="canDoThis"/>
  <user username="bigCheese" password="yes!" roles="canDoThis,canDoThat"/>
</tomcat-users>
```

The `tomcat-users.xml` file is shared by all applications, but this doesn't prevent you from using the roles only for specific applications. To password-protect all the pages inside a particular folder of an application, you have to edit the `WEB-INF/web.xml` file in the application's root directory. Listing 2-11 shows you the code you need to insert inside the `<web-app>` element to limit the access of the pages in the folder `/tests/auth/this/` to users with the role `canDoThis`, and of the pages in the folder `/tests/auth/that/` to users with the role `canDoThat`. I've highlighted the three main tags.

Listing 2-11. web.xml Fragment

```
  <security-role>
    <role-name>canDoThis</role-name>
    <role-name>canDoThat</role-name>
  </security-role>
  <security-constraint>
```

```
    <web-resource-collection>
      <web-resource-name>This</web-resource-name>
      <url-pattern>/tests/auth/this/*</url-pattern>
      </web-resource-collection>
    <auth-constraint>
      <role-name>canDoThis</role-name>
      </auth-constraint>
    </security-constraint>
  <security-constraint>
    <web-resource-collection>
      <web-resource-name>That</web-resource-name>
      <url-pattern>/tests/auth/that/*</url-pattern>
      <http-method>GET</http-method>
      </web-resource-collection>
    <auth-constraint>
      <role-name>canDoThat</role-name>
      </auth-constraint>
    </security-constraint>
  <login-config>
    <auth-method>BASIC</auth-method>
    </login-config>
```

As you can see, you first declare the security roles defined in tomcat-users.xml. Then you define two security constraints. Each security constraint can include several resources and authority constraints. The <url-pattern> sub-elements state which folders or pages require protection. Finally, you state that the BASIC authentication method should be applied.

To test it, you can copy to the usual %CATALINA_HOME%\webapps\ROOT\tests\ folder the whole auth folder you will find in the code available for this chapter. It contains two subfolders named this and that, each containing a trivial index.html that displays the name of the enclosing folder, and an index.html that lets you choose between the two subfolders.

That's it! After you have restarted Tomcat, type in a browser http://localhost:8080/tests/auth and choose to enter either this or that. When you choose the first time, the browser will ask you to provide user identification and a password, as shown in Figure 2-5.

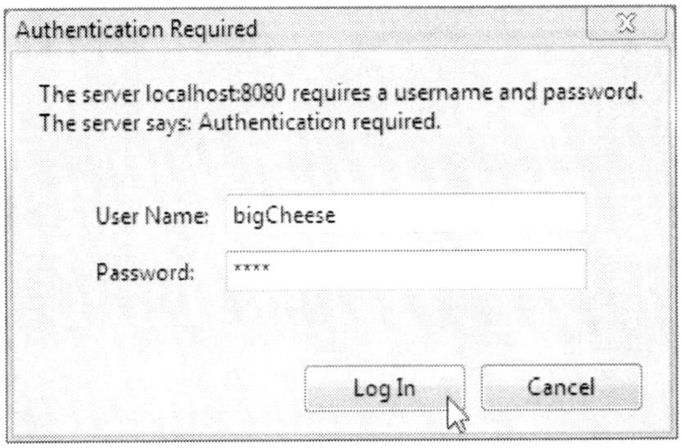

Figure 2-5. Basic authentication

If you try to access a forbidden directory (e.g., the that folder as user aBloke), you get an error message like that shown in Figure 2-6.

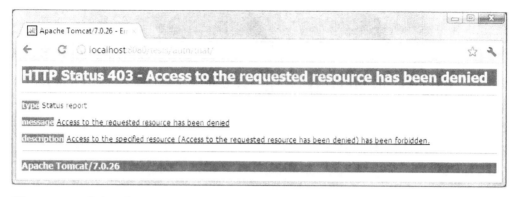

Figure 2-6. Failed authentication

The only way of logging out is to close the browser and reopen it. After logging in, the getAuthType method will return "BASIC" instead of null, getRemoteUsers will return "bigCheese" instead of null, isUserInRole("canDoThat") will return true, and getUserPrincipal() will return an object of type Principal containing the name "bigCheese".

Example: Reading the Request Body

You can read the request content with either getInputStream or getReader (but not both for the same request). Listing 2-12 shows you an example with getInputStream.

Listing 2-12. req_getInputStream.jsp

```
<%@page language="java" contentType="text/html"%>
<%@page import="java.util.*, java.io.*"%>
<%
  int    len = request.getContentLength();
  byte[] buf = null;
  int    n = 0;
  if (len > 0) {
    buf = new byte[len];
    n = request.getInputStream().read(buf);
    }
  %>
<html><head><title>Test request.getInputStream</title></head><body>
  <form action="" method="post" enctype="multipart/form-data">
    <input type="hidden" name="oneTwoThree" value="123"/>
    <input type="file" name="fil"/>
    <input type="submit"/>
    </form>
  <table border="1">
    <tr><td>getContentType()</td><td><%=request.getContentType()%></td></tr>
    <tr><td>getContentLength()</td><td><%=len%></td></tr>
<%
    out.print("<tr><td>getInputStream(): " + n + "</td><td><pre>");
```

```
      for (int k = 0; k < n; k++) out.print((char)buf[k]);
      out.println("</pre></td></tr>");
  %>
    </table>
</body></html>
```

Listing 2-13 shows you an example with getReader. There are several methods to read the content, but the important thing to keep in mind is that getInputStream returns data in binary form and unbuffered, while getReader returns buffered characters.

Listing 2-13. req_getReader.jsp

```
<%@page language="java" contentType="text/html"%>
<%@page import="java.util.*, java.io.*"%>
<%
  int    len = request.getContentLength();
  String s = "";
  if (len > 0) {
    char[] cbuf = new char[len];
    int    n = request.getReader().read(cbuf, 0, len);
    s = new String(cbuf);
    }
  %>
<html><head><title>Test request.getReader</title></head><body>
  <form action="" method="post">
    <input type="hidden" name="oneTwoThree" value="123"/>
    <input type="hidden" name="fourFiveSix" value="456"/>
    <input type="submit"/>
    </form>
  <table border="1">
    <tr><td>getContentType()</td><td><%=request.getContentType()%></td></tr>
    <tr><td>getContentLength()</td><td><%=len%></td></tr>
    <tr><td>getReader(): <%=s.length()%></td><td><pre><%=s%></pre></td></tr>
    </table>
</body></html>
```

Figures 2-7 and 2-8 show the output of req_getInputStream.jsp generated by Opera and by IE respectively.

Figure 2-7. Output of req_getInputStream.jsp when viewed with Opera

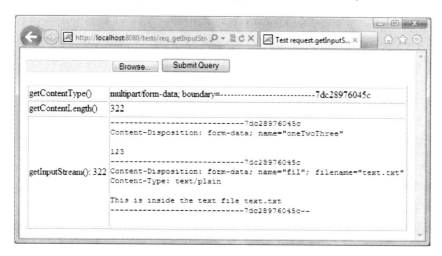

Figure 2-8. Output of req_getInputStream.jsp when viewed with IE

I've uploaded the file named text.txt, which only contains the text This is inside the test file text.txt. In the real world, the file would perhaps contain a formatted document, an image, or a video clip. With this example, you can also get an idea of the multipart format. As you can see, the content type actually contains a definition of the boundary, which is then used inside the request body to separate its parts. Each part consists of a header followed by an empty line and its content. Notice that the two browsers generate boundaries with different formats. I chose the outputs of Opera and IE because they generate the shortest and longest requests. This is entirely due to the different number of characters used for the boundaries.

Figure 2-9 shows the output of req_getReader.jsp.

Figure 2-9. *Output of req_getReader.jsp*

The `response` Object

The `response` variable gives you access within your JSP page to the HTTP response to be sent back to the client. It is an instance of the `org.apache.catalina.connector.ResponseFacade` class, which Tomcat defines to implement the interfaces `javax.servlet.http.HttpServletResponse` and `javax.servlet.ServletResponse`.

The `HttpServletResponse` interface includes the definition of 41 status codes (of type `public static final int`) to be returned to the client as part of the response. The HTTP status codes are all between 100 and 599. The range 100–199 is reserved to provide information, 200–299 to report successful completion of the requested operation, 300–399 to report warnings, 400–499 to report client errors, and 500–599 to report server errors. You will find the full list of errors at `http://www.w3.org/Protocols/rfc2616/rfc2616-sec10.html`.

The normal status code is `SC_OK (200)`, and the most common error is `SC_NOT_FOUND (404)`, which occurs when the client requests a page that doesn't exist. Working with Tomcat, the most common server error is `SC_INTERNAL_SERVER_ERROR (500)`. You get it when there is an error in a JSP. You can use these constants as arguments of the `sendError` and `setStatus` methods.

The `session` Object

The term *session* refers to all the interactions a client has with a server from the moment the user views the first page of an application to the moment they quit the browser (or the session expires because too much time has elapsed since the last request).

When Tomcat receives an HTTP request from a client, it checks whether the request contains a cookie that by default is named `JSESSIONID`. If it doesn't find it, it creates the cookie with a unique value and attaches it to the response. This establishes the beginning of a session. If the client's browser accepts cookies, it attaches that cookie to all subsequent requests it sends to the same server.

The `session` variable lets your JSP pages store information associated with each individual user. For example, following a user login, you can set a session attribute to the access level of that user, so that all the pages of your application can check it before performing their function. In its simplest form, you could set up such a mechanism like this:

```
session.setAttribute("MyAppOperator", "");
```

Then, you can use the following code to check it:

```
boolean isOperator = (session.getAttribute("MyAppOperator")  != null);
if (isOperator) { ...
```

You can save in a session-scoped attribute much more than a simple access level. You only need to define a class to hold the preferences (e.g., UserPrefs), fill in an object of that type (named, say, preferences) when the user logs in, and save it as a session's attribute, like in the following example:

```
session.setAttribute("upref", preferences);
```

In all the pages of your application, you can then retrieve that information with something like this:

```
UserPrefs preferences = (UserPrefs)session.getAttribute("upref");
```

By doing so, as long as the user keeps his or her browser running and the session doesn't timeout, you don't need to reload the user's preferences from a database.

The variable session is an instance of the org.apache.catalina.session.StandardSessionFacade class, which Tomcat defines to implement the javax.servlet.http.HttpSession interface.

The session object supports a dozen methods, including setMaxInactiveInterval, which lets you specify the timeout in seconds (the default is 1800 s = 30 minutes). This didn't work with older versions of Tomcat, but I tested it with Tomcat 7 and it correctly sets the timeout. You can also set the timeout for your application to a given number of minutes by inserting a <session-config> element in your application's \WEB-INF\web.xml file. To do so, you need to place the following code inside the <web-app> element:

```
<session-config>
  <session-timeout>write here the timeout in minutes</session-timeout>
</session-config>
```

Alternatively, you can also change Tomcat's default timeout by insetting the <session-config> element in the \conf\web-xml file you find inside the Tomcat home directory.

Directive Elements

JSP pages use directive elements to pass to Tomcat data about themselves. This data influences the translation process from a script file to a Java servlet class. As directives only play a role when a JSP page is re-compiled after you modify it, they have no specific effect on the individual HTML responses.

There are three directives that you can use in JSP pages: page, include, and taglib. Their syntax is as follows:

```
<%@directive-name attr1="value1" [attr2="value2"...] %>
```

The page Directive

The page directive defines several page-dependent properties expressed through attributes. These properties should appear only once in a JSP page (unless the multiple instances all have the same value, but why should you do that?). You can write more than one page directive in a JSP page, and they will all apply. Their order or position within the page is generally irrelevant.

This directive is used in all JSP pages. Typically, a JSP page starts with a page directive to tell Tomcat that the scripting language is Java and that the output is to be HTML:

```
<%@page language="java" contentType="text/html"%>
```

This is almost always followed by one or more further page directives to tell Tomcat which external class definitions your code needs. For example:

```
<%@page import="java.util.ArrayList"%>
<%@page import="java.util.Iterator"%>
<%@page import="myBeans.OneOfMyBeans"%>
```

It is *not* good coding practice to import whole class libraries, as in

```
<%@page import="java.util.*"%>
```

because any relaxation of control, sooner or later, creates problems. In any case, as you can see in the following example, you don't need to write a separate directive for each class you need to include:

```
<%@page import="java.util.ArrayList, java.util.Iterator"%>
```

In addition to language, contentType, and import, the page directive also supports autoFlush, buffer, errorPage, extends, info, isELIgnored, isErrorPage, isScriptingEnabled, isThreadSafe, pageEncoding, session, and trimDirectiveWhitespaces.

Listing 2-14 shows you a simple program that utilizes the isThreadSafe attribute to test concurrency.

Listing 2-14. concurrency.jsp

```
<%@page language="java" contentType="text/html"%>
<%@page isThreadSafe="false"%>
<%! int k = 0;%>
<html><head><title>Concurrency</title></head><body>
<%
  out.print(k);
  int j = k + 1;
  Thread.sleep(5000);
  k = j;
  out.println(" -> " + k);
  %>
</body></html>
```

The program declares the instance variable k, copies it to the variable j, increments j, waits for five seconds, and copies the incremented j back to k. It also displays k at the beginning and at the end.

If you reload the page several times, you'll see that k is increased every time the page refreshes. Now view the page in another browser (not just another browser window, because caching plays funny tricks); for example, view it in Chrome if you normally use Firefox. If you keep reloading the page in the two browsers, you'll see the k keeps increasing regardless of which browser you're looking at. This is because k is an instance variable.

Now reload the page in the first browser and then immediately in the second browser. Do you notice how the second browser takes longer to refresh? This is because you've set isThreadSafe="false", and Tomcat doesn't execute the servlet code for the two requests at the same time. However, k keeps increasing across the browsers with each page refresh.

Now remove the page directive that sets isThreadSafe to false and repeat the test. When you reload the page on both browsers almost simultaneously, they refresh the page at the same time but with the same value of k! This is because the second execution of the servlet starts while the first one is "holding" for five seconds.

I introduced the five-second delay to be sure that you would see the problem. Without the delay, the time interval between incrementing j and saving it back to k would be vanishingly small. Therefore, you might keep trying for years and never see the problem. Nevertheless, to rely on "it will never happen" when developing code, especially when concurrency plays a role, is a very bad practice. Other factors might influence the timing, and suddenly you might start seeing a problem once a day or even more rarely. It could have a damaging effect on how users consider your web site.

The price paid for playing it safe with isThreadSafe is that it can slow down execution significantly. Fortunately, there's a better way to make the threads safe than relying on Tomcat. Look at Listing 2-15.

Listing 2-15. concurrency2.jsp

```
<%@page language="java" contentType="text/html"%>
<%!
  int k = 0;
  Object syncK = new Object();
  %>
<html><head><title>Concurrency</title></head><body>
<%
  synchronized(syncK) {
    out.print(k);
    int j = k + 1;
    Thread.sleep(5000);
    k = j;
    out.println(" -> " + k);
    }
  %>
</body></html>
```

You protect the critical part of the code by enclosing it in a synchronized block. The syncK variable, being defined in a declaration element, is an instance variable shared like k among all the requests. I haven't used k because synchronized requires an object. In this simple case, instead of creating a new object specifically to protect the code, I could have used this, representing the servlet itself. But in general, if there were more than one block of code to protect, it wouldn't be a good idea. The best strategy to maximize efficiency, besides staying locked as little as possible, is to use specific locks.

I spent a bit of time on the attribute isThreadSafe because concurrency often is not well understood or implemented and causes intermittent bugs that are devilish to eliminate.

Earlier in this chapter, you have already seen how to use errorPage and isErrorPage (in "The Exception Object"), and trimDirectiveWhitespaces, autoFlush, and buffer (in "The Out Object"). Here is a brief description of the remaining attributes of the page directive:

- **extends** tells Tomcat which class the servlet should extend.

- **info** defines a string that the servlet can access with its getServletInfo() method.

- **isELIgnored** tells Tomcat whether to ignore EL expressions.

- **isScriptingEnabled** tells Tomcat whether to ignore scripting elements.

- **pageEncoding** specifies the character set used in the JSP page itself.

- **session** tells Tomcat to include or exclude the page from HTTP sessions.

The bottom line is that, in most occasions, you can leave these additional attribute set to their default values.

The `include` Directive

The include directive lets you insert into a JSP page the unprocessed content of another text file. For example, the following line of code includes a file named some_jsp_code with the extension jspf:

```
<%@include file="some_jsp_code.jspf"%>
```

JSPF stands for *JSP Fragment*, although more recently, chunks of JSP code have been called *JSP Segments*, rather than Fragments. In fact, any text file with any extension will do.

As Tomcat does the merging before any translation, the raw content of the included file is pasted into the page without any check. All the HTML tags and JSP variables defined before the line containing the directive are available to the included code. This directive can be very useful, but use it sparingly, because it can easily lead to unmaintainable code, with bits and pieces spread all over the place.

The `taglib` Directive

You can extend the number of available JSP tags by directing Tomcat to use external self-contained tag libraries. The taglib directory identifies a tag library and specifies what prefix you use to identify its tags. For example, this code

```
<%@taglib uri="http://mysite.com/mytags" prefix="my"%>
```

makes it possible for you to write the following line as part of your JSP page:

```
<my:oneOfMyTags> ... </my:oneOfMyTags>
```

The following code includes the core JSP Standard Tag Library:

```
<%@taglib uri="http://java.sun.com/jsp/jstl/core" prefix="c"%>
```

You will find the description of JSTL and how to use it in Chapter 4. In section "JSP's Tag Extension Mechanism" of the same chapter, I'll explain the possible advantages of creating your own libraries of tags and how to do it. For the time being, simply remember that the taglib directive tells Tomcat what libraries to load and where they are.

Summary

In this chapter, you learned all scripting and directive JSP elements.

I started by explaining the Java syntax used in scriptlets and the implicit objects defined by Tomcat, with several examples showing how to use them.

After that, I described the JSP directives.

In the next chapter, you will learn how to build complex JSP applications.

CHAPTER 3

JSP Application Architectures

In the first two chapters, you learned a large portion of JSP's components through brief examples. In this chapter, I will tell you how everything fits together in complex applications.

The insertion of Java code into HTML modules opens up the possibility of building dynamic web pages, but to say that it is possible doesn't mean you can do it efficiently and effectively. If you start developing complex applications exclusively by means of scripting elements, you'll rapidly reach the point where the code will become difficult to maintain. The key problem with mixing Java and HTML, as in "Hello World!", is that the application logic and the way the information is presented in the browser are mixed. Often, the business application designers and the web-page designers are different people with complementary and only partially overlapping skills. While application designers are experts in complex algorithms and databases, web designers focus on page composition and graphics. The architecture of your JSP-based applications should reflect this distinction. The last thing you want to do is blur the roles within the development team and end up with everybody doing what somebody else is better qualified to do. And even if you develop everything yourself, by keeping presentation and application logic separate, you will build more stable and more maintainable applications.

The Model 1 Architecture

The simplest way to separate presentation and logic is to move the bulk of the application logic from JSP to Java classes (i.e., Java beans), which can then be used within JSP (see Figure 3-1). This is called the JSP Model 1 architecture.

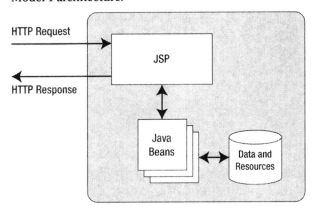

Figure 3-1. JSP Model 1 architecture

Although Model 1 is acceptable for applications containing up to a few thousand lines of code, the JSP pages still have to handle the HTTP requests, and this can cause headaches for the page designers.

The Model 2 Architecture

A better solution, more suitable for larger applications, is to split the functionality further and use JSP exclusively to format the HTML pages. This solution comes in the form of the JSP Model 2 architecture, also known as the model-view-controller (MVC) design pattern (see Figure 3-2).

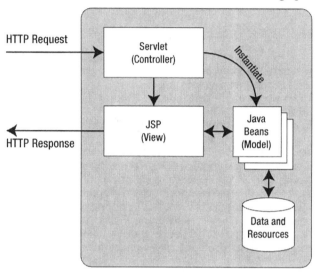

Figure 3-2. JSP Model 2 architecture

With this model, a servlet processes the request, handles the application logic, and instantiates Java beans. JSP obtains data from the beans and can format the response without having to know anything about what's going on behind the scenes. To illustrate this model, I will describe a sample application called *E-bookshop*, a small application to sell books online. E-bookshop is not really functional, because the list of books is hard-coded in the application rather than stored in a database. Also, nothing happens once you confirm the order. However, this example serves the purpose of showing you how Model 2 lets you completely separate business logic and presentation. Later in this chapter, I will introduce a better version of an online bookshop application that will accompany us through the rest of the book.

Figure 3-3 shows the E-bookshop's home page, which you see when you type http://localhost:8080/ebookshop in your browser's address field.

Figure 3-3. The E-bookshop home page

You can select a book by clicking on the drop-down list, as shown in Figure 3-3, type in the number of copies you need, and then click the Add to Cart button. Every time you do so, the content of your shopping cart appears at the bottom of the window, as shown in Figure 3-4.

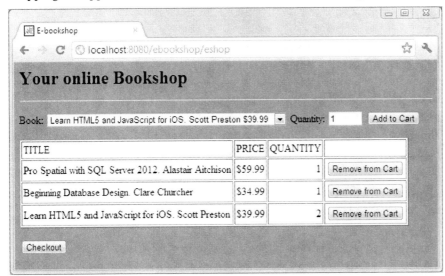

Figure 3-4. The E-bookshop home page displaying the shopping cart

You can remove an item from the shopping cart or go to the checkout. If you add additional copies of a book to the cart, the quantity in the cart increases accordingly.

If you click on the Checkout button, you'll see the page shown in Figure 3-5.

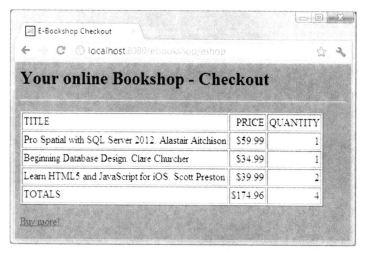

Figure 3-5. *The E-bookshop checkout page*

If you click on the Buy more! link, you'll go back to the home page with an empty shopping cart, ready for more shopping.

The E-bookshop Home Page

Listing 3-1 shows the home page http://localhost:8080/ebookshop/index.jsp. For ease of reading, I've highlighted the JSP directives and scriptlets in bold.

Listing 3-1. *The E-bookshop Home Page index.jsp*

```
<%@page language="java" contentType="text/html"%>
<%@page trimDirectiveWhitespaces="true"%>
<%@page session="true" import="java.util.Vector, ebookshop.Book"%>
<html>
<head>
  <title>E-bookshop</title>
  <style type="text/css">
    body {background-color:gray; font-size=10pt;}
    H1 {font-size:20pt;}
    table {background-color:white;}
    </style>
  </head>
<body>
  <H1>Your online Bookshop</H1>
  <hr/><p/>
<% // Scriptlet 1: check whether the booklist is ready
  Vector<ebookshop.Book> booklist =
      (Vector<ebookshop.Book>)session.getValue("ebookshop.list");
  if (booklist == null) {
    response.sendRedirect("/ebookshop/eshop");
```

```jsp
    }
  else {
    %>
      <form name="addForm" action="eshop" method="POST">
        <input type="hidden" name="do_this" value="add">
        Book:
        <select name=book>
<%  // Scriptlet 2: copy the booklist to the selection control
        for (int i = 0; i < booklist.size(); i++) {
          out.println("<option>" + (String)booklist.elementAt(i) + "</option>");
          }
    %>
        </select>
        Quantity: <input type="text" name="qty" size="3" value="1">
        <input type="submit" value="Add to Cart">
        </form>
      <p/>
<%  // Scriptlet 3: check whether the shopping cart is empty
    Vector shoplist =
        (Vector<ebookshop.Book>)session.getAttribute("ebookshop.cart");
    if (shoplist != null  &&  shoplist.size() > 0) {
    %>
      <table border="1" cellpadding="2">
      <tr>
      <td>TITLE</td>
      <td>PRICE</td>
      <td>QUANTITY</td>
      <td></td>
      </tr>
<%  // Scriptlet 4: display the books in the shopping cart
      for (int i = 0; i < shoplist.size(); i++) {
        Book aBook = shoplist.elementAt(i);
    %>
        <tr>
          <form name="removeForm" action="eshop" method="POST">
            <input type="hidden" name="position" value="<%=i%>">
            <input type="hidden" name="do_this" value="remove">
            <td><%=aBook.getTitle()%></td>
            <td align="right">$<%=aBook.getPrice()%></td>
            <td align="right"><%=aBook.getQuantity()%></td>
            <td><input type="submit" value="Remove from Cart"></td>
            </form>
          </tr>
<%
        } // for (int i..
    %>
      </table>
      <p/>
      <form name="checkoutForm" action="eshop" method="POST">
        <input type="hidden" name="do_this" value="checkout">
        <input type="submit" value="Checkout">
        </form>
```

```
<%
      } // if (shoplist..
    } // if (booklist..else..
  %>
  </body>
</html>
```

First, index.jsp (as shown in Scriptlet 1) checks whether the list of books to be sold is available and, if it isn't, it passes the control to the servlet, which then must initialize the book list. In a real online bookshop, the book list would be very long and kept in a database. Note that JSP doesn't *need to know* where the list is kept. This is the first hint at the fact that application logic and presentation are separate. You'll see later how the servlet fills in the book list and returns control to index.jsp. For now, let's proceed with the analysis of the home page.

If Scriptlet 1 discovers that the book list exists, it copies it into the select control one by one (as shown in Scriptlet 2). Notice how JSP simply creates each option by writing to the out stream. When the buyer clicks on the Add to Cart button after selecting a title and possibly changing the number of copies, the home page posts a request to the eshop servlet with the hidden parameter do_this set to add. Once more, the servlet takes care of updating or creating the shopping cart by instantiating the class Book for each new book added to the cart. This is application logic, not presentation of information.

Scriptlet 3 checks whether a shopping cart exists. index.jsp, being completely data-driven, doesn't remember what has happened before, so it runs every time from the beginning. Therefore, it checks for the presence of a shopping cart even when the buyer sees the book list for the very first time.

Scriptlet 4 displays the items in the shopping cart, each one with its own form. If the buyer decides to delete an entry, index.jsp sends a request to the servlet with the hidden parameter do_this set to remove.

The sole purpose of the last two scriptlets is to close the curly brackets of ifs and fors. However, notice that the form to ask the servlet to do the checkout is only displayed to the buyer when the shopping cart isn't empty. This is possible because Tomcat, when converting a JSP page into a Java servlet, processes all scriptlets together, without expecting each one of them individually to contain a complete block of code. HTML elements can then be enclosed within a Java block statement spanning two scriptlets.

If the buyer clicks on the Checkout button, index.jsp will send a request to the servlet with the hidden parameter do_this set to checkout.

Finally, notice the use of the expression elements <%=i%>, <%=aBook.getTitle()%>, <%=aBook.getPrice()%>, and <%=aBook.getQuantity()%>.The first expression, <%=i%>, is the position of the book within the shopping cart. The other three are the execution of methods of an object of type Book, which the servlet instantiated for each new book added to the cart.

You've probably noticed that the address shown in the browser is http://localhost:8080/ebookshop/eshop. This is actually the address of the Java servlet that controls the application.

The E-bookshop Servlet

Listing 3-2 shows the source code of the servlet. Later in this chapter, you will find information on the folder structure you need and on how to compile the Java modules. In this section and in the following one, I will explain how the code works.

Listing 3-2. ShoppingServlet.java

```
package ebookshop;
import java.util.Vector;
```

```java
import java.io.IOException;
import javax.servlet.ServletException;
import javax.servlet.ServletConfig;
import javax.servlet.ServletContext;
import javax.servlet.RequestDispatcher;
import javax.servlet.http.HttpServlet;
import javax.servlet.http.HttpServletRequest;
import javax.servlet.http.HttpSession;
import javax.servlet.http.HttpServletResponse;
import ebookshop.Book;

public class ShoppingServlet extends HttpServlet {

  public void init(ServletConfig conf) throws ServletException  {
    super.init(conf);
    }

  public void doGet (HttpServletRequest req, HttpServletResponse res)
      throws ServletException, IOException {
    doPost(req, res);
    }

  public void doPost (HttpServletRequest req, HttpServletResponse res)
      throws ServletException, IOException {
    HttpSession session = req.getSession(true);
    @SuppressWarnings("unchecked")
    Vector<Book> shoplist =
      (Vector<Book>)session.getAttribute("ebookshop.cart");
    String do_this = req.getParameter("do_this");

    // If it is the first time, initialize the list of books, which in
    // real life would be stored in a database on disk
    if (do_this == null) {
      Vector<String> blist = new Vector<String>();
      blist.addElement("Learn HTML5 and JavaScript for iOS. Scott Preston $39.99");
      blist.addElement("Java 7 for Absolute Beginners. Jay Bryant $39.99");
      blist.addElement("Beginning Android 4. Livingston $39.99");
      blist.addElement("Pro Spatial with SQL Server 2012. Alastair Aitchison $59.99");
      blist.addElement("Beginning Database Design. Clare Churcher $34.99");
      session.setAttribute("ebookshop.list", blist);
      ServletContext    sc = getServletContext();
      RequestDispatcher rd = sc.getRequestDispatcher("/");
      rd.forward(req, res);
      }
    else {

      // If it is not the first request, it can only be a checkout request
      // or a request to manipulate the list of books being ordered
      if (do_this.equals("checkout"))  {
        float dollars = 0;
        int    books = 0;
        for (Book aBook : shoplist) {
```

```java
        float price = aBook.getPrice();
        int   qty = aBook.getQuantity();
        dollars += price * qty;
        books += qty;
        }
      req.setAttribute("dollars", new Float(dollars).toString());
      req.setAttribute("books", new Integer(books).toString());
      ServletContext    sc = getServletContext();
      RequestDispatcher rd = sc.getRequestDispatcher("/Checkout.jsp");
      rd.forward(req, res);
      } // if (..checkout..

    // Not a checkout request - Manipulate the list of books
    else {
      if (do_this.equals("remove")) {
        String pos = req.getParameter("position");
        shoplist.removeElementAt((new Integer(pos)).intValue());
        }
      else if (do_this.equals("add")) {
        boolean found = false;
        Book aBook = getBook(req);
        if (shoplist == null) {  // the shopping cart is empty
          shoplist = new Vector<Book>();
          shoplist.addElement(aBook);
          }
        else {  // update the #copies if the book is already there
          for (int i = 0; i < shoplist.size() && !found; i++) {
            Book b = (Book)shoplist.elementAt(i);
            if (b.getTitle().equals(aBook.getTitle())) {
              b.setQuantity(b.getQuantity() + aBook.getQuantity());
              shoplist.setElementAt(b, i);
              found = true;
              }
            } // for (i..
          if (!found) {  // if it is a new book => Add it to the shoplist
            shoplist.addElement(aBook);
            }
          } // if (shoplist == null) .. else ..
        } // if (..add..

      // Save the updated list of books and return to the home page
      session.setAttribute("ebookshop.cart", shoplist);
      ServletContext sc = getServletContext();
      RequestDispatcher rd = sc.getRequestDispatcher("/");
      rd.forward(req, res);
      } // if (..checkout..else
    } // if (do_this..
  } // doPost

  private Book getBook(HttpServletRequest req) {
    String myBook = req.getParameter("book");
    int    n = myBook.indexOf('$');
```

```
    String title = myBook.substring(0, n);
    String price = myBook.substring(n+1);
    String qty = req.getParameter("qty");
    return new Book(title, Float.parseFloat(price), Integer.parseInt(qty));
    } // getBook
}
```

As you can see, the init() method only executes the standard servlet initialization, and the doGet() method simply executes doPost(), where all the work is done. If you were to remove the doGet() method, you would effectively forbid the direct call of the servlet. That is, if you typed http://localhost:8080/ebookshop/eshop in your browser, you would receive an error message that says the requested resource isn't available. As it is, you can type the URL with or without trailing eshop.

The highlighted line shows that I suppressed a warning. Normally, a warning tells you that something might be wrong. Therefore, it is not good to have spurious warnings, because they might distract you from noticing warnings you should fix. The use of @suppressWarnings is in general bad practice and encourages you to use a sloppy programming style. In this particular case, the compiler complained about the typecasting of a generic Object to a Vector, but I knew that the attribute ebookshop.cart was of type Vector<book>.

When you analyze index.jsp, you can see that it passes control to the servlet on four occasions, as listed here from the point of view of the servlet:

1. **If no book list exists**: This happens at the beginning, when the buyer types http://localhost:8080/ebookshop/. The servlet executes without any parameter, initializes the book list, and passes control straight back to index.jsp.

2. **When the buyer clicks on Add to Cart**: The servlet executes with do_this set to add and a parameter containing the book description. Normally, this would be done more elegantly with a reference to the book rather than the whole description, but we want to keep things as simple as possible. The servlet creates a cart if necessary and adds to it a new object of type Book or, if the same book is already in the cart, updates its quantity. After that, it passes the control back to index.jsp.

3. **When the buyer clicks on Remove from Cart**: The servlet executes with do_this set to remove and a parameter containing the position of the book within the cart. The servlet removes the book in the given position by deleting the object of type Book from the vector representing the cart. After that, it passes the control back to index.jsp.

4. **When the buyer clicks on Checkout**: The servlet executes with do_this set to checkout. The servlet calculates the total amount of money and the number of books ordered, adds them as attributes to the HTTP request, and passes the control to Checkout.jsp, which has the task of displaying the bill.

More on E-bookshop

By now, it should be clear to you how the servlet is in control of the application and how JSP is only used to present the data. To see the full picture, you only need to see Book.java, the Java bean used to represent a book, and Checkout.jsp, which displays the bill. Listing 3-3 shows the code for Book.java.

Listing 3-3. Book.java

```java
package ebookshop;
public class Book {
  String title;
  float  price;
  int    quantity;
  public Book(String t, float p, int q) {
    title    = t;
    price    = p;
    quantity = q;
  }
  public String getTitle()         { return title; }
  public void   setTitle(String t) { title = t; }
  public float  getPrice()         { return price; }
  public void   setPrice(float p)  { price = p; }
  public int    getQuantity()      { return quantity; }
  public void   setQuantity(int q) { quantity = q; }
}
```

In a more realistic case, the class Book would contain much more information, which the buyer could use to select the book. Also, the class attribute title is a misnomer, as it also includes the author names, but you get the idea. Listing 3-4 shows the code for Checkout.jsp.

Listing 3-4. Checkout.jsp

```jsp
<%@page language="java" contentType="text/html"%>
<%@page session="true" import="java.util.Vector, ebookshop.Book" %>
<html>
<head>
  <title>E-Bookshop Checkout</title>
  <style type="text/css">
    body {background-color:gray; font-size=10pt;}
    H1 {font-size:20pt;}
    table {background-color:white;}
    </style>
</head>
<body>
  <H1>Your online Bookshop - Checkout</H1>
  <hr/><p/>
  <table border="1" cellpadding="2">
    <tr>
      <td>TITLE</td>
      <td align="right">PRICE</td>
      <td align="right">QUANTITY</td>
    </tr>
<%
    Vector<Book> shoplist =
        (Vector<Book>)session.getAttribute("ebookshop.cart");
    for (Book anOrder : shoplist) {
%>
```

```
        <tr>
          <td><%=anOrder.getTitle()%></td>
          <td align="right">$<%=anOrder.getPrice()%></td>
          <td align="right"><%=anOrder.getQuantity()%></td>
          </tr>
<%
      }
    session.invalidate();
  %>
      <tr>
        <td>TOTALS</td>
        <td align="right">$<%=(String)request.getAttribute("dollars")%></td>
        <td align="right"><%=(String)request.getAttribute("books")%></td>
        </tr>
      </table>
  <p/>
  <a href="/ebookshop/eshop">Buy more!</a>
  </body>
</html>
```

Checkout.jsp displays the shopping cart and the totals precalculated by the servlet, and it invalidates the session so that a new empty shopping cart will be created if the application is restarted from the same browser window.

Note that you could have included the checkout logic in index.jsp and made its execution dependent on the presence of the two totals. However, I wanted to show you a more structured application. It's also better design to keep different functions in different JSP modules. In fact, I could have also kept the shopping cart in a separate JSP file. In real life, I would have certainly done so. In addition, I would have saved the styles in a Cascading Style Sheets (CSS) file rather than repeating them in all JSP sources. Finally, there is close to no error checking and reporting. You could easily crash this application. In a real case, you would add an error page as explained in the previous chapter.

Before we move on, you'll certainly find it interesting to see the dynamic HTML page that actually reaches the browser after adding one item to the shopping cart (see Listing 3-5).

Listing 3-5. HTML Generated by index.jsp

```
<html>
<head>
  <title>E-bookshop</title>
  <style type="text/css">
    body {background-color:gray; font-size=10pt;}
    H1 {font-size:20pt;}
    table {background-color:white;}
    </style>
  </head>
<body>
  <H1>Your online Bookshop</H1>
  <hr/><p/>
<form name="addForm" action="eshop" method="POST">
      <input type="hidden" name="do_this" value="add">
      Book:
      <select name=book>
<option>Learn HTML5 and JavaScript for iOS. Scott Preston $39.99</option>
```

```
<option>Java 7 for Absolute Beginners. Jay Bryant $39.99</option>
<option>Beginning Android 4. Livingston $39.99</option>
<option>Pro Spatial with SQL Server 2012. Alastair Aitchison $59.99</option>
<option>Beginning Database Design. Clare Churcher $34.99</option>
</select>
    Quantity: <input type="text" name="qty" size="3" value="1">
    <input type="submit" value="Add to Cart">
    </form>
  <p/>
<table border="1" cellpadding="2">
    <tr>
    <td>TITLE</td>
    <td>PRICE</td>
    <td>QUANTITY</td>
    <td></td>
    </tr>
<tr>
        <form name="removeForm" action="eshop" method="POST">
          <input type="hidden" name="position" value="0">
          <input type="hidden" name="do_this" value="remove">
          <td>Pro Spatial with SQL Server 2012. Alastair Aitchison </td>
          <td align="right">$59.99</td>
          <td align="right">1</td>
          <td><input type="submit" value="Remove from Cart"></td>
          </form>
        </tr>
</table>
    <p/>
    <form name="checkoutForm" action="eshop" method="POST">
      <input type="hidden" name="do_this" value="checkout">
      <input type="submit" value="Checkout">
      </form>
</body>
</html>
```

Neat, isn't it?

You now have in your hands the full code of a nontrivial Java/JSP application, but you still need to know how to make these four modules work together.

E-bookshop's Folder Structure

Figure 3-6 shows the structure of the E-bookshop application. First of all, create the root folder of the application, named ebookshop, inside %CATALINA_HOME%\webapps\. Then, create the folder hierarchy and place in it the four source files index.jsp, Checkout.jsp, ShoppingServlet.java, and Book.java as shown.

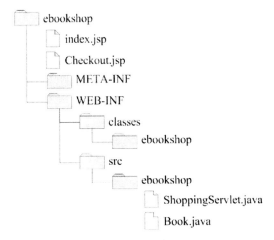

ebookshop
  index.jsp
  Checkout.jsp
  META-INF
  WEB-INF
    classes
      ebookshop
    src
      ebookshop
        ShoppingServlet.java
        Book.java

Figure 3-6. *The E-bookshop folder structure*

To get the application to work, you first need to compile the two Java modules from the command line with javac, as explained in the "Java Test" section of Chapter 1. Then copy the two .class files from WEB-INF\src\ebookshop\ to WEB-INF\classes\ebookshop\. Alternatively, if you feel lazy (!), you can copy to WEB-INF the little batch file shown in Listing 3-6 and double-click it. Note that if you want to launch it from the command line, you have first to attach to WEB-INF, otherwise it won't find the src folder.

Listing 3-6. *compile_it.bat*

```
@echo off
set aname=ebookshop
set /P fname=Please enter the java file name without extension:
set fil=%aname%\%fname%
echo *** compile_it.bat: compile src\%fil%.java
javac -verbose -deprecation -Xlint:unchecked -classpath ➥
  "C:\Program Files\Apache Software Foundation\Tomcat\lib\servlet-api.jar";classes ➥
  src\%fil%.java
javac -verbose -deprecation -Xlint:unchecked -classpath classes src\%fil%.java
if %errorlevel% GTR 1 goto _PAUSE
echo *** compile_it.bat: move the class to the package directory
move /y src\%fil%.class classes\%fil%.class
:_PAUSE
pause
```

The batch file opens a command-line window automatically and asks you to type the name of a Java file (without the extension). It then compiles the file and moves the resulting class into the classes\ebookshop\ subfolder. The line with javac invokes the Java compiler with the switches that maximize both the checks the compiler does on your sources and the information you get.

Notice the classpath switch, which tells the compiler to look for classes in the local directory and in Tomcat's lib folder in addition to the usual places where the Java libraries are kept. This is necessary because ShoppingServlet.java imports the javax.servlet package and the class Book and, without the classpath switch, the compiler wouldn't know where to find them. This also means that you have to compile Book.java *before* ShoppingServlet.java.

When executing your application, Tomcat looks for classes in the WEB-INF\classes\ folder immediately inside the root folder of your application (i.e., bookshop\), which in turn is immediately inside webapps. The directory structure inside WEB-INF\classes\ must reflect what you write in the package statement at the beginning of the Java sources, which is:

```
package ebookshop;
```

If you had written this instead:

```
package myLibs.ebookshop;
```

you would have had to insert a myLibs folder below classes and above ebookshop. To avoid confusion, note that the package name has nothing to do with the name of the application. That is, you could have named the package (and, therefore, the folder below classes\) qwertyuiop instead of ebookshop. In fact, you could have dispensed with the package statement altogether and placed your classes directly inside the classes folder. Finally, you could have also created a JAR file (i.e., a Java ARchive), but we'll talk about that later.

Before you're ready to go, you still need to write an additional file where you describe the structure of your application to Tomcat. This web deployment descriptor, shown in Listing 3-7, *must* be named web.xml and placed in WEB-INF.

Listing 3-7. web.xml

```
<?xml version="1.0" encoding="ISO-8859-1"?>
<web-app xmlns="http://java.sun.com/xml/ns/j2ee"
    xmlns:xsi="http://www.w3.org/2001/XMLSchema-instance"
    xsi:schemaLocation=~CCC
"http://java.sun.com/xml/ns/j2ee http://java.sun.com/xml/ns/j2ee/web-app_2_4.xsd"
    version="2.4">
  <display-name>Electronic Bookshop</display-name>
  <description>
    E-bookshop example for
    Beginning JSP, JSF and Tomcat: from Novice to Professional
    </description>
  <servlet>
    <servlet-name>EBookshopServlet</servlet-name>
    <servlet-class>ebookshop.ShoppingServlet</servlet-class>
    </servlet>
  <servlet-mapping>
    <servlet-name>EBookshopServlet</servlet-name>
    <url-pattern>/eshop</url-pattern>
    </servlet-mapping>
</web-app>
```

The two crucial lines are those highlighted in bold. The first one tells Tomcat that the servlet is in classes\ebookshop\ShoppingServlet.class. The second one tells Tomcat that the requests will refer to the servlet as /eshop. As the root folder of this application (i.e., the folder immediately inside webapps) is ebookshop, Tomcat will then route to this servlet all the requests it will receive for the URL http://servername:8080/ebookshop/eshop.

The element <servlet-name> in both <servlet> and <servlet-mapping> is only needed to make the connection between the two. An alternative to declaring the servlet in web.xml is to use an annotation in ShoppingServlet.java. To test it out, remove from web.xml both the servlet and the servlet-mapping elements. Then, insert into ShoppingServlet.java two lines as shown in the following code fragment:

```
import ebookshop.Book;
import javax.servlet.annotation.WebServlet;
@WebServlet(value="/eshop")
public class ShoppingServlet extends HttpServlet {
```

Regardless of how you declare the servlet, if you now open a browser and type
http://localhost:8080/ebookshop/, you should see the application's home page.

You might be wondering about the purpose of the META-INF folder. Place inside that folder a file
named MANIFEST.MF and containing the following single line:

```
Manifest-Version: 1.0
```

Move the webapps\ebookshop folder to the Desktop, open it and select all four items in it. Then, right-
click on them and select "Send To ➤ Compressed (Zipped) Folder". When asked to provide a file name,
type ebookshop. Windows will create a file named ebookshop.zip. Change its extension to war (which
stands for Web ARchive) and move it to Tomcat's webapps folder. After a short while, Tomcat will
automatically unpack the WAR file into a folder named ebookshop identical to the one you started with.

The manifest file contains information about the files packaged in a JAR file, and A WAR file is just a
JAR with a particular function. You can find a specification for the manifest file at
http://docs.oracle.com/javase/7/docs/technotes/guides/jar/jar.html#JAR%20Manifest.

WAR files are the best way to deploy your applications to more than one server: copy them into
webapps, and Tomcat will do the rest for you. What could be easier than that?

Eclipse

Although it's possible to build web applications by compiling Java modules from the command line, it's
more efficient to use an Integrated Development Environment (IDE). This way, you can concentrate on
the more creative part of developing software, rather than fix inconsistency and fiddle with folder
hierarchies.

An IDE integrates all the applications that you need to develop software—from a source editor and a
compiler, to tools to automate the application building process and a debugger—into a single
application. When developing in Java or in another OO language, an IDE also includes tools to visualize
class and object structure as well as inheritance and containment. Another advantage of using an IDE is
that it propagates changes you make to individual modules. For example, if you rename a class, the IDE
can automatically update its occurrences throughout your project files.

As the applications you develop become more complex, it makes more and more sense to use an
IDE. That's why, before continuing to our next project, I will tell you how to install and configure Eclipse.

Eclipse is an extremely powerful and extensible IDE, well suited for web application development.
The Eclipse Foundation makes a new release of the Eclipse IDE once a year. Each yearly release has a
different name. To develop the examples contained in this book, I used Indigo 3.7.2 of February 16, 2012.

Once you've installed Eclipse to develop web applications, you can use it for any other software
development task, including, for example, developing and debugging applications written in Java, C++,
and even Fortran, which is still widely used in the scientific community.

Furthermore, whatever task related to software development you need to perform, it's likely that
somebody has already developed an Eclipse plug-in for it. The web site
http://marketplace.eclipse.org/ lists more than 1,300 plug-ins organized in dozens of categories. In
fact, Eclipse itself consists of a core platform that executes plug-ins, plus a series of plug-ins that
implement most of its functionality. Therefore, the standard packages available for download from the
Eclipse web site already include dozens of plug-ins.

In this section, I'll only explain how to install the standard Eclipse configuration for Java EE
development, which is what you need as you go through the rest of this book.

First of all, you need to download the package. To do so, go to http://www.eclipse.org/downloads/ and click on the Windows 32 bit link of Eclipse IDE for Java EE Developers, as shown in Figure 3-7.

Figure 3-7. Downloading Eclipse

The web site will suggest a mirror site for the download and provide the MD5 checksum. The installation of Eclipse is very easy: expand the downloaded eclipse-jee-indigo-SR2-win32.zip file and move the eclipse folder to a convenient place. For no particular reason, I chose to move it to C:\. Old habits are difficult to change. You might like to move the Eclipse folder to C:\Program Files\.

To execute Eclipse, double-click eclipse.exe, which you find immediately inside the eclipse folder.

When it starts, Eclipse asks you to select a workspace. The workspace is the folder where Eclipse stores your development projects. Therefore, it makes sense to place it on a drive or in a directory that you back up regularly. Before clicking on the OK button, check the box marked "Use this as the default and do not ask again". It will make your life easier. I chose C:\Users\Giulio\, which is my user's home directory.

The first time it executes, Eclipse displays a Welcome screen. To enter the screen where you do development, click on the Workbench icon, as shown in Figure 3-8.

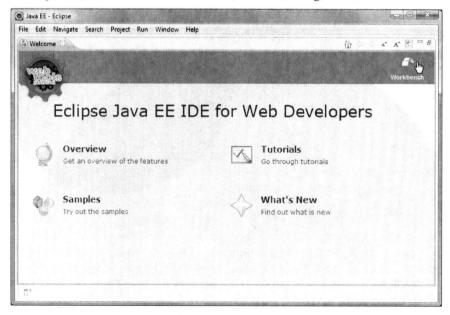

Figure 3-8. Eclipse–the Welcome screen

Once you see the Workbench screen, select the Servers tab and click on the new server wizard link, as shown in Figure 3-9.

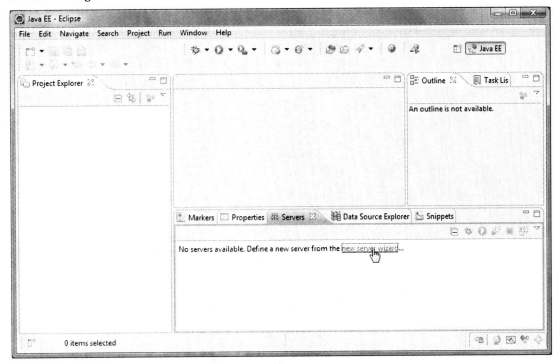

Figure 3-9. Eclipse–the Workbench screen

The screen that comes up is where you tell Eclipse to use Tomcat 7, as shown in Figure 3-10.

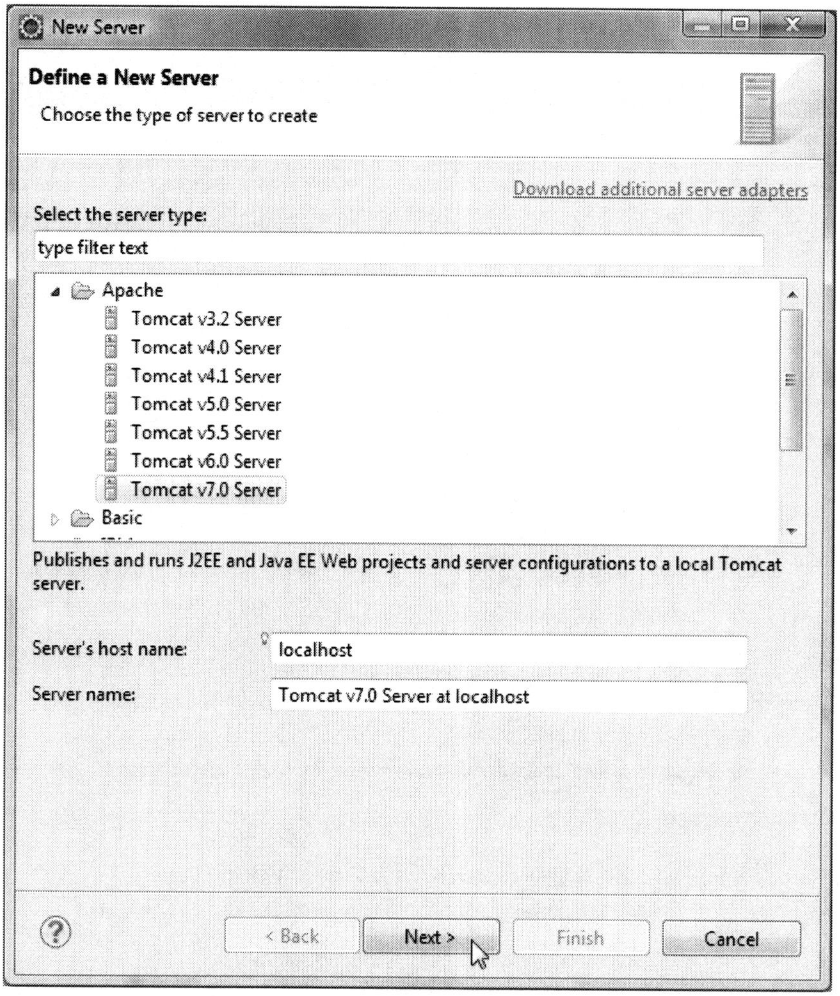

Figure 3-10. Eclipse–choosing Tomcat 7 as localhost

Next (and last), you need to tell Eclipse where to find Tomcat 7 and what version of JDK to use, as shown in Figure 3-11.

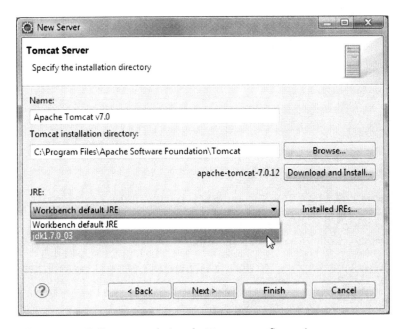

Figure 3-11. Eclipse–completing the Tomcat configuration

Now, if you have done everything correctly, Tomcat 7 should appear under the Servers tab of the Workbench. I have explained this configuration procedure because Eclipse is a very complex application, and it is easy to get lost among the many options.

For the same reason, to be on the safe side, I will also explain how to create a new web project. Later, you will learn how to import into Eclipse the example projects included in the software package of this book.

Creating a New Web Project

In the menu bar of the Workbench, select File ➤ New ➤ Dynamic Web Project, type a project name (e.g., test), and click on the Next button. In the new screen, named Java, click again on the Next button. In the new screen, named Web Module, tick the box Generate web.xml deployment descriptor (i.e., the web.xml file) before clicking on the Finish button.

The new project will appear in the Project Explorer pane (i.e., on the left hand side) of the Workbench. Expand it as shown in Figure 3-12, right-click on the Web Content folder and select "New ➤ JSP File".

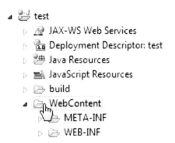

Figure 3-12. *Eclipse–the test project*

In the new JSP screen that appears, replace the default name `NewFile.jsp` with `index.jsp` and click on the `Finish` button.

Eclipse shows the newly created file in the `Project Explorer` pane and opens it in the central pane of the Workbench for you to edit. Listing 3-8 shows its content. For me, the newly created file is located in `C:\Users\Giulio\workspace\test\WebContent\`. If, for any reason, you edit the file with some other editor, to see the latest version within Eclipse, you need to right-click it in Eclipse's Project Explorer and select `Refresh`. But I suggest that you stick to Eclipse with all editing, because it is very easy to make a mistake otherwise.

Listing 3-8. *index.jsp of the Test Project*

```
<%@ page language="java" contentType="text/html; charset=ISO-8859-1"
    pageEncoding="ISO-8859-1"%>
<!DOCTYPE html PUBLIC "-//W3C//DTD HTML 4.01 Transitional//EN"
"http://www.w3.org/TR/html4/loose.dtd">
<html>
<head>
<meta http-equiv="Content-Type" content="text/html; charset=ISO-8859-1">
<title>Insert title here</title>
</head>
<body>

</body>
</html>
```

Replace "Insert title here" with "My first project" (or whatever you like, of course), and write "Hello from Eclipse!" between <body> and </body>. Then save the file.

Caution You must stop the Tomcat service in Windows before using Tomcat from within Eclipse, and vice-versa.

Position the cursor on the test project folder shown in the Project Explorer, right-click, and select `Run As ▶ Run on Server`. When a screen comes up, click on `Finish`. You will be rewarded with what is shown in Figure 3-13.

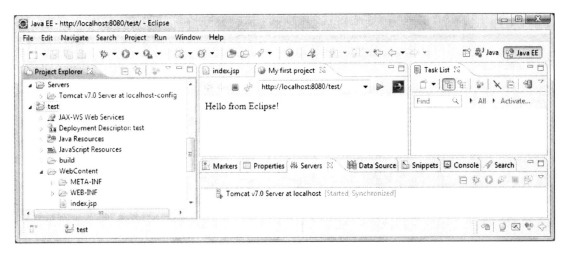

Figure 3-13. *Eclipse–the output of the first project*

It might seem very convenient that Eclipse can launch Tomcat and show the output within the Workbench. In practice though, it has a couple of drawbacks. First of all, because of the side and bottom panes, the space available in the central pane is limited. As a result, most web pages are "too squeezed" to display correctly.

You can maximize the web pane by double-clicking on the title bar, but there is also a more important reason: Eclipse doesn't always display everything. It should copy all files from the project folder to a Tomcat work directory, but it doesn't! It tends to "lose" CSS files and images. This means that, except for a quick check of simple features, you might do what I do and use Tomcat externally.

To see the output of the test project outside Eclipse, first of all, stop the "internal" Tomcat by right-clicking it under the Servers tab of the Workbench and selecting Stop. Then, start the Tomcat service in Windows.

Right-click the test-project folder as you did to launch it within Eclipse, but this time select Export ➤ WAR File.

When the WAR Export screen appears, the only thing you have to do is browse to select the destination, which should be %CATALINA_HOME%\webapps\test.war, and click Finish.

In a browser, type http://localhost:8080/test to see the output of the project. This works because, as I showed to you at the end of the previous section, Tomcat automatically expands all WAR files it discovers in its webapps folder, without any need to restart it. And because by default Tomcat looks for index.html, index.htm, and index.jsp. If you want, you can change the default by adding the following element to the body of the web-app element of web.xml:

```
<welcome-file-list>
    <welcome-file>whatever.jsp</welcome-file>
</welcome-file-list>
```

Importing a WAR file

In the next section, I will introduce you to the eshop application. You will find the web archive for the application in the software for this chapter, and the easiest way to work on the application is to import it into Eclipse.

The first step is to select the menu item `Import...` in the `File` menu. When the `Select` dialog opens, scroll down to the folder named `Web`, open it, select `WAR file`, and click `Next >`, as shown in Figure 3-14.

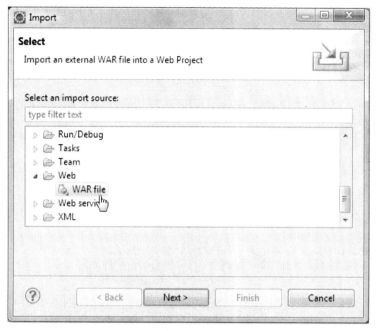

Figure 3-14. *Eclipse–selecting to import a WAR file*

When the next dialog comes up, browse to select `eshop.war` and click on `Finish`. Eclipse will create the eshop project for you.

Eclipse Occasional Bugs

Eclipse is a very complex package developed by several people in parallel. As a result, bugs occasionally creep in.

While developing the applications for this book, one such bug suddenly appeared: Eclipse reported that a function of a JSP Standard Tag Library didn't exist.

Eclipse validates JSP files but doesn't do anything with them. Therefore, I ignored the reported error and deployed the application to Tomcat, which executed it without any problem.

I don't know why Eclipse started reporting that nonexistent error. If you search the Internet, you will find that several people have had some problems with Eclipse's validation of JSPs.

When problems like that occur, as long as they don't affect your application, you don't really need to do anything. You could reinstall Eclipse, but that might not cure them, or they might reappear later.

A Better Online Bookshop

The online bookshop you saw at the beginning of this chapter was a good introduction to the MVC architecture, but in order to explore the use of databases, other JSP features, and JSF, we need an example with more substance. In this section, I will introduce the eshop application, which will remain with us through the rest of the book. Taking an object-oriented approach, I'll begin by specifying the objects that the application needs to handle, the operations which those objects support, and the roles of the people who perform those operations.

Each role corresponds to a separate user interface, and the two main roles are the administrator and the customer. The administrators manage products, orders, and customer records, but for our purposes, it is sufficient to implement the public interface of a customer buying from a catalog.

Objects and Operations

In eshop we won't keep track of orders and customers. Once the customer goes to the checkout, enters credit-card information, and checks out, we'll save the order, but we won't do anything with it. In the real world, we'd have to process the purchase by charging the credit card account and dispatching the order.

In fact, if you decided to deploy this application "out there" to sell books or other items, you would be better off interfacing with PayPal or another online payment service, rather than accepting credit cards. But the purpose of this example is to help you learn JSP and JSF without getting bogged down in details of other services. For that, the credit-card option is fine. Obviously, in the real world, you would have to consider using secure communication and encrypted data, but that would go beyond the scope of this example.

Product Categories

It makes sense to group the products into categories, especially if the catalog is diversified and substantial. As eshop only sells books, its categories refer to broad book subjects, such as action novels, science fiction, and web development.

Each category has a *name* and an *identifier*. The identifier is guaranteed to be unique, thereby allowing us to refer to each category without ambiguity. Normally, a category would have additional attributes, like description, status, date of creation, etc. To implement the customer interface, the only operation you need with such a bare-bones category definition is obtaining a category name given its ID.

Books

Each book has a *title*, an *author*, a *price*, a unique *identifier*, a *category ID*, and an image of the *front cover*. Customers must be able to select books from a category, search for books, display the book details, and put books into a shopping cart.

Shopping Cart

The minimum amount of information stored in a shopping cart is a list of items, each consisting of a book identifier and the number of ordered copies. I decided to duplicate in the shopping cart title, description, and price of the books instead of using their book IDs. Besides simplifying the application, this also protects the customer from book updates that might occur while he or she is still shopping. In a more sophisticated application, when some book attributes change, you might want to inform the customers who've placed the book in their cart but haven't yet completed the checkout. You wouldn't be able to do so without saving the original information. Obviously, this only avoids a problem due to concurrent access of data (more about that in Chapter 6). To protect the information from more serious occurrences like server failures, you would have to implement more general solutions, like saving session data on non-volatile storage and server clustering,

Customers must be able to change the number of copies of each book in the cart, remove a book altogether, and go to the checkout. They should also be able to display the shopping cart at any time.

Order

Although this sample application doesn't cover orders, it's useful to specify the structure of an order. You need two separate classes: one to represent the ordered items, and one with the customer's data.

For each ordered item, you need to save the book data obtained from the shopping cart. Additionally, for each order, you need to save the customer data and a unique order number.

The Customer Interface

Figure 3-15 shows eshop's home page. The top section includes a link to the shopping cart, while the sidebar on the left features a search box and a list of categories. The other pages only differ in the central panel, which in the home page contains a welcoming message.

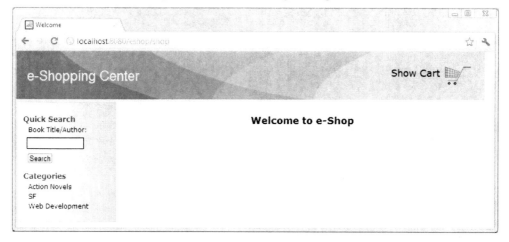

Figure 3-15. *E-shop's home page*

Figure 3-16 shows the panel containing the list of books in a category.

Select Catalog

Category: **Web Development**

Title	Author	Price	Details
Web Standards	Leslie Sikos	44.99	Details
Getting Started with CSS	David Powers	24.99	Details

Figure 3-16. *A book category on E-shop*

Figure 3-17 shows the details of a book.

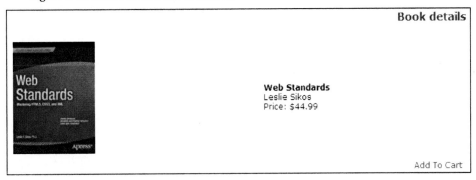

Figure 3-17. *A book's details on E-shop*

Figure 3-18 shows the shopping cart with a couple of items.

Shopping Cart

Title	Author	Price	Quantity		Subtotal	Delete
Web Standards	Leslie Sikos	44.99	2	Update	89.98	Delete
Getting Started with CSS	David Powers	24.99	1	Update	24.99	Delete

Total: 114.97

Check Out

Figure 3-18. *E-shop's shopping cart*

Pretty straightforward, isn't it?

The E-shop Architecture

E-shop is an MVC application. The data and the business logic (the model) reside in a database and Java classes; the user interface (the view) is implemented in JSP; and the handler of client requests (the controller) is an HTTP Java servlet.

When the servlet receives a client HTTP request, it instantiates the model's central class and forwards the request to the appropriate JSP page. The JSP page obtains data from the model and generates the HTML response. The model isn't aware of what the JSP pages do with the data it provides, and the JSP pages aren't aware of where and how the model keeps the data.

The Model

The central model class is called `DataManager`. Its purpose is to hide all database operations from the JSP pages. `DataManager` supports some methods that have to do with initialization and connecting to the database, which we'll look at in later chapters. For the time being, we're more interested in the methods that implement the business logic of the application. Table 3-1 lists these methods.

Table 3-1. DataManager Methods

Type	Method
String	getCategoryName(int categoryId)
Hashtable	getCategories()
ArrayList	getSearchResults(String keyword)
ArrayList	getBooksInCategory(String categoryId)
Book	getBookDetails(int bookId)
long	insertOrder(String contactName, String deliveryAddress, String ccName, String ccNumber, String ccExpiryDate, Hashtable shoppingCart)

Their purpose should be pretty clear. I would just like to make a couple of points concerning insertOrder. First, the value it returns is the order ID to be given back to the client. Second, in a more realistic case, all parameters, with the exception of the shopping cart, would be replaced by a customer ID, typically the customer's e-mail address. In this simple application, however, as it doesn't keep track of the customers, there are no permanent customer records and customer IDs.

The Controller

The controller servlet extends javax.servlet.http.HttpServlet and is named ShopServlet.

Servlet Initialization

Tomcat executes the servlet method init immediately after instantiating the servlet (see Listing 3-9). You will find the code of the whole project in the software package for this chapter. To install it, open the folder named eshop project and copy either the folder eshop or the file eshop.war to Tomcat's webapps folder. To launch the application, view the URL http://localhost:8080/eshop/shop.

Listing 3-9. ShopServlet.java - init Method

```
public void init(ServletConfig config) throws ServletException {
   System.out.println("*** initializing controller servlet.");
   super.init(config);

   DataManager dataManager = new DataManager();
   dataManager.setDbUrl(config.getInitParameter("dbUrl"));
   dataManager.setDbUserName(config.getInitParameter("dbUserName"));
   dataManager.setDbPassword(config.getInitParameter("dbPassword"));
```

```
ServletContext context = config.getServletContext();
context.setAttribute("base", config.getInitParameter("base"));
context.setAttribute("imageUrl", config.getInitParameter("imageUrl"));
context.setAttribute("dataManager", dataManager);

try { // load the database JDBC driver
  Class.forName(config.getInitParameter("jdbcDriver"));
  }
catch (ClassNotFoundException e) {
  System.out.println(e.toString());
  }
}
```

As you can see, the initialization consists of three main activities: instantiating and configuring the data manager, saving some parameters for later use by the JSP pages (remember that JSP can access the servlet context via the implicit variable application), and loading the driver necessary to access the database—JDBC stands for Java DataBase Connector.

Notice that all these activities are done by setting servlet context attributes to values obtained through this method:

```
config.getInitParameter("init-parameter-name")
```

These values are stored in the WEB-INF\web.xml file, as shown in Listing 3-10.

Listing 3-10. Partial web.xml

```
<web-app ...>
  ...
  <servlet>
    ...
    <init-param>
      <param-name>dbUrl</param-name>
      <param-value>jdbc:mysql://localhost:3306/shop</param-value>
      </init-param>
    ...
    </servlet>
  ...
  <web-app ...>
```

By defining the critical initialization parameters in web.xml, you can change the parameters without having to modify the application code. Table 3-2 shows the initialization parameters defined for this application.

Table 3-2. Servlet Initialization Parameters

Name	Value
base	/eshop/shop
imageUrl	/eshop/images/

Name	Value
jdbcDriver	com.mysql.jdbc.Driver
dbUrl	jdbc:mysql://localhost:3306/shop
dbUserName	root
dbPassword	*none*

For ease of use, I didn't make the database password-protected, but this is obviously something you'd want to do in real life. I will explain how to install and use MySQL in Chapter 5. Then, the initialization parameters associated with the database will make complete sense. For the time being, the essential thing to keep in mind is how to define the initialization parameters.

From Chapter 2, you know that Tomcat makes available to JSP the servlet context by defining the implicit object application. Therefore, for example, the value set in ShopServlet.init() with context.setAttribute("imageUrl", ...) is available to JSP as the value returned by application.getAttribute("imageUrl").

Request Handling

Depending on what the user does, the page currently being displayed in the browser sends to the servlet a request with a specific value of the action parameter. The servlet then forwards each request to a JSP page determined by that value. For example, the page that shows the shopping cart also includes a button to check out. If the user clicks on it, the page will send to the servlet a request with the action parameter set to "checkOut".

The View

Table 3-3 shows the list of all JSP pages in the application. I will explain them in the next chapters, as we look at the different aspects of the application.

Table 3-3. JSP Pages

Name	Function	Mode of Access
index.jsp	The initial page welcoming a new user	
LeftMenu.jsp	Standard page sidebar	Included in all non-menu pages
TopMenu.jsp	Standard page header	Included in all non-menu pages
SelectCatalog.jsp	Lists books of a category	LeftMenu.jsp
SearchOutcome.jsp	Lists books selected through a search	LeftMenu.jsp

Name	Function	Mode of Access
BookDetails.jsp	Shows the details of one book	SelectCatalog.jsp and SearchOutcome.jsp
ShoppingCart.jsp	Displays the shopping cart	TopMenu.jsp and ShoppingCart.jsp
Checkout.jsp	Requests a customer's payment data	ShoppingCart.jsp
OrderConfirmation.jsp	Confirms acceptance of an order	Checkout.jsp

Additionally, you have a style-sheet file named eshop.css.

A typical user session proceeds as follows:

1. The user starts by accessing http://your-web-site/eshop/shop and sees the welcome page with a left-side menu containing a search box and a list of book categories. The user then can:

    - Type a word in the search box and hit the Search button, or select a book category.

    - Select one of the books by clicking on the corresponding Details link. The application then replaces the list of books with an image of the front cover of the book and all the information available in the database about that book.

    - Add the book to the shopping cart. The application then automatically takes the user to the shopping cart, where it is possible to update the number of copies or delete the book entry.

    - Repeat the previous steps until the user is ready to submit the order. From the shopping cart page, the user can then click on the Check Out link.

2. The check-out page asks the user to provide his or her personal and financial data. When the user clicks on the Confirm Order button, the page tells the application to memorize the order.

At any time, the user can add books through the left-side menu or go to the shopping cart through the top-side menu to modify the order.

Summary

In this chapter, I described the application architectures suitable for web applications and provided the example E-bookshop to explain how the Model-View-Controller architecture works.

You then learned how to install the Eclipse IDE, how to configure it to use the latest versions of Java and Tomcat, and how to create JSP applications from scratch. It was necessary at this point because, with E-bookshop, we had reached the limit of what was reasonable to do without an IDE.

Finally, I introduced the E-shop project, which, in different versions, I will use to complete the description of JSP and to explain JSF.

In the next three chapters, I'll take you through the remaining functionality of JSP. In particular, the next chapter will be dedicated to the action elements. To do that, I will use simple dedicated examples and the relevant aspects of the eshop application.

CHAPTER 4

JSP in Action

In Chapter 2, you learned that there are three types of JSP elements: scripting, directives, and actions. I described the first two types directly in Chapter 2, and the time has come to look at JSP actions. Actions, like scriptlets, are processed when a page is requested. In this chapter, you will learn how to use JSP standard actions, how to create actions of your own design, and how to use some of the actions contained in the JSP Standard Tag Library. Besides small specific examples, you will also learn the role of actions in the eshop application that I introduced in the previous chapter. Actions can do everything that scripting elements can do, as you will see at the end of the next chapter, when I will tell you how to write JSP code without any scripting element at all.

JSP Standard Actions

While Tomcat executes directive elements when translating a page, it executes action elements when processing a client's HTTP request.

JSP actions specify activities to be performed when a page is requested and can therefore operate on objects and affect the response. They normally take the following form:

```
<jsp:action-name attr1="value1" [attr2="value2"...]> ... </jsp:action-name>
```

However, actions can also have a body, like in the following example:

```
<jsp:action-name attribute-list>
  <jsp:subaction-name subaction-attribute-list/>
  </jsp:action-name>
```

There are eight JSP standard actions (forward, include, useBean, setProperty, getProperty, text, element, and plugin) and five additional actions that can only appear in the body of other actions (param, params, attribute, body, and fallback).

Actually, to be precise, there are two additional action elements—invoke and doBody—that you cannot invoke from within JSP pages. More about them later in this chapter. There is also a further standard action—root—that I will explain at the end of the next chapter.

Actions: forward, include, and param

The forward action lets you abort execution of the current page and transfer the request to another page:

```
<jsp:forward page="myOtherPage.jsp">
  <jsp:param name="newParName" value="newParValue"/>
  </jsp:forward>
```

The include action is similar to forward, the main difference being that it returns control to the including page after the included page has completed execution. The output of the included page is appended to the output generated by the including page up to the point where the action is executed.

As shown in the example, jsp:param lets you define a new parameter for the invoked page, which also has access to the parameters already available to the invoking page.

Here is another example of a forward action:

```
<% String dest = "/myJspPages/" + someVar; %>
<jsp:forward page="<%=dest%>">
  <jsp:param name="newParName" value="newParValue"/>
  </jsp:forward>
```

This is 100 percent equivalent to the following scriptlet:

```
<%
  String dest = "/myJspPages/" + someVar;
  RequestDispatcher rd = application.getRequestDispatcher(dest + "?newParName=newParValue");
  rd.forward(request, response);
  %>
```

Tomcat clears the output buffer upon executing the forward action. Therefore, the HTML code generated up to that point by the current page is lost. But if the current page has already filled the response buffer by the time it is aborted with forward, that part of the response will have already left the server. This will probably result in a bad page sent to the client. Therefore, you have to be very careful when invoking forward from within a page that generates a large output.

You don't have to worry about such a problem with include, because Tomcat doesn't clear the output buffer when it executes that action.

With both forward and include, the destination page must be a well-formed and complete JSP page. The forward action must satisfy the additional requirement of generating a complete and valid HTML page, because the output of the destination page is what goes back to the client's browser in the HTML response. The destination page of an include action might even generate only a single character, although in most cases it provides HTML code. For example, the top bar of the eshop application is generated in the page TopMenu.jsp (see Listing 4-1) and included in seven JSP pages with this code:

```
<jsp:include page="TopMenu.jsp" flush="true"/>
```

The flush attribute (default false) ensures that the HTML generated so far by the including page is sent to the client before executing the included page. Note that the included page is not allowed to change the response headers or the status code.

Listing 4-1. TopMenu.jsp

```
<%@page language="java" contentType="text/html"%>
<%
  String base = (String)application.getAttribute("base");
  String imageUrl = (String)application.getAttribute("imageUrl");
  %>
<div class="header">
  <div class="logo">
    <p>e-Shopping Center</p>
    </div>
  <div class="cart">
    <a class="link2" href="<%=base%>?action=showCart">Show Cart
      <img src="<%=imageUrl%>/cart.gif" border="0"/></a>
```

```
      </div>
    </div>
```

TopMenu.jsp generates the HTML code in Listing 4-2 (shown after I removed the empty lines).

Listing 4-2. HTML Generated by TopMenu.jsp

```
<div class="header">
  <div class="logo">
    <p>e-Shopping Center</p>
    </div>
  <div class="cart">
    <a class="link2" href="/eshop/shop?action=showCart">Show Cart
      <img src="/eshop/images//cart.gif" border="0"/></a>
    </div>
  </div>
```

Notice that TopMenu.jsp uses styles (such as class="header") that aren't loaded or defined within the same file. If you're wondering how that's possible, you probably don't clearly understand the distinction between source JSP and output HTML. The JSP code in TopMenu.jsp is executed on the server, and it produces HTML code, which is then appended to the output buffer. JSP *doesn't need* style sheets. It is the generated HTML that needs them when it's interpreted by the client's browser.

You might think that <jsp:include page="..."/> is the same as <%@include file="..."%>, but this is definitely not the case. The most important difference is that while the include directive includes the content of a file without any processing, the include action includes the *output* of the included resource. If the resource is a JSP page, this makes a big difference. In practical terms, this also explains why JSP pages to be included with jsp:include must be well-formed and complete pages rather than simply JSP fragments.

To illustrate a subtle consequence of the different mechanisms of inclusion, I have prepared a small test page (see Listing 4-3). To try it out, copy to the usual test folder (webapps\ROOT\tests\) the folder named jsp_includes that you will find in the software package for this chapter, and then type localhost:8080/tests/jsp_includes/includes.jsp in a web browser.

Listing 4-3. includes.jsp

```
<%@page language="java" contentType="text/html"%>
<html><head><title>A</title></head><body>
<table border="1">
  <tr><th>incl B</th><th>incl C</th><th>C contains</th></tr>
  <tr><td>jsp:include</td><td>jsp:include</td><td><jsp:include page="d/b_act.jsp"/></td></tr>
  <tr><td>jsp:include</td><td>@include</td><td><jsp:include page="d/b_dir.jsp"/></td></tr>
  <tr><td>@include</td><td>jsp:include</td><td><%@include file="d/b_act.jsp"%></td></tr>
  <tr><td>@include</td><td>@include</td><td><%@include file="d/b_dir.jsp"%></td></tr>
  </table>
</body></html>
```

As you can see, I first included the d/b_act.jsp and d/b_dir.jsp files with an include action and then with an include directive. The two files contain these lines, respectively:

```
<%@page language="java" contentType="text/html"%><jsp:include page="c.txt"/>
<%@page language="java" contentType="text/html"%><%@include file="c.txt"%>
```

I placed a c.txt file (only containing the letter A) in the directory of includes.jsp and a second c.txt file (only containing the letter B) in the d directory. Figure 4-1 shows the result of running includes.jsp.

***Figure 4-1.** The output of includes.jsp*

As you can see, includes.jsp displays the letter B in all cases except when you implement the outer inclusion with the directive and the inner inclusion with the action. This means that only with that particular combination of file inclusions, includes.jsp accesses the c.txt file that is in the same directory. In the other three cases, includes.jsp accesses the c.txt file that is in the d directory, together with b_act.jsp and b_dir.jsp. To understand these results, you have to know that when Tomcat translates a JSP page into a Java class, it replaces <jsp:include page="fname"/> with an execution of the method org.apache.jasper.runtime.JspRuntimeLibrary.include(request, response, "fname", out, false), while <%@include file="fname"%> results in the copying of the *content* of the fname file. Therefore, in the third case of the example, the <jsp:include page="c.txt"/> inside b_act.jsp is replaced with an include(request, response, "c.txt", out, false), and then the whole b_act.jsp is copied into includes.jsp. That's why the servlet picks up the file in the directory of includes.jsp. The fact that b_act.jsp was in a different directory was lost when its include directive was replaced by the file content.

I decided to spend a bit of time on this issue because the inclusion mechanism is often misunderstood and causes many people to knock their heads against the wall when files seem to disappear.

Action: useBean

The useBean action declares a new JSP scripting variable and associates a Java object to it. For example, the following code declares the variable dataManager of type eshop.model.DataManager:

```
<jsp:useBean id="dataManager" scope="application" class="eshop.model.DataManager"/>
```

This is the same data manager instantiated and configured in ShopServlet.java as you saw in Chapter 3 (Listing 3-9). JSP uses this variable to access the data without having to worry about its location and implementation. Within eshop, this is the only way for JSP (the View) to interact with the data manager (the Model). For example, when a user selects a book and clicks on the link to add it to the shopping cart, the controller servlet executes ShoppingCart.jsp with an argument set to the book identifier. Then, ShoppingCart.jsp executes a method of the data manager (see Table 3-1) to obtain the book details, which are actually stored in a MySQL database:

```
Book book = dataManager.getBookDetails(bookId);
```

The result is stored in an object of type book, from which JSP can obtain individual book attributes by executing simple get methods such as book.getTitle() and book.getAuthor().

jsp:useBean accepts the attributes beanName, class, id, scope, and type, of which only id is mandatory.

If you type <jsp:useBean id="objName"/>, Tomcat will check whether an object named objName exists in pageContext. If it exists, Tomcat will create a variable named objName of the same type as the object, so that you can access the object in subsequent JSP scripting elements. If the object doesn't exist, Tomcat will throw a java.lang.InstantiationException.

If you type <jsp:useBean id="objName" scope="*aScope*"/> with *aScope* set to one of the words page, request, session, or application, Tomcat will behave as described in the previous paragraph, but it will look for the objName object in the given scope rather than in the page context. In other words, page is the default scope.

Also jsp:useBean can create new objects. Whether useBean does it and what type of variable it makes available for JSP scripting depends on the three remaining attributes: class, type, and beanName.

■ **Caution** The use of jsp:useBean is not for the faint hearted!

If you specify class and set it to a fully qualified class name (i.e., with its package, as in java.lang.String) but specify neither type nor beanName, Tomcat will instantiate an object of the given class in the scope you specify with the attribute scope (or in the page scope by default).

If together with class you also specify type, Tomcat will set the data type of the new object to the value of the type attribute. You can set the type attribute to the same class as the class attribute (which is equivalent to omitting type), to a superclass of class, or to an interface implemented by class.

If instead of class you specify the beanName attribute, Tomcat will behave as if you had specified class, but only after attempting to find a serialized bean of that class. Serializing a bean means that the object's data is converted to a byte stream and saved in a file with the extension ser. Tomcat expects to find serialized objects in the same folder containing the application classes. For example, a serialized bean of the xxx.yyy.Zzz class is expected to be in the WEB-INF\classes\xxx\yyy\Zzz.ser file. This mechanism lets you save an object in a file and then load it into your JSP page. You can actually have several serialized beans of the same class (e.g., Zzz.ser, Zzz_test.ser, Zzz25.ser, and Abc.ser). Fortunately, the designers of JSP have thought this issue through and allowed you to set the value of beanName at request time (the other attributes must be hard-coded), so that you can parameterize your page for what concerns loading serialized objects.

Finally, if you specify type and set it to a fully qualified class name but specify neither class nor beanName, Tomcat won't instantiate any object and will instead look for it in the given scope. If it finds it, Tomcat will make it available as an object of the given type rather than of the class from which it was instantiated. If what I just explained sounds confusing, you might decide to follow a simple rule: forget that jsp:useBean supports the attributes class and beanName. Let the servlet do the work. Just pay attention that the servlet creates the objects in the correct scope. In the previous chapter, the initialization method of the eshop servlet (see Listing 3.9) first instantiated the dataManager object and then saved it in the application scope.

Caution Don't confuse the scope of a bean as specified with the useBean attribute scope with the scope of the scripting variable that Tomcat associates to the bean

---

As an example of useBean scopes, the following code instantiates a MyClass object that remains available as long as the session remains valid:

```
<jsp:useBean class="myPkg.MyClass" id="myObj" scope="session"/>
```

You'll be able to access it via a scripting variable named myObj in any page within the same session with the following statement:

```
<jsp:useBean id="myObj" type="myPkg.MyClass" scope="session"/>
```

However, the scope of the scripting variable myObj is determined by where within your page you execute useBean, as with the declaration of any other scripting variable. If you find this confusing, consider this: in the page containing the second useBean, you don't have access to the scripting variable myObj until you execute the useBean action. Before that, the scripting variable is undefined, although the bean called myObj already exists, as it was instantiated by the first useBean in a previously executed page. This tells you that the scripting variable referring to the object and the actual object are two different things with two different scopes, even if they share the same name.

Incidentally, the first useBean (with class, id, and scope) is completely equivalent to this:

```
<%
MyClass myName = new MyClass();
session.setAttribute("myObj", myObj);
%>
```

and the second useBean (with id, type, and scope) is the same as this:

```
<%
MyClass myObj = (MyClass)session.getAttribute("myObj");
%>
```

This representation should make completely clear that the object and the scripting variable are two different entities. In the second scriptlet, you could even decide to call the scripting variable with a different name.

Because of all the options implemented by combining its attributes, as I said at the beginning, useBean is somewhat tricky to use. But you can always come back to this page in case of doubt!

Actions: setProperty and getProperty

A bean property is nothing else than an attribute of a bean's class, but only when you define for that attribute the standard get and put methods . To make it completely clear, both get and put must be there. Otherwise, that class attribute is *not* a bean property.

Additionally, you must name the two methods respectively get and put, followed by the full name of the attribute with the first letter capitalized. For example, if you define the attribute named myAttr, you must name the two attributes getMyAttr and setMyAttr. Otherwise, again, Tomcat will not recognize the attribute as a bean property.

An example from the eshop application will convince you that you are better off if Tomcat recognizes an attribute as a property. The JSP page `OrderConfirmation.jsp` has the following two elements:

```
<jsp:useBean id="customer" class="eshop.beans.Customer"/>
<jsp:setProperty property="*" name="customer"/>
```

The useBean action instantiates an object of type Customer and assigns it to the variable named customer. The action is equivalent to:

```
Customer customer = new Customer();
```

By defining property="*", the setProperty action tells Tomcat to set all bean properties of the newly created object. What setProperty does *not* say is to what values they should be set. This is because the values come from request parameters named *exactly* like the properties. Check out the definition of the Customer class, shown in Listing 4-4.

Listing 4-4. *Customer.java*

```
package eshop.beans;

public class Customer {
  private String contactName = "";
  private String deliveryAddress = "";
  private String ccName = "";
  private String ccNumber = "";
  private String ccExpiryDate = "";

  public String getContactName() {
    return contactName;
    }
  public void setContactName(String contactName) {
    this.contactName = contactName;
    }

  public String getDeliveryAddress() {
    return deliveryAddress;
    }
  public void setDeliveryAddress(String deliveryAddress) {
    this.deliveryAddress = deliveryAddress;
    }

  public String getCcName() {
    return ccName;
    }
  public void setCcName(String ccName) {
    this.ccName = ccName;
    }

  public String getCcNumber() {
    return ccNumber;
    }
  public void setCcNumber(String ccNumber) {
```

```
    this.ccNumber = ccNumber;
    }

  public String getCcExpiryDate() {
    return ccExpiryDate;
    }
  public void setCcExpiryDate(String ccExpiryDate) {
    this.ccExpiryDate = ccExpiryDate;
    }
  }
```

As you can see, the Customer class defines private attributes and then the methods to access them, so that they can be recognized as properties.

▪ **Caution** The use of property="*" can have confusing outcomes if parameters and attributes are not correctly matched

---

So far so good. Not so interesting. But what is interesting is that the setProperty action

```
<jsp:setProperty property="*" name="customer"/>
```

is equivalent to the following:

```
customer.setContactName(request.getParameter("contactName");
customer.setDeliveryAddress(request.getParameter("deliveryAddress");
customer.setCcName(request.getParameter("ccName");
customer.setCcNumber(request.getParameter("ccNumber"));
customer.setCcExpiryDate(request.getParameter("ccExpiryDate"));
```

The implementation with the action is more compact and, most importantly, it remains valid regardless of whether you add or remove customer attributes. And that's what makes setProperty worthwhile.

Also jsp:getProperty is useful, because it sends the value of a property to the output. For example, suppose you define MyClass as shown in Listing 4-5.

Listing 4-5. MyClass.java

```
package MyClasses;
import java.io.Serializable;
public class MyClass implements java.io.Serializable {
  public static final long serialVersionUID = 1L;
  private int i;
  public MyClass() {i = 0;}
  public void setI(int i) {this.i = i;}
  public int getI() {return i;}
  }
```

As you can see, the integer attribute i is a property. Listing 4-6 shows a JSP page that uses both getProperty and setProperty.

Listing 4-6. myObj.jsp

```
<%@page language="java" contentType="text/html"%>
<%@page import="java.util.*, MyClasses.MyClass"%>
<%@page trimDirectiveWhitespaces="true"%>
<html><head><title>myObj</title></head><body>
<jsp:useBean id="obj" class="MyClasses.MyClass" scope="session">
  <jsp:setProperty name="obj" property="i" value="11"/>
  </jsp:useBean>
<jsp:getProperty name="obj" property="i"/>
<jsp:setProperty name="obj" property="i" value="22"/>
<jsp:getProperty name="obj" property="i"/>
</body></html>
```

As you can see, myObj.jsp instantiates the bean object with useBean and initializes its attribute by executing setProperty within the body of useBean. The advantage of doing it that way is that Tomcat only attempts to execute the sub-action setProperty if the instantiation of the bean succeeds.

The two executions of getProperty send the value of i to the output. As a result, myObj.jsp generates the following HTML page:

```
<html><head><title>myObj</title></head><body>
1122</body></html>
```

The example also shows that in setProperty you can replace the value attribute with param. Then, Tomcat sets the attribute to the value of the identically named request parameter. Notice how the page directive with trimDirectiveWhitespaces set to true only leaves a single newline, after <body>, because it is in the HTML template. It results in 11 and 12 being "fused" into 1122. Not necessarily what you would like to have.

Action: text

You can use the jsp:text action to write template text. Its syntax is straightforward:

```
<jsp:text>Template data</jsp:text>
```

Its body cannot contain other elements; it can only contain text and EL expressions.

Actions: element, attribute, and body

With the actions element, attribute, and body, you can define XML elements dynamically within a JSP page. One reason why you might like to define XML elements dynamically is that your JSP page, instead of generating a web page to be displayed in a browser, might need to generate an XML file used to exchange data with other modules and applications. The word *dynamically* is important, because it means that you can generate the XML elements at request time rather than statically at compile time.

The JSP page shown in Listing 4-7 generates the HTML output shown in Listing 4-8. It is a meaningless page, only designed to show you how to use these actions. Don't look for a meaning that doesn't exist!

Listing 4-7. actel_element_attribute.jsp

```
<%@page language="java" contentType="text/html"%>
<html>
<head><title>Action elements: element, attribute</title></head>
<body>
<jsp:element name="myElem">
  <jsp:attribute name="myElemAttr">myElemAttr's value</jsp:attribute>
  <jsp:body>myElem's body</jsp:body>
  </jsp:element>
<br/>
<jsp:include page="text.txt"/>
<br/>
<jsp:include>
  <jsp:attribute name="page">text.txt</jsp:attribute>
  </jsp:include>
</body>
</html>
```

Listing 4-8. The Output of actel_element_attribute.jsp

```
<html>
<head><title>Action elements: element, attribute</title></head>
<body>
<myElem myElemAttr="myElemAttr's value">myElem's body</myElem>
<br/>
This is inside the test file text.txt
<br/>
This is inside the test file text.txt
</body>
</html>
```

I have highlighted two parts of the listings. The first highlight shows how to use the actions element, attribute, and body to generate an XML element. Be aware that if you drop the action body, the XML element generated by element will have an empty body, as in the following example:

```
<myElem myElemAttr="myElemAttr's value"/>
```

The second highlight shows how you can use attribute to move the page attribute of include to be inside the body of the include action. The content of the file text.txt is unimportant. You'll find a one-line file in the jsp_element folder of the software package for this chapter.

Actions: plugin, params, and fallback

These three actions let you embed an object in a web page. For example, Listing 4-9 shows you how to embed an applet with plugin, how to pass to it a line of text with params, and how to inform the user with fallback if the applet fails to start. To test it, copy the file plugin.jsp from the jsp_plugin folder of the software package for this chapter to the usual tests folder, and then browse localhost:8080/tests/plugin.jsp.

The plugin action generates for you the appropriate browser-dependent HTML construct to embed the applet.

Listing 4-9. plugin.jsp

```
<%@page language="java" contentType="text/html"%>
<html><head><title>Action: plugin</title></head><body>
<jsp:plugin type="applet" code="MyApplet.class"
  codebase="/tests" height="100" width="100">
  <jsp:params>
    <jsp:param name="line" value="Well said!"/>
    </jsp:params>
  <jsp:fallback>Unable to start plugin</jsp:fallback>
  </jsp:plugin>
</body></html>
```

If you want to try it yourself, Listing 4-10 shows you the code for a simple applet.

Listing 4-10. MyApplet.java

```
import java.awt.*;
import java.applet.*;
public class MyApplet extends Applet {
  String line;
  public void init() {
    line = getParameter("line");
    }
  public void paint(Graphics page) {
    page.setColor(Color.red);
    page.fillRect(0, 0, 50, 50);
    page.setColor(Color.green);
    page.fillRect(50, 0, 50, 50);
    page.setColor(Color.blue);
    page.fillRect(0, 50, 50, 50);
    page.setColor(Color.yellow);
    page.fillRect(50, 50, 50, 50);
    page.setColor(Color.black);
    page.drawString(line, 10, 40);
    }
  }
```

And Figure 4-2 shows what you should see in your browser. To test it, compile the applet, place both plugin.jsp and MyApplet.class in the folder %CATALINA_HOME%\webapps\ROOT\tests\, and type localhost:8080/tests/plugin.jsp in your browser. Note that Tomcat doesn't do anything with the applet itself. It only sends it to the client when requested to do so. That's why the applet class doesn't need to be placed in the WEB-INF folder like the other classes you have encountered so far.

Figure 4-2. *The output of plugin.jsp*

`jsp:plugin` accepts the attributes `type`, `jreversion`, `nspluginurl`, and `iepluginurl`. The example used `type` to specify that the plugin was an applet; `jreversion` lets you specify the version number of the JRE specification you require (the default is 1.2); and `nspluginurl` and `iepluginurl` let you specify where the JRE plug-in can be downloaded for Netscape Navigator and Internet Explorer, respectively. However, I doubt that you will ever use the last three attributes.

Comments and Escape Characters

The comment delimiters `<%-- .. --%>` have in JSP the same function as `/* .. */` in Java. You can also use them to "switch off" JSP elements, as shown here:

```
<%-- <jsp:include page="whatever.jsp"/> --%>
```

They can also span over several lines.

■ **Note** Regular HTML comments such as `<!-- ... -->` won't work with JSP

JSP comments have the advantage over HTML comments in that they are not sent to the client. Their content is therefore invisible to the user.

To include the sequence of characters `<%` and `%>` in template text, you have to "break" them with a backslash, like in `<\%` and `%\>`, so that the JSP engine doesn't interpret them as the beginning and end of scripting elements. Alternatively, you can replace the inequality signs with their corresponding HTML entities, as in `&lt;%` and `%&gt;`.

JSP's Tag Extension Mechanism

You can define your own actions to replace lengthy scriptlets. By "hiding" functions behind custom tags, you can increase modularity and maintainability of your pages.

To write in a JSP page a statement like

```
<myPrefix:myActionTag attributeName="myAttributeName"/>
```

you need to follow the following steps:

1. Define Java classes that provide the functionality of the new actions, including the definition of their attributes (e.g., `myAttributeName`). These classes are called *tag handlers*.

2. Provide a formalized description of your action elements, so that Tomcat knows how to handle them. For example, you need to specify which actions can have a body and which attributes can be omitted. Such a description is called a tag library descriptor (TLD).

3. In the JSP pages, tell Tomcat that the pages need your *tag library* and specify the prefix that you want to identify those custom tags with.

I will take you through these steps, beginning with bodyless actions, which are simpler to implement.

Bodyless Custom Actions

A bodyless action is an element that, not having an end tag, cannot enclose a body between start and end tags. As an example, let's say you want to develop an action that prints the day of the week of any given date:

```
<wow:weekday date="date"/>
```

With the date attribute accepting values in the form yyyy-mm-dd and defaulting to the current date. All the examples of this section on bodyless actions and the following section of bodied actions are in the software package for this chapter. To test them, copy the folder `tags` to Tomcat's `webapps` folder.

Step 1: Define the Tag Handler

A tag handler for a bodyless custom tag is a class that implements the interfaces `java.io.Serializable` and `javax.servlet.jsp.tagext.Tag`. Remember that to satisfy an interface, you have to implement all the methods it defines.

To satisfy `Serializable`, you only need to define a unique identifier, like this:

```
static final long serialVersionUID = 1L;
```

The value identifies the version of your class and the objects you instantiate from it. It is then used when deserializing objects to check that class and object match. As long as you don't have several versions of the class and swap objects between JVMs, you don't really need to worry about it. However, to satisfy the `Tag` interface, you have to define the methods listed in Table 4-1.

Table 4-1. The Methods of the Tag Interface

Method	Description
int doEndTag()	Processes the end tag
int doStartTag()	Processes the start tag

Method	Description
Tag getParent()	Provides a reference to the closest enclosing tag handler
void release()	Removes all the references to objects
void setPageContext(PageContext pc)	Sets the current page context
void setParent(Tag t)	Sets the closest enclosing tag handler

Fortunately, the javax.servlet.jsp.tagext.TagSupport class makes life easier by implementing the Tag interface with default methods and other useful methods. Therefore, you only need to extend TagSupport and overwrite the methods you need for your weekday action. You certainly don't need getParent, because the action isn't going to be used in the body of other actions. You don't need doStartTag either, because the action is bodyless, and, as a consequence, you don't have separate start and end tags. In conclusion, you only need to overwrite doEndTag with a method containing all the functionality of the weekday tag.

Listing 4-11 shows you the code of the whole tag handler.

Listing 4-11. WeekdayTag.java

```java
package tags;

import javax.servlet.jsp.JspException;
import javax.servlet.jsp.tagext.TagSupport;
import java.util.Date;
import java.text.SimpleDateFormat;
import java.util.Calendar;
import java.util.GregorianCalendar;

public class WeekdayTag extends TagSupport {
  static final long serialVersionUID = 1L;
  static final String[] WD = {"","Sun","Mon","Tue","Wed","Thu","Fri","Sat"};
  private String date;

  public void setDate(String date) {
    this.date = date;
    }

  public int doEndTag() throws JspException {
    GregorianCalendar cal = new GregorianCalendar();
    SimpleDateFormat fmt = new SimpleDateFormat("yyyy-MM-dd");
    fmt.setLenient(true);
    if (date != null && date.length() > 0) {
      Date d = new Date();
      try {
        d = fmt.parse(date);
        }
      catch (Exception e) {
        throw new JspException("Date parsing failed: " + e.getMessage());
```

```
      }
    cal.setTime(d);
    }
  try {
    pageContext.getOut().print(WD[cal.get(Calendar.DAY_OF_WEEK)]);
    }
  catch (Exception e) {
    throw new JspException("Weekday writing failed: " + e.getMessage());
    }
  return EVAL_PAGE;
  }
}
```

You need the setDate method because Tomcat uses it to pass the value of the action's date attribute to the tag handler. The corresponding getDate method isn't present, because it is never used and can be omitted. That said, you might argue that working with incomplete Java beans, sooner or later, will get you into trouble. If the action is executed without the date attribute, the date variable defined in doEndTag remains set to null, and the calendar cal, which is used to determine the day of the week, remains set to the current date. On the other hand, if a date attribute is specified in the action, its value is parsed and used to set the calendar.

Notice that the tag handler is named like the tag but with the first letter capitalized and with the Tag suffix. This is a good practice to follow, although you can name your handlers whatever you like. You'll see in a moment how to make the association between a tag and its handler.

The return value EVAL_PAGE means that execution should continue with the page code following the custom action. Use SKIP_PAGE to abort the page.

In any case, you must place your handlers in WEB-INF\classes\. For example, as WeekDayTag.java belongs to the package named tags, its compiled class must go into the folder WEB-INF\classes\tags\.

Step 2: Define the TLD

The TLD is an XML file that describes your tags so that Tomcat knows how to deal with them. Listing 4-11 shows the full TLD for the custom tag library.

Listing 4-11. wow.tld

```
<?xml version="1.0" encoding="UTF-8"?>
<taglib xmlns="http://java.sun.com/xml/ns/javaee"
    xmlns:xsi="http://www.w3.org/2001/XMLSchema-instance"
    xsi:schemaLocation="http://java.sun.com/xml/ns/javaee ~CCC
http://java.sun.com/xml/ns/j2ee/web-jsptaglibrary_2_1.xsd"
    version="2.1">
  <description>Example of a simple tag library</description>
  <tlib-version>1.0</tlib-version>
  <short-name>wow</short-name>
  <tag>
    <description>Displays the day of the week</description>
    <display-name>weekday</display-name>
    <name>weekday</name>
    <tag-class>tags.WeekdayTag</tag-class>
    <body-content>empty</body-content>
    <attribute>
```

```
        <name>date</name>
        <type>java.lang.String</type>
        <rtexprvalue>true</rtexprvalue>
      </attribute>
    </tag>
  </taglib>
```

As you can see, the outermost element is taglib, which contains a tag element for each custom action (in this case, only weekday). Apart from tag, all taglib sub-elements in the example are for information purposes or to be used by tools and can be omitted.

The tag element contains an attribute sub-element for each action attribute (in this case, only date). Of the tag sub-elements in the example, you can omit description and display-name. The sub-element name defines the custom action name; tag-class specifies the fully qualified class name of the tag handler; and body-content specifies the action to be bodyless.

The sub-element tag-class is what gives you the freedom to name your tag handlers anything you like. The sub-element body-content is mandatory and can only have one the following three values: empty, scriptless, or tagdependent. The value scriptless is the default and means that the body cannot contain scripting elements, while EL expressions and JSP actions are accepted and processed normally. The value tagdependent means that the body content is passed to the tag handler as it is, without any processing. This is useful if the body contains character sequences, such as <%, that would confuse Tomcat.

Note that up to JSP 2.0, body-content was mandatory, and body-content="JSP" was valid. This is no longer the case with JSP 2.1.

The attribute element in the example has three sub-elements: name, which sets the action attribute name; type, which sets the class name of the attribute value; and rtexprvalue, which decides whether the attribute accepts values at request time.

If you had used a type other than String, the value passed to the tag handler would have been of that type. For example, with an attribute defined like this:

```
<attribute>
  <name>num</name>
  <type>java.lang.Integer</type>
</attribute>
```

you would have included the following code in the tag handler:

```
private int num;
public void setNum(Integer num) {
  this.num = num.intValue();
  }
```

When processing the start tag of the custom action, Tomcat would have parsed the string passed to the action (as in num="23") to obtain the Integer value for the tag handler.

If you had omitted the rtexprvalue sub-element or set it to false, you would have been forced to pass to the date attribute only constant values, such as "2007-12-05", instead of runtime values such as "<%=aDate%>". (rtexpr stands for real-time expression).

Inside WEB-INF, create a folder named tlds and place wow.tld there.

Step 3: Use the Custom Action

Listing 4-12 shows you a simple JSP page to test the weekday custom action.

Listing 4-12. weekday.jsp

```
1: <%@page language="java" contentType="text/html"%>
2: <%@taglib uri="/WEB-INF/tlds/wow.tld" prefix="wow"%>
3: <% String d = request.getParameter("d"); %>
4: <html><head><title>weekday bodyless tag</title></head><body>
5: weekday today: <wow:weekday/><br/>
6: weekday <%=d%>: <wow:weekday date="<%=d%>"/>
7: </body></html>
```

Line 2 contains the `taglib` directive, line 4 uses weekday without the `date` attribute, and line 6 passes the request parameter d to the action. It's as simple as that.

If you type in your browser `http://localhost:8080/tags/weekday.jsp?d=2012-12-25`, you get two lines, such as Today: Wed and 2012-12-25: Tue. If you type the URL without the query, the second line of the output becomes null: Wed. On the other hand, if you type a query with a bad date, such as d=2012-1225, Tomcat shows you an error page with a back trace that begins as follows:

```
org.apache.jasper.JasperException: javax.servlet.ServletException: ➡
  javax.servlet.jsp.JspException: ➡
    Date parsing failed: Unparseable date: "2012-1225"
```

To try out the example, you can simply copy the folder named tags from the code of Chapter 4 to Tomcat's webapps folder. You can then execute the example by typing in your browser `localhost:8080/tags/weekday.jsp`.

Note that if you modify the tag handler, you need to recompile it from the command line. To do so, type the following two commands:

```
cd c:\program files\apache software foundation\tomcat\webapps\tags\web-inf\classes\tags
javac -classpath "C:\Program Files\Apache Software Foundation\Tomcat\lib\jsp-api.jar" ➡
  WeekDayTag.java
```

You then also have to restart Tomcat.

Bodied Custom Actions

To show you the differences from the bodyless action, I will implement a version of the weekday action that expects the date in its body instead of in an attribute:

```
<wow:weekdayBody>date</wow:weekdayBody>
```

Step 1: Define the Tag Handler

Similar to bodyless actions, the tag handlers for bodied actions need to implement an interface, only this time it's `javax.servlet.jsp.tagex.BodyTag` instead of `Tag`. Again, similarly to bodyless actions, the API provides a convenient class that you can use as a basis: `javax.servlet.jsp.tagext.BodyTagSupport`. However, as opposed to what you did in the tag handler for a bodyless action, you cannot simply replace the `doEndTag` method, because the action body will have come and gone by the time you reach the end tag. You first have to overwrite `doAfterBody`.

An additional complication concerns the default date: if you write the action with an empty body, as follows:

```
<wow:weekdayBody></wow:weekdayBody>
```

the method doAfterBody won't be executed at all. How can you then print out the default day?

The answer is simple: you have to overwrite the doEndTag method and write the default date from there in case there is no body. Listing 4-13 shows the end result.

Listing 4-13. WeekdayBodyTag.java

```java
package tags;

import javax.servlet.jsp.JspException;
import javax.servlet.jsp.tagext.BodyTagSupport;
import java.util.Date;
import java.text.SimpleDateFormat;
import java.util.Calendar;
import java.util.GregorianCalendar;

public class WeekdayBodyTag extends BodyTagSupport {
  static final long serialVersionUID = 1L;
  static final String[] WD = {"","Sun","Mon","Tue","Wed","Thu","Fri","Sat"};
  private boolean bodyless = true;   /* 1 */

  public int doAfterBody() throws JspException {
    String date = getBodyContent().getString();   /* 2 */
    if (date.length() > 0) {
      GregorianCalendar cal = new GregorianCalendar();
      Date d = new Date();
      SimpleDateFormat fmt = new SimpleDateFormat("yyyy-MM-dd");
      fmt.setLenient(true);
      try {
        d = fmt.parse(date);
        }
      catch (Exception e) {
        throw new JspException("Date parsing failed: " + e.getMessage());
        }
      cal.setTime(d);
      try {
          getPreviousOut().print(WD[cal.get(Calendar.DAY_OF_WEEK)]);   /* 3 */
          }
        catch (Exception e) {
          throw new JspException("Weekday writing failed: " + e.getMessage());
          }
      bodyless = false;   /* 4 */
      }
    return SKIP_BODY;
    }

  public int doEndTag() throws JspException {
    if (bodyless) {   /* 5 */
      GregorianCalendar cal = new GregorianCalendar();
      try {
        pageContext.getOut().print(WD[cal.get(Calendar.DAY_OF_WEEK)]);
        }
      catch (Exception e) {
```

```
        throw new JspException("Weekday writing failed: " + e.getMessage());
      }
    }
    return EVAL_PAGE;
  }
}
```

Lines 1, 4, and 5 implement the mechanism to ensure that you write the default date but only when the body is empty. In line 1, you define a boolean instance variable called bodyless and set it to true. If there is no body to process, doAfterBody does not run, and doEndTag in line 5 prints the default day of the week. If, on the other hand, there is a body to process, doAfterBody in line 4 sets bodyless to false, and doEndTag does nothing.

Line 2 shows you how to get the body content, and line 3 how to get the method to print the date while processing the body. The method has been named getPreviousOut to remind you that there can be actions within actions, in which case you'll want to append the output of an inner action to that of an outer one.

Step 2: Define the TLD

To define the new action, you only need to add the <tag> shown in Listing 4-14 after the <tag> for the bodyless weekday action.

Listing 4-14. The tag Element for weekdayBody

```
<tag>
  <description>Displays the day of the week</description>
  <display-name>weekdayBody</display-name>
  <name>weekdayBody</name>
  <tag-class>tags.WeekdayBodyTag</tag-class>
  <body-content>scriptless</body-content>
</tag>
```

Notice that you define the body-content sub-element as scriptless even though it is the default. The purpose is to make the code more readable. It's just a matter of taste.

Step 3: Use the Custom Action

Listing 4-15 shows a modified version of weekday.jsp to handle the bodied tag.

Listing 4-15. weekday_b.jsp for the Bodied Action

```
<%@page language="java" contentType="text/html"%>
<%@taglib uri="/WEB-INF/tlds/wow.tld" prefix="wow"%>
<html><head><title>weekday bodied tag</title></head><body>
weekdayBody today: <wow:weekdayBody></wow:weekdayBody><br/>
weekdayBody ${param.d}: <wow:weekdayBody>${param.d}</wow:weekdayBody><br/>
</body></html>
```

Notice that I replaced the request.getParameter("d") logic with the simpler and more elegant EL expression ${param.d}. You have to use an EL expression in any case, because scripting elements aren't

97

allowed in the body of an action. Therefore, you couldn't have used <%=d%>. You will learn how to use EL in the next section of this chapter.

░ **Tip** Many tag libraries are available on the Internet. JSTL provides many actions that you can use and reuse, which I will write about in the next section. It certainly pays, in terms of both quality and efficiency, to avoid developing actions from scratch unless they give you clear and quantifiable benefits. You will find more info on JSTL at www.oracle.com/technetwork/java/index-jsp-135995.html.

Tag Files

Tag files are special JSP files that replace tag handlers written in Java. After all, JSP basically *is* Java.

Do you remember when I told you in Chapter 2 that the only available directive elements are page, include, and taglib? Well, I lied. There are three more directives: tag, attribute, and variable. The reason I didn't mention them is that you can only use them in tag files. Now that you know how to develop custom tag libraries with Java, I can tell you how to develop them using the JSP syntax and the newly revealed directives. The examples of this section are in the folder tag files of the software package for this chapter. To install them, follow the instructions contained in README.txt.

Bodyless Tag

Listing 4-16 shows the tag-file version of the tag handler WeekdayTag.java that you saw in Listing 4-11.

Listing 4-16. weekday.tag

```
<%@tag import="java.util.Date, java.text.SimpleDateFormat"
       import="java.util.Calendar, java.util.GregorianCalendar"%>
<%@attribute name="date" required="false"%>
<%
  final String[] WD = {"","Sun","Mon","Tue","Wed","Thu","Fri","Sat"};
  GregorianCalendar cal = new GregorianCalendar();
  if (date != null && date.length() > 0) {
    SimpleDateFormat fmt = new SimpleDateFormat("yyyy-MM-dd");
    fmt.setLenient(true);
    Date d = fmt.parse(date);
    cal.setTime(d);
    }
  out.print(WD[cal.get(Calendar.DAY_OF_WEEK)]);
  %>
```

The tag directive of a tag file replaces the page directive of a JSP page, and the attribute directive lets you define an input parameter. As Tomcat handles the tag exceptions for us, I removed the try/catch constructs, which certainly makes the code more readable. Another simplification is in sending the result to the output, because in the tag file the implicit variable out makes it unnecessary to invoke pageContext.getOut().

Listing 4-17 shows how you modify weekday.jsp of Listing 4-12 to use the tag file.

Listing 4-17. weekday_t.jsp

```
<%@page language="java" contentType="text/html"%>
<%@taglib tagdir="/WEB-INF/tags" prefix="wow"%>
<% String d = request.getParameter("d"); %>
<html><head><title>weekday bodyless tag</title></head><body>
weekday today: <wow:weekday/><br/>
weekday <%=d%>: <wow:weekday date="<%=d%>"/><br/>
</body></html>
```

As you can see, the only difference is that the attribute uri="/WEB-INF/tlds/wow.tld" of the taglib directive has become tagdir="/WEB-INF/tags".

To keep the uri attribute, you need to declare the tag file in a TLD, as shown in Listing 4-18.

Listing 4-18. wow.tld for a Tag File

```
<?xml version="1.0" encoding="UTF-8"?>
<taglib xmlns="http://java.sun.com/xml/ns/javaee"
    xmlns:xsi="http://www.w3.org/2001/XMLSchema-instance"
    xsi:schemaLocation="http://java.sun.com/xml/ns/javaee ~CCC
http://java.sun.com/xml/ns/j2ee/web-jsptaglibrary_2_1.xsd"
    version="2.1">
  <description>My library of tag files</description>
  <tlib-version>1.0</tlib-version>
  <short-name>wow</short-name>
  <uri>tagFiles</uri>
  <tag-file>
    <description>Displays the day of the week</description>
    <display-name>weekday</display-name>
    <name>weekday</name>
    <path>/WEB-INF/tags/weekday.tag</path>
    </tag-file>
</taglib>
```

Then, in the taglib directive of weekday_t.jsp, you can replace tagdir="/WEB-INF/tags" with uri="tagFiles".

As an example of the variable directive, replace in weekday.tag the line

```
out.print(WD[cal.get(Calendar.DAY_OF_WEEK)]);
```

with the following two:

```
%><%@variable name-given="dayw" scope="AT_END"%><%
jspContext.setAttribute("dayw", WD[cal.get(Calendar.DAY_OF_WEEK)]);
```

The action will then save the string with the day of the week into the attribute dayw instead of sending it directly to the output. To display the action's result from within weekday_t.jsp, insert the following expression element after executing the action:

```
<%=pageContext.getAttribute("dayw")%>
```

As you will see later in this chapter, you can also replace the somewhat cumbersome expression element with the more compact EL expression ${dayw}.

Bodied Tag

Listing 4-19 shows the tag file equivalent to the tag handler WeekdayBodyTag.java, which you saw in Listing 4-13. I wrote it by modifying the tag file weekday.tag that implemented the bodyless tag as shown in Listing 4-16. Listing 4-20 is the tag-file equivalent to weekday_b.jsp (see Listing 4-15), which invoked the bodied tag handler. I wrote it by modifying weekday_t.jsp of Listing 4-17, which used the bodyless tag file.

Listing 4-19. weekdayBody.tag

```
<%@tag import="java.util.Date, java.text.SimpleDateFormat"
       import="java.util.Calendar, java.util.GregorianCalendar"%>
<jsp:doBody var="dateAttr"/>
<%
  String date = (String)jspContext.getAttribute("dateAttr");
  final String[] WD = {"","Sun","Mon","Tue","Wed","Thu","Fri","Sat"};
  GregorianCalendar cal = new GregorianCalendar();
  if (date.length() > 0) {
    SimpleDateFormat fmt = new SimpleDateFormat("yyyy-MM-dd");
    fmt.setLenient(true);
    Date d = fmt.parse(date);
    cal.setTime(d);
    }
  out.print(WD[cal.get(Calendar.DAY_OF_WEEK)]);
  %>
```

The standard action element jsp:doBody evaluates the body of the weekdayBody action and stores its output as a string into the page-scoped attribute dateAttr. The first line of the scriptlet then copies the attribute into the JSP variable named date. After that, the bodied tag file is identical to the bodyless one. This was not really necessary, but the subsequent code accesses the date twice, first to check that it isn't empty and then to parse it. I didn't like to invoke the getAttribute method twice. It seemed less tidy.

If you omit the attribute var, doBody sends the body's result to the output; if you replace var with varReader, the result is stored as a java.io.Reader object instead of a java.lang.String; and if you add the attribute scope, you can specify var / varReader to be defined as a request, session, or application attribute, instead of in the page scope.

You should know that jsp:invoke is very similar to jsp:doBody but operates on a JSP fragment instead of the action body. For example, by writing the following two lines in a tag file

```
<%@attribute name="fragName" fragment="true"%>
<jsp:invoke fragment="fragName"/>
```

you pass to it a JSP fragment. Like doBody, invoke admits the attributes var, varReader, and scope. Both standard actions can only be used within tag files.

Listing 4-20. weekday_bt.jsp

```
<%@page language="java" contentType="text/html"%>
<%@taglib tagdir="/WEB-INF/tags" prefix="wow"%>
<html><head><title>weekday bodied tag</title></head><body>
weekdayBody today: <wow:weekdayBody></wow:weekdayBody><br/>
weekdayBody ${param.d}: <wow:weekdayBody>${param.d}</wow:weekdayBody><br/>
</body></html>
```

The tag Directive

In the previous section, you encountered the import attribute of the tag directive. Table 4-2 lists the other attributes that are available. They are all optional.

Table 4-2. Attributes of the tag Directive

Attribute	Description
description	The name says it all.
display-name	A short name intended for tools. The default is the name of the tag file without the .tag extension.
body-content	Same as the <body-content> tag in a TLD (see the comments after Listing 4-11).
dynamic-attributes	If the attribute is present, its value identifies a scoped attribute where you store a map with names and values of the dynamic attributes you use when executing the tag.
example	A string with a brief description of an example.
small-icon	Path, relative from the tag file, of a small icon intended for tools.
large-icon	Yes, you guessed correctly!
language	Equivalent to its namesake of the page directive.
pageEncoding	Ditto.
isELIgnored	Ditto.

The attribute Directive

You have already encountered the attributes name and required. Table 4-3 briefly describes the remaining ones (all optional).

Table 4-3. Attributes of the attribute Directive

Attribute	Description
description	This attribute is almost universal.
rtexprvalue	Same as the equally-named tag in a TLD (see the comments after Listing 4-11).
type	Ditto.

Attribute	Description
fragment	If set to true, it means that the attribute is a JSP fragment to be evaluated by the tag file. If false (the default), the attribute is a normal one and is therefore evaluated by Tomcat before being passed to the tag file. Do not specify rtexprvalue or type when you set fragment to true. Tomcat will set them for you respectively to true and javax.servlet.jsp.tagext.JspFragment.
example	A string with a brief description of an example.
small-icon	Path, relative from the tag file, of a small icon intended for tools.

There are also two mutually exclusive pairs of attributes that are associated with JavaServer Faces: deferredValue / deferredValueType and deferredMethod / deferredMethodSignature. Let's not put the cart before the oxen.

The variable Directive

Table 4-4 briefly describes all the attributes.

Table 4-4. Attributes of the variable Directive

Attribute	Description
description	No surprises here.
name-given / name-from-attribute	You have seen name-given in the example. One of these two attributes must be present. The value of name-given cannot be the same of the value of the name attribute of an attribute directive or the value of a dynamic-attributes attribute of a tag directive. See after the end of this table for an explanation of how to use name-from-attribute.
alias	It works together with name-from-attribute. Again, see below.
scope	Can be AT_BEGIN, AT_END, or NESTED (the default). Once more, too much text to keep it in this table. See below.
variable-class	The name of the class of the variable (default is java.lang.String).
declare	Set to false (the default is true) if the variable is *not* declared.

While name-given provides the name of a JSP attribute (which, as you will see in the next section, coincides with the name of an EL variable), name-from-attribute provides the name of another JSP attribute containing the name of the JSP attribute you are interested in. Then, alias provides the name of an EL variable local to the tag file that Tomcat synchronizes with the JSP attribute. For example, if you declare:

```
<%@variable alias="ali" name-from-attribute="attrName"%>
```

Tomcat, before continuing execution of the tag file, makes available to it the page-scoped attribute named ali and sets it to the value of the attribute named attrName. This name redirection makes possible for JSP pages that use differently named attributes to use the same tag file. For example, a.jsp might include the line

```
session.setAttribute("greet", "Good morning!");
```

and b.jsp might have

```
application.setAttribute("novel", "Stranger in a Strange Land");
```

If a.jsp contains

```
pageContext.setAttribute("attrName", "greet");
```

and b.jsp

```
pageContext.setAttribute("attrName", "novel");
```

they can both invoke the tag file that includes the variable directive shown above. The tag file will then have an ali attribute containing "Good morning!" in the first case and "Stranger in a Strange Land" in the second case.

The attribute scope tells when Tomcat creates or updates the attribute in the calling page with the value of the attribute that is local to the tag file (perhaps a name like *synchronization* would have been clearer than scope). With AT_BEGIN, Tomcat does it before the tag file invokes a segment or immediately before exiting the tag file; with NESTED, only before invoking a segment; and with AT_END, only before leaving the tag file. Additionally, with NESTED, Tomcat saves the value of the calling-page attribute upon entering the tag file and restores it upon leaving it. But this only if an attribute with the given name exists in the calling page before entering the tag file.

JSTL and EL

Many developers have implemented similar custom actions to remove or at least reduce the need for scripting elements. Eventually, a new effective standard known as JSTL was born.

However, JSTL is of little use without the Expression Language (EL), which lets you access and manipulate objects in a compact and efficient way and can be used within the body of actions. I will first introduce you to EL, so that you'll be well prepared to understand the JSTL examples.

But first of all, you have to download two libraries from http://jstl.java.net/download.html. If you follow the two links "JSTL API" and "JSTL Implementation", you will reach two pages from which you can download respectively javax.servlet.jsp.jstl-api-1.2.1.jar and javax.servlet.jsp.jstl-1.2.1.jar (or the equivalent files for the version that will be current when you will be reading this book).

Copy them to %CATALINA_HOME%\lib\ and restart Tomcat.

JSP Expression Language

EL was introduced in JSP 2.0 as an alternative to the scripting elements. You can use EL expressions in template text and also in action attributes specified to be capable of accepting runtime expressions. You will find a good reference at http://java.sun.com/products/jsp/syntax/2.0/syntaxref207.html#1010522.

EL Expressions

EL supports two representations: ${expr} and #{expr}. To explain when you can or should use them, I must first clarify the distinction between lvalues and rvalues.

The *l* stands for *left*, and the *r* stands for *right*. These values refer to the fact that in most computer languages, the assigned value is on the right-hand side of an assignment statement, while the value to be assigned to it is on the left-hand side. For example, the Java statement

```
ka[k] = j*3;
```

means that the result of the evaluation of j*3 (an rvalue) is to be assigned to the value resulting from the evaluation of ka[k] (an lvalue). Clearly, an lvalue must be a reference to something you can assign values to (a variable or some attribute of an object), while there is no such restriction on rvalues.

Suppose that you have a page with a form. Wouldn't it be nice if you could specify *directly in the input elements of the form* the references to where the user's inputs should be stored? For example, it'd be nice to specify something like <input id="firstName" value="*variableName*">, with *variableName* specifying where you want to store the input typed by the user. Then, when the form is submitted, there should be a mechanism to automatically take the user's input and store it where you specified. Perhaps you could also define a new attribute of the input element to provide a validating method. Inside the input element, you would then already have everything you need to accept the user's input, validate it, and store it away.

This sounds great, but if you set the value attribute of the input element to ${formBean.firstName}, this evaluates to an rvalue. The value of the firstName attribute of formBean is assigned to the value attribute of the input element, and that's it. You need a way of *deferring* evaluation of formBean.firstName and use it as an *lvalue* when you really need it—that is, when you handle the form that was submitted.

You achieve that by replacing the $ before the EL braces with a #. The # tells Tomcat to defer evaluation and use its result as an lvalue or an rvalue, depending on the context. EL expressions with the dollar sign are evaluated like everything else. In any other aspect, parsing and evaluation of the two representations are identical. You will use the #-representation when we will talk about JSF. For now, you can learn about EL using the $-representation.

Using EL Expressions

The expr in ${expr} can contain literals, operators, and references to objects and methods. Table 4-5 shows some examples and their results.

Table 4-5. EL Expressions

EL Expression	Result
${1 <= (1/2)}	false
${5.0 > 3}	true
${100.0 == 100}	true
${'a' < 'b'}	true

EL Expression	Result
`${'fluke' gt 'flute'}`	false
`${1.5E2 + 1.5}`	151.5
`${1 div 2}`	0.5
`${12 mod 5}`	2
`${empty param.a}`	true if the request parameter a is null or an empty string
`${sessionScope.cart.nItems}`	The value of the nItems property of the session-scoped attribute named cart
`${aBean.aProp}`	The value of the aProp property of the aBean bean
`${aMap[entryName]}`	The value of the entry named entryName in the map named aMap

The operators behave in general like in Java, but with one important difference: the equality operator (==) applied to string variables compares their contents, not whether the variables refer to the same instance of a string. That is, it behaves like Java's `String.equals()` method.

In addition to EL operators identical to Java operators, you also have most of their literal equivalents: not for !, div for /, mod for %, lt for <, gt for >, le for <=, ge for >=, eq for ==, ne for !=, and for && , and or for ||. You also have the unary operator empty, to be used as shown in one of the examples in Table 4-2.

The EL operators '.' (i.e., the dot) and [] (i.e., indexing) are more powerful and forgiving than the corresponding Java operators.

When applied to a bean, as in `${myBean.prop}`, the dot operator is interpreted as an indication that the value of the property should be returned, as if you'd written `myBean.getProp()` in a scripting element. As a result, for example, the line of code

`${pageContext.servletContext.servletContextName}`

is equivalent to this:

`<%=pageContext.getServletContext().getServletContextName()%>`

Furthermore, `${first.second.third}`, equivalent to `<%=first.getSecond().getThird()%>`, returns null when `first.second` evaluates to null, although in the expression, we try to dereference it with `.third`. The JSP scripting equivalent would throw a `NullPointerException`. For this to work, all classes must implement the getter methods of properly formed Java beans.

Array indexing allows you to try to access an element that doesn't exist, in which case it simply evaluates to null. For example, if you have an array of ten elements, the EL expression `${myArray[999]}` returns null instead of throwing an `ArrayIndexOutOfBoundsException`, as Java would have done. It is not as bad as in the plain old "C" language, in which an index out of bounds would have returned the value it found in memory. With EL, you can check for null. And in general you should do so, because you cannot rely on an exception being thrown, as it would be in Java.

You can use both the dot and indexing operator to access maps. For example, the following two EL expressions both return the value associated with the key named myKey:

```
${myMap.myKey}
${myMap["myKey"]}
```

There is a tiny difference, though: you cannot use the dot operator if the name of the key contains a character that confuses EL. For example, ${header["user-agent"]} is OK, but ${header.user-agent} doesn't work, because the dash between user and agent in the second expression is interpreted as a minus sign. Unless you have a variable named agent, both header.user and agent evaluate to null and, according to the EL specification document, ${null - null} evaluates to zero. Therefore, the second expression would return a zero. You would encounter a different, but potentially more serious, problem if you had a map key containing a dot. For example, you could use ${param["my.par"]} without problems, but ${param.my.par} would probably result in a null or, almost certainly, in something other than what you are looking for. This would be bad in any case, because null is a possible valid outcome. I suggest you use the bracketed form in all occasions and simply forget this issue.

Similar to JSP, EL contains implicit objects, which you find listed in Table 4-6.

Table 4-6. *EL's Implicit Objects*

Object	Description
pageContext	The context of the JSP page. In particular, pageContext.servletContext gives you a reference to the same object referenced in JSP by the implicit variable application. Similarly, pageContext.session is equivalent to JSP's session, pageContext.request to JSP's request, and pageContext.response to JSP's response.
param	Maps a request parameter name to its first value.
paramValues	Maps a request parameter name to an array of its values.
header	Maps a request header name to its first value.
headerValues	Maps a request header name to an array of its values.
cookie	Maps a cookie name to a single cookie.
initParam	Maps the name of a context initialization parameter to its value.
pageScope	Maps page-scoped variable names to their values.
requestScope	Maps request-scoped variable names to their values.
sessionScope	Maps session-scoped variable names to their values.
${aBean.aProp}	The value of the aProp property of the aBean bean
applicationScope	Maps application-scoped variable names to their values.

> ▮ **Caution** You *cannot* use JSP scripting variables within EL expressions.

You've probably noticed that EL doesn't include any way of declaring variables. Within EL expressions, you can use variables set with the `c:set` JSTL core action (which I will describe in the next section) or scoped attributes. For example, all of the following definitions let you use the EL expression `${xyz}`:

```
<c:set var="xyz" value="33"/>
<% session.setAttribute("xyz", "44"); %>
<% pageContext.setAttribute("xyz", "22"); %>
```

However, you have to pay attention to scope precedence. The variable set with `c:set` and the attribute in `pageContext` *are the same variable*. That is, `c:set` defines an attribute in the page context. The attribute in `sessionContext` is a different variable, and you cannot access it with `${xyz}` because it is "hidden" behind the attribute with the same name in the page context. To access a session attribute, you have to prefix its name with `sessionScope`, as in `${sessionScope.xyz}`. If you don't specify a scope, EL looks first in the page, then in the request, then in the session, and finally in the application scope.

> ▮ **Caution** You cannot nest EL expressions. Expressions such as `${expr1[${expr2}]}` are illegal.

You can make composite expressions consisting of several EL expressions and additional text, as in the following example:

```
<c:set var="varName" value="Welcome ${firstName} ${lastName}!"/>
```

However, you cannot mix the `${}` and `#{}` forms.

JSP Standard Tag Library

JSTL consists of five tag libraries, as listed in Table 4-7. If you are wondering, i18n stands for *internationalization*, abbreviated by replacing the eighteen letters in the middle with the number 18.

Table 4-7. JSTL Tag Libraries

Area	Functionality
Core	Variable support, flow control, URL management, and miscellaneous
i18n	Locale, message formatting, and number and date formatting
Functions	String manipulation and length of collection objects
SQL	Handling of databases

Area	Functionality
XML	XML core, flow control, and transformation

Table 4-8 lists all the tags defined in the five libraries.

Table 4-8. The JSTL Tags

Core	i18n	Functions	Database	XML
c:catch	fmt:bundle	fn:contains	sql:dateParam	x:choose
c:choose	fmt:formatDate	fn:containsIgnoreCase	sql:param	x:forEach
c:forEach	fmt:formatNumber	fn:endsWith	sql:query	x:if
c:forTokens	fmt:message	fn:escapeXml	sql:setDataSource	x:otherwise
c:if	fmt:param	fn:indexOf	sql:transaction	x:out
c:import	fmt:parseDate	fn:join	sql:update	x:param
c:otherwise	fmt:parseNumber	fn:length		x:parse
c:out	fmt:requestEncoding	fn:replace		x:set
c:param	fmt:setBundle	fn:split		x:transform
c:redirect	fmt:setLocale	fn:startsWith		x:when
c:remove	fmt:setTimeZone	fn:substring		
c:set	fmt:timeZone	fn:substringAfter		
c:url		fn:substringBefore		
c:when		fn:toLowerCase		
		fn:toUpperCase		
		fn:trim		

As you have already seen in a couple of examples, to use the JSTL libraries in JSP pages, you must declare them in taglib directives as follows:

```
<%@taglib prefix="c" uri="http://java.sun.com/jsp/jstl/core"%>
<%@taglib prefix="fmt" uri="http://java.sun.com/jsp/jstl/fmt"%>
<%@taglib prefix="fn" uri="http://java.sun.com/jsp/jstl/functions"%>
<%@taglib prefix="sql" uri="http://java.sun.com/jsp/jstl/sql"%>
<%@taglib prefix="x" uri="http://java.sun.com/jsp/jstl/xml"%>
```

I will describe JSTL-XML in Chapter 5, where I will talk about XML, and JSTL-SQL in Chapter 6, dedicated to database access from JSP. In the following sections of this chapter, I will describe JSTL-core and JSTL-i18n. I will not talk about the functions because they are pretty self-explanatory.

The Core Library

To explain some of the most used actions, I will go back to the example req_params.jsp, of Chapter 1 (Listing 1-6) and replace its scriptlets with JSTL actions. Listing 4-16 shows you how you do it.

c:out, c:set, and c:forEach (and fn:length)

Listing 4-16. req_params_jstl.jsp

```
01: <%@page language="java" contentType="text/html"%>
02: <%@taglib prefix="c" uri="http://java.sun.com/jsp/jstl/core"%>
03: <%@taglib prefix="fn" uri="http://java.sun.com/jsp/jstl/functions"%>
04: <html><head><title>Request Parameters with JSTL</title></head><body>
05:   Map size = <c:out value="${fn:length(paramValues)}"/>
06:   <table border="1">
07:     <tr><td>Map element</td><td>Par name</td><td>Par value[s]</td></tr>
08:     <c:set var="k" value="0"/>
09:     <c:forEach var="par" items="${paramValues}"><tr>
10:       <td><c:out value="${k}"/></td>
11:       <td><c:out value="'${par.key}'"/></td>
12:       <td><c:forEach var="val" items="${par.value}">
13:         <c:out value="'${val}'"/>
14:         </c:forEach></td>
15:       <c:set var="k" value="${k+1}"/>
16:     </tr></c:forEach>
17:   </table>
18: </body></html>
```

Notice that, as there are no scripting elements, I have removed the importing of Java libraries.

Lines 2 and 3 show the taglib directives for JSTL core and functions. In Line 5, you can see how to use the fn:length function to determine the size of the EL implicit object paramValues and the c:out action to send the value of an EL expression to the output. You could have just written the naked EL expression, but c:out automatically converts characters that have special HTML meaning to the corresponding HTTP entities. For example, it writes & instead of &. Therefore, it's better to use c:out.

c:set initializes an index in line 8 and increments it in line 15. In lines 9 and 12, c:forEach lets you go through the elements of maps and arrays.

If you type in your browser

```
http://localhost:8080/tests/req_params_jstl.jsp?a=b&c=d&a=zzz&empty=&empty=&1=22
```

you'll get the same output shown in Figure 1-12 for req_params.jsp (see Figure 4-3). Although, to be completely correct, the format of the HTML will be different.

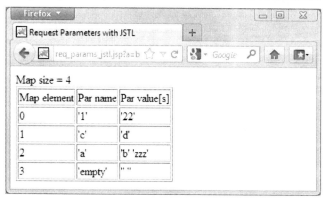

Figure 4-3. *Output of req_params_jstl.jsp*

In essence, c:out is for EL expressions what an expression scripting element is for JSP (i.e., Java) expressions. Beside the attribute value, it supports default, to provide a fallback output, and escapeXml, that you set to false to prevent the escaping of XML characters, which are escaped by default.

With c:set, besides defining var and value, you can also specify the scope of the variable with the attribute scope. Finally, in alternative to var, you can use the pair of attributes property and target to specify which property of which object you want to modify.

In the example, you have seen that c:forEach lets you loop over a list of objects with the two attributes var and items. Alternatively, you can go through a list by means of the attributes begin, where 0 indicates the first element, end, and step. Further, if you define the name of a variable by setting the attribute varStatus, c:forEach will store in it an object of type javax.servlet.jsp.jstl.core.LoopTagStatus.

As these attributes are pretty straightforward, the best way for you to become familiar with them is to write a small page and see what happens when you set them to different values.

Before moving on, have a look at Table 4-9. It lists what types of objects you can assign to the attribute items and, correspondingly, what type of objects you get in the variable defined through var.

Table 4-9. *c:forEach Types*

items	var
Array of instances of class C	Instance of C
Array of primitive values (e.g., of int)	Wrapped element (e.g., in Integer)
String of comma-delimited substrings	Substring
java.util.Collection	Element obtained by invoking iterator()
java.util.Map	Instance of java.util.Map.Entry

items	var
java.util.Iterator	An Iterator element
java.util.Enumeration	An Enumeration element
javax.servlet.jsp.jstl.sql.Result	SQL rows

c:if, c:choose, c:when, and c:otherwise

The JSTL versions of Java's if and switch are particularly useful tags. For example, the body of the following action is executed only if the EL expression calculates to true:

```
<c:if test="EL-expression"> ... </c:if>
```

Unfortunately, there is no c:else, but the JSTL version of switch (c:choose) is much more powerful than its Java counterpart. In fact, it's more like a chain of if .. else:

```
<c:choose>
  <c:when test="EL-expression-1"> ... </c:when>
  <c:when test="EL-expression-2"> ... </c:when>
  ...
  <c:otherwise> ... </c:otherwise>
</c:choose>
```

Besides test, which lets you define the condition you want to test, c:if supports the two attributes var and scope, which c:if uses to store the condition's result.

There is no attribute supported by c:choose and c:otherwise, and c:when only supports test.

c:catch, c:remove, and c:url

With c:catch you can catch the exceptions that occur within its body. It accepts a var attribute, where it stores the result of the exception, of type java.lang.Throwable. For example, the following two lines will insert into the output the string "java.lang.ArithmaticException: / by zero".

```
<c:catch var="e"><% int k = 1/0; %></c:catch>
<c:if test="${e != null}"><c:out value="${e}"/></c:if>
```

c:remove lets you remove the variable defined in its pair of attributes var and scope.

c:url formats a string into a URL, which it then inserts into the output, like in the following example:

```
<a href="<c:url value="/tests/hello.jsp"/>">Hello World</a>
```

Notice the nested double quotes. This is not a problem, because Tomcat processes the action on the server and replaces it with a string representing the URL. The client doesn't see the inner double quotes.

You can also specify a var/scope pair of attributes to store the generated URL into a scoped variable and the attribute context to refer to another application. If you use the bodied form of c:url, you can define with c:param additional parameters that will be appended to the URL.

c:import, c:redirect, and c:param

c:import and c:redirect are generalized versions of the standard actions jsp:include and jsp:forward. The main difference is that the JSTL actions are not limited to the scope of the current application. They let you include or forward to any URL via the attribute url, which is in both cases the only attribute required.

The general syntax of c:import is as follows:

```
<c:import url="expr1" context="expr2" charEncoding="expr3" var="name" scope="scope">
  <c:param name="expr4" value="expr5"/>
  ...
  </c:import>
```

By now, everything should be pretty clear to you. The only thing worth mentioning is that the default value for charEncoding is "ISO-8859-1". I prefer to use UTF-8 because it is equally supported by all operating systems. Also, UTF-8 can handle non-European languages and has become the de-facto standard on the Web. In case you are curious, UTF stands for UCS Transformation Format, where UCS means Universal Character Set.

c:redirect is equivalent to invoking javax.servlet.http.HttpServletResponse.sendRedirect and only admits the two attributes url and context. When designing a web site, you might find it useful to remember that c:redirect changes the page that the user sees, thereby affecting the setting of bookmarks, while with jsp:forward, the user remains unaware of the page change.

c:forTokens

In addition to c:forEach, the JSTL provides a form of string tokenizer, which lets you easily extract from a string the sub-strings separated by one or more delimiters.

If you have a comma as a single delimiter, you can use c:forEach, but if you have more than one delimiter, or if the only delimiter is not a comma, c:forTokens is for you.

The general syntax of c:forTokens is as follows:

```
<c:forTokens var="name" items="expr1" delims="expr2" varStatus="name"
    begin="expr3" end="expr4" step="expr5">
  ...
</c:forTokens>
```

The i18n Library: Writing Multi-Lingual Applications

You can take one of two approaches to internationalizing a web application: you can either provide a different version of the JSP pages for each locale and select them via a servlet when processing each request, or you can save locale-specific data in separate resource bundles and access them via i18n actions. The JSTL internationalization actions support both, but I will concentrate on the second approach, where the work of switching between languages is actually done in JSP.

fmt:setLocale, fmt:setBundle, fmt:setMessage, and fmt:param

Suppose that you want to support English and Italian. The first thing you have to do is identify all the strings that are going to be different in the two languages and define two bundles, one for each language (see Listings 4-17 and 4-18).

Listing 4-17. MyBundle_en.java

```
package myPkg.i18n;
import java.util.*;
public class MyBundle_en extends ListResourceBundle {
  public Object[][] getContents() {return contents;}
  static final Object[][] contents = {
    {"login.loginmess","Please login with ID and password"},
    {"login.submit","Submit"},
    {"login.choose","Choose the language"},
    {"login.english","English"},
    {"login.italian","Italian"}
    };
  }
```

Listing 4-18. MyBundle_it.java

```
package myPkg.i18n;
import java.util.*;
public class MyBundle_it extends ListResourceBundle {
  public Object[][] getContents() {return contents;}
  static final Object[][] contents = {
    {"login.loginmess","Loggati con ID e parola d'ordine"},
    {"login.submit","Invia"},
    {"login.choose","Scegli la lingua"},
    {"login.english","Inglese"},
    {"login.italian","Italiano"}
    };
  }
```

As you can see, a bundle is nothing other than a Java class that extends the class java.util.ListResourceBundle. In this example, you will only find a simple login page, but in reality, you'll have to include all the language-specific messages of your application. I used the prefix login to show you that it's possible to group messages within a bundle. You can compile the Java files from the command line with javac to obtain the two files MyBundle_en.class and MyBundle_it.class. Place both files inside the WEB-INF\classes\myPkg\i18n\ folder of your application's root directory, as you would do with any other custom class.

Listing 4-19 shows the login page that supports two languages. To try it out, copy the folder named international from the software package for this chapter to webapps. Then type in your browser localhost:8080/international.

Listing 4-19. index.jsp of a Multilingual Application

```
01: <%@page language="java" contentType="text/html"%>
02: <%@taglib prefix="c" uri="http://java.sun.com/jsp/jstl/core"%>
03: <%@taglib prefix="fmt" uri="http://java.sun.com/jsp/jstl/fmt"%>
04: <c:set var="langExt" value="en"/>
05: <c:if test="${param.lang!=null}">
06:   <c:set var="langExt" value="${param.lang}"/>
07:   </c:if>
08: <fmt:setLocale value="${langExt}"/>
```

113

```
09: <fmt:setBundle basename="myPkg.i18n.MyBundle"
10:    var="lang" scope="session"/>
11: <html><head><title>i18n</title></head><body>
12: <h1><fmt:message key="login.loginmess" bundle="${lang}"/></h1>
13: <form method="post" action="home.jsp">
14:    <input name=id>
15:    <input name=passwd>
16:    <input type="submit"
17:      value="<fmt:message key="login.submit" bundle="${lang}"/>"
18:      >
19: <h2><fmt:message key="login.choose" bundle="${lang}"/></h2>
20: <a href="index.jsp?lang=en">
21:    <fmt:message key="login.english" bundle="${lang}"/>
22:    </a>
23:  
24: <a href="index.jsp?lang=it">
25:    <fmt:message key="login.italian" bundle="${lang}"/>
26:    </a>
27: </body></html>
```

Lines 4-7 ensure that the page variable langExt is not null by setting it to en when the page is requested the first time. Line 8 sets the locale to the requested language code. The list of valid language codes is defined in the International Organization for Standardization (ISO) 639 standard. They're in lowercase (e.g., it for Italian), so you can't confuse them with the country codes defined in the ISO 3166 standard, which are in uppercase (e.g., IT for Italy).

In line 9, you set the bundle. Notice that it looks like the fully qualified class name of the two bundle classes but without the trailing underscore and language code. This is exactly how it should be done. Otherwise, the JSTL won't find your messages. After executing fmt:setBundle, the session variable lang points to the bundle in the correct language, thanks to the locale and the basename attribute.

After that, an element like the following one will insert in the appropriate language the message identified by the value of the key attribute:

```
<fmt:message key="keyName" bundle="${lang}"/>
```

Notice how the double quotes are nested in line 17 without causing any problem. This is because the actions are processed first. By the time Tomcat arrives to process the HTML, only the outer double quotes remain.

Figure 4-4 shows what the page looks like the first time you view it.

Figure 4-4. *The first time you view index.jsp*

Figure 4-5 shows how the page looks when you choose Italian by clicking on the corresponding bottom link.

Figure 4-5. The Italian version of index.jsp

If Tomcat cannot find a bundle, it will display the key name preceded and followed by three question marks, as shown in Figure 4-6. This indicates that you must have made a mistake in the directory names.

Figure 4-6. index.jsp cannot find the messages.

Besides value, `fmt:setLocale` admits two additional attributes. The first one, `scope`, defines the scope of the locale. In the example, the default (i.e., page) is used, but scope lets you, for example, save the locale as a session attribute. The remaining attribute, `variant`, lets you specify non-standardized locales.

`fmt:setMessage` also supports a `var`/`scope` pair of attributes to let you store the generated string into a scoped variable. You can also place the sub-action `fmt:param` inside the body of `fmt:message` and set its attribute `value` to a string that you want to append to the message.

fmt:bundle, fmt:setTimeZone, and fmt:timeZone

Similar to `fmt:SetBundle` is `fmt:bundle`, but while you choose the `basename` the same way you do with `fmt:setBundle`, you cannot store your choice in a scoped variable. Instead, the basename you choose applies to all elements inside the body of fmt:bundle. Additionally, fmt:bundle also supports the attribute prefix, which extends the basename. For example, if you replace lines 9-10 in Listing 4-19 with

`<fmt:bundle basename="myPkg.i18n.MyBundle" prefix="login.">`

and insert `</fmt:bundle>` immediately above the last line, you then replace the existing line 21:

`<fmt:message key="login.english" bundle="${lang}"/>`

with:

`<fmt:message key="english"/>`

fmt:setTimeZone sets the current time zone to what specified in the attribute value, like in

`<fmt:setTimeZone value="America/Los_Angeles"/>`

but it can also store a time zone into a scoped variable specified by the var/scope attribute pair.

When you define a time zone with fmt:timeZone, on the other hand, it only applies to the elements that appear in the body of the action.

fmt:parseNumber and fmt: formatNumber

fmt:parseNumber and fmt:formatNumber deal with numbers, percentages, and currencies. Both actions can store their result into a scoped variable through the usual var/scope pair of attributes, or send it to the output if those attributes are missing.

Note that fmt:formatNumber is bodyless and expects to find the number to be formatted in the value attribute. fmt:parseNumber also supports value in its bodyless form, but if the attribute is missing, it takes as input the content of its body.

Both actions support a type attribute that can have the values "number", "currency", or "percent".

Both actions also support a pattern attribute that lets you specify in detail a custom format. Table 4-10 lists the available symbols.

Table 4-10. Pattern Symbols for the Number-Actions

Symbol	Meaning
0	A digit
E	Exponential form
#	A digit; 0 when absent
.	Decimal period
,	Group of digits separator
;	Format separator
-	Default negative prefix

Symbol	Meaning
%	Displays a percent sign after multiplying the number by 100
?	Displays a per mille sign after multiplying the number by 1000
¤	Place marker for the actual currency sign
X	Place marker for any other character used in the prefix or suffix
'	To quote special characters in the prefix or suffix

Try out fmt:formatNumber with different patterns and see what you get. Some symbols are obvious, others, less so.

Additionally, fmt:parseNumber supports the attributes parseLocale, integerOnly (that you must set to false when parsing a floating-point number), and timeZone.

Yet, on the other hand, fmt:formatNumber supports the attributes currencyCode (only when type is set to "currency"), currencySymbol (ditto), groupingUsed (set to false if you don't want a separator between triplets of integer digits), maxIntegerDigits, minIntegerDigits, maxFractionDigits, and minFractionDigits. The last four attributes specify the maximum and minimum number of digits you want before and after the decimal point.

fmt:ParseDate, fmt:formatDate, and fmt:requestEncoding

Like fmt:parseNumber and fmt:formatNumber, fmt:ParseDate and fmt:formatDate can store their result into a scoped variable or send it to the output. Also, fmt:formatDate is bodyless while fmt:parseDate can be either bodyless or bodied. Not surprisingly, both actions support the timeZone attribute, and the format attributes dateStyle (with possible values "full", "long", "medium", "short", or "default"), and timeStyle (ditto). The Date-actions also support a pattern attribute. See Table 4-11 for a list of available symbols.

Table 4-11. Pattern Symbols for the Date-Actions

Symbol	Meaning
G	Era designator (e.g., AD)
y	Year
M	Month
d	Day of the month
h	Hour (12-hour time)
H	Hour (24-hour time)

Symbol	Meaning
m	Minute
s	Second
S	Millisecond
E	Day of the week
D	Day of the year
F	Day of the week within the month (e.g., 2 means 2nd Tue of the month)
w	Week of the year
W	Week of the month
a	AM/PM
k	Hour (12-hour time)
K	Hour (24-hour time)
z	Time zone
'	Escape for text
''	Quote

Additionally, fmt:parseDate supports the attributes parseLocale, and fmt:formatDate supports type (with possible values "date", "time", and "both").

With the remaining i18n action, fmt:requestEncoding, you specify what character encoding you expect for the text that the user types in forms. For example:

```
<fmt:requestEncoding value="UTF-8"/>
```

This action makes sense because the locale of the user might be different from the locale of the page. Note that if you develop a custom action that uses the method ServletResponse.setLocale() to set the locale of the response, it will take precedence over the character encoding set in fmt:requestEncoding.

Summary

In this chapter, you have learned everything about JSP standard actions and how to develop custom actions with JSP's tag extension mechanism.

You saw detailed examples that explained how to develop and use custom actions with and without body, both implemented with tag handlers and with tag files.

After explaining the Expression Language, I described in general terms the JSP Standard Tag Library and explained in detail the core and the internationalization tags.

In the next chapter, I will introduce you to XML, an understanding of which is essential for developing professional web applications.

CHAPTER 5

XML and JSP

HTML is probably the first markup language most of us came into contact with. It's a great language, but it's not without its problems.

For example, HTML mixes content data with the way the information is presented, thereby making it difficult to present the same data in different ways and to standardize presentations across multiple sets of data. Cascading Style Sheets (CSS) significantly reduces this problem but doesn't completely eliminate it, and it also forces you to learn yet another language.

Another problem, partly due to the way in which HTML is defined, is that the browsers are very forgiving about inconsistently written pages. In many cases, they're able to render pages with unquoted attribute values and tags that aren't closed properly. This encourages sloppiness in coding and wastes computer resources.

XML (whose standard is available at `http://www.w3.org/TR/xml`) lets you organize information into a treelike structure in which each item of information represents a leaf. Its power and flexibility lies in the idea of defining its syntax and a mechanism for defining tags. This makes it possible for you to define your own markup language tailored for the type of information you're dealing with. This also lets you define XHTML, a version of HTML clean of inconsistencies, as a well-formatted XML file.

Also, XML is the perfect vehicle for exchanging structured information. In fact, XML's purpose is precisely to describe information.

I have introduced XML starting from HTML, because you're familiar with HTML and they're both markup languages. However, the usefulness of XML goes well beyond providing a better syntax for HTML. The great advantage of using XML in preference to proprietary formats whenever information needs to be structured is that standardized parsers make the manipulation of XML documents easy. In this chapter, you will also learn how to parse an XML document in JSP with XML custom tags and XPath.

Many organizations, both private and public, have turned to XML to standardize the representation of information in their respective areas.

Some initiatives are very ambitious, like for example the development of a Universal Business Language (UBL) to generate XML-based standards of business documents like purchase orders and invoices (see `http://ubl.xml.org`).

Other initiatives, like the Real Estate Transaction Markup Language (RETML) to standardize the encoding of real estate transactions, have already gone through years of refinements and associated tool development and are being adopted.

Still other initiatives, like the Mind Reading Markup Language (MRML) might just serve the purpose of having fun (see `http://ifaq.wap.org/computers/mrml.html`).

OASIS, a not-for-profit consortium that promotes the establishment of open standards for the exchange of information, lists in `http://xml.coverpages.org/xmlApplications.html` almost 600 XML applications and initiatives.

CASCADING STYLE SHEETS

The concept of style sheets has its origins in desktop publishing. Style sheets are used to separate presentation from content. The term cascading refers to the fact that you can write a series of style sheets, whereby each one builds upon and refines the styles defined in the more general ones.

The W3C has generated two standards that are relevant when talking about style sheets associated with HTML pages: Cascading Style Sheets, level 1 (CSS1), and Cascading Style Sheets, level 2 (CSS2). (See http://www.w3.org/TR/REC-CSS1 and http://www.w3.org/TR/REC-CSS2, respectively.)

You need the following three components to define styles: `selector {property: value}`

The selector is the HTML element you want to define, the property is the name of one of the element's attributes, and the value is the attribute value. You can define several attributes for the same element by separating them with a semicolon, and you can style several elements with a single definition by separating them with a comma. To define more than one style for the same element, you can associate a class name to each separate style. For example:

```
<style type="text/css">
  p {font-size: 130%}
  p.bold {font-weight: bold}
  p.italic {font-style: italic}
</style>
```

Then, you can use the styles as follows:

```
<p>This is a default paragraph, large size</p>
<p class="bold">This is a large and bold paragraph</p>
<p class="bold italic">This is a large, bold, and italic paragraph</p>
<p class="italic" style="font-size: 100%;">This is an italic normal sized paragraph</p>
```

You can place `style` elements inside the head or body HTML elements of your pages, or define styles for individual elements by placing style definitions separated by semicolons in their `style` attribute.

The XML Document

To explain XML, I'll start by giving you a simple example that will accompany us throughout this chapter. For this purpose, I'll use the file shown in Listing 5-1. We will go back to the eshop example in the next chapter. But, to explain XML, it is better to look at a simple example without being distracted by the complexity of the application that has nothing to do with the task at hand.

Listing 5-1. enterprises.xml

```
<?xml version="1.0" encoding="UTF-8"?>
<starfleet>
  <title>The two most famous starships in the fleet</title>
  <starship name="USS Enterprise" sn="NCC-1701">
    <class name="Constitution"/>
    <captain>James Tiberius Kirk</captain>
```

```
    </starship>
  <starship name="USS Enterprise" sn="NCC-1701-D">
    <class name="Galaxy"/>
    <captain>Jean-Luc Picard</captain>
    </starship>
  </starfleet>
```

The first line defines the standard and the character set used in the document. The tags are always closed, either with an end tag when they have a body (e.g., `<title>...</title>`) or with a slash if they're empty (e.g., `<class .../>`). There can be repeated tags (e.g., starship), and the attribute names are not unique (e.g., name).

As you can see, the tags reflect the logical structure of the data, although there are certainly many ways of structuring the same information. Each tag identifies an *element node* labeled with a name (e.g., starfleet, title, and class, also called an *element type*), often characterized by *attributes* that consist of a *name* and a *value* (e.g., sn="NCC-1701"), and possibly containing *child nodes* (e.g., captain inside starship), also called *sub-elements*.

XML documents can also contain processing instructions for the applications that handle them (enclosed between `<?` and `?>`), comments (enclosed between `<!--` and `-->`), and document-type declarations (more about that later). Notice that enterprises.xml doesn't provide any information concerning how the data it contains might be presented.

XML relies on the less-than sign to identify the tags. Therefore, if you want to use it for other purposes, you have to escape it by writing the four characters `&lt;` instead. To escape larger blocks of text, you can use the CDATA section, as in the following example:

```
<![CDATA[<aTag>The tag's body</aTag>]]>
```

Looking at enterprises.xml, you might ask yourself why sn is an attribute of starship, while captain is a child element. Couldn't you make captain an attribute, as in the following example?

```
<starship name="USS Enterprise" sn="NCC-1701" captain="Jean-Luc Picard">
```

Yes, you could. It all depends on what you think you might like to do with the element in the future. With captain defined as an element, you can define attributes for it, such as its birth date. This wouldn't be possible if you had defined captain as an attribute. And the same applies to the class element. You could also replace the starship attributes name and sn with two children elements, but how much sense would it make?

We have to make one last consideration about empty vs. bodied elements. By defining the captain's name as the body of the element, as in:

```
<captain>Jean-Luc Picard</captain>
```

you make it impossible for it to have children elements. Alternatively, you could have defined this:

```
<captain name="Jean-Luc Picard"></captain>
```

perhaps shortened, as in:

```
<captain name="Jean-Luc Picard"/>
```

Defining Your Own XML Documents

The usefulness of being able to use XML tags tailored to your needs is greatly expanded by the possibility of formally specifying them in a separate document. This enables you to verify the validity of the XML documents and also to communicate their structure to others. Without a specification in a standardized format, you would have to describe your document structure in plain language or via examples. It wouldn't be the most efficient way, and it certainly wouldn't be good enough for automatic validation. The two most widely used methods to specify document structures are XML DTDs and XML schemas. You will see later on in this chapter that you can select which method your XML document uses for validation by adding an appropriate element to it.

XML DTDs

DTDs are better known than XML schemas, which have been developed more recently. They are also easier to understand. DTDs were originally developed for the XML predecessor, Standard Generalized Markup Language (SGML), and they have a very compact syntax. Listing 5-2 shows how a DTD for enterprises.xml would look.

Listing 5-2. starfleet.dtd

```
01: <!ELEMENT starfleet (title,starship*)>
02: <!ELEMENT title (#PCDATA)>
03: <!ELEMENT starship (class,captain)>
04: <!ATTLIST
05:     starship name CDATA #REQUIRED
06:     sn CDATA #REQUIRED>
07: <!ELEMENT class EMPTY>
08: <!ATTLIST class name CDATA #REQUIRED>
09: <!ELEMENT captain (#PCDATA)>
```

Line 1 defines the starfleet element as consisting of one title element and an undefined number of starship elements. Replacing the asterisk with a plus sign would require starship to occur at least once, and a question mark would mean zero or one starships. If you replaced starship with (starship|shuttle), it would mean that you could have a mix of starship and shuttle elements following the title (just as an example, because you haven't defined shuttle).

Line 2 specifies title to be a string of characters (the PC of PCDATA stands for *parsed character*). Line 7 shows how to specify that an element not be allowed to have a body. To complete the description of how to define elements, I only need to add that if you replaced EMPTY with ANY, it would mean that the element could contain any type of data.

Lines 4–6 specify the attributes for starship. The general format of an attribute list declaration is as follows:

```
<!ATTLIST elementName attributeName attributeType defaultValue>
```

where *attributeType* can have a dozen of possible values, including CDATA (to indicate character data), an enumeration of all strings allowed (enclosed in parentheses and with bars as separators, as in (left|right|center)), ID (to indicate a unique identifier), and IDREF (the ID of another element). The *defaultValue* can be a quoted value (e.g., "0" or "a string"), the keyword #REQUIRED (to indicate that it's mandatory), the keyword #IMPLIED (to indicate that it can be omitted), or the keyword #FIXED followed by a value (to force the attribute to have that value).

XML Schemas

The most significant difference from DTDs is that the schemas are in XML syntax themselves. This makes the schemas more extensible and flexible than DTDs. Furthermore, schemas can perform a more sophisticated validation thanks to their support data types. As the schemas are in XML format, you can store, handle, and style schemas like any other XML document. W3C describes standardized XML schemas in three documents: http://www.w3.org/TR/xmlschema-0/ (a primer to get you started), http://www.w3.org/TR/xmlschema-1/ (about structures), and http://www.w3.org/TR/xmlschema-2/ (about data types). Unfortunately, schemas are complicated, and the standards aren't exactly easy to read and understand. In this section, I am only going to describe a sub-set of schemas that will get you by in most situations.

Let's see the XML schema for enterprises.xml (see Listing 5-3).

Listing 5-3. starfleet.xsd

```
01: <?xml version="1.0" encoding="UTF-8"?>
02: <xsd:schema xmlns:xsd="http://www.w3.org/2001/XMLSchema"
03:     xmlns="http://localhost:8080/xml-validate/xsd"
04:     targetNamespace="http://localhost:8080/xml-validate/xsd"
05:     elementFormDefault="qualified"
06:     attributeFormDefault="unqualified"
07:     >
08:   <xsd:annotation>
09:     <xsd:documentation xml:lang="en">
10:       Schema for Starfleet
11:       </xsd:documentation>
12:   </xsd:annotation>
13:   <xsd:element name="starfleet">
14:     <xsd:complexType>
15:       <xsd:sequence>
16:         <xsd:element name="title" type="xsd:string" maxOccurs="1"/>
17:         <xsd:element name="starship" type="ShipType" maxOccurs="unbounded"/>
18:       </xsd:sequence>
19:     </xsd:complexType>
20:   </xsd:element>
21:   <xsd:complexType name="ShipType">
22:     <xsd:all>
23:       <xsd:element name="class" type="ClassType" minOccurs="1"/>
24:       <xsd:element name="captain" type="xsd:string" minOccurs="1"/>
25:     </xsd:all>
26:     <xsd:attribute name="name" type="xsd:string" use="required"/>
27:     <xsd:attribute name="sn" type="xsd:string" use="required"/>
28:   </xsd:complexType>
29:   <xsd:complexType name="ClassType">
30:     <xsd:attribute name="name" type="xsd:string" use="required"/>
31:   </xsd:complexType>
32: </xsd:schema>
```

Lines 2–7 establish that this schema conforms to the standard XML schema and define the schema's namespace and how XML files are supposed to refer to elements and attributes. To understand it all, you need to learn quite a bit about namespaces and schemas. The whole matter is quite tricky, and the error messages you get when you try to validate an XML document with a schema are sometimes implicit (more about this later). For example, if you remove the setting of elementFormDefault to "qualified" and try to validate a correct XML document, you will get the following error message:

```
*** Validation Error: org.xml.sax.SAXParseException; systemId: ➥
file:///C:/Program%20Files/Apache%20Software%20Foundation/Tomcat/webapps/xml- ➥
validate/xml/enterprises_schema.xml; lineNumber: 7; columnNumber: 10; ➥
cvc-complex-type.2.4.a: Invalid content was found starting with element 'title'. ➥
One of '{title}' is expected.
```

How can it be that the validator expects the element title but complains when it encounters title? It has to do with the fact that normally the element tags include a prefix and a colon before the element name, like in xsd:element, and that schema and the XML document must be consistent.

Lines 8–12 are essentially a comment.

Lines 13–20 specify the starfleet element, which is of a complex type, as defined in Line 14. This means that starfleet can have attributes and/or can contain other elements. Line 15 tells you in which way starfleet is complex: it contains a sequence of elements. Elements in xsd:sequence must appear in the order in which they are specified (in this case, title followed by starship).

Line 16 specifies that title is of type xsd:string, which is a primitive type hard-coded in the standard XML Schema. Line 16 also tells you that there can be maximum one title per starfleet. It is also possible to define minOccurs, and the default for both minOccurs and maxOccurs is 1. This means that by omitting minOccurs, you make title mandatory.

Line 17 declares that the starship element is of type ShipType, which is defined somewhere else in starfleet.xsd. This is an alternative to defining the type of an element inside its body, as we did with the starfleet element. Naming a type lets you use it for several element definitions and as a base for more complex types. However, I have only extracted the type specification from the body of starship to make the code more readable. maxOccurs="unbounded" states that there can be as many starship elements in starfleet as you need.

Lines 21–28 define the type of the starship element. It's a complex type, but it's different from that of starfleet. The xsd:all group means that there can only be up to one element each of all those listed, in any order. This would normally mean that each starship could be empty or contain a class, a captain, or both as children. However, we want to make ship class and captain mandatory. To achieve this result, we specified the attribute minOccurs="1" for both elements.

Lines 26–27 define the two attributes of starship. The use attribute lets you specify that they are mandatory.

If you now look again at enterprises.xml, you'll notice that the class element has an attribute (name). Because of this attribute, you must define its type as complex, although class has no body. This is done in lines 29–31. As you can see, you specify an empty body by creating a complex type without sub-elements.

Occurrence Constraints

In starfleet.xsd, we used three attributes to limit the number of occurrences: minOccurs and maxOccurs when declaring elements, and use when declaring attributes. While the constraints for elements accept non-negative integers as values (with 1 as the default), use can only have one of the following values: required, optional (the default), and prohibited. You can use two additional attributes when declaring either elements or attributes: default and fixed.

When applied to an attribute, default supplies the value of an optional attribute in case it is omitted when you define its element in the XML document (it is an error to provide a default for attributes that are required). Note that when you define elements in an XML document, they're always created with all their attributes, whether you explicitly define them in the XML document or not, because their existence is determined by their presence in the schema. When applied to an element, default refers to the element content, but it never results in the creation of elements. It only provides content for empty elements. For example: `<xsd:attribute name="country" type="xsd:string" default="USA"/>`.

The `fixed` constraint forces an attribute value or an element content to have a particular value. You can still define a value in the XML document, but it must match the fixed value assigned in the schema.

Primitive and Derived Types

With `xsd:string`, you've already seen an example of primitive types. Table 5-1 summarizes the full list of primitive types.

Table 5-1. XML Primitive Types

Type	Example/Description
anyURI	Either an absolute or a relative URI
base64Binary	MIME encoding consisting of A-Z, a-z, 0-9, +, and /, with A = 0 and / = 63
boolean	For example, `true` and `false`
date	Like the date portion of `dateTime`, but with the addition of the time zone
dateTime	For example, `2007-12-05T15:00:00.345-05:00` means 345 milliseconds after 3 PM Eastern Standard Time (EST) of December 5th, 2007; fractional seconds can be omitted
decimal	For example, `123.456`
double	Formatted like `float`, but uses 64 bits
duration	For example, PaYbMcDTdHeMfS means a years, b months, c days, d hours, e minutes, and f seconds; a minus at the beginning, when present, indicates "in the past"
float	32-bit floating point; for example, `1.2e-4`
gDay	For example, `25`
gMonth	For example, `12`
gMonthDay	For example, `12-25`
gYear	For example, `2007`
gYearMonth	For example, `2007-12`; g stands for Gregorian calendar, which is the calendar we use

Type	Example/Description
hexBinary	Hexadecimal encoding; for example, 1F represents the number 31 and corresponds to a byte containing the bit sequence 01111111
NOTATION	Externally defined formats
QName	Qualified XML name; for example, xsd:string
string	For example, "This is a string"
time	Like the time portion of dateTime

The XML Schema standard also defines additional types called *derived*, among which are those listed in Table 5-2.

Table 5-2. XML Derived Types

Type	Example/Description
byte	An integer number between -2^7 (-128) and 2^7-1 (127)
int	An integer number between -2^{31} (-2,147,483,648) and 2^{31}-1 (2,147,483,647)
integer	An integer number
language	A natural language code as specified in the ISO 639 standard (e.g., FR for French and EN-US for American English)
long	An integer number between -2^{63} (-9,223,372,036,854,775,808) and 2^{63}-1 (9,223,372,036,854,775,807)
negativeInteger	An integer number < 0
nonNegativeInteger	An integer number >= 0
nonPositiveInteger	An integer number <= 0
normalizedString	A string that doesn't contain any carriage return, line feed, or tab characters
positiveInteger	An integer number > 0
short	An integer number between -2^{15} (-32,768) and 2^{15}-1 (32,767)
token	A string that doesn't contain any carriage return, line feed, tab characters, leading or trailing spaces, or sequences of two or more consecutive spaces

Type	Example/Description
unsignedByte	An integer number between 0 and 2^8-1 (255)
unsignedInt	An integer number between 0 and 2^{32}-1 (4,294,967,295)
unsignedLong	An integer number between 0 and 2^{64}-1 (18,446,744,073,709,551,615)
unsignedShort	An integer number between 0 and 2^{16}-1 (65,535)

Simple Types

If you need to modify an already defined type without adding attributes or other elements, you can define a so-called *simple type* instead of recurring to a complex one. For example, the following code defines a string that can only contain up to 32 characters:

```
<xsd:simpleType name="myString">
  <xsd:restriction base="xsd:string">
    <xsd:maxLength value="32"/>
    </xsd:restriction>
  </xsdLsimpleType>
```

Besides maxLength, you can also apply the length and minLength attributes to listlike types. Additionally, you can use the whiteSpace and pattern attributes.

The possible values for whiteSpace are preserve (the default), replace, and collapse. With replace, all carriage return, line feed, and tab characters are replaced with simple spaces. With collapse, leading and trailing spaces are removed, and sequences of multiple spaces are collapsed into single spaces.

With pattern, you define a regular expression that must be matched. For example, the following code specifies that only strings consisting of at least one letter of the alphabet are valid:

```
<xsd:pattern value="[A-Za-z]+"
```

For non-list types, you can also use the attributes minExclusive, minInclusive, maxExclusive, maxInclusive, totalDigits, fractionDigits, and enumeration. For example, this code defines a number with three decimal figures >= 10 and < 20:

```
<xsd:simpleType name="xxyyyType">
  <xsd:restriction base="xsd:decimal">
    <xsd:totalDigits value="6"/>
    <xsd:fractionDigits value="3"/>
    <xsd:minInclusive value="10.000"/>
    <xsd:maxExclusive value="20.000"/>
    </xsd:restriction>
  </xsd:simpleType>
```

And here's an example of enumeration:

```
<xsd:simpleType name="directionType">
  <xsd:restriction base="xsd:string">
    <xsd:enumeration value="left"/>
    <xsd:enumeration value="right"/>
```

```
    <xsd:enumeration value="straight"/>
    </xsd:restriction>
</xsd:simpleType>
```

REGULAR EXPRESSIONS

A regular expression is a string that matches a set of strings according to certain rules. Unfortunately, there is no standard syntax for regular expressions. They are used with several applications, including text editors (e.g., vi) and programming languages (e.g., Perl), and in Unix commands and scripting. W3C defines the syntax for regular expressions to be used in XML schemas (http://www.w3.org/TR/xmlschema-2/#regexs). Here I give you a summary of that definition in plain English.

The basic component of a regular expression is called an *atom*. It consists of a single character (specified either individually or as a *class* of characters enclosed between square brackets) indicating that any of the characters in the class are a match. For example, both "a" and "[a]" are regular expressions matching the lowercase character 'a', while "[a-zA-Z]" matches all letters of the English alphabet.

Things can get complicated, because you can also subtract a class from a group or create a *negative group* by sticking a ^ character at the beginning of it. For example, "[(^abc) - [ABC]]" matches any character with the exclusion of the characters 'a', 'b', and 'c' in uppercase or lowercase. This is because the group ^abc matches everything with the exclusion of the three letters in lowercase, and the subtraction of [ABC] removes the same three letters in uppercase. Obviously, you could have obtained the same effect with the regular expression "[^aAbBcC]".

The characters \|.-^?*+{}()[] are special and must be escaped with a backslash. You can also use \n for newlines, \r for returns, and \t for tabs.

With atoms, you can build *pieces* by appending to it a *quantifier*. Possible quantifiers are ? (the question mark), + (the plus sign), * (the asterisk), and {n,m}, with n <= m indicating non-negative integers. The question mark indicates that the atom can be missing; the plus sign means any concatenation of one or more atoms; the asterisk means any concatenation of atoms (including none at all); and {n,m} means any concatenation of length >= n and <= m (e.g., "[a-z]{2,7}" means all strings containing between two and seven lowercase alphabetic characters). If you omit m but leave the comma in place, you leave the upper limit unbounded. If, on the other hand, you also omit the comma, you define a string of fixed length (e.g., "[0-9]{3}" means a string of exactly three numeric characters). You can concatenate pieces simply by writing them one after the other. For example, to define an identifier consisting of alphanumeric characters and underscores but beginning with a letter, you could write the expression "[a-zA-Z]{1}[a-zA-Z0-9_]*". The general term *branch* is used to indicate a single piece or a concatenation of pieces when the distinction is not relevant.

To specify partial patterns, you can insert at the beginning and/or at the end of each atom a sequence formed with a period and an asterisk. For example, ".*ABC.*" identifies all strings containing in any position the substring ABC. Without dot-asterisk wildcarding, "ABC" only matches a string of exactly three characters of length.

Several branches can be further composed by means of vertical bars to form a more general regular expression. For example, "[a-zA-Z]* | [0-9]*" matches all strings composed entirely of letters or of digits but not a mix of the two.

Instead of defining a new simple type by imposing a restriction, you can also specify that it consists of a list of items of an existing simple type. For example, the following code defines a type consisting of a series of directions:

```
<xsd:simpleType name="pathType">
  <xsd:list itemType="directionType"/>
  </xsd:simpleType>
```

Finally, besides xsd:restriction and xsd:list, you can define a new simple type by means of xsd:union, which lets you combine two different preexisting types. For example, the following code defines a type that can be either a number between 1 and 10 or one of the strings "< 1" and "> 10":

```
<xsd:simpleType name="myNumber">
  <xsd:union>
    <xsd:simpleType>
      <xsd:restriction base="xsd:positiveInteger">
        <xsd:maxInclusive value="10"/>
        </xsd:restriction>
      </xsd:simpleType>
    <xsd:simpleType>
      <xsd:restriction base="xsd:string">
        <xsd:enumeration value="< 1"/>
        <xsd:enumeration value="> 10"/>
        </xsd:restriction>
      </xsd:simpleType>
    </xsd:union>
  </xsd:simpleType>
```

Complex Types

You've already seen some examples of complex types in starfleet.xsd. There are three models that you can use to group the elements contained in a complex type: sequence (in which the elements must appear in the specified sequence), all (in which there can only be up to one element each of all those listed, but they can appear in any order), and choice (in which the contained elements are mutually exclusive). Note that while all can only contain individual elements, sequence and choice can contain other groups. For example, the fragment:

```
<xsd:sequence>
  <xsd:choice>
    <xsd:element name="no" ... />
    <xsd:all>
      <xsd:element name="yes1" ... />
      <xsd:element name="yes2" ... />
      </xsd:all>
    </xsd:choice>
  <xsd:element name="whatever" ... />
```

```
</xsd:sequence>
```

defines an element that contains one of the following combinations of elements:

- whatever
- no, whatever
- yes1, whatever
- yes2, whatever
- yes1, yes2, whatever
- yes2, yes1, whatever

Complex type definitions provide many additional options, but are not always easy to handle. One might even argue that they've been overengineered. Therefore, to describe them in detail would exceed the scope of this manual. Nevertheless, the information I have provided on primitive and simple types, together with the description of the three model groups, is already enough to cover most cases.

Validation

An XML document is said to be *valid* if it passes the checks done by a validating parser against the document's DTD or XML schema. For the parser to be able to operate, the XML document must be *well formed*, which means that all tags are closed, the attributes are quoted, the nesting is done correctly, and so on. A validating parser, besides checking for well formedness, also checks for validity.

You actually have to validate two documents: the XML file and the DTD or XML Schema. In the example, those are enterprises.xml and starfleet.dtd/starfleet.xsd, respectively. The simplest way to do the validation is to use a development environment like Eclipse, which validates the documents as you type.

An alternative is to use online services. For example, the tool available at http://xmlvalidation.com can check XML files, DTD files, and XML schemas. To validate your schema, you can also use the online tool by W3C, which provides an authoritative check. Go to http://www.w3.org/2001/03/webdata/xsv and look at the second section, which should look as shown in Figure 5-1.

Caution The fact that your XML schema is valid doesn't mean at all that you will not get any error when validating an XML file, because inconsistencies can easily creep in.

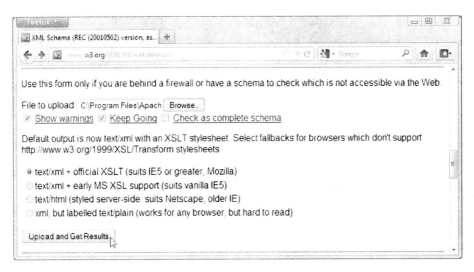

Figure 5-1. *Validating the schema with W3C*

Click on the `Browse...` button, select `starfleet.xsd` (or the schema you want to get checked), and then click on `Upload and Get Results`. You should see a page like that shown in Figure 5-2.

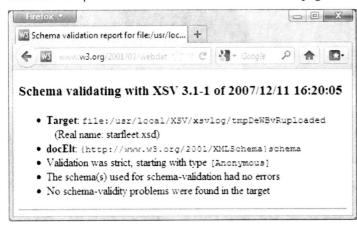

Figure 5-2. *Validation results*

In general, you need to go through three steps to validate an XML document:

1. Associate the document to the DTD/schema against which it is to be validated.

2. Define an exception handler to specify what happens when a validation error is detected.

3. Parse the document with a validating parser, which validates your XML document against the DTD/schema.

133

PARSERS

A parser is a piece of software that breaks down a document into *tokens*, analyzes the syntax of the tokens to form valid expressions, and finally interprets the expressions and performs corresponding actions.

The parsing process therefore implies a validation of the document. The DOM (standardized by W3C) and Simple API for XML (SAX) define, among other things, interfaces to perform XML parsing.

DOM parsers build a tree of nodes after loading the whole document in memory. Therefore, they require quite a bit of memory. SAX, on the other hand, parses the documents from streams, and therefore has a smaller memory footprint. The flexibility of the DOM also costs in terms of performance, and DOM implementations tend to be slower than SAX implementations, although they might overall be more efficient with small XML files that don't stretch memory usage. The two most widely used packages implementing DOM and SAX are Xerces and Java API for XML Processing (JAXP). You can download the documentation for JAXP from `http://java.sun.com/xml/downloads/jaxp.html`. In case you are interested, Xerces is also available for other languages, such as C++.

Xerces are the developer of SAX, and the version of SAX included in JAXP is not identical to the original one. Several people reported bugs in the JAXP version, although I have used it in all the examples of this chapter without any problem. You can install the Xerces version downloaded from `http://xerces.apache.org/`. All you need to do is click on "Xerces2 Java 2.11.0 - zip" under the heading `Xerces2` (there might be a newer version when you go there), expand `Xerces-J-bin.2.11.0.zip`, and copy `xercesimpl.jar` and `xml-apis.jar` to Tomcat's `lib` folder. `xml-apis.jar` contains DOM level 3, SAX 2.0.2, and the JAXP 1.4 APIs; `xercesImpl.jar` contains the implementation of these APIs as well as of the XNI API (the Xerces Native Interface). I have included `starfleet_validate_sax_schema_xerces.jsp` in the software package of this chapter as an example.

Using JSP to Validate XML against a DTD

To validate an XML file against a DTD, you must first associate the XML document with the DTD by adding a DOCTYPE declaration to the XML file. The declaration, which you should insert immediately after the `<?xml...?>` line, is as follows:

```
<!DOCTYPE starfleet SYSTEM "http://localhost:8080/xml-validate/dtd/starfleet.dtd">
```

Notice that the file `starfleet.dtd` doesn't need to be in the WEB-INF\dtds\ folder. We had to place the DTDs there because Tomcat expected them there, but if you do the validation yourself, Tomcat is out of the loop. You can therefore place your DTDs wherever you like.

The next step is the definition of an exception handler. This is a Java object of a class that extends `org.xml.sax.helpers.DefaultHandler` and replaces three of its methods: `warning`, `error`, and `fatalError`. Once the handler is registered with the parser, the parser executes the appropriate method upon encountering a validation problem. The default behavior of `DefaultHandler` is to do nothing. Therefore, you need to overwrite the methods in order to report the errors. Listing 5-4 shows you the code of a possible handler. It's really up to you to decide what level of reporting you'd like to have, but I have decided to report all validation problems and interrupt the parsing.

Listing 5-4. ParsingExceptionHandler.java

```java
package myPkg;
import org.xml.sax.helpers.DefaultHandler;
import org.xml.sax.SAXParseException;
public class ParsingExceptionHandler extends DefaultHandler {
  public SAXParseException parsingException = null;
  public String errorLevel = null;
  public void warning(SAXParseException e) {
    errorLevel = "Warning";
    parsingException = e;
    }
  public void error(SAXParseException e) {
    errorLevel = "Error";
    parsingException = e;
    }
  public void fatalError(SAXParseException e) {
    errorLevel = "Fatal error";
    parsingException = e;
    }
}
```

As you can see, it's pretty simple. You define two public attributes: one to save the exception generated by the parser, and one to save the error level. You then update the two attributes in each one of the three methods. After each parsing, you can check one of the attributes for null in order to determine whether the parsing succeeded or not. Compile this module from the DOS command line with javac ParsingExceptionHandler.java and copy the resulting .class file into the WEB-INF\classes\myPkg folder of your application directory.

You are now ready to perform the validation. Listing 5-5 shows you a JSP page that implements a SAX parser.

Listing 5-5. starfleet_validate_sax.jsp (first cut)

```jsp
<%@page language="java" contentType="text/html"%>
<%@page import="javax.xml.parsers.SAXParserFactory"%>
<%@page import="javax.xml.parsers.SAXParser"%>
<%@page import="org.xml.sax.InputSource"%>
<%@page import="myPkg.ParsingExceptionHandler"%>
<html><head><title>Starfleet validation (SAX - DTD)</title></head><body>
<%
  SAXParserFactory factory = SAXParserFactory.newInstance();
  factory.setValidating(true);
  SAXParser parser = factory.newSAXParser();
  InputSource inputSource = new InputSource("webapps/xml-validate/xml/enterprises.xml");
  ParsingExceptionHandler handler = new ParsingExceptionHandler();
  parser.parse(inputSource, handler);
  %>
</body></html>
```

After instantiating the parser factory and setting its `validating` property to `true`, you direct the factory to create a SAX parser. Then you instantiate the `InputSource` class to access the XML document and the exception handler. After that, all you need to do is execute the parser.

This implementation is not very nice, though, because it causes the dumping of a stack trace whenever the validation fails. It is better to wrap the parsing inside a `try`/`catch` as shown in Listing 5-6, so that you can display validation errors without stack trace.

Note that before you can execute the improved version of `starfleet_validate_sax.jsp`, you need to download the `StringEscapeUtils` from Apache Commons. Their purpose is to convert special characters to their corresponding HTML entities, so that they display correctly in your web page. Go to `http://commons.apache.org/lang/download_lang.cgi` and click on the link `commons-lang3-3.1-bin.zip`.

To install it in Tomcat, unzip the file, copy `commons-lang3-3.1.jar` to `%CATALINA_HOME%\lib\`, and restart Tomcat.

■ **Tip** In alternative to copying libraries to Tomcat's `lib` folder, you can make them available to a particular application by placing them in the `WEB-INF\lib` folder of the application (create it if it's not yet there). In that way, the library will not be generally available, but you will not run the risk of later needing a different version of the same library for another application and introducing a conflict when both versions are in Tomcat's `lib` folder.

Listing 5-6. starfleet_validate_sax.jsp

```
<%@page language="java" contentType="text/html"%>
<%@page import="javax.xml.parsers.SAXParserFactory"%>
<%@page import="javax.xml.parsers.SAXParser"%>
<%@page import="org.xml.sax.InputSource"%>
<%@page import="org.apache.commons.lang3.StringEscapeUtils"%>
<%@page import="myPkg.ParsingExceptionHandler"%>
<html><head><title>Starfleet validation (SAX - DTD)</title></head><body>
<%
  SAXParserFactory factory = SAXParserFactory.newInstance();
  factory.setValidating(true);
  SAXParser parser = factory.newSAXParser();
  InputSource inputSource = new InputSource("webapps/xml-validate/xml/enterprises.xml");
  ParsingExceptionHandler handler = new ParsingExceptionHandler();
  try { parser.parse(inputSource, handler); }
  catch (Exception e) { }
  if (handler.errorLevel == null) {
    out.println("The document is valid.");
  }
  else {
    out.println(
      "*** Validation " + handler.errorLevel + ": "
      + StringEscapeUtils.escapeHtml4(handler.parsingException.toString())
    );
  }
%>
</body></html>
```

Now, if you type `http://localhost:8080/xml-validate/with-dtd/starfleet_validate_sax.jsp` in a browser, you should get a one-liner confirming that `enterprises.xml` is correct.

When you introduce an error in the XML document, for example by mistyping the closing tag as in `<captain>James Tiberius Kirk</catain>`, you get the following message:

```
*** Validation Fatal error: org.xml.sax.SAXParseException; systemId: ➥
file:///C:/Program%20Files/Apache%20Software%20Foundation/Tomcat/webapps/xml- ➥
validate/xml/enterprises.xml; lineNumber: 7; columnNumber: 35; The element type ➥
"captain" must be terminated by the matching end-tag "</captain>".
```

Good, isn't it? Notice that it is a fatal error. Incidentally, the angle brackets around `/captain` is why you need to escape the message with `StringEscapeUtils`. If you remove the line altogether, you get this message:

```
*** Validation Error: org.xml.sax.SAXParseException; systemId: ➥
file:///C:/Program%20Files/Apache%20Software%20Foundation/Tomcat/webapps/xml- ➥
validate/xml/enterprises.xml; lineNumber: 7; columnNumber: 16; The content of ➥
element type "starship" is incomplete, it must match "(class,captain)".
```

Notice that it is an error, rather than a fatal error. I confess that I tried to get a warning message but didn't succeed. If you do, please let me know.

To use a DOM parser instead of SAX, make a copy of `starfleet_validate_sax.jsp`, name it `starfleet_validate_dom.jsp`, and replace six lines with seven new lines, as shown in Listing 5-7.

Listing 5-7. starfleet_validate_dom.jsp

```
<%@page language="java" contentType="text/html"%>
<%@page import="javax.xml.parsers.DocumentBuilderFactory"%>
<%@page import="javax.xml.parsers.DocumentBuilder"%>
<%@page import="org.xml.sax.InputSource"%>
<%@page import="org.apache.commons.lang3.StringEscapeUtils"%>
<%@page import="myPkg.ParsingExceptionHandler"%>
<html><head><title>Starfleet validation (DOM - DTD)</title></head><body>
<%
  DocumentBuilderFactory factory = DocumentBuilderFactory.newInstance();
  factory.setValidating(true);
  DocumentBuilder parser = factory.newDocumentBuilder();
  InputSource inputSource = new InputSource("webapps/xml-validate/xml/enterprises.xml");
  ParsingExceptionHandler handler = new ParsingExceptionHandler();
  parser.setErrorHandler(handler);
  try { parser.parse(inputSource); }
  catch (Exception e) { }
  if (handler.errorLevel == null) {
    out.println("The document is valid.");
    }
  else {
    out.println(
        "*** Validation " + handler.errorLevel + ": "
      + StringEscapeUtils.escapeHtml4(handler.parsingException.toString())
      );
    }
%>
```

```
</body></html>
```

Using JSP to Validate XML against a Schema

The procedure used to validate an XML file against a schema is almost identical to the procedure explained in the previous section for validating against a DTD.

To avoid confusion, I made copies of enterprises.xml and starfleet_validate_sax.jsp and renamed them respectively enterprises_schema.xml and starfleet_validate_sax_schema.jsp.

In enterprises_schema.xml, to change from DTD to schema, you only need to remove the DOCTYPE declaration and add to the starfleet tag some attributes:

```
<starfleet
    xmlns="http://localhost:8080/xml-validate/xsd"
    xmlns:xsi="http://www.w3.org/2001/XMLSchema-instance"
    xsi:schemaLocation="http://localhost:8080/xml-validate/xsd  ➥
http://localhost:8080/xml-validate/xsd/starfleet.xsd"
    >
```

Listing 5-8 shows starfleet_validate_sax_schema.jsp with the differences from starfleet_validate_sax.jsp highlighted in bold.

Listing 5-8. starfleet_validate_sax_schema.jsp

```
<%@page language="java" contentType="text/html"%>
<%@page import="javax.xml.parsers.SAXParserFactory"%>
<%@page import="javax.xml.parsers.SAXParser"%>
<%@page import="org.xml.sax.InputSource"%>
<%@page import="org.apache.commons.lang3.StringEscapeUtils"%>
<%@page import="myPkg.ParsingExceptionHandler"%>
<html><head><title>Starfleet validation (SAX - schema)</title></head><body>
<%
  SAXParserFactory factory = SAXParserFactory.newInstance();
  factory.setValidating(true);
  factory.setNamespaceAware(true);
  factory.setFeature("http://apache.org/xml/features/validation/schema", true);
  SAXParser parser = factory.newSAXParser();
  InputSource inputSource =
    new InputSource("webapps/xml-validate/xml/enterprises_schema.xml");
  ParsingExceptionHandler handler = new ParsingExceptionHandler();
  try { parser.parse(inputSource, handler); }
  catch (Exception e) { }
  if (handler.errorLevel == null) {
    out.println("The document is valid.");
    }
  else {
    out.println(
        "*** Validation " + handler.errorLevel + ": "
      + StringEscapeUtils.escapeHtml4(handler.parsingException.toString())
      );
    }
  %>
```

```
</body></html>
```

As you can see, apart from updating the page title and the name of the XML file, you only need to switch on two features of the parser that tell it to use a schema instead of a DTD.

What I said about changing `SAX` to `DOM` in `starfleet_validate_sax.jsp` also applies to `starfleet_validate_sax_schema.jsp`. You will find `starfleet_validate_dom_schema.jsp` in the software package for this chapter.

JSTL-XML and XSL

The XML actions specified in JSTL are meant to address the basic XML needs that a JSP programmer is likely to encounter.

To make XML file contents easier to access, the W3C specified the XML Path Language (XPath). The name XPath was chosen to indicate that it identifies paths within XML documents (see `http://www.w3.org/TR/xpath`). The JSTL-XML actions rely on that language to identify XML components.

To avoid confusion between EL expressions and XPath expressions, the actions that require an XPath expression always use the `select` attribute. In this way, you can be sure that all expressions outside `select` are EL expressions. Several XML actions are the XPath-counterparts of equivalent core actions, with the attribute `select` replacing the attribute `value` (when present). They are: `x:choose`, `x:forEach`, `x:if`, `x:out`, `x:otherwise`, `x:set`, and `x:when`.

The remaining three actions are `x:parse` and the pair `x:transform` and `x:param`. But before you can learn about them, we have to talk about the Extensible Stylesheet Language (XSL).

XSL is a language for expressing style sheets that describe how to display and transform XML documents. The specification documents are available from `http://www.w3.org/Style/XSL/`.

While CSS only needs to define how to represent the predefined HTML tags, XSL has to cope with the fact that there are no predefined tags in XML! How do you know whether a `<table>` element in an XML file represents a table of data as you know it from HTML or an object around which you can sit for dinner?

That's why XSL is more than a style-sheet language. It actually includes three parts:

- **XPath**: The language to navigate in XML documents I already mentioned.

- **XSLT**: A language to transform XML documents that can completely change their structure.

- **XSL Formatting Objects (XSL-FO)**: A language for formatting XML documents.

I will only explain XPath and XSLT, because XSL-FO is concerned with *page formatting* (page size, margins, headers, footers, citations, footnotes, and so on), which is very different from the screen formatting and hyperlinking you need for web pages.

Just to give you an idea, XSL-FO divides the output into pages, the pages into regions (body, header, footer, and left and right sidebars), the regions into block areas, the block areas into line areas, and the line areas into inline areas. You can define several attributes of these fields and then "flow" your content into them. XSL-FO also provides constructs for lists and tables similar to those you know from HTML.

XPath

XPath expressions identify a set of XML nodes through patterns. Extensible Stylesheet Language Transformations (XSLT) templates (see later in this chapter for XSLT examples) then use those patterns when they apply transformations. Possible XPath nodes can be any of the following: document/root, comment, element, attribute, text, processing instruction, and namespace.

Note Processing instructions in an XML document provide information for the application that uses the document.

For example, take a look at the following XML document:

```
<?xml version="1.0" encoding="UTF-8"?>
<whatever xmlns:zzz="http://myWeb.com/whatever">
  <!-- bla bla -->   <?myAppl "xyz"?>
  <item name="anything">
    <subitem>The quick brown fox</subitem>
    </item>
  </whatever>
```

The document (or root) node is `<whatever>`, `<!-- bla bla -->` is a comment node, `<subitem>...</subitem>` is an element node, `name="anything"` is an attribute node, the string `The quick brown fox` is a text node, `<?myAppl "xyz"?>` is a processing-instruction node, and `xmlns:zzz="http://myWeb.com/whatever"` is a namespace node.

As with URLs, XPath uses a slash as a separator. Absolute paths start with a slash, while all other paths are relative. Similar to file directories, a period indicates the current node, while a double period indicates the parent node.

Several nodes with the same name are distinguished by indexing them, as Java does with array elements. For example, let's say you have the following XML code:

```
<a> <b>whatever</b> <b>never</b> </a>
<c> <non_b>no</non_b> <b>verywell</b> </c>
<a> <b attr="zz">nice</b> <b attr="xxx">ok</b> </a>
```

The pattern `/a/b` selects the four `<b>` elements, which contain `whatever`, `never`, `nice`, and `ok`. The `<b>` element with `verywell` isn't selected, because it's inside `<c>` instead of `<a>`. The pattern `/a[1]/b[0]` selects the `<b>` element with `nice`. Attribute names are prefixed by an @. For example, `/a[1]/b[1]/@attr` refers to the attribute that has the value `xxx` in the example.

A clever thing in XPath: you can use conditions as indices. For example, `/a/b[@attr="zz"]` selects the same `<b>` element selected by `/a[1]/b[0]`, while `/a[b]` selects all `<a>` elements that have `<b>` as a child (in the example, both), and `/a[b="never"]` selects the first `<a>` element. A final example: `/a/b[@attr][0]` selects the first `<b>` element that is contained in an `<a>` and has the attribute `attr` (i.e., it selects once again the element `/a[1]/b[0]`).

XPath defines several operators and functions related to node sets, positions, or namespaces, and it defines string, numeric, boolean, and conversion operations.

A *node set* is a group of nodes considered collectively. A node set resulting from the execution of an XPath expression doesn't necessarily contain several nodes. It can consist of a single node or even none. Keep in mind that the nodes belonging to a node set can be organized in a tree, but not necessarily. For example, the expression `$myDoc//C` identifies all `C` elements in a document that was parsed into the variable `myDoc`. It is unlikely that they form a tree.

Within XPath, you have access to the implicit JSP objects you're familiar with. Table 5-3 lists the mappings.

Table 5-3. XPath Mappings of Implicit JSP Objects

JSP	XPath
pageContext.findAttribute("attrName")	$attrName
request.getParameter("parName")	$param:paramName
request.getHeader("headerName")	$header:headerName
cookie's value for name foo	$cookie:foo
application.getInitParameter("initParName")	$initParam:initParName
pageContext.getAttribute("attrName", PageContext.PAGE_SCOPE)	$pageScope:attrName
pageContext.getAttribute("attrName", PageContext.REQUEST_SCOPE)	$requestScope:attrName
pageContext.getAttribute("attrName", PageContext.SESSION_SCOPE)	$sessionScope:attrName
pageContext.getAttribute("attrName", PageContext.APPLICATION_SCOPE)	$applicationScope:attrName

Before we look at an XPath example, I would like to give you a more rigorous reference of its syntax and explain some terms that you are likely to encounter "out there."

To identify a node or a set of nodes, you need to navigate through the tree structure of an XML document from your current position within the tree (the *context node*) to the target. The path description consists of a series of steps separated by slashes, whereby each step includes the navigation direction (the *axis specifier*), an expression identifying the node[s] (the *node test*), and a condition to be satisfied (the *predicate*) enclosed between square brackets.

A slash at the beginning indicates that the path begins at the root node, while paths relative to the context node begin without a slash. Two consecutive colons separate the axis specifier and the node test. For example, this code identifies the second attribute of all B elements immediately below the root element A:

```
/child::A/child::B/attribute::*[position()=2]
```

You can express the same path with an abbreviated syntax, as follows:

```
/A/B/@*[2]
```

where child, ::, and position()= are simply omitted, and attribute is represented by @.

Table 5-4 shows the possible axis specifiers and their abbreviated syntax.

Table 5-4. Axis Specifiers

Specifier	Abbreviated Syntax
ancestor	Not available (n/a)
ancestor-or-self	n/a
attribute	@
child	Default; do not specify it
descendant	//
descendant-or-self	n/a
following	n/a
following-sibling	n/a
namespace	n/a
parent	(i.e., two dots)
preceding	n/a
preceding-sibling	n/a
self	(i.e., a single dot)

As node tests, you can use node names with or without a namespace prefix, or you can use an asterisk to indicate all names. With abbreviated syntax, an asterisk on its own indicates all element nodes, and @* indicates all attributes.

You can also use node() as a node test to indicate all possible nodes of any type. Similarly, comment() indicates all comment nodes, text() indicates all text nodes, and processing-instruction() indicates all processing instruction nodes.

For example, the following code selects all elements B descendant of A that have the attribute xx set to 'z':

A//B[@xx='z']

while to select all elements C anywhere in the tree that have the attribute yy you can do this:

//C[@yy]

To form expressions, besides the operators you have already seen (i.e., slash, double slash, and square brackets), you have available all standard arithmetic and comparison operators (i.e., +, -, *, div, mod, =, !=, <, <=, >, and >=). Additionally, you have and and or for boolean operations, and the union operator | (i.e., the vertical bar) to merge two node sets.

References to variables are indicated by sticking a dollar sign before them, as shown in the following example:

```
<x:parse doc="${sf}" varDom="dom"/>
<x:forEach var="tag" select="$dom//starship">
```

where I parse an XML document into the variable dom and then use $dom when I refer to it in an XPath expression.

An XPath Example

So far, everything has been pretty dry and abstract. To spice things up a bit, we are going to write a JSP page that parses an XML file, selects its elements and attributes, and displays them in a HTML table. Listing 5-9 shows the XML file we'll play with, starfleet.xml. It is an expanded version of the file enterprises.xml (Listing 5-1) you have already encountered in the validation section of this chapter.

Listing 5-9. starfleet.xml

```
<?xml version="1.0" encoding="UTF-8"?>
<starfleet>
  <starship name="Enterprise" sn="NX-01">
    <class commissioned="2151">NX</class>
    <captain>Jonathan Archer</captain>
    </starship>
  <starship name="USS Enterprise" sn="NCC-1701">
    <class commissioned="2245">Constitution</class>
    <captain>James Tiberius Kirk</captain>
    </starship>
  <starship name="USS Enterprise" sn="NCC-1701-A">
    <class commissioned="2286">Constitution</class>
    <captain>James T. Kirk</captain>
    </starship>
  <starship name="USS Enterprise" sn="NCC-1701-B">
    <class commissioned="2293">Excelsior</class>
    <captain>John Harriman</captain>
    </starship>
  <starship name="USS Enterprise" sn="NCC-1701-C">
    <class commissioned="2332">Ambassador</class>
    <captain>Rachel Garrett</captain>
    </starship>
  <starship name="USS Enterprise" sn="NCC-1701-D">
    <class commissioned="2363">Galaxy</class>
    <captain>Jean-Luc Picard</captain>
    </starship>
  <starship name="USS Enterprise" sn="NCC-1701-E">
    <class commissioned="2372">Sovereign</class>
    <captain>Jean-Luc Picard</captain>
    </starship>
  </starfleet>
```

Notice that it doesn't include the DOCTYPE element necessary for DTD validation or the namespace declarations necessary for schema validation. This is because in this example we are not going to do any validation. Listing 5-10 shows the JSP page that does the conversion to HTML, and Figure 5-3 shows its output as it appears in a web browser.

Listing 5-10. *starfleet.jsp*

```
01: <%@page language="java" contentType="text/html"%>
02: <%@taglib uri="http://java.sun.com/jsp/jstl/core" prefix="c"%>
03: <%@taglib uri="http://java.sun.com/jsp/jstl/xml" prefix="x"%>
04: <c:import url="starfleet.xml" var="sf"/>
05: <x:parse doc="${sf}" varDom="dom"/>
06: <html><head>
07:   <title>Parsing starfleet.xml</title>
08:   <style>th {text-align:left}</style>
09:   </head>
10: <body>
11: <table border="1">
12:   <tr><th>Name</th><th>S/N</th><th>Class</th><th>Year</th><th>Captain</th></tr>
13:   <x:forEach var="tag" select="$dom//starship">
14:     <tr>
15:       <td><x:out select="$tag/@name"/></td>
16:       <td><x:out select="$tag/@sn"/></td>
17:       <td><x:out select="$tag/class"/></td>
18:       <td><x:out select="$tag/class/@commissioned"/></td>
19:       <td><x:out select="$tag/captain"/></td>
20:     </tr>
21:   </x:forEach>
22:   </table>
23: </body>
24: </html>
```

In line 4, you load the XML file in memory, and in line 5, you parse it into an object of type org.apache.xerces.dom.DeferredDocumentImpl, which implements the standard interface org.w3c.dom.Document of a Document Object Model (DOM). In lines 13–21, you loop through all the starship tags of the DOM, regardless of how "deep" they are in the structure. You can achieve this with the double slash. Inside the x:forEach loop, the variable tag refers in turn to each starship, and you can display the information contained in attributes and sub-elements. Notice that the select paths inside the loop always start with the slash. This is because the root element in each loop iteration is a starship tag, not starfleet, which is the root element of the document.

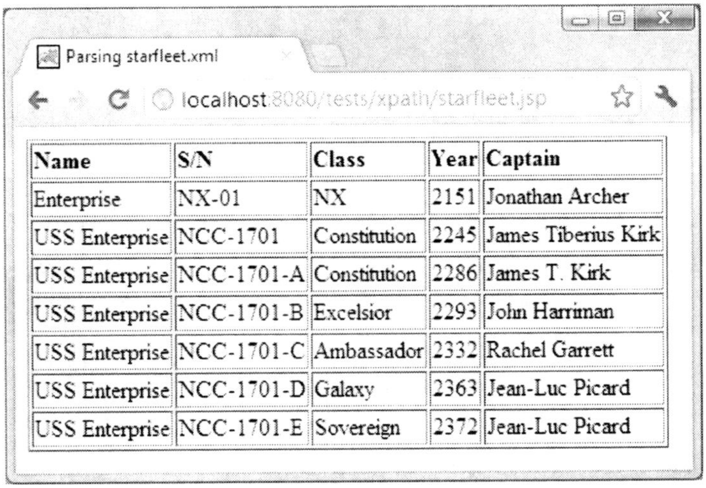

Figure 5-3. Starfleet information

x:parse

With `starfleet.jsp`, you have just seen an example of how to use `x:parse` and XPath to convert XML into HTML. Table 5-5 summarizes all attributes that `x:parse` supports. You will find a good reference for `x:parse` at `http://www.ibm.com/developerworks/java/library/j-jstl0520/`.

Table 5-5. x:parse Attributes

Attribute	Description
doc	Source XML document to be parsed
varDom	Name of the EL variable to store the parsed XML data as an object of type org.w3c.dom.Document
scopeDom	Scope for varDom
filter	Filter of type org.xml.sax.XMLFilter to be applied to the source XML
systemId	System identifier for parsing the XML source. It is a URI that identify the origin of the XML data, potentially useful to some parsers
var	Name of the variable to store the parse XML data (of implementation-dependent type)
scope	Scope for var

Instead of storing the XML source code in the attribute doc, you can also make x:parse a bodied action and store the source XML in its body.

XSLT: Transformation from One XML Format to Another

At the beginning of this chapter, I showed you the file enterprises.xml (Listing 5.1) and, later on, to explain XPath, I expanded it to starfleet.xml (Listing 5-9).

But the information contained in enterprises.xml is not just a sub-set of the larger starfleet.xml, because also the encoding is different. In particular, the differences from starfleet.xml are:

- The presence of a title element

- The removal in the class element of the commissioned attribute

- The replacement of the class body with an attribute named name

Listing 5-11 shows you an XSL style sheet that lets you extract enterprises.xml from starfleet.xml.

Listing 5-11. enterprises.xsl

```
01: <?xml version="1.0" encoding="UTF-8"?>
02: <xsl:stylesheet version="1.0" xmlns:xsl="http://www.w3.org/1999/XSL/Transform">
03: <xsl:output method="xml" version="1.0" encoding="UTF-8" indent="yes"/>
04: <xsl:template match="/">
05:   <starfleet>
06:     <title>The two most famous starships in the fleet</title>
07:     <xsl:for-each select="starfleet/starship">
08:       <xsl:if test="@sn='NCC-1701' or @sn='NCC-1701-D'">
09:         <xsl:element name="starship">
10:           <xsl:attribute name="name">
11:             <xsl:value-of select="@name"/>
12:           </xsl:attribute>
13:           <xsl:attribute name="sn">
14:             <xsl:value-of select="@sn"/>
15:           </xsl:attribute>
16:           <xsl:element name="class">
17:             <xsl:attribute name="name">
18:               <xsl:value-of select="class"/>
19:             </xsl:attribute>
20:           </xsl:element>
21:           <xsl:copy-of select="captain"/>
22:         </xsl:element>
23:       </xsl:if>
24:     </xsl:for-each>
25:   </starfleet>
26: </xsl:template>
27: </xsl:stylesheet>
```

Lines 1 and 2 state that the file is in XML format and specify its namespace. In line 2, you could replace xsl:stylesheet with xsl:transform, because the two keywords are considered synonyms.

Line 3 specifies that the output is also an XML document. XML is the default output format, but by writing it explicitly, you can also request that the output be indented. Otherwise, by default, the generated code would be written on a single very long line. The element also lets you specify an encoding other than ISO-8859-1.

The xsl:template element associates a template to an element, and in line 4, you write match="/" to specify the whole source document. In lines 5–6 and 25, you write the enterprise and title elements to the output.

The loop between lines 7 and 24 is where you scan all the starship elements. Immediately inside the loop, you select the two starships you're interested in with an xsl:if. In XSL, you could have also used the choose/when/otherwise construct that you encountered in Chapter 4 when I described JSTL-core, but in this case, it would not be appropriate, because you do not need an else.

The actual work is done in lines 9–22. The xsl:element and xsl:attribute elements create a new element and a new attribute, respectively, while xsl:value-of copies data from the source XML file to the output. Notice that the XPath expressions in the select attributes are relative to the current element selected by xsl:for-each. Also, notice that the only difference between the source and the output is handled in lines 17–19, where you assign to the name attribute of the class element what was originally in the element's body. The class attribute commissioned is simply ignored, so that it doesn't appear in the output.

The xsl:copy-of element copies the whole element to the output, including attributes and children elements. If you only want to copy the element tag, you can use xsl:copy.

XSL includes more than 30 elements, but the dozen or so that I have just described cover the vast majority of what you are likely to need. You will find the official documentation about XSLT at http://www.w3.org/TR/xslt.

XSLT: Transformation from XML to HTML

As you have seen, you can use XPath in a JSP page to navigate through an XML document and display it in HTML format. In this section, I'm going to show you how you can use XSLT to transform the same starfleet.xml directly into HTML. The two strategies are subtly different: with JSP, you pick up the nodes one by one and display them in HTML; with XSLT, you specify how the nodes of the XML files are to be mapped into HTML elements.

Let's cut to the chase and go directly to the XSLT file, shown in Listing 5-12.

Listing 5-12. starfleet.xsl

```
<?xml version="1.0" encoding="UTF-8"?>
<xsl:stylesheet version="1.0" xmlns:xsl="http://www.w3.org/1999/XSL/Transform">
<xsl:output method="html" version="4.0" encoding="UTF-8" indent="yes"/>
<xsl:template match="/">
<html><head>
  <title>Styling starfleet.xml</title>
  <style>th {text-align:left}</style>
  </head>
<body>
<h2>The Most Famous Starships in the Fleet</h2>
<table border="1">
  <tr><th>Name</th><th>S/N</th><th>Class</th><th>Commissioned</th><th>Captain</th></tr>
  <xsl:for-each select="starfleet/starship">
    <xsl:sort select="class/@commissioned"/>
    <tr>
      <td><xsl:value-of select="@name"/></td>
      <td><xsl:value-of select="@sn"/></td>
      <td><xsl:value-of select="class"/></td>
```

```
      <td><xsl:value-of select="class/@commissioned"/></td>
      <td><xsl:value-of select="captain"/></td>
      </tr>
    </xsl:for-each>
  </table>
</body>
</html>
</xsl:template>
</xsl:stylesheet>
```

After the first example (Listing 5-11), it should be clear how this works. There is just one point I would like to clarify: if you wanted to, you could omit the third line because, although the default output format is XML, XSL automatically recognizes that you're generating HTML if the first tag it encounters is <html>. Nevertheless, I recommend that you define the output format explicitly so that you can set HTML version, encoding, and indentation.

XSL Transformation: Browser Side vs. Server Side

I still haven't told you how to apply an XSL style sheet to an XML file to perform the transformation. This is because I first have to clarify the distinction between browser-side vs. server-side transformation.

Browser-Side XSL Transformation

All browsers can process XML and XSL. For example, let's say you copy enterprises_schema.xml from the xml-validate\xml\ subfolder of the software package for this chapter to the webapps\ROOT\tests\ folder of the Tomcat directory. By typing http://localhost:8080/tests/enterprises_schema.xml in most browsers, you see the file with little markers on the left of each element, as shown in Figure 5-4, where I used Chrome. By clicking on the markers, you can collapse or expand the elements as if they were folders. Firefox and IE use -/+ as markers. Opera is the only widely used browser that doesn't support this feature.

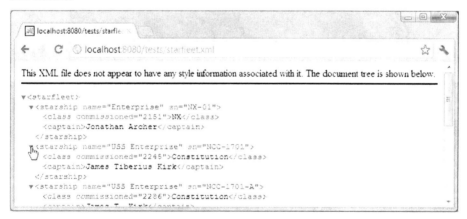

Figure 5-4. Browsing an XML file without XSL

The browsers can provide this feature because they "know" how to display XML. The message at the top of the page indicates that the browser displays the file as a node tree in a generic way because `enterprises_schema.xml` doesn't refer to any XSL style sheet. (Just so you know, Firefox displays the same message, IE doesn't display any message, and Opera simply states "`This document had no style information`".) But all browsers color code the different components.

Making the association is simple: copy `starfleet.xsl` from the sub-folder `xml-style\xsl\` of the software package for this chapter to the usual `tests` folder and insert the following processing instruction immediately below the first line of `enterprises_schema.xml` (i.e., the line with `<?xml...?>`):

```
<?xml-stylesheet type="text/xsl" href="starfleet.xsl"?>
```

Now, if you ask the browser to display `http://localhost:8080/test/enterprises_schema.xml`, it will know what style sheet to use. The `href` attribute expects a URL. Therefore, in general, you can also set it to URLs such as "`http://localhost:8080/tests/starfleet.xsl`" or "`/tests/starfleet.xsl`". I chose to write the relative URL, because I am keeping both files in the same `test` folder and it makes our lives easier. In any case, Figure 5-5 shows the result.

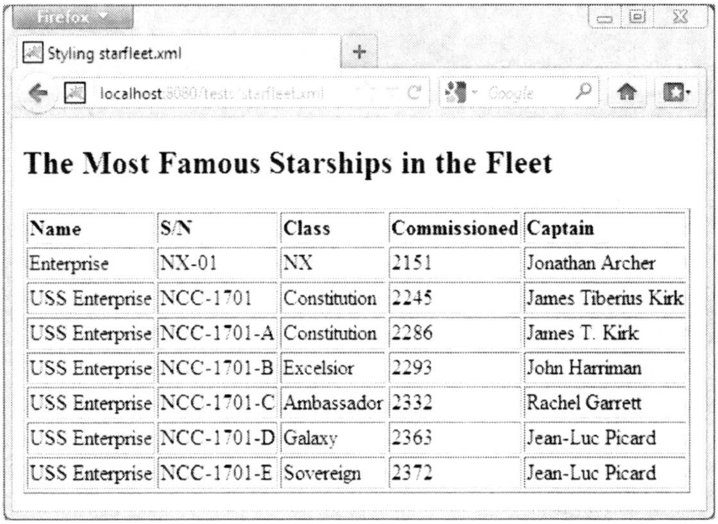

Figure 5-5. *Browsing an XML file with XSL*

Actually, there is one small advantage in keeping XML and XSL files in the same folder: you can view the XML file in a browser by just drag-and-dropping it onto the browser window. This doesn't work if you use an absolute URL in the `href`.

But I need to expand on this concerning Google Chrome. For the drag-and-drop trick to work, the browser must allow a file to access another file. Chrome, for security reasons, doesn't. You can force it to do this operation by starting it with the switch `--allow-file-access-from-files`. To do so, right-click Chrome's icon in the quick-start bar or on the desktop, display its properties, and append the switch to the application's path you see in the target field. It's easy, but I advise you not to weaken the security of the browser.

With any browser, if you view the page source, you'll see the XML file, because it is the browser that does the transformation from XML to HTML. Therefore, the source file is in fact the XML document.

One thing to keep in mind is that the user can also easily obtain your XSL file, because its URL is shown in the XML source. For example, if you copy `starfleet.xml` from the `xml-style\xsl\` sub-folder of the software package for this chapter to the tests folder and view it in a browser with the URL http://localhost:8080/tests/starfleet.xml, you can display its source and discover the relative URL of the style sheet. Then, you only need to type http://localhost:8080/tests/starfleet.xsl to see the XSL file.

Server-Side XSL Transformation

You can do the transformation on the server and make its output available, rather than making the XML and XSL files visible to the user. In that way, you can keep XML and XSL in private folders. Listing 5-13 shows you how to do the XSL server-side transformation with a JSP page.

Listing 5-13. enterprises_transform.jsp

```
01: <%@page language="java" contentType="text/html"%>
02: <%@page import="java.io.File"%>
03: <%@page import="java.io.FileOutputStream"%>
04: <%@page import="javax.xml.transform.TransformerFactory"%>
05: <%@page import="javax.xml.transform.Transformer"%>
06: <%@page import="javax.xml.transform.Source"%>
07: <%@page import="javax.xml.transform.SourceLocator"%>
08: <%@page import="javax.xml.transform.TransformerException"%>
09: <%@page import="javax.xml.transform.Result"%>
10: <%@page import="javax.xml.transform.stream.StreamSource"%>
11: <%@page import="javax.xml.transform.stream.StreamResult"%>
12: <%@page import="myPkg.TransformerExceptionHandler"%>
13: <%
14:    File inFile = new File("webapps/xml-style/xsl/starfleet.xml");
15:    File xslFile = new File("webapps/xml-style/xsl/enterprises.xsl");
16:    String outFilename = "webapps/xml-style/out/enterprises_out.xml";
17:    TransformerExceptionHandler handler = new TransformerExceptionHandler();
18:    try {
19:      TransformerFactory factory = TransformerFactory.newInstance();
20:      Transformer transformer = factory.newTransformer(new StreamSource(xslFile));
21:      transformer.setErrorListener(handler);
22:      Source source = new StreamSource(inFile);
23:      Result result = new StreamResult(new FileOutputStream(outFilename));
24:      transformer.transform(source, result);
25:    }
26:    catch (TransformerException e) {
27:    }
28:    if (handler.errorLevel == null) {
29:      out.println("Transformation completed.");
30:    }
31:    else {
32:      out.println(
33:         "*** Transformation " + handler.errorLevel + ": "
34:      + handler.transformationException
35:      );
36:    }
37:  %>
```

150

It looks more complicated than it actually is. Moreover, I have hard-coded the file names for simplicity, but you can add to the JSP page a simple input form to set `inFile` and `xslFile`, and you'll have a small utility you can use to transform all XML files. Following the MVC architecture, you should place the application logic in a servlet (i.e., the Controller), not in a JSP page. But I just wanted to show you in the simplest possible way how this is done in JSP/Java.

`enterprises_transform.jsp` performs the XML transformation on the server side as follows:

1. It instantiates a generic `TransformerFactory` and uses it to create a `Transformer` that implements the XSL (lines 19 and 20).

2. In line 21, it registers with the transformer the exception handler that was instantiated in line 17. This is similar to what you did to handle validation exceptions.

3. It opens an input stream to read the XML file and an output stream to write the document that will result from the transformation (lines 22 and 23).

4. It finally does the transformation (line 24).

The exception reporting is almost a carbon copy of the method I described when talking about validation (Listings 5-5 to 5-7), and the exception handler for transformations (Listing 5-14) is compiled and used exactly like the handler for validations shown in Listing 5-4.

Listing 5-14. TransformerExceptionHandler.java

```
package myPkg;
import javax.xml.transform.TransformerException;
public class TransformerExceptionHandler
    implements javax.xml.transform.ErrorListener {
  public TransformerException transformationException = null;
  public String errorLevel = null;
  public void warning(TransformerException e) {
    errorLevel = "Warning";
    transformationException = e;
    }
  public void error(TransformerException e) {
    errorLevel = "Error";
    transformationException = e;
    }
  public void fatalError(TransformerException e) {
    errorLevel = "Fatal error";
    transformationException = e;
    }
  }
```

The JSP page `enterprises_transform.jsp` applies the style sheet `enterprises.xsl` to `starfleet.xml` to produce `enterprises_out.xml`. If you change the file names in lines 15–16 to `starfleet.xsl`, and `starfleet_out.html`, the same page will generate a file that, when viewed in a browser, will appear identical to what you see in Figure 5-5.

My apologies if you find all these variations of XML files somewhat confusing. My purpose is to show you most of the possibilities you have for validating and converting XML files. In real life, you will pick the solution that suits your needs best and stick to it. In any case, I'm not done yet, because there is still one way of implementing server-side transformations that I want to show you.

x:transform and x:param

x:transform applies an XSL style sheet to an XML document. Table 5-6 summarizes its attributes.

Table 5-6. x:transform Attributes

Attribute	Description
doc	The well-formed source XML document to be transformed. It can be an object of type java.lang.String, java.io.Reader, javax.xml.transform.Source, org.w3c.dom.Document, or an object resulting from x:parse or x:set.
xslt	The transformation style sheet of type java.lang.String, java.io.Reader, or javax.xml.transform.Source.
var	Name of the EL variable to store the transformed XML document as an object of type org.w3c.dom.Document
scope	Scope for var
docSystemId	System identifier for parsing the XML source. It is a URI that identifies the origin of the XML data, potentially useful to some parsers
xsltSystemId	Like docSystemId but for the XSL style sheet.

Listing 5-15 shows the JSP page starfleet_tag_transform.jsp, which performs on the server the same transformation done by the browser when displaying what is shown in Figure 5-5.

Listing 5-15. starfleet_tag_transform.jsp

```
<%@page language="java" contentType="text/html"%>
<%@taglib prefix="c" uri="http://java.sun.com/jsp/jstl/core"%>
<%@taglib prefix="x" uri="http://java.sun.com/jsp/jstl/xml"%>
<c:import url="/xsl/starfleet.xml" var="xml"/>
<c:import url="/xsl/starfleet.xsl" var="xsl"/>
<x:transform doc="${xml}" xslt="${xsl}"/>
```

Type http://localhost:8080/xml-style/starfleet_tag_transform.jsp in your browser. You will see the familiar table shown in Figure 5-5.

At this point you might ask: why on earth did we go through the complex implementation of enterprise_transform.jsp and TransformerExceptionHandler.java (Listings 5-13 and 5-14) when we can achieve an equivalent result with six lines of code?

There are two reasons: the first one is that you might in the future encounter a situation in which you need to do it the "hard way"; the second reason is that I like to "peek under the hood" every now and then, and I thought you might like to do the same.

JSP in XML Syntax

JSP pages with scripting elements aren't XML files. This implies that you cannot use XML tools when developing JSP pages. However, it is possible to write JSP in a way to make it correct XML. The trick is to use standard JSP actions, JSTL with EL, and possibly non-JSTL custom actions. Actually, there are some "special standard" (pun intended!) JSP actions defined to support the XML syntax (jsp:root, jsp:output, and jsp:directive). In any case, such XML modules are called *JSP documents*, as opposed to the *JSP pages* written in the traditional non-XML-compliant way.

As a first example, let's convert the hello.jsp page shown in Listing 1-4 to a hello.jspx document. Listing 5-16 shows a partial hello.jspx that only writes "Hello World!". We'll convert the scriptlet that displays the dynamic information later.

Listing 5-16. *Partial hello.jspx*

```
01: <?xml version="1.0" encoding="UTF-8"?>
02: <jsp:root
03:   xmlns:jsp="http://java.sun.com/JSP/Page"
04:   xmlns:c="http://java.sun.com/jsp/jstl/core"
05:   xmlns:fn="http://java.sun.com/jsp/jstl/functions"
06:   version="2.1"
07:   >
08: <jsp:directive.page
09:   language="java"
10:   contentType="application/xhtml+xml;charset=UTF-8"
11:   />
12: <html>
13: <head><title>Hello World in XHTML</title></head>
14: <body>
15:   <jsp:text>Hello World!</jsp:text>
15: </body>
16: </html>
17: </jsp:root>
```

Line 1 states that the file is XML-compliant. The root element in lines 2–7 has several purposes. For example, it lets you use the jsp extension instead of the recommended jspx. It's also a convenient place where you can group namespace declarations (xmlns). The namespace declaration for the JSTL core tag library is the XML equivalent of the taglib directive in JSP pages. You don't need to specify the JSP namespace in JSP pages, but you cannot omit it in a JSP document; otherwise, the jsp: tags won't be recognized.

Lines 8–11 are the XML equivalent of the page directive of JSP pages. Also the include directive has its XML-equivalent with the element <jsp:directive.include file="*relativeURL*"/>.

Notice that the string "Hello World!" in Line 15 is enclosed within the jsp:text element. This is necessary, because in XML you cannot have "untagged" text.

To be consistent and make possible the full validation of the generated HTML, you should also include the proper DOCTYPE. The best way to do this is to use the attributes of the jsp:output action, which was specifically designed for this purpose. You only need to replace the <html> tag in line 12 with the following three elements:

```
<jsp:output omit-xml-declaration="false"/>
<jsp:output
  doctype-root-element="html"
```

```
doctype-public="-//W3C//DTD XHTML 1.0 Strict//EN"
doctype-system="http://www.w3.org/TR/xhtml1/DTD/xhtml1-strict.dtd"
/>
<html xmlns="http://www.w3.org/1999/xhtml">
```

Yes, it's quite a bit of work just to write "Hello World!", but this overhead is going to stay the same for JSP documents of any size. The first line causes the `<?xml ... ?>` elements to be written at the beginning of the generated HTML page, while the second element generates the `DOCTYPE`.

If you look at the HTML page generated by this preliminary version of `hello.jspx`, you'll see that all the HTML code is in a single line. If you want to have newlines between HTML tags in the output, you have to write them. You can actually do this with the `jsp:text` action. For example, all the `jsp:text` elements in the following code fragment contain a newline (which you can see) followed by two spaces (which you cannot see in the listing but are there):

```
<html xmlns="http://www.w3.org/1999/xhtml"><jsp:text>
  </jsp:text><head><title>Hello World in XHTML</title></head><jsp:text>
  </jsp:text><body>Hello World!</body><jsp:text>
  </jsp:text></html>
```

As the `jsp:text` content is sent to the output as it is, the HTML generated will be written over several lines and indented:

```
<html xmlns="http://www.w3.org/1999/xhtml">
  <head><title>Hello World in XHTML</title></head>
  <body>Hello World!</body>
  </html>
```

The other possibility is to use a CDATA section to enclose the whole HTML:

```
<![CDATA[<html xmlns="http://www.w3.org/1999/xhtml">
  <head><title>Hello World in XHTML</title></head>
  <body>Hello World!</body>
  </html>]]>
```

This way, the whole block will be sent to the client as it is, uninterpreted. However, it seems an admission of defeat to send off code that could have been validated for XML compliance at the source. Don't you think?

IE AND XHTML

Microsoft only managed to include in their Internet Explorer full support of XHTML with IE9. Unfortunately, IE9 requires at least Windows Vista. If you are running XP, you are not in luck.

But also if you are running Vista, in order to install IE9, you first need to install Service Pack 2, which is *not* an automatic update. Further, while all other browsers have no problems in recognizing XHTML in a page with content type "text/html", IE requires that you specify the mime type of the page to be "application/xhtml+xml".

For your information, in April 2012, http://en.wikipedia.org/wiki/Web_browsers reported that IE [still] counted for approximately 26 percent of worldwide browser usage. At about the same time, http://www.statowl.com claimed that about 36 percent of the IEs installed were version 9. This means that almost 17% of people were then not able to view XHTML pages. By the time you are reading this, that percentage will have significantly decreased, not only because more people will have upgraded to the last version of IE but also because many will have switched to using chrome, android, or other browsers.

Now you're finally ready to tackle the conversion of the scriptlet in hello.jsp to XML syntax. Listing 5-17 shows the complete hello.jspx.

Listing 5-17. hello.jspx

```
<?xml version="1.0" encoding="UTF-8"?>
<jsp:root
  xmlns:jsp="http://java.sun.com/JSP/Page"
  xmlns:c="http://java.sun.com/jsp/jstl/core"
  xmlns:fn="http://java.sun.com/jsp/jstl/functions"
  version="2.1"
  >
<jsp:directive.page
  language="java"
  contentType="application/xhtml+xml;charset=UTF-8"
  />
<jsp:output omit-xml-declaration="false"/>
<jsp:output
  doctype-root-element="html"
  doctype-public="-//W3C//DTD XHTML 1.0 Strict//EN"
  doctype-system="http://www.w3.org/TR/xhtml1/DTD/xhtml1-strict.dtd"
  />
<html xmlns="http://www.w3.org/1999/xhtml">
<head><title>Hello World in XHTML</title></head>
<body>
  <jsp:text>Hello World!</jsp:text>
  <br/>
  <jsp:text>Your IP address is ${pageContext.request.remoteAddr}</jsp:text>
  <br/>
  <jsp:text>and your browser is </jsp:text>
  <c:set var="usAg" value="${header['user-agent']}"/>
  <c:choose>
    <c:when test="${fn:contains(usAg, 'MSIE')}">
      <jsp:text>MS InternetExplorer</jsp:text>
      </c:when>
    <c:when test="${fn:contains(usAg, 'Firefox')}">
      <jsp:text>Mozilla Firefox</jsp:text>
      </c:when>
    <c:when test="${fn:contains(usAg, 'Opera')}">
      <jsp:text>Opera</jsp:text>
      </c:when>
    <c:when test="${fn:contains(usAg, 'Chrome')}">
      <jsp:text>Google Chrome</jsp:text>
      </c:when>
    <c:when test="${fn:contains(usAg, 'Safari')}">
      <jsp:text>Apple Safari</jsp:text>
```

```
      </c:when>
    <c:otherwise><jsp:text>unknown</jsp:text></c:otherwise>
      </c:choose>
</body>
</html>
</jsp:root>
```

Note In JSP documents, you cannot use expressions such as ${whatever > 0}, because the greater-than signs are illegal within XML. Instead, use the gt form, such as ${whatever gt 0}.

As a second example, of converting a JSP page to a JSP document, you can compare starfleet.jspx (Listing 5-18) with the original starfleet.jsp (Listing 5-10).

Listing 5-18. starfleet.jspx

```
<?xml version="1.0" encoding="UTF-8"?>
<jsp:root
  xmlns:jsp="http://java.sun.com/JSP/Page"
  xmlns:c="http://java.sun.com/jsp/jstl/core"
  xmlns:x="http://java.sun.com/jsp/jstl/xml"
  version="2.1"
  >
<jsp:directive.page
  language="java"
  contentType="application/xhtml+xml;charset=UTF-8"
  />
<jsp:output omit-xml-declaration="false"/>
<jsp:output
  doctype-root-element="html"
  doctype-public="-//W3C//DTD XHTML 1.0 Strict//EN"
  doctype-system="http://www.w3.org/TR/xhtml1/DTD/xhtml1-strict.dtd"
  />
<c:import url="starfleet.xml" var="sf"/>
<x:parse doc="${sf}" varDom="dom"/>
<html xmlns="http://www.w3.org/1999/xhtml">
<head>
  <title>Parsing starfleet.xml</title>
  <style>th {text-align:left}</style>
  </head>
<body>
<table border="1">
  <tr><th>Name</th><th>S/N</th><th>Class</th><th>Year</th><th>Captain</th></tr>
  <x:forEach var="tag" select="$dom//starship">
    <tr>
      <td><x:out select="$tag/@name"/></td>
      <td><x:out select="$tag/@sn"/></td>
      <td><x:out select="$tag/class"/></td>
```

```
        <td><x:out select="$tag/class/@commissioned"/></td>
        <td><x:out select="$tag/captain"/></td>
      </tr>
    </x:forEach>
  </table>
</body>
</html>
</jsp:root>
```

The first 17 lines are identical to the corresponding lines of hello.jspx, while the rest of the document is identical to the corresponding lines of starfleet.jsp, with the only addition of the closing tag for jsp:root. This is because starfleet.jsp didn't include any scripting element or untagged text.

Summary

In this chapter, you learned about the structure and the syntax of XML documents, DTDs, and XML schemas.

You then saw several ways of how to validate XML documents against DTDs and schemas.

Next, I introduced you to XSL and explained examples of XPath use and of transformation from XML to XML and from XML to HTML.

To conclude, I showed how you can convert JSP pages with directives and scripting elements into JSP documents that are fully XML-compliant.

In the next chapter, we'll talk about databases.

CHAPTER 6

Databases

In many cases, a web application is nothing more than a front end for a database (DB). In fact, what makes web pages dynamic is precisely the fact that there is a significant amount of data behind them.

A database consists of organized data—that is, the data itself and a *schema* that provides data structures. Nowadays, most databases are organized in *tables*. You can define the table characteristics independently of the actual data you're going to store into it. This is another instance of the separation of formatting and content, which you've already encountered in Chapter 3, when we discussed web applications.

A database management system (DBMS), such as MySQL or PostgreSQL, is a software package that lets you create, retrieve, update, and delete (CRUD) both items of data and elements of the schema.

Therefore, when talking about a database, you need to distinguish between three aspects:

- The data it contains.

- The structure you impose on the data in order to CRUD it efficiently.

- The software that allows you to manipulate both the data itself and the database structure (the DBMS).

Working with a database means that you're interacting with its DBMS. You can do that through a command line interface (CLI), through graphical user interfaces (GUIs) provided by the DBMS vendor and third parties, or programmatically through an API. In general, you use all three methods, each for a different purpose. The CLI is best suited for setting up the initial data structure and for testing, the API is for your web application to interact with the database to perform its tasks, and the GUI is what you use to check individual data items or fix one-off problems.

In this chapter's examples, I'll use MySQL as the DBMS of choice, because, first, it's available for free, and second, it's the most widely used of the freely available DBMSs. As such, it has been proven to work reliably in all sorts of environments. At the end of this chapter, I'll briefly talk about possible alternatives to MySQL.

MySQL

In this section, I will explain how to install MySQL. You actually need three packages: the MySQL database server, a connector to access MySQL databases from Java (a JDBC), and the MySQL Workbench, an application that lets you easily inspect and modify databases via a comfortable GUI.

To install MySQL, do the following:

1. Go to http://dev.mysql.com/downloads/ and click on the big green button labeled "Download".

2. Ensure that the selected platform is "Microsoft Windows" and click on the "Download" button.

3. Before you can download the package, you will have to login as a user, or register to be one. Then, after selecting a mirror site, you will be able to download the MSI installer mysql-installer-5.5.21.0.msi (or a more recent version of it). This package contains all three components of MySQL. Be aware that Workbench requires ".NET 4.0" and the "Visual C++ 2010 Redistributable Package". The MySQL installer will guide you to download and install them if needed. Alternatively, you can go to http://dev.mysql.com/resources/wb52_prerequisites.html to make sure you have everything in place beforehand.

4. When you execute the MySQL installer, choose the "Full" installation.

5. By default, MySQL keeps all databases in "C:\Program Data\MySQL\MySQL Server 5.5". I chose to change the datapath to "C:\Program Data\MySQL\data\", because it was more convenient for access and for backup.

6. Choose "Standard Configuration", and tick both option boxes before clicking on "Next >". The first option is to run MySQL as a service from startup. The second one lets you use MySQL from the command line.

7. Keep the default configuration: developer machine, enabled TCP/IP, and create Windows service MySQL55.

8. The version of the installer I had forced me to choose a password to access the databases.

If you go to the Services control panel as explained for Tomcat, you should see the service MySQL55 running.

For the examples of this book, as all databases are accessed locally and don't contain valuable data, I decided I didn't need a password.

To remove the password I had been forced to choose during installation, I opened a command window, attached to the directory "C:\Program Files\MySQL\MySQL Server 5.5\bin\" and typed the command "mysqladmin -u root -p password". The program asked me to enter the password, which I did, and then asked me twice to enter the new password, to which I replied both times by pressing Enter.

These MySQL packages that contain all components do not necessarily include the latest versions of the connectors and of the Workbench. I didn't particularly care about having the latest Workbench, because I intended to use it only to check simple database generated from JSP. But I was keen to have the latest Java connector. Therefore, I went to http://dev.mysql.com/downloads/connector/j/ and downloaded mysql-connector-java-5.1.18.zip.

To install a JDBC, you only need to copy its JAR file into %CATALINA_HOME%\lib\. The MySQL installer puts it into C:\Program Files\MySQL\MySQL Connector J\.

For easy access, you should create a shortcut pointing to the Workbench application and place it in the quickstart bar or on the desktop. The application path will look like this:

C:\Program Files\MySQL\MySQL Workbench CE 5.2.37\MySQLWorkbench.exe.

MySQL Test

Listing 6-1 shows an SQL script to create a simple database, which we will use in the E-shop application you first encountered in Chapter 3. For your reference, I have written a summary of the SQL language in Appendix B.

Listing 6-1. shop_create.sql

```
01    drop database shop;
02    create database shop;
03    create table shop.categories (
04      category_id integer not null auto_increment unique,
05      category_name varchar(70),
07      primary key (category_id)
08      );
09    create table shop.books (
10      book_id integer not null auto_increment unique,
11      title varchar(70),
12      author varchar(70),
13      price double precision,
14      category_id integer,
15      primary key (book_id)
16      );
17    create index category_id_key on shop.categories (category_id);
18    create index book_id_key on shop.books (book_id);
19    alter table shop.books add index category_id (category_id),
20      add constraint category_id foreign key (category_id)
21      references shop.categories (category_id)
22      ;
```

Line 01 removes the database. It reports an error when you use it the first time, because there is no database to delete, but it also lets you re-run the script to re-create the database from scratch. It isn't something you would normally do in a non-test environment.

Line 02 creates a blank database named shop.

Lines 03 to 08 create a table to store book categories.

Lines 09 to 16 create a table to store book records.

Line 17 creates an index to speed up the search of categories.

Line 18 creates an index to speed up the search of books when selected by their IDs.

Lines 19 to 22 create an index to speed up the search of books when selected by their categories.

To execute the SQL script, you can use either the Command Line Client or the Workbench. You will find the script in the software package for this chapter.

To use the Command Line Client, click on "Start" and select "Programs ➤ MySQL ➤ MySQL Server 5.5 ➤ MySQL 5.5 Command Line Client". This opens a command-line window where you will first have to type the password to access the server. If you have removed the password as I suggested, you only need to hit Enter. The Client will respond by displaying the "mysql> " prompt. Open shop_create.sql with a text editor, copy everything into the clipboard, and paste it onto the Command Line Client. Listing 6-2 shows what you will get.

Listing 6-2. Log of shop_create.sql

```
Enter password:
Welcome to the MySQL monitor.  Commands end with ; or \g.
Your MySQL connection id is 1
Server version: 5.5.21 MySQL Community Server (GPL)

Copyright (c) 2000, 2011, Oracle and/or its affiliates. All rights reserved.

Oracle is a registered trademark of Oracle Corporation and/or its
affiliates. Other names may be trademarks of their respective
owners.

Type 'help;' or '\h' for help. Type '\c' to clear the current input statement.

mysql> drop database shop;
ERROR 1008 (HY000): Can't drop database 'shop'; database doesn't exist
mysql> create database shop;
Query OK, 1 row affected (0.00 sec)

mysql> create table shop.categories (
    ->    category_id integer not null auto_increment unique,
    ->    category_name varchar(70),
    ->    primary key (category_id)
    ->    );
Query OK, 0 rows affected (0.13 sec)

mysql> create table shop.books (
    ->    book_id integer not null auto_increment unique,
    ->    title varchar(70),
    ->    author varchar(70),
    ->    price double precision,
    ->    category_id integer,
    ->    primary key (book_id)
    ->    );
Query OK, 0 rows affected (0.19 sec)

mysql> create index category_id_key on shop.categories (category_id);
Query OK, 0 rows affected (0.37 sec)
Records: 0  Duplicates: 0  Warnings: 0

mysql> create index book_id_key on shop.books (book_id);
Query OK, 0 rows affected (0.36 sec)
Records: 0  Duplicates: 0  Warnings: 0

mysql> alter table shop.books add index category_id (category_id),
    ->    add constraint category_id foreign key (category_id)
    ->    references shop.categories (category_id)
    ->    ;
Query OK, 0 rows affected (0.33 sec)
Records: 0  Duplicates: 0  Warnings: 0
```

If you repeat the operation, you'll see that something like "Query OK, 2 rows affected (0.56 sec)" will replace the "ERROR 1008" message.

You can achieve the same result with the Workbench. After launching it, double-click on the link "Local MySQL55" that appears under the heading "Open Connection to Start Querying". This will open a window as shown in Figure 6-1.

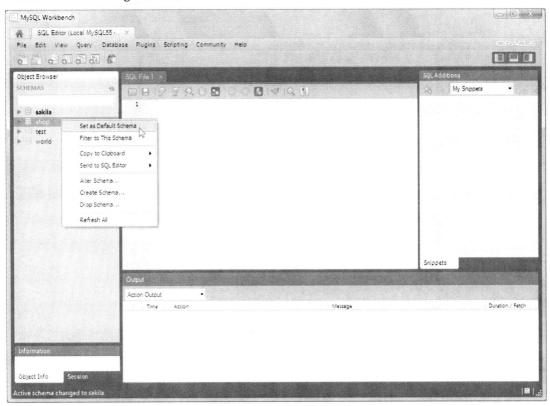

Figure 6-1. MySQL Workbench

If you have already created the shop database from the command line, you will see the corresponding entry in the Object Browser. If you right-click it, you will be able to choose the default database, although it is not necessary for you to do so.

In any case, to load the SQL script, click on the folder icon in the menu bar of the central pane. You can then open shop_create.sql or paste its content into the central pane. To execute it, click on the lightning icon. Figure 6-2 shows what happens when you do so.

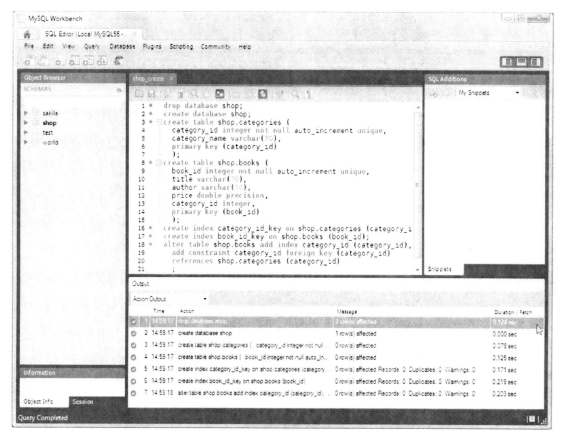

Figure 6-2. Creating the shop database with the Workbench

Now that the database is in place, insert book categories and book records by executing the SQL script shown in Listing 6-3.

Listing 6-3. shop_populate.sql

```
USE shop;
INSERT INTO categories (
    category_id
  , category_name
  )
  VALUES
    (1,'Web Development')
  , (2,'SF')
  , (3,'Action Novels')
  ;
INSERT INTO books (
    book_id
```

```
, title
, author
, price
, category_id
)
VALUES
  (1,'Pro CSS and HTML Design Patterns','Michael Bowers',44.99,1)
, (2,'Pro PayPal E-Commerce','Damon Williams',59.99,1)
, (3,'The Complete Robot','Isaac Asimov',8.95,2)
, (4,'Foundation','Isaac ASimov',8.95,2)
, (5,'Area 7','Matthew Reilly',5.99,3)
, (6,'Term Limits','Vince Flynn',6.99,3)
;
```

Note that you only need the "USE shop;" command if you execute the script from the command line.
After populating the database, you can look at the book records by typing a SELECT command in the central pane of Workbench (or at the "mysql> " prompt of the Command Line Client). For example, "select * from books;" will list all the books you have inserted, as shown in Figure 6-3.

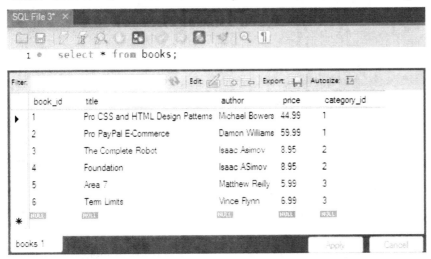

Figure 6-3. List of all books

MySQL/Tomcat Test

To be sure that everything works, you still need to check that you can access the database from Tomcat using JSP. That is, that Tomcat is able to use the JDBC connector. To do so, you can use the JSP page shown in Listing 6-4, which lists all books in the database.

Listing 6-4. jdbc.jsp

```
01    <%@page language="java" contentType="text/html"%>
02    <%@page import="java.sql.*"%>
03    <html><head><title>JDBC test</title></head><body>
04    <%
05       Class.forName("com.mysql.jdbc.Driver");
06       Connection conn = DriverManager.getConnection(
07          "jdbc:mysql://localhost:3306/shop", "root", "");
08       Statement stmt = conn.createStatement();
09       ResultSet rs = stmt.executeQuery("select * from books");
10    %><table border= "1"><%
11       ResultSetMetaData resMetaData = rs.getMetaData();
12       int nCols = resMetaData.getColumnCount();
13    %><tr><%
14       for (int kCol = 1; kCol <= nCols; kCol++) {
15          out.print("<td><b>" + resMetaData.getColumnName(kCol) + "</b></td>");
16       }
17    %></tr><%
18       while (rs.next()) {
19          %><tr><%
20          for (int kCol = 1; kCol <= nCols; kCol++) {
21             out.print("<td>" + rs.getString(kCol) + "</td>");
22          }
23          %></tr><%
24       }
25    %></table><%
26       conn.close();
27    %>
28    </body></html>
```

Here is how jdbc.jsp obtains the list of books from the database and then displays them:

  05:    Load JDBC to connect to the database server.
  06–07: Connect to the database.
  08:    Create an empty statement to query the database.
  09:    Execute the query to list all books and store the result set into a local variable.
  11:    Obtain information on the structure of the result set.
  12:    Obtain the number of columns of the result set.
  13–17: Display the column names.
  18–23: List the books one per row.
  26:    Close the connection to the database server.

Don't worry if things are not completely clear. Later in this chapter, I will explain in detail how you access a database from Java. For the time being, I just want to give you an example of how you can test database connectivity with a simple JSP page.

To execute the page, place it into the usual test folder. Figure 6-4 shows how the generated page appears in a web browser.

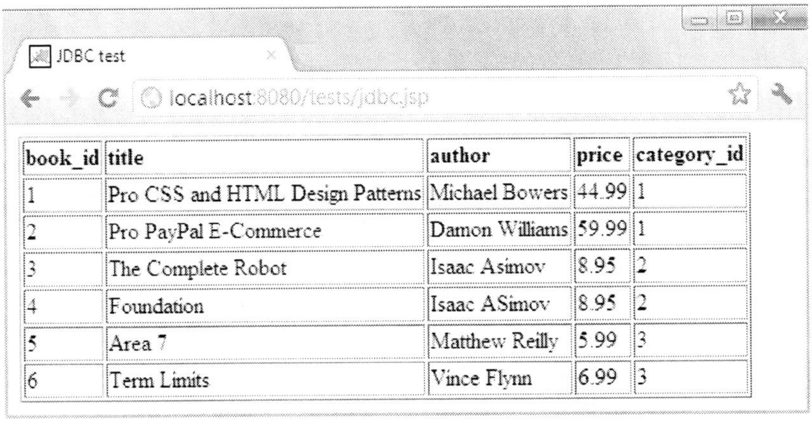

book_id	title	author	price	category_id
1	Pro CSS and HTML Design Patterns	Michael Bowers	44.99	1
2	Pro PayPal E-Commerce	Damon Williams	59.99	1
3	The Complete Robot	Isaac Asimov	8.95	2
4	Foundation	Isaac ASimov	8.95	2
5	Area 7	Matthew Reilly	5.99	3
6	Term Limits	Vince Flynn	6.99	3

***Figure 6-4.** jdbc.jsp output*

In a more realistic situation, you would replace the category identifiers with the category names, but I want to keep this first example as simple as possible.

There is one thing, though, that deserves a comment: it is bad practice to hard code in a page the name of the database, of the user ID, and of the access password. Sooner or later, you might need to change one of those parameters, and the last thing you want to do is to go through all your pages to do it. The initialization parameters exist precisely to avoid such error-prone procedure.

First, you need to include the parameter definitions in the `web.xml` file that's inside the `WEB-INF` folder of your application's root directory. You need to insert the lines shown in Listing 6-5 within the body of the `web-app` element.

***Listing 6-5.** web.xml Fragment to Define Initialization Parameters*

```
<context-param>
  <param-name>dbName</param-name>
  <param-value>my-database-name</param-value>
  </context-param>
<context-param>
  <param-name>dbUser</param-name>
  <param-value>my-userID</param-value>
  </context-param>
<context-param>
  <param-name>dbPass</param-name>
  <param-value>my-password</param-value>
  </context-param>
```

In the example, `my-database-name` would be `jdbc:mysql://localhost:3306/shop`, `my-userID` would be `root`, and `my-password` would be the empty string (i.e., nothing).

To access the parameters from within any JSP page, you then just need to type something like the following:

```
String dbName = application.getInitParameter("dbName");
String dbUser = application.getInitParameter("dbUser");
String dbPass = application.getInitParameter("dbPass");
```

After that, you can replace lines 6 and 7 of the example with:

```
Connection conn = DriverManager.getConnection(dbName, dbUser, dbPass);
```

Database Basics

In some cases, a DB might contain a small amount of data, have a simple structure, and reside together with the application software on a home PC. In other cases, at the higher end of the scale, it might hold millions of records, have a data structure of great complexity, and run on a cluster of powerful servers (e.g., with MySQL Cluster).

In any case, regardless of size, environment, and complexity, the DBMS is organized around the client/server architecture. The system on which your DB resides is the *server*, and the system from which you need to access your DB is the *client*, even when they're one and the same PC. Therefore, in order to be able to work with data and a data structure, you first have to establish a connection from the client to the database on the server. To be able to do so, you need the following three pieces of information:

- The URL of your server

- A user ID that allows you to access the DB

- The password that goes together with the User ID

Once you establish the connection, you can then begin to manipulate the DB structure and its content via SQL statements. Be aware that although you need to provide a User ID and password when you connect to the server, this doesn't automatically mean that a user has access to all databases on the same server. You can (and, in most cases, should) allow access to specific databases to some users and not others. In fact, you can define one or more new users for each new database you create and group them according to the capabilities they are required to have (i.e., database administrators, developers, etc.). This ensures total confidentiality of data when several users share a database server. It's good practice to define different users for different applications so that you don't risk "cross-polluting" data.

In 1986, the American National Standards Institute (ANSI) adopted SQL as a standard, and ISO followed suit one year later. The current standard is ISO/IEC 9075, but, unfortunately, it's not freely available. If you want to have it, you have to buy it from ANSI or ISO. The SQL standard has been widely adopted, and, as a result, most of what I'm going to say concerning SQL actually applies to all DBMSs. As you can imagine, there are still proprietary additions and variations that, in some cases, make SQL less portable than what it could and should be, but it won't affect us.

The SQL standard specifies at least 27 basic statements with numerous variants. They are alter, based on, begin, close, commit, connect, create, declare, delete, describe, disconnect, drop, end, event, execute, fetch, grant, insert, open, prepare, revoke, rollback, select, set, show, update, and whenever (see Appendix B for the details). In total, at the last count, 231 words were reserved by SQL as keywords. Therefore, it should be clear that in this chapter, I couldn't possibly give you more than a small introduction to SQL. Appendix B provides a more detailed SQL reference to help you along. Also, if you search Apress for "SQL", you will get a list of more than a hundred books. "Beginning SQL Queries" (www.apress.com/9781590599433) might be a good starting point.

The basic structural elements of a DB are rows, columns, tables, and indices. In non-SQL terms, rows are data records, columns identify the record fields, tables are named collections of records, and indices are ordered lists of records.

To design a database for a web application, you basically associate a table to each Java class that represents the data you need to store permanently. Each attribute of your class then becomes a column of your table. In a sense, to express it in OO terminology, each row corresponds to an instantiation of your class containing different data. For example, in the E-shop application, book categories are modeled to reflect the Java class shown in Listing 6-6.

Listing 6-6. Category.java

```
package eshop.beans;

public class Category {
  private int id;
  private String name;

  public Category(int id, String name) {
    this.id = id;
    this.name = name;
    }

  public int getId() { return id; }
  public void setId(int id) { this.id = id; }

  public String getName() { return name; }
  public void setName(String name) { this.name = name; }
  }
```

Accordingly, to store categories in the shop database, you can use the following SQL statement to create a table named categories, extracted from shop_create.sql (see Listing 6.1):

```
create table shop.categories (
  category_id integer not null auto_increment unique,
  category_name varchar(70),
  primary key (category_id)
  );
```

Each SQL statement consists of a verb that defines the operation to be done (create table in this example), the identifier of the object operated on (shop.categories in this example), and one or more operation parameters, often enclosed in parentheses. When more than one object or parameter is needed, they're usually comma-separated. In the example, the first two parameters define the DB columns category_id and category_name. Notice how the attributes specified in the SQL statement match those defined in the Java class. When creating this table, I also told MySQL to create an index of category_id by declaring the column to contain unique values and designating it as the primary key of the table. The purpose is to speed up DB operations, although in this case, given the small size of the table, it obviously won't make any practical difference.

Use this code, which creates three new rows, to store new records in a DB, extracted from shop_populate.sql (see Listing 6.2):

```
insert into categories (category_id, category_name)
  values (1,'Web Development'), (2,'SF'), (3,'Action Novels');
```

Incidentally, be aware that SQL, contrary to Java, is not case-sensitive.

Use the powerful select SQL statement to read data. It lets you create complex queries that include sorting the data. Here's a simple example:

```
select category_id, category_name from categories where category_id = '2';
```

To retrieve all columns of a table, you replace the comma-separated list of columns with an asterisk. The where clause can consist of several conditions composed by means of logical operators.

You use the update statement to modify row contents:

```
update categories set category_name = 'SF' where category_id = '2';
```

Using delete you can remove rows:

```
delete from categories where category_id > '3';
```

You can also operate on the data structure. To do so, you use the alter statement, as in the following example:

```
alter table categories add new_column_name column-definition;
```

This lets you add a column to an existing table. If you replace add with modify or drop, the alter statement will let you redefine a column or remove it.

In general, the SQL statements are grouped depending on their purposes. Table 6-1 gives you a summary of their classification.

Table 6-1. Classification of SQL Statements

Group	Description
Data Definition Language (DDL)	Statements used to define the DB structure (e.g., create, alter, drop, and rename)
Data Manipulation Language (DML)	Statements used to manage data (e.g., select, insert, update, and delete)
Data Control Language (DCL)	Statements used to control access to the data (e.g., grant, used to give access rights to a user, and revoke, used to withdraw them)
Transaction ControL (TCL)	Statements used to group together DML statements into logical transactions (e.g., commit and rollback)

In this chapter, I'll explain how to execute any SQL statement, but we'll concentrate mainly on DML.

SQL Scripts

As I have already said, a CLI is useful to initialize a database. As a CLI, MySQL makes available the program "MySQL Command Line Client," which starts in a DOS window and attempts at once to establish a connection as the default User ID to the default server. If you've set up MySQL as I suggested at the beginning of this chapter, the default user will be root and the default host will be localhost. After providing the correct password, you get a mysql> prompt and can start executing SQL statements.

You can play around with the commands, but the best way to use the CLI is with SQL scripts. These are plain-text files containing the statements you want to execute. At the mysql prompt, you only need to type backslash-period-space (\.) followed by the script file name, and off you go. In fact, you must use scripts if you want to ensure that your steps are repeatable and correctable. Listing 6-7 shows the third (and last) SQL script needed to configure the database of the E-shop application.

Listing 6-7. shop_orders.sql

```
USE shop;
create table shop.order_details (

    id double precision not null auto_increment unique,
    book_id integer,
    title varchar(70),
    author varchar(70),

    quantity integer,
    price double precision,
    order_id double precision,
    primary key (id)
    );
create table shop.orders (
    order_id double precision not null auto_increment unique,
    delivery_name varchar(70),
    delivery_address varchar(70),
    cc_name varchar(70),
    cc_number varchar(32),
    cc_expiry varchar(20),
    primary key (order_id)
    );
create index order_details_id_key on shop.order_details (id);
alter table shop.order_details add index order_id (order_id),
    add constraint order_id foreign key (order_id)
    references shop.orders (order_id)
    ;
create index order_id_key on shop.orders (order_id);
```

Notice that the primary (i.e., unique) keys of both order_details and orders are automatically generated by MySQL as ever increasing numbers, while the primary keys of books and categories are hard-coded in shop_create.sql (see Listing 6.1). As the category and book IDs are not visible to the user, I could have let MySQL generate them as well. I didn't do it because the book and category records are created by hand anyway, and to add an ID didn't seem a big deal. Perhaps it is due to my tendency to minimize the use of automatic mechanisms when they are not necessary, in order to retain more control. The downside of this is of course that manual entries are in general more error prone and require more maintenance effort.

To write comments in an SQL script, you enclose them between /* and */, like Java's block comments.

Java API

You operate on databases by executing SQL statements. To do so from within Java/JSP, you need an API consisting of several interfaces, classes, and method definitions. The API is included in the class libraries java.sql and javax.sql of JDK version 7. Additionally, you also need a driver that implements that API for the specific DBMS (i.e., MySQL) in the native code of your system (i.e., an Intel/Windows PC). To work with MySQL, you use as driver the MySQL Connector/J version 5, which is a type 4 JDBC driver (see sidebar).

JDBC DRIVERS

The JDBC API lets you access databases from Java. There are four types of JDBC implementations (i.e., drivers).

JDBC drivers of type 1 are actually JDBC-ODBC bridges, because they access databases via an Open Database Connectivity (ODBC) driver. At the end of this chapter, we'll show you how to use the bridge included in the Java Virtual Machine (JVM).

JDBC drivers of type 2 use vendor-specific, native, client-side libraries. In other words, they interface to non-Java functions provided by the DBMS vendor, which in turn interfaces to the databases. These drivers are more efficient compared to those of type 1, but you can only use them locally.

JDBC drivers of type 3 are Java drivers that, instead of communicating directly with the databases, rely on a middleware package that sits on an application server.

JDBC drivers of type 4 are written entirely in Java and communicate directly with the DBMS server. This is the type you want!

Connecting to the Database

The first step to access a database from Java is to load the driver, without which nothing will work. To do so, you execute the method Class.forName("com.mysql.jdbc.Driver"). In the E-shop application, you do this in the init method of the servlet (see Listing 3-9).

To be able to switch from MySQL to other DBMSs without much effort, store the driver name in an init parameter defined in WEB-INF\web.xml as follows:

```
<init-param>
  <param-name>jdbcDriver</param-name>
  <param-value>com.mysql.jdbc.Driver</param-value>
  </init-param>
```

This way, you can load it as follows when initializing the servlet:

```
java.lang.Class.forName(config.getInitParameter("jdbcDriver"));
```

Once you load the driver, you also need to connect to the database before you can access its content. In the E-shop application, you do this by executing a data manager (of type DataManager, defined in WEB-INF\classes\eshop\model\DataManager.java) method, as shown in the following line of code:

```
java.sql.Connection connection = dataManager.getConnection();
```

The data manager's getConnection method, in turn, obtains the connection from the JDBC driver, as shown in the fragment in Listing 6-8.

Listing 6-8. The DataManager.getConnection Method

```
public Connection getConnection() {
  Connection conn = null;
  try {
    conn = DriverManager.getConnection(getDbURL(), getDbUserName(), getDbPassword());
    }
  catch (SQLException e) {
    System.out.println("Could not connect to DB: " + e.getMessage());
    }
  return conn;
  }
```

To be able to change the database, the user ID, or the password without having to rebuild the application, you define them in servlet initialization parameters as you did for the name of the JDBC driver and as I showed earlier in this chapter:

```
dbURL: jdbc:mysql://localhost:3306/shop
dbUserName: root
dbPassword: none
```

Port 3306 is the default for MySQL and can be configured differently. Obviously, in real life, you would use a different user and, most importantly, define a password.

Once you finish working with a database, you should always close the connection by executing `connection.close()`. E-shop does it via another data manager's method, as shown in Listing 6-9.

Listing 6-9. The DataManager.putConnection Method

```
public void putConnection(Connection conn) {
  if (conn != null) {
    try { conn.close(); }
    catch (SQLException e) { }
    }
  }
```

Before you can start hacking at your database, you still need to create an object of type `java.sql.Statement`, as it is through the methods of that object that you execute SQL statements. Use this code to create a statement:

```
Statement stmt = connection.createStatement();
```

Once you're done with one statement, you should release it immediately with `stmt.close()`, because it takes a non-negligible amount of space, and you want to be sure that it doesn't hang around while your page does other things.

Accessing Data

The `Statement` class has 40 methods, plus some more inherited ones. Nevertheless, two methods are likely to satisfy most of your needs: `executeQuery` and `executeUpdate`.

The executeQuery Method

You use this method to execute a select SQL statement, like this:

```
String sql = "select book_id, title, author from books where category_id=1"
    + " order by author, title";
ResultSet rs = stmt.executeQuery(sql);
```

In the example, the method returns in the variable rs of type java.sql.ResultSet all the books in category 1, sorted by author name and title. The rows in the result set only contain the columns specified in the select statement, which in this example are book_id, title, and author.

At any given time, you can only access the row of the result set pointed to by the so-called *cursor*, and by default you can only move the cursor forward. The usual way of accessing the rows of the result set is to start from the first one and "go down" in sequence. For example, with the shop database, the following code:

```
while (rs.next()) {
    out.println(rs.getString(3) + ", " + rs.getString(2) + "<br/>");
}
```

would produce the following output:

```
Damon Williams, Pro PayPal E-Commerce
Michael Bowers, Pro CSS and HTML Design Patterns
```

The next method moves the cursor down one row. After the cursor goes past the last row, next() returns false, and the while loop terminates. Initially, the cursor is positioned *before* the first row. Therefore, you have to execute next() once in order to access the very first row.

Besides next(), there are other methods that let you reposition your cursor. Five of them return a boolean such as next(), which returns true if the cursor points to a row. They are absolute(*row-position*), first(), last(), previous(), and relative(*number-of-rows*). The beforeFirst() and afterLast()methods also move the cursor but are of type void, because they always succeed. The isBeforeFirst(), isFirst(), isLast(), and isAfterLast() methods check whether the cursor is in the corresponding positions, while getRow() returns the position of the row currently pointed to by the cursor.

Keep in mind that in order to be able to move the cursor around, you have to specify a couple of attributes when you create the statement—that is, *before* you actually execute the query. This is how you do it:

```
Statement stmt = connection.createStatement(
    ResultSet.TYPE_SCROLL_INSENSITIVE,
    ResultSet.CONCUR_READ_ONLY
);
```

ResultSet.TYPE_SCROLL_INSENSITIVE is what allows you to move the cursor forth and back within the result set. This parameter can only have one of the following two other values: ResultSet.TYPE_FORWARD_ONLY (the default) and ResultSet.TYPE_SCROLL_SENSITIVE. The difference between SENSITIVE and INSENSITIVE is that with INSENSITIVE, you're not affected by changes made to the result set while you're working with it (more about this in a moment). This is probably what you want.

ResultSet.CONCUR_READ_ONLY states that you don't want to modify the result set. This is the default, and it makes sense in most cases. The alternative is to specify ResultSet.CONCUR_UPDATABLE, which allows you to insert, delete, and modify result rows. Now you can see why you might like to use ResultSet.TYPE_SCROLL_SENSITIVE as the first parameter: it lets you see the modifications made to the result set after you started working with it, rather than showing how it was before those changes. On the other hand, in a complex application with several threads operating on the same result set, you'll probably prefer to ignore the changes made in other threads. In such a situation, it would have to be 100 percent clear which thread would be allowed to modify which rows; otherwise, you'd end up with a mess.

ResultSet provides several methods for retrieving a column value in different formats, given a column position or its label. For example, the following two methods will return the same value:

```
long bookID = rs.getLong(1);
long bookID = rs.getLong("book_id");
```

The column position refers to the columns specified in the select statement. Notice that the column numbering begins with 1, not with 0 as is customary in Java. The types available are Array, BigDecimal, Blob, boolean, byte, byte[], Clob, Date, double, float, InputStream, int, long, NClob, Object, Reader, Ref, RowId, short, SQLXML, String, Time, Timestamp, and URL (see Appendix B for more details). For most of these types exists a corresponding update method, which lets you modify a column. For example, the following code writes "Joe Bloke" in the author column of the current row of the result set:

```
rs.updateString("author", "Joe Bloke");
```

Note that there are no update methods for the types InputStream, Reader, and URL. You can also set a column to null with the methods updateNull(*column-index*) and updateNull(*column-label*).

ResultSet provides more than two dozen additional methods that let you do things such as transfer changes from an updated result set to the actual database or refresh a row that somebody else might have modified in the actual database after you performed the query. One method that you might find useful returns the column position in your result set given its name:

```
int findColumn(column-label)
```

The result set is automatically disposed of when the corresponding statement is closed. Therefore, you don't really need to execute rs.close(), as long as you immediately close the statement when you no longer need it.

The executeUpdate Method

You can use this method to execute the SQL statements insert, update, and delete. For example, if you want to add a new book category to the E-shop example, you do something like this:

```
String sql = "insert into categories (category_id, category_name)"
    + " values (4, 'Comic Books')";
stmt.executeUpdate(sql);
```

You don't need to define all the columns, because the undefined fields are set automatically to their corresponding default values. That said, as I haven't specified any default in the definition of the categories table, the following statement would result in the field category_name being set to null:

```
stmt.executeUpdate("insert into categories (category_id) values (4)");
```

To avoid this occurrence, I could have defined the category_name column with a default:

```
category_name varchar(70) default 'Miscellanea'
```

Transactions

In E-shop, I have defined two separate tables for data associated with a book order: one for the customer data, and one for the individual books ordered (see Listing 6-7). It would be bad if you completely lost an order, but perhaps it would be even worse if you lost some items and only processed a partial order. It would also be a problem if you saved the order details in the database but failed to save the customer data. That would leave some "orphaned" book items with no information concerning the buyer. You don't need to worry about this if you save the customer data first: then, by the time you start saving the order details, the customer record is already on disk. But how do you ensure that the database only contains complete orders?

Normally, when you execute an SQL insert, the data is immediately stored into the database. To ensure the completion of orders, you could keep track of the updates you've already successfully executed and reverse them if you cannot complete the whole order. However, this would be very complicated, and there would be no guarantee of success. Moreover, in a more complex application, there might be several operations proceeding simultaneously and causing the same database records to be accessed concurrently. The solution is a built-in, foolproof mechanism capable of ensuring that some complex transactions are done "in one shot" or not at all.

This mechanism is actually quite simple. It works like this:

1. Immediately after connecting to the DB with conn = DriverManager.getConnection(...), execute conn.setAutoCommit(false). This tells MySQL not to make permanent changes to the database until you confirm them.

2. Perform all the updates that form your complex transaction. Be sure that you place them inside a try block as part of a try/catch construct.

3. In the catch block, include the statement conn.rollback(). If one of the updates fails, an SQLException will be thrown, and when the catch block is executed, the rollback will cause MySQL to "forget" the uncommitted updates.

4. When all the updates have completed without being interrupted by any exception, execute conn.commit() to tell MySQL that it can finalize the updates.

DB Access in E-shop

As I mentioned in Chapter 3, all database operations are concentrated in the data model of an MVC architecture. JSP modules interact with the database by executing methods of the DataManager class, which accept and/or return data in the form of Java beans. By mediating DB access via the data manager and Java beans, you ensure that the view and the model can be developed independently.

Figure 6-5 shows the structure of the model.

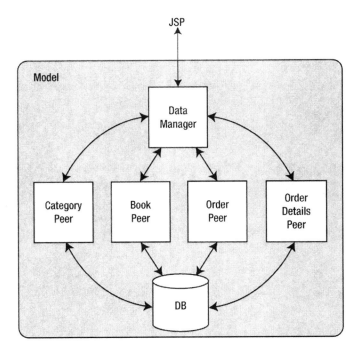

Figure 6-5. *The data model structure*

The DataManager class sets up and closes connections to the database; however, concerning table access, it only acts as a clearinghouse. Specific classes perform the actual operations on individual tables. In this way, you ensure that changes to individual tables have the minimum impact on the application. This is actually an example of the Java EnterPrise Edition pattern called Data Access Object (DAO).

For example, the JSP page that displays the book details obtains the information concerning the requested book by executing the following method of the data manager:

```
public Book getBookDetails(int bookID) {
  return BookPeer.getBookById(this, bookID);
  }
```

It is the getBookByID method in BookPeer.java that performs the actual database access, as shown in Listing 6-10.

Listing 6-10. *The BookPeer.getBookID Method*

```
01: public static Book getBookById(DataManager dataManager, int bookID) {
02:   Book book = null;
03:   Connection connection = dataManager.getConnection();
04:   if (connection != null) {
05:     try {
06:       Statement s = connection.createStatement();
07:       String sql = "select book_id, title, author, price from books"
08:           + " where book_id=" + bookID;
```

```
09:        try {
10:           ResultSet rs = s.executeQuery(sql);
11:           if (rs.next()) {
12:              book = new Book();
13:              book.setId(rs.getString(1));
14:              book.setTitle(rs.getString(2));
15:              book.setAuthor(rs.getString(3));
16:              book.setPrice(rs.getDouble(4));
17:           }
18:        }
19:        finally { s.close(); }
20:        }
21:     catch (SQLException e) {
22:        System.out.println("Could not get book: " + e.getMessage());
23:        }
24:     finally {
25:        dataManager.putConnection(connection);
26:        }
27:     }  return book;
28:  }
```

In line 3, you open the database connection by invoking a method of the data manager that also reports an error in case of failure. Then you start a try block where you do the actual work. In the corresponding catch block, you display an error message (line 22), and in the finally block (line 25), you close the DB connection. Remember that the finally block is executed whether the try succeeds or not. In this way, you ensure that the connection is closed in case of failure.

Inside the outermost try (lines 5–20), you create a statement and set up the query string before starting a second try block (lines 9–17). Similar to what you did concerning the connection, you use the finally block to close the statement (line 19).

This is a technique of general applicability: every time you do something that needs to be undone, take care of it immediately inside a try block by placing the "undoing" statement in the corresponding finally. In this way, you'll be sure not to leave any "ghosts" behind you. It's true that Java's garbage-collection mechanism should take care of removing unreferenced objects, but it's good practice to clean up behind yourself as you go, especially when you're dealing with databases and potentially large objects, such as statements and result sets. At the very least, your application will work more efficiently. And it feels good to write "clean" code.

Line 10 is where you actually execute the query. You know that you're not going to get more than one row in the result set, because the book_id is a unique key of the book table.

You might be thinking, "Why should I go through the data manager at all? Couldn't I simply execute the BookPeer method from JSP?" Well, you could, but it wouldn't be clean, and dirtiness sooner or later causes problems.

Furthermore, consider the more complex case in which you want to save an order. From the JSP point of view, you only want to call a method of the data manager that takes care of both the customer's data and the shopping cart. Behind the scenes, though, two different tables need to be updated: one for the orders and one for the order details. Therefore, it makes a lot of sense to execute the overall transaction in the data manager (see Listing 6-11) while leaving the updates of individual tables to the peer classes.

Listing 6-11. The DataManager.insertOrder Method

```java
public long insertOrder(Customer customer, Hashtable shoppingCart) {
  long returnValue = OL;
  long orderId = System.currentTimeMillis();
  Connection connection = getConnection();
  if (connection != null) {
    Statement stmt = null;
    try {
      connection.setAutoCommit(false);
      stmt = connection.createStatement();
      try {
        OrderPeer.insertOrder(stmt, orderId, customer);
        OrderDetailsPeer.insertOrderDetails(stmt, orderId, shoppingCart);
        try { stmt.close(); }
        finally { stmt = null; }
        connection.commit();
        returnValue = orderId;
      }
      catch (SQLException e) {
        System.out.println("Could not insert order: " + e.getMessage());
        try { connection.rollback(); }
        catch (SQLException ee) { }
      }
    }
    catch (SQLException e) {
      System.out.println("Could not insert order: " + e.getMessage());
    }
    finally {
      if (stmt != null) {
        try { stmt.close(); }
        catch (SQLException e) { }
      }
      putConnection(connection);
    }
  }
  return returnValue;
}
```

The two lines in bold show you how the data manager asks the peer classes of the tables orders and order_details to do the update. Notice that you pass to them the same statement and order ID. Listing 6-12 shows insertOrder, one of the two methods that do the updates.

Listing 6-12. The OrderPeer.insertOrder Method

```java
public static void insertOrder(Statement stmt, long orderId,
    Customer customer) throws SQLException {
  String sql = "insert into orders (order_id, delivery_name,"
      + " delivery_address, cc_name, cc_number, cc_expiry) values ('"
      + orderId + "','" + customer.getContactName() + "','"
      + customer.getDeliveryAddress() + "','"
```

```
                 + customer.getCcName() + "','" + customer.getCcNumber()
                 + "','" + customer.getCcExpiryDate() + "')"
                 ;
       stmt.executeUpdate(sql);
       }
```

Listing 6-13 shows the other method, insertOrderDetails.

Listing 6-13. The OrderDetailsPeer.insertOrderDetails Method

```
public static void insertOrderDetails(Statement stmt, long orderId,
       Hashtable shoppingCart) throws SQLException {
    String sql;
    Enumeration enumList = shoppingCart.elements();
    while (enumList.hasMoreElements()) {
      CartItem item = (CartItem)enumList.nextElement();
      sql = "insert into order_details (order_id, book_id, quantity,"
           + " price, title, author) values ('" + orderId + "','"
           + item.getBookID() + "','" + item.getQuantity() + "','"
           + item.getPrice() + "','" + item.getTitle() + "','"
           + item.getAuthor() + "')"
           ;
      stmt.executeUpdate(sql);
      }
    }
```

The methods throw the SQL exception rather than catch it locally, so that the data manager's method catches it.

What about the XML Syntax?

In the previous chapter, you have learned about writing JSP documents instead of JPS pages. What impact does that have on what I just said about database access? None! This is a consequence of the MVC model: JSP is the view, while only the model has to do with databases.

However, the switch from traditional to XML syntax has an impact on how you execute the data manager methods. For example, you can write the JSP page OrderConfirmation.jsp to save an order in the database with a couple of scriptlets, as shown in Listing 6-14.

Listing 6-14. OrderConfirmation.jsp

```
01: <%@page language="java" contentType="text/html"%>
02: <%@page import="java.util.Hashtable"%>
03: <jsp:useBean id="dataManager" scope="application"
04:   class="eshop.model.DataManager"/>
05: <html>
06: <head>
07:   <meta http-equiv="Content-Type" content="text/html; charset=UTF-8"/>
08:   <title>Order</title>
09:   <link rel="stylesheet" href="/eshop/css/eshop.css" type="text/css"/>
10: </head>
11: <body>
12: <jsp:include page="TopMenu.jsp" flush="true"/>
```

```
13: <jsp:include page="LeftMenu.jsp" flush="true"/>
14: <div class="content">
15:    <h2>Order</h2>
16:    <jsp:useBean id="customer" class="eshop.beans.Customer"/>
17:    <jsp:setProperty property="*" name="customer"/>
18: <%
19:     long orderId = dataManager.insertOrder(
20:                         customer,
21:                         (Hashtable)session.getAttribute("shoppingCart")
22:                         );
23:     if (orderId > 0L) {
24:       session.invalidate();
25:  %>
26:      <p class="info">
27:        Thank you for your purchase.<br/>
28:        Your Order Number is: <%=orderId%>
29:      </p>
30: <%
31:       }
32:     else {
33:       %><p class="error">Unexpected error processing the order!</p><%
34:       }
35:  %>
36:   </div>
37: </body>
38: </html>
```

Or you can write the JSP document OrderConfirmation.jspx, as shown in Listing 6-15. I have included the whole E-shop project converted to XML format in the software package for this chapter. You will find it both in WAR format and already expanded in the folder named eshopx. To launch it, similarly to eshop, type http://localhost:8080/eshopx/shop.

Listing 6-15. OrderConfirmation.jspx

```
01: <?xml version="1.0" encoding="UTF-8"?>
02: <jsp:root
03:    xmlns:jsp="http://java.sun.com/JSP/Page"
04:    xmlns:c="http://java.sun.com/jsp/jstl/core"
05:    xmlns:eshop="urn:jsptld:/WEB-INF/tlds/eshop.tld"
06:    version="2.1"
07:    >
08: <jsp:directive.page
09:    language="java"
10:    contentType="application/xhtml+xml;charset=UTF-8"
11:    />
12: <jsp:output omit-xml-declaration="false"/>
13: <jsp:output
14:    doctype-root-element="html"
15:    doctype-public="-//W3C//DTD XHTML 1.0 Strict//EN"
16:    doctype-system="http://www.w3.org/TR/xhtml1/DTD/xhtml1-strict.dtd"
17:    />
18: <c:url var="cssUrl" value="/css/eshop.jspx"/>
```

```
19: <html xmlns="http://www.w3.org/1999/xhtml">
20: <head>
21:   <title>Order</title>
22:   <link rel="stylesheet" href="${cssUrl}" type="text/css"/>
23: </head>
24: <body>
25: <jsp:include page="TopMenu.jspx" flush="true"/>
26: <jsp:include page="LeftMenu.jspx" flush="true"/>
27: <div class="content">
28:   <h2>Order</h2>
29:   <jsp:useBean id="customer" class="eshop.beans.Customer"/>
30:   <jsp:setProperty property="*" name="customer"/>
31:   <eshop:insertOrder var="orderID" customer="${customer}"/>
32:   <c:choose>
33:     <c:when test="${orderID > 0}">
34:       <p class="info">
35:         Thank you for your purchase.<br/>
36:         Your Order Number is: <c:out value="${orderID}"/>
37:       </p>
38:     </c:when>
39:     <c:otherwise>
40:       <p class="error">Unexpected error processing the order!</p>
41:     </c:otherwise>
42:   </c:choose>
43: </div>
44: </body>
45: </html>
46: </jsp:root>
```

Let's concentrate on the highlighted code, where the actual work is done. The saving of the order information in the database, which you do in the JSP page (Listing 6-14) by executing a data manager's method (lines 19–22), you do in the JSP document (Listing 6-15) by executing a custom action (line 31). The same custom action also invalidates the session (which was done in line 24 of the JSP page).

The if/else Java construct in lines 23, 31–32, and 34 of the JSP page becomes in the JSP document the JSTL core construct choose/when/otherwise in lines 32–33, 38–39, and 41–42.

Informing the user of the order acceptance is in HTML and remains basically the same (JSP lines 26–29 become JSPX lines 34–37). In fact, you could have replaced the scripting expression of the JSP page with the EL expression of the JSP document, making the code identical.

The introduction of the custom action insertOrder is necessary because scriptlets, being Java code, can make assignments and execute methods, while EL expressions cannot. Therefore, when you remove scriptlets because they're not valid XML code, you have to move the computation to Java beans or custom actions.

In line 5 of OrderConfirmation.jspx, you declare eshop.tld, which contains the definition of the insertOrder action (see Listing 6-16).

Listing 6-16. InsertOrderTag Definition in eshop.tld

```
<tag>
  <description>Insert an order into storage</description>
  <display-name>insertOrder</display-name>
  <name>insertOrder</name>
  <tag-class>eshop.tags.InsertOrderTag</tag-class>
```

```
<body-content>empty</body-content>
<attribute>
  <name>var</name>
  <required>true</required>
  <rtexprvalue>true</rtexprvalue>
  </attribute>
<attribute>
  <name>customer</name>
  <required>true</required>
  <rtexprvalue>true</rtexprvalue>
  </attribute>
</tag>
```

As you can see, you pass two parameters to the custom action: the name of the variable where the order ID is to be returned, and an object containing the customer data (name, address, and credit-card information). You don't absolutely need the second parameter, because the action code could have retrieved the customer data from the page context as follows:

```
(Customer)pageContext.getAttribute("customer")
```

On the other hand, you could have passed to the action a third parameter referencing the shopping cart, but I decided to let the action retrieve it from the session as follows:

```
(Hashtable)pageContext.getSession().getAttribute("shoppingCart")
```

It's not always obvious what constitutes a better design. I felt that the shopping cart, being a session attribute, was obviously shared across JSP documents. Therefore, it was OK for the action to retrieve it directly from the session. The customer data, however, was a page attribute, normally not shared with other modules. Passing it "behind the scenes" to a Java class didn't seem appropriate. Listing 6-17 shows you the action code in its entirety.

Listing 6-17. InsertOrderTag.java

```
package eshop.tags;

import java.util.Hashtable;
import javax.servlet.http.HttpSession;
import javax.servlet.jsp.tagext.TagSupport;
import javax.servlet.ServletContext;

import eshop.beans.CartItem;
import eshop.beans.Customer;
import eshop.model.DataManager;

public class InsertOrderTag extends TagSupport {
  static final long serialVersionUID = 1L;
  private String var;
  private Customer customer;

  public void setVar(String var) {
    this.var = var;
    }

  public void setCustomer(Customer customer) {
```

```
      this.customer = customer;
      }

  public int doEndTag() {
    ServletContext context = pageContext.getServletContext();
    DataManager dataManager =(DataManager)context.getAttribute("dataManager");
    HttpSession session = pageContext.getSession();
    @SuppressWarnings("unchecked")
    Hashtable<String, CartItem> cart =
        (Hashtable<String, CartItem>)session.getAttribute("shoppingCart");
    long orderID = dataManager.insertOrder(customer, cart);
    if (orderID > OL) session.invalidate();
    pageContext.setAttribute(var, new Long(orderID).toString());
    return EVAL_PAGE;
    }
  }
```

Notice how you obtain the servlet context (corresponding to the JSP implicit object application) from pageContext, and from it the data manager, so that you can then execute the same insertOrder method you invoked directly from within the JSP page.

The highlighted line shows that I suppressed a warning. I did it because Eclipse kept complaining about typecasting of a generic Object to the Hashtable type. Normally, a warning tells you that something might be wrong. The use of @suppressWarnings is usually bad practice and encourages a sloppy programming style. In this particular case, I was left with no choice, because Eclipse's warning was unjustified.

Possible Alternatives to MySQL

There's no general reason why you shouldn't use MySQL in your applications. Nevertheless, you do have alternatives worth mentioning. I have only tested E-shop with MySQL, but I expect it to work exactly the same with other DBMSs.

If you switch DBMSs, there's a good chance that you'll just need to change the values of the init parameters jdbcDriver and dbUrl in web.xml from these values for MySQL:

```
com.mysql.jdbc.Driver
jdbc:mysql://localhost:3306/shop
```

to the values for the other DBMS.

For example, for PostgreSQL (http://www.postgresql.org/), the values would look like this:

```
org.postgresql.Driver
jdbc:postgresql://localhost/shop
```

For Firebird (http://www.firebirdsql.org/), the values could look like this:

```
org.firebirdsql.jdbc.FBDriver
jdbc:firebirdsql:localhost/3050:D:\\Firebird Datafiles\\shop.fdb
```

Sun Microsystems reports that 221 different JDBC drivers exist (see http://developers.sun.com/product/jdbc/drivers). Therefore, you should be able to find the driver you need to connect to any database, although it might not be freely available.

If you don't find the right JDBC driver or if it's too expensive, you might be able to use the JDBC-ODBC bridge included in the JVM to connect to any ODBC-compliant database. ODBC refers to an API supported by many database vendors on basically all operating systems. With the JDBC-ODBC bridge, you can also access Microsoft Excel files as if they were a database. For example, let's suppose that you have the spreadsheet shown in Figure 6-6.

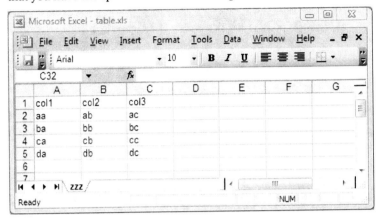

Figure 6-6. table.xls

To be able to access it via the JDBC-ODBC bridge, you first need to associate the file with an ODBC data source. To do so, go to Start ➤ Settings ➤ Control Panel ➤ Administrative Tools ➤ Data Sources (ODBC). There, click on the System DSN tab and then on the Add button, as shown in Figure 6-7.

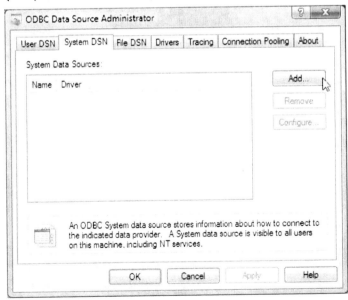

Figure 6-7. ODBC Data Source control panel

This opens the Create New Data Source dialog. Scroll the list of possible data sources until you find Microsoft Excel Driver (*.xls). Select it and click on the Finish button. Despite the name of the button, you're not done yet! A new dialog called ODBC Microsoft Excel Setup opens, which lets you select the Excel file and associate it with a data source name. See Figure 6-8.

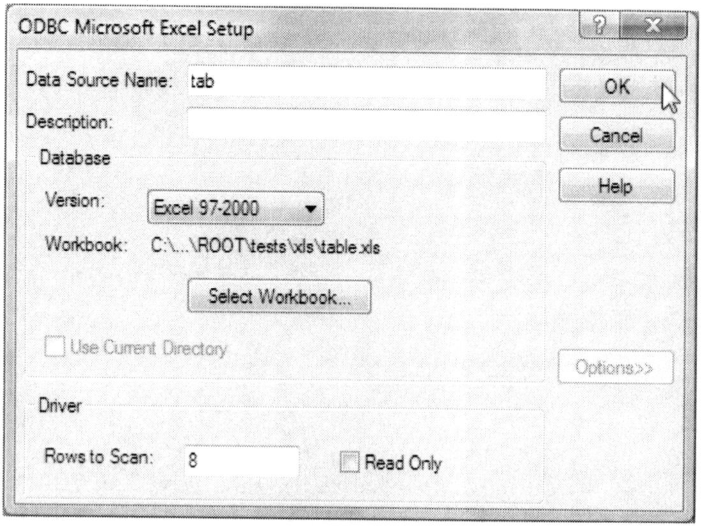

Figure 6-8. ODBC Microsoft Excel setup

Click on the Select Workbook... button to select the file. Notice that I have placed table.xls in ROOT\tests\xls\, together with the JSP page to access it, but it doesn't need to be there. Also, I have chosen tab as a data source name, but you're free to choose any name.

Listing 6-18 shows you a little JSP page to access table.xls as if it were a database.

Listing 6-18. xls.jsp

```
<%@page language="java" contentType="text/html"%>
<%@page import="java.sql.*"%>
<html><head><title>XLS - ODBC test</title></head><body>
<%
  Class.forName("sun.jdbc.odbc.JdbcOdbcDriver").newInstance();
  Connection conn = DriverManager.getConnection ("jdbc:odbc:tab");
  Statement stmt = conn.createStatement();
  ResultSet rs = stmt.executeQuery("select * from [zzz$]");
%><table border= "1"><%
  ResultSetMetaData resMetaData = rs.getMetaData();
  int nCols = resMetaData.getColumnCount();
%><tr><%
  for (int kCol = 1; kCol <= nCols; kCol++) {
    out.print("<td><b>" + resMetaData.getColumnName(kCol) + "</b></td>");
    }
%></tr><%
  while (rs.next()) {
```

```
  %><tr><%
  for (int kCol = 1; kCol <= nCols; kCol++) {
    out.print("<td>" + rs.getString(kCol) + "</td>");
    }
  %></tr><%
  }
 %></table><%
 conn.close();
 %>
</body></html>
```

Notice that in the select statement, I have used [zzz$] as a table name to access the worksheet named zzz. Figure 6-9 shows the output of xsl.jsp.

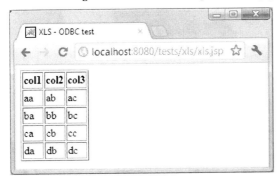

Figure 6-9. The output of xls.jsp

One word of warning: you will fail to establish the Java connection if you have the file already open in Excel, because Excel opens it exclusively. It will not fail if, when you set up the data source as shown in Figure 6-8, you tick the Read Only box.

Summary

In this chapter, I introduced you to working with databases and SQL. I explained how to access databases from JSP via the Java SQL API. In particular, I showed you how to establish a connection, insert data, and perform queries. To complete the summary of essential DB operations, I also described how to group elementary updates into transactions.

To bring it all together, I described the design of database operations in the E-shop application and showed you their implementation both with scriptlets and with the XML syntax. Finally, I mentioned possible alternatives to MySQL and described how you can access a spreadsheet from JSP as if it were a database.

Brace yourself, because in the next chapter I will finally talk about JSF!

CHAPTER 7

JavaServer Faces 2.2

In this chapter, I'll introduce you to JSF and show you how to use it to create user interfaces for web-based applications. Within the MVC application architecture I described in Chapter 3 (refer to Figure 3-2), JSF takes the place of the controller, thereby mediating every interaction between JSP (the View) and the Model, which encapsulates the application data. JSF makes the development of web applications easier by:

- Letting you create user interfaces from a set of standard UI components wired to server-side objects

- Making available four custom tag libraries to handle those UI components

- Providing a mechanism for extending the standard UI components

JSF transparently saves state information of the UI components and repopulates forms when they redisplay. This is possible because the states of the components live beyond the lifespan of HTTP requests. JSF operates by providing a controller servlet and a component model that includes event handling, server-side validation, data conversion, and component rendering. Not surprisingly, JSF doesn't change the basic page life cycle that you already know from JSP: the client makes an HTTP request, and the server replies with a dynamically generated HTML page.

The user interface of a JSF application, called a *view*, consists of a tree of UI component objects of types based on the javax.faces.component.UIComponent class. Some components are simple, such as a button or a text field. Others are complex, such as a table or a tree control element.

Be warned that JSF isn't very easy to use, and it requires a non-negligible initial effort to get it going. However, the reward comes once you've familiarized yourself with JSF and can then develop user interfaces more quickly and efficiently. You will find the latest version of JSF in the master Project Object Model (POM) file for Oracle's JSF Implementation, at http://mvnrepository.com/artifact/org.glassfish/javax.faces/. The file includes binaries, documentation, and dependencies of JSF's recent releases. To be able to use JSF, you will need to copy javax.faces-2.1.7.jar (or a newer version) to Tomcat's lib folder and restart Tomcat.

You can download the latest JSF specification (JSR-344 – JSF 2.2) by going to http://jcp.org/en/jsr/detail?id=344 and clicking on the download page link.

Let's begin with a simple JSF application, so that you can see how JSF works in practice.

The simplef Application

You should start by copying into Tomcat's webapps the folder named simplef you will find in the software package for this chapter. You can try it out by typing http://localhost:8080/simplef/ in your web browser. Figure 7-1 is an example of what you'll see.

Figure 7-1. The first page of simplef

As you can see, there isn't much to it. If you type, say, "qwerty," and click Submit, you will see the page shown in Figure 7-2.

Figure 7-2. The second page of simplef

Apart from the URL, which is not what you might expect, everything is pretty boring. If you click on Another, you go back to the first page, as shown in Figure 7-3.

Figure 7-3. Back to the first page of simplef

Again, nothing to get excited about. But notice that the string you typed in the first page appeared in the second one and again in the first one as the default for the input field. What is exciting in this example is how easily this was accomplished with JSF. Listings 7-1 and 7-2 show the two JSP pages of the example.

Listing 7-1. first.jsp

```
<%@taglib uri="http://java.sun.com/jsf/html" prefix="h"%>
<%@taglib uri="http://java.sun.com/jsf/core" prefix="f"%>
<html><head><title>First Page</title></head><body>
<f:view>
  <h:form>
    <h:outputText value="Type something here: "/>
    <h:inputText value="#{aStringBean.str}" />
    <h:commandButton action="goOn" value="Submit" />
    </h:form>
```

```
    </f:view>
</body></html>
```

Listing 7-2. second.jsp

```
<%@taglib uri="http://java.sun.com/jsf/html" prefix="h"%>
<%@taglib uri="http://java.sun.com/jsf/core" prefix="f"%>
<html><head><title>Second page</title></head><body>
<f:view>
  <h:form>
    <h:outputText value="&quot;#{aStringBean.str}&quot; " />
    <h:commandButton action="goBack" value="Another" />
    </h:form>
</f:view>
</body></html>
```

The first two lines of both JSP pages load two of the JSF libraries I mentioned at the beginning of the chapter. The two libraries, core and html, contain all custom-tag definitions that implement JSF.

The first JSF element you encounter in both pages is f:view, which is a container for all JSF actions. The next one is h:form, the JSF element that generates the pair <form>..</form> of HTML tags. The three JSF elements h:outputText, h:inputText, and h:commandButton generate respectively the three HTML elements .., <input type="text"../>, and <input type="submit"../>. If you had used h:commandLink instead of h:commandButton, JSF would have generated a hyperlink with the HTML-tag a and the attribute href instead of a submit button.

Notice that the value attributes of h:inputText in first.jsp and h:outputText in second.jsp contain the EL expression #{aStringBean.str}. This is the first time you encounter a practical example of an EL expression representing an lvalue (see the Expression Language section in Chapter 4).

The expression ${aStringBean.str} (for the record: illegal in this case) would have been evaluated by Tomcat immediately. Tomcat would have replaced it with the value obtained by executing the method aStringBean.getStr().

But, with the # replacing the $, the only thing that happens is that JSF assigns an identifier to the attribute str of the object aStringBean.

Listing 7-3 shows the HTML page that first.jsp generates (reformatted by me for easy reading).

Listing 7-3. HTML generated by first.jsp

```
<html><head><title>First Page</title></head><body>
<form id="id_1" name="id_1" method="post"
    action="/simplef/first.jsf;jsessionid=E48B69EEB4C81EB74C85C1ABCFBB8AE0"
    enctype="application/x-www-form-urlencoded"
    >
<input type="hidden" name="id_1" value="id_1"/>
Type something here: <input type="text" name="id_1:id_3"/>
<input type="submit" name="id_1:id_4" value="Submit"/>
<input type="hidden" name="javax.faces.ViewState" id="javax.faces.ViewState"
    value="5073854143807380359:-1196606070653851981" autocomplete="off"
    />
</form>
</body></html>
```

Whenever you see id, the generated code actually contained j_id_jsp_58993504, but I did a global replace with id because I found the long automatically generated strings somewhat distracting.

The two lines in bold are the result of the three JSF elements h:outputText, h:inputText, and h:commandButton.

JSF assigned to #{aStringBean.str} the identifier j_id_jsp_58993504_1:j_id_jsp_58993504_3. When processing on the server the request your browser sends when you click on Submit, JSF will assign the value you have typed (e.g., the string "qwerty") to the str attribute of the object aStringBean. This is the delayed evaluation I mentioned in Chapter 4. By saving the string in this way, JSF will have it available for the value of h:outputText in second.jsp and as the default value for h:inputText in first.jsp when it will need to render that page again.

To continue the explanation of how JSF works, I would like to direct your attention to the fact that the URLs that appear in the browser do not match the names of the JSP pages. For example, you start the application by typing in your browser http://localhost:8080/simplef/. What trick then takes you to first.jsp? If you open the default JSP page index.jsp that you find inside the simplef folder, you will see the one-liner shown in Listing 7-4.

Listing 7-4. index.jsp

```
<html><body><jsp:forward page="/first.jsf"/></body></html>
```

But in the same folder there is no file named first.jsf! To begin understanding what happens, you have to look at the web.xml file (see Listing 7.5).

Listing 7-5. web.xml

```
<?xml version="1.0" encoding="UTF-8"?>
<web-app version="2.5" xmlns="http://java.sun.com/xml/ns/javaee"
  xmlns:xsi="http://www.w3.org/2001/XMLSchema-instance"
  xsi:schemaLocation="http://java.sun.com/xml/ns/javaee http://java.sun.com/xml/ns/javaee/web-
app_2_5.xsd">
<servlet>
  <servlet-name>Faces Servlet</servlet-name>
  <servlet-class>javax.faces.webapp.FacesServlet</servlet-class>
  <load-on-startup>1</load-on-startup>
  </servlet>
<servlet-mapping>
  <servlet-name>Faces Servlet</servlet-name>
  <url-pattern>*.jsf</url-pattern>
  </servlet-mapping>
</web-app>
```

It defines a servlet of type javax.faces.webapp.FacesServlet. It is the JSF servlet, which I have informally called "JSF". It is that servlet that assigns IDs to attributes and transfers data between pages. web.xml also maps the extension jsf to the servlet, thereby forcing all requests for pages with extension jsf to be sent to it.

This reveals part of the mystery: when you type http://localhost:8080/simplef/ in your browser, Tomcat executes index.jsp, which forwards the request to first.jsf (which actually doesn't exist). But, because of the servlet mapping in web.xml, Tomcat diverts your request to the JSF servlet.

The rest of the mystery is easily explained: JSF replaces the extension jsf with jsp, which means that the request can finally reach first.jsp. The extension jsp is the default, but you can replace it by inserting in the web-app element of web.xml an element like that shown in Listing 7-6.

Listing 7-6. Defining the JSF default suffix in web.xml

```
<context-param>
  <param-name>javax.faces.DEFAULT_SUFFIX</param-name>
  <param-value>.jspx</param-value>
</context-param>
```

The next mystery that we have to solve is how the request generated by the form in first.jsp reaches second.jsp. In other words, how does the action "goOn" cause a request to reach second.jsp?

To solve this second mystery, you have to look at another file you find in WEB-INF: faces-config.xml (see Listing 7-7).

Listing 7-7. faces-config.xml

```
<?xml version="1.0" encoding="UTF-8"?>
<faces-config xmlns="http://java.sun.com/xml/ns/javaee"
    xmlns:xi="http://www.w3.org/2001/XInclude"
    xmlns:xsi="http://www.w3.org/2001/XMLSchema-instance"
    xsi:schemaLocation="http://java.sun.com/xml/ns/javaee ~CCC
http://java.sun.com/xml/ns/javaee/web-facesconfig_2_0.xsd"
    version="2.0"
    >
  <managed-bean>
    <managed-bean-name>aStringBean</managed-bean-name>
    <managed-bean-class>AString</managed-bean-class>
    <managed-bean-scope>session</managed-bean-scope>
    <managed-property>
      <property-name>str</property-name>
      <property-class>java.lang.String</property-class>
      <null-value></null-value>
    </managed-property>
  </managed-bean>
  <navigation-rule>
    <from-view-id>/first.jsp</from-view-id>
    <navigation-case>
      <from-outcome>goOn</from-outcome>
      <to-view-id>/second.jsp</to-view-id>
    </navigation-case>
  </navigation-rule>
  <navigation-rule>
    <from-view-id>/second.jsp</from-view-id>
    <navigation-case>
      <from-outcome>goBack</from-outcome>
      <to-view-id>/first.jsp</to-view-id>
    </navigation-case>
  </navigation-rule>
</faces-config>
```

Concentrate for the time being on the part I have highlighted. It tells JSF that, when the page first.jsp ends with outcome goOn (i.e., executes h:commandButton with action goOn), control should go to second.jsp. In a more complex application, first.jsp would include different actions, which would correspond to different navigation-case elements. Then, the JSF servlet would have a function analogous to that of a Java switch statement.

We are almost there. The next thing that needs some explanation is the managed-bean element that you see in faces-config.xml immediately above the first navigation rule. It tells JSF to manage a session-scoped object named aStringBean of type AString, and to manage its attribute named str, which should be initialized to null. This also means that the JSF servlet will instantiate the object automatically.

This is where the name aStringBean you saw in the EL expressions of both first.jsp and second.jsp comes from. I could have chosen any name, but it is good practice to end the names of such managed beans with Bean.

Also, the default scope is request. But by specifying session, I ensured that the aStringBean is not destroyed after the first request. In the example, it would have meant that the input element in the second execution of first.jsp would have been without default. The request scope would have been sufficient to "remember" the default if first.jsp had executed itself instead of second.jsp. Note that you should be careful not to go overboard with storing information in the session, because you could affect the performance of your application. Remember that every new user causes a new session to be created.

The last piece that you need in order to complete the resolution of the JSF puzzle is the definition of the class AString. For this see Listing 7-8.

Listing 7-8. AString.java

```
import java.io.Serializable;
public class AString implements Serializable {
  String str;
  public String getStr() { return str; }
  public void setStr(String s) { str = s; }
  }
```

For simplef to work, AString.class should be in the classes sub-directory of WEB-INF.

AString is the simplest possible bean that you need for JSF. Actually, you could drop the import statement and remove the implementation of Serializable. They are there because it makes possible for Tomcat to save the object to disk and to retrieve it from disk. The server possibly uses a hard disk to park session data when it is under a heavy load or when it is restarted. This is one more reason for keeping the session's size as contained as possible. Note that Tomcat can only save objects that it is able to convert to output streams of data, and that requires the objects to be serializable.

The bottom line is that, to be completely safe, your managed beans should be serializable when defined to be in the session scope. But you don't absolutely need to do it. It means that under heavy load conditions, some sessions might be abruptly terminated.

░ **Tip** You will find that sometimes, if you make a mistake when developing a JSF application that causes it to fail, the application will not work again when you revert back to the version you had before making a mistake. It has to do with caching. In a development environment, the simplest way to fix it is to restart your browser and Tomcat.

An Alternative to <managed-bean>

Java annotations are a way of providing information about classes or objects. You saw an example of an annotation in Chapter 6 (see Listing 6.17), where I used @SuppressWarnings ("unchecked") to tell the Java compiler how to behave when processing the statement that followed.

JSF supports annotations that you can use in a Java bean to replace the <managed-bean> element of faces-config.xml. In other words, if you use an annotated version of AString.java as shown in Listing 7-9, you can completely remove the <managed-bean> element from the faces-config.xml shown in Listing 7-7.

Listing 7-9. AString.java (annotated)

```
import javax.faces.bean.ManagedBean;
import javax.faces.bean.SessionScoped;
import javax.faces.bean.ManagedProperty;
@ManagedBean(name="aStringBean")
@SessionScoped
public class AString {
  @ManagedProperty(value="#{AString.str}")
  String str;
  public String getStr() { return str; }
  public void setStr(String s) { str = s; }
  }
```

I think it is pretty self-explanatory. If you remove the parenthesized assignment following @ManagedBean, in JSP you have to use as bean-object name the class name with its first letter changed from uppercase to lowercase.

For simplicity, I have included in the software package for this chapter a separate folder with the annotated version of simplef. You will find in there the WAR file, which you can easily import into Eclipse or drop into Tomcat's webapps folder, and an already expanded folder (which you can also drop into webapps).

The simplefx and simpleh Applications

In the previous section, I showed you how to build a simple JSF application with JSP pages. To use JSF with JSP documents (i.e., in XML format), you only have to make minimal changes. To convert first.jsp (Listing 7.1) to first.jspx, you only need to make the standard changes described in the last section of Chapter 5 and replace the two JSF taglib actions with the corresponding namespace declarations, as shown in Listing 7-10.

Listing 7-10. first.jspx

```
<?xml version="1.0" encoding="UTF-8"?>
<jsp:root
  xmlns:jsp="http://java.sun.com/JSP/Page"
  xmlns:f="http://java.sun.com/jsf/core"
  xmlns:h="http://java.sun.com/jsf/html"
  version="2.1"
  >
<jsp:directive.page
  language="java"
```

```
    contentType="application/xhtml+xml;charset=UTF-8"
  />
<jsp:output omit-xml-declaration="false"/>
<jsp:output
  doctype-root-element="html"
  doctype-public="-//W3C//DTD XHTML 1.0 Strict//EN"
  doctype-system="http://www.w3.org/TR/xhtml1/DTD/xhtml1-strict.dtd"
  />
<html xmlns="http://www.w3.org/1999/xhtml">
<head><title>First Page</title></head>
<body>
<f:view>
  <h:form>
    <h:outputText value="Type something here: "/>
    <h:inputText value="#{aStringBean.str}"/>
    <h:commandButton action="goOn" value="Submit"/>
    </h:form>
  </f:view>
</body>
</html>
</jsp:root>
```

After converting second.jsp to second.jspx in the same way, you also need to insert into web.xml the context-param element shown in Listing 7-6, otherwise JSF will keep looking for files with extension jsp. Finally, to complete the conversion to XML you will need to make a global replace from jsp to jspx in faces-config.xml, so that the navigation rules will keep working. You will find all the updated sources in the folder simplefx as part of the software package for this chapter.

Notice that we didn't need to do any conversion inside the body elements of the JSP pages. This is because there were no scripting elements to convert. With JSTL, JSF, and other custom actions that you acquire or develop yourself, you can write JSP in XML format without much effort.

There is another reason for switching from JSP pages to JSP documents: it will unlock for you pieces of JSF 2.0 functionality that otherwise you wouldn't be able to use. One example is *implicit navigation*.

You saw that in faces-config.xml you need to specify to which document you want the control to move when you request a particular action from within a particular document. The navigation elements for the simplexf applications are those shown in Listing 7-11.

Listing 7-11. Navigation Rules for simplexf

```
<navigation-rule>
  <from-view-id>/first.jspx</from-view-id>
  <navigation-case>
    <from-outcome>goOn</from-outcome>
    <to-view-id>/second.jspx</to-view-id>
    </navigation-case>
  </navigation-rule>
  <navigation-rule>
  <from-view-id>/second.jspx</from-view-id>
  <navigation-case>
    <from-outcome>goBack</from-outcome>
    <to-view-id>/first.jspx</to-view-id>
    </navigation-case>
  </navigation-rule>
```

In particular, the first navigation rule tells JSF that when it executes the element `<h:commandButton action="goOn" value="Submit"/>` in `first.jspx`, it should transfer control to `second.jspx` (which JSF renames `second.jsf` so that a subsequent request from the user goes back to the JSF servlet).

From release 2.0 of 2009, JSF lets you navigate without defining navigation rules in `faces-config.xml`, provided that:

- the action's value (i.e., what you write in the `from-outcome` element of `faces-config.xml`) is identical to the name of the destination document (without its extension and the dot), and

- the extension of the destination document is `xhtml`.

Pity that the JSF Expert Group didn't provide the choice of other extensions. Isn't it? But you don't need to worry, because JSP documents don't need the extension `jspx`!

In the software package for this chapter, you will find yet another version of what originally was the `simplef` application. I named it `simpleh`. The only differences from the previous version (`simplefx`) are:

- `first.jspx` has become `first.xhtml`

- `second.jspx` has become `second.xhtml`

- In first.xhtml, the action `"goOn"` has become `"second"`

- In second.xhtml, the action `"goBack"` has become `"first"`

- In `web.xml`, the element `context-param` is no longer there, because the extensions `jspx` have gone

- The file `faces-config.xml` has disappeared, because it no longer serves any purpose.

XHTML pages used to develop JSF applications are called *facelets*. Giving the `xhtml` extension to JSP documents is only a way of generating the XHTML pages with JSP rather than coding them by hand.

Note If somebody tells you that JSP is out and facelets are in, tell them that things are not as black-and-white as they think! But please be careful when mixing JSF and JSP/JSTL, because it can be confusing. Also, before implementing complex pieces of code with JSP, you might like to investigate whether you can do it more simply with JSF.

The JSF Life Cycle

Now that you have seen an example of JSF, let's have a closer look at how JSF does its job. For that, refer to Figure 7-4. Note that the figure only shows what JSF does when the user types valid values into the input fields of the page that sends the request. Read on for more details.

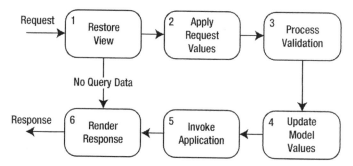

Figure 7-4. The JSF life cycle

1. **Restore View**: The JSF servlet builds the view of the requested page as a component tree that contains the information associated with all components of the page. If the page is requested for the first time, JSF creates an empty view, wires event handlers and validators (if any) to its components, and saves it in a FacesContext object, before jumping directly to Render Response. By saving the view, JSF makes it possible to repopulate the page if necessary—for example, when the user doesn't fill out a form as required. If the same page was displayed before and component states were saved, JSF uses that information to restore the page to its current state.

2. **Apply Request Values**: JSF goes through the component tree and executes each component's decode method, which extracts values from the request parameters, or possibly from cookies or headers. It also automatically converts the parameters that are associated with object properties of nonstring types. Conversion errors cause error messages to be queued to the FacesContext object. In some cases, typically when the user clicks on controls, the servlet also generates request events and queues them to FacesContext. For components that have the immediate event-handling property set to true, JSF also validates them and saves them in their component instances within FacesContext.

3. **Process Validation**: The servlet invokes the validate methods for all components of the validators that had been registered during Restore View. The validation rules are those you define or, by default, those predefined by JSF. For each validate method that returns false, the servlet marks the component as invalid and queues an error message to the FacesContext. At the end of this phase, if there are validation errors, JSF jumps directly to Render Response, so that error messages can be displayed to the user.

4. **Update Model Values**: During this phase, the values of the components are copied to the corresponding properties of the managed beans that are wired to them. JSF does it by executing the component method updateModel, which also performs type conversions when necessary. Conversion errors cause error messages to be queued to FacesContext.

5. **Invoke Application**: During this phase, the servlet processes the application-level events by executing the corresponding handlers. When the user submits a form or clicks on a link of a JSF application, the JSF servlet generates a

corresponding application-level event. One of the tasks you have to do when developing a JSF application is to assign a handler to each one of the possible application events. This is where you also specify what should happen next, by returning outcomes that you have linked to possible next pages, either with a navigation case or implicitly, as I showed you in the previous section.

6. **Render Response:** The servlet creates a response component tree and delegates the rendering of the page to Tomcat. Each component renders itself as Tomcat goes through the corresponding JSF tags. At the end of this phase, the state of the response is saved so that the servlet can access it during the Restore View phase of subsequent requests to the same page.

Event Handling

Before looking at an application, I need to spend a few words on the JSF mechanism to handle events, because you cannot really understand how JSF works unless you know a thing or two about event handling.

As an example, let's see what role the event handling plays when a user clicks on a Submit button. The JSF UI components used to represent button HTML elements are objects of type javax.faces.component.html.HtmlCommandButton, which is a class extending the more general javax.faces.component.UICommand. As with any other HTML page, by clicking on the Submit button in a JSF application, the user triggers the sending to the server of an HTTP request that contains the ID of the button as a parameter name.

As I've already mentioned, during the Apply Request Values phase, JSF executes the decode method of each component of the page. First, the decode method scans the parameter names to see whether one matches the ID of the component the method belongs to. In our example, the decode method of the UICommand object associated with the button clicked by the user finds the component ID among the request parameters, precisely because the user clicked the button. As a result of finding its own ID, the component instantiates an event object of type javax.faces.event.ActionEvent and queues it up.

At this point, you have to distinguish between situations in which all the input fields of a form need to be validated and those in which only a partial validation is appropriate. For example, in an online shop such as the eshop application, the shopper must be able to add further books to the shopping cart even after reaching the checkout page, where the shopper is asked to provide payment information. To make that possible, you must ensure that the validation of the payment data is skipped if the user selects a book category or searches for new titles. If you allowed the validation of empty or partially filled payment fields to proceed, the application would report one or more errors and prevent the shopper from going back to look for new books.

You solve this issue by specifying that the handling of both the book search and the category selection be done during Apply Request Values, while leaving the handling of the payment data to follow the normal life cycle. If it turns out that the user wants to shop for new books rather than complete the checkout, control then jumps directly to the Render Response phase, thereby skipping the intermediate phases where payment data would have been validated and processed.

In the next chapter, you will see in detail how this is done in the JSF version of eshop.

The JSF Tag Libraries

The first two sections of this chapter showed you examples of simple JSF applications that used a handful of elements: f:view, h:form, h:outputText, h:inputText, and h:commandButton. You will recall that the prefix h was associated with the HTML component library, and the prefix f with the JSF core library. Besides those two libraries, JSF 2 consists of two additional custom-tag libraries: `facelets`, normally associated with the prefix `ui`, and `composite`, with prefix `composite`.

In the rest of this chapter, I will briefly describe the four libraries and show you more examples. In the next chapter, I will describe how to use more of the tags by referring to a JSF-version of the `eshop` application.

You can find a complete list of tags with associated documentation at `http://java.sun.com/javaee/javaserverfaces/reference/api/`.

The `html` Library

As its name suggests, JSF's HTML library collects the tags associated with rendering HTML components. As you have already seen in the examples (e.g., with `h:inputText`), you associate objects of your data model to the corresponding components by assigning value expressions that refer to the objects to specific attributes of the component tags (e.g., `<h:inputText value="#{aStringBean.str}"/>`).

Although in most cases the names of the tags should already tell you their purpose, I have summarized the correspondence between tags and HTML elements in Table 7-1.

Table 7-1. html Tags and HTML Elements

Tag Name	HTML Element
h:body	body
h:button	input type="button"
h:column	--
h:commandButton	input type="submit"
h:commandLink	a
h:dataTable	table
h:doctype	`<!DOCTYPE>` declaration
h:form	form
h:graphicImage	img
h:head	head
h:inputHidden	input type="hidden"
h:inputSecret	input type="password"
h:inputText	input type="text"
h:inputTextarea	input type="textarea"

Tag Name	HTML Element
h:link	a
h:message	span or text
h:messages	span or text
h:outputFormat	span or text
h:outputLabel	label
h:outputLink	a
h:outputScript	script
h:outputStylesheet	link
h:outputText	span or text
h:panelGrid	table
h:panelGroup	div or span
h:selectBooleanCheckbox	input type="checkbox"
h:selectManyCheckbox	multiple input type="checkbox"
h:selectManyListbox	select and multiple option
h:selectManyMenu	select and multiple option
h:selectOneListbox	select and multiple option
h:selectOneMenu	select and multiple option
h:selectOneRadio	multiple input type="radio"

Caution The elements h:head and h:body are only valid in documents with extension xhtml

The h:select* Elements

There are seven JSF HTML tags to render selections. To show how they differ from each other, I created in Eclipse the small project testf. You will find it in the testf project subfolder of the software package for this chapter. If you copy testf.war to Tomcat's webapps folder, after a few seconds, you will be able to try it out by typing http://localhost:8080/testf/ in your web browser. Figure 7-5 shows you what you will see in your browser after selecting values in the controls (and hitting the Submit button, although it is not necessary to do so).

Figure 7-5. *The output of testf*

Listing 7-12 shows the JSP document.

Listing 7-12. *index.jspx for the testf Project*

```
<?xml version="1.0" encoding="UTF-8"?>
<jsp:root
  xmlns:jsp="http://java.sun.com/JSP/Page"
  xmlns:f="http://java.sun.com/jsf/core"
  xmlns:h="http://java.sun.com/jsf/html"
  version="2.1"
  >
<jsp:directive.page
```

```
  language="java"
  contentType="application/xhtml+xml;charset=UTF-8"
  />
<jsp:output omit-xml-declaration="false"/>
<jsp:output
  doctype-root-element="html"
  doctype-public="-//W3C//DTD XHTML 1.0 Strict//EN"
  doctype-system="http://www.w3.org/TR/xhtml1/DTD/xhtml1-strict.dtd"
  />
<html xmlns="http://www.w3.org/1999/xhtml">
<head><title>Test</title></head>
<body><f:view><h:form id="form">
  <h:panelGrid columns="2" border="1" cellpadding="5">

    <h:outputText value="h:selectBooleanCheckbox"/>
    <h:panelGroup>
      <h:selectBooleanCheckbox id="checkbox" value="#{myBean.oneValue}"/>
      <h:outputText value=" just a checkbox"/>
      </h:panelGroup>

    <h:outputText value="h:selectManyCheckbox"/>
    <h:selectManyCheckbox id="checkboxes" value="#{myBean.choices1}">
      <f:selectItems value="#{myBean.selects}"/>
      <f:selectItem itemLabel="everything" itemValue="42"/>
      </h:selectManyCheckbox>

    <h:outputText value="h:selectManyListbox"/>
    <h:selectManyListbox id="listboxes" value="#{myBean.choices2}">
      <f:selectItems value="#{myBean.selects}"/>
      <f:selectItem itemLabel="too much" itemValue="999"/>
      </h:selectManyListbox>

    <h:outputText value="h:selectManyMenu"/>
    <h:selectManyMenu id="menus" value="#{myBean.choices3}"
        style="min-height:48px">
      <f:selectItems value="#{myBean.selects}"/>
      <f:selectItem itemLabel="ninenty-nine" itemValue="99"/>
      </h:selectManyMenu>

    <h:outputText value="h:selectOneListbox"/>
    <h:selectOneListbox id="listbox" value="#{myBean.choice1}">
      <f:selectItems value="#{myBean.selects}"/>
      <f:selectItem itemLabel="nine" itemValue="9"/>
      </h:selectOneListbox>

    <h:outputText value="h:selectOneMenu"/>
    <h:selectOneMenu id="menu" value="#{myBean.choice2}">
      <f:selectItem itemLabel="zero" itemValue="0"/>
      <f:selectItems value="#{myBean.selects}"/>
      </h:selectOneMenu>
```

```
    <h:outputText value="h:selectOneRadio"/>
    <h:selectOneRadio id="radio" value="#{myBean.choice3}">
      <f:selectItem itemLabel="nothing" itemValue="-1"/>
      <f:selectItems value="#{myBean.selects}"/>
    </h:selectOneRadio>

    </h:panelGrid>
    <h:commandButton value="Submit"/>
  </h:form></f:view></body>
</html>
</jsp:root>
```

I have highlighted in bold the selection components. h:selectBooleanCheckbox renders a single checkbox; h:selectManyCheckbox, h:selectManyListbox, and h:selectManyMenu render multiple selections; and h:selectOneListbox, h:selectOneMenu, and h:selectOneRadio render single selections.

In all cases in which you can select one or more of several items, I have included a hard-coded item in addition to a list of items provided by the managed bean through an attribute I chose to name selects:

```
<f:selectItems value="#{myBean.selects}"/>
```

The tags wire to each HTML control a different property of the managed bean. Notice the use of the core JSF tags f:selectItem and f:selectItems to provide the information needed for the options of the HTML select elements.

From this example, you can also see how to use h:panelGrid and h:panelGroup to render an HTML table. Differently from HTML, where you need to identify rows with tr elements and cells within rows with td elements, with h:panelGrid you specify at the beginning the number of columns, and all the components between its begin and end tags "flow" from left to right into the table. If you need more than one component within the same cell, you group them together with h:panelGroup.

Listing 7-13 shows the managed bean used to hold the items you select in the browser.

Listing 7-13. myPkg.MyBean.java for the testf Project

```
package myPkg;
import java.util.ArrayList;
import javax.faces.model.SelectItem;

public class MyBean {
  @SuppressWarnings("unchecked")
  private ArrayList<String>[] choices = new ArrayList[3];
  private String choice1, choice2, choice3;
  private Object oneValue;
  private SelectItem[] selects;

  public MyBean() {
    selects = new SelectItem[3];
    selects[0] = new SelectItem("1", "one");
    selects[1] = new SelectItem("2", "two");
    selects[2] = new SelectItem("3", "three");
    for (int kC = 0; kC < choices.length; kC++) {
      choices[kC] = new ArrayList<String>();
      }
```

```
        }

// ---------- Getters
public Object[] getChoices1() { return choices[0].toArray(); }
public Object[] getChoices2() { return choices[1].toArray(); }
public Object[] getChoices3() { return choices[2].toArray(); }
public String getChoice1() { return choice1; }
public String getChoice2() { return choice2; }
public String getChoice3() { return choice3; }
public Object getOneValue() { return oneValue; }
public SelectItem[] getSelects() { return selects; }

// ---------- Setters
public void setChoices(Object[] cc, int kC) {
        int len=0;
        if (cc != null) len = cc.length;
        if (len != 0) {
          choices[kC].clear();
          choices[kC] = new ArrayList<String>(len);
          for (int k = 0; k < len; k++) {
            choices[kC].add((String)cc[k]);
            }
          }
        }
public void setChoices1(Object[] cc) { setChoices(cc, 0); }
public void setChoices2(Object[] cc) { setChoices(cc, 1); }
public void setChoices3(Object[] cc) { setChoices(cc, 2); }
public void setChoice1(String c) { choice1 = c; }
public void setChoice2(String c) { choice2 = c; }
public void setChoice3(String c) { choice3 = c; }
public void setOneValue(Object v) { oneValue = v; }
}
```

There isn't really much to explain. JSF takes care of executing the initialization method of the bean, which initializes three values to be provided for selection through the select attribute and sets up the arrays needed to save the user's choices.

Notice that I haven't written a setter method for select. This is because I didn't need to modify the values stored there. What you should never do is to omit the getter methods, because JSF expects to be able to read the properties.

The core Library

JSF's core library gives you access to APIs that are independent of a particular render kit:

- **Converters**. Converters let you convert between the data types of the components and those of your application objects.

- **Listeners**. Based on the JavaBean version 1.0.1 mechanism, you register a listener with a component to handle events that the component generates.

- **Events**. After the listener is registered with a component, the FacesServlet fires the events by invoking an event notification method of the corresponding listener.

- **Validators**. Validators examine the value of a component and ensure that it conforms to a set of predefined rules.

In the previous examples, you have already encountered f:view, f:selectItem, and f:selectItems. Most of the core tags perform operations on components. Table 7-2 provides the list of all core tags and the corresponding operations. In the table, I have highlighted in italics the few operations that do not apply to individual components. As for the HTML library, you will find more information about the core in Chapter 9.

Table 7-2. core Tags

Tag Name	Operation
f:actionListener	Adds an action listener
f:ajax	*Registers an Ajax behavior for one or more components*
f:attribute	Sets an attribute
f:convertDateTime	Add a date-time converter
f:converter	Adds a converter
f:convertNumber	Adds a number converter
f:event	Adds a system-event listener
f:facet	Adds a facet
f:loadBundle	*Loads a resource bundle into a Map*
f:metadata	*Declares the metadata facet for a view*
f:param	Adds a parameter
f:phaseListener	*Adds a phase listener to a view*
f:selectItem	Specifies an item for :selectMany* and h:selectOne*
f:selectItems	Specifies items for :selectMany* and h:selectOne*
f:setPropertyActionListener	Adds an action listener that sets a property
f:subview	*Container for all JSF actions on pages included via jsp:include or c:import*
f:validateBean	Adds a bean validator

Tag Name	Operation
f:validateDoubleRange	Adds a double-range validator
f:validateLength	Adds a length validator
f:validateLongRange	Adds a long-range validator
f:validateRegex	Adds a validator against a regular expression
f:validateRequired	Adds a check that a value is present
f:validator	Adds a validator
f:valueChangeListener	Adds a value change listener
f:view	*Container for all JSF actions of a page*
f:viewAction	*Specifies an application-specific action*
f:viewParam	*Adds a parameter to the metadata facet of a view*

I expect that you will find many of the tags listed in Table 7-2 obscure. You will be able to understand most of them after the next sections and chapters, but the use of some of them definitely falls outside the scope of this book.

If you are curious about what a facet is, I can tell you that it is a named sub-component specific to a particular component. For example, h:gridPanel (which renders an HTML table) supports the two facets header and footer. If you include <f:facet "header"><h:outputText value="Whatever"/></f:facet> anywhere within the body of h:gridPanel, the rendered table will have the header "Whatever".

I will talk about converters and validators in the next chapter, where I will describe a JSF version of the eshopx project I introduced in Chapter 6. In this chapter, as an interesting example of core tags, I will describe how to use f:ajax, which was first added to the core library with release 2.0. In order to do that, I will first tell you about Ajax in general, and show you how it was used before the introduction of f:ajax.

What's Ajax?

Asynchronous JavaScript and XML (Ajax) is a mechanism for letting JavaScript communicate with the server *asynchronously*—that is, without reloading the page. This is possible by means of the JavaScript built-in object XMLHttpRequest. For those who are not familiar with JavaScript, I have added some notes about it in Appendix A.

In practical terms, it works like this: you create an XMLHttpRequest object within JavaScript, use it to send a request to the server, get the response, and, presto, you have fresh data for your web page without having to reload it. Well, it sounds easy, but it's not obvious how to do it, and it's even more tricky to maintain. To explain how to use Ajax, I'll show you a simple example of a page that displays the server time. First, you need to write a JSP page to return the time (see Listing 7-14).

Listing 7-14. time.jsp

```
<%@page language="java" contentType="text/html"
  %><%@page import="java.util.*"
  %><% out.print(new GregorianCalendar().getTime()); %>
```

I've removed all the spaces and newlines before and after the print statement, including a newline at the end. This ensures that only the time is returned. If you type the URL of this script in a browser, you'll get something like this:

```
Sat Jun 23 21:56:27 EST 2012
```

You'll perhaps see some other time zone, but the format will be identical. A good place to check out the abbreviation for your time zone is http://www.timeanddate.com/library/abbreviations/timezones/.

Now that you have a way of getting the server time, you can write the page to display it with Ajax, as shown in Listing 7-15.

Listing 7-15. ajax.xhtml

```
<?xml version="1.0" encoding="UTF-8"?>
<!DOCTYPE html PUBLIC "-//W3C//DTD XHTML 1.0 Transitional//EN"
    "http://www.w3.org/TR/xhtml1/DTD/xhtml1-transitional.dtd"
    >
<html xmlns="http://www.w3.org/1999/xhtml">
<head>
  <title>Example of Ajax</title>
  <script type="text/javascript" src="ajax.js"></script>
  </head>
<body>
  <form name="tForm" action="">
    <span>The time on the server is:</span>
    <input type="text" name="tElement" readonly="readonly" size="30"/>
    <input type="button" value="Update"
        onclick="ajaxFun('tForm', 'tElement');"
        />
  </form>
  </body>
</html>
```

As you can see, I've highlighted two lines. The first is where you load the file ajax.js, which contains the JavaScript code to support the Ajax operation. The second line is where you execute the ajaxFun JavaScript function whenever you click the Update button. Notice that you pass to ajaxFun the names of the form and of the input element to be updated. You could have hard-coded the string "tForm.tElement" within JavaScript, but it would have been bad programming practice to use within ajax.js identifiers defined elsewhere. Global variables invariably lead to code that's a nightmare to maintain and should be avoided whenever possible.

To complete this brief introduction to Ajax, I still need to show you the JavaScript code. However, before I do that, check out Figure 7-6 to see how the browser renders the page. To test the application, copy the ajax folder from the software package for this chapter to Tomcat's webapps folder and type in your browser http://localhost:8080/ajax/.

Figure 7-6. *Server time with Ajax*

Listing 7-16 shows the JavaScript code.

Listing 7-16. *ajax.js*

```javascript
function ajaxFun(tf, te){
  var tElem = eval("document." + tf + "." + te)
  var ajaxReq;
  try { // Firefox, Opera, IE 9, Chrome
    ajaxReq = new XMLHttpRequest();
    }
  catch (e) { // older IEs
    try{
      ajaxReq = new ActiveXObject("Msxml2.XMLHTTP");
      }
    catch (e) {
      try{ // still older IEs
        ajaxReq = new ActiveXObject("Microsoft.XMLHTTP");
        }
      catch (e) {
        alert("Your browser does not support Ajax!");
        return false;
        }
      }
    }
  ajaxReq.open("GET", "time.jsp");
  ajaxReq.send(null);
  ajaxReq.onreadystatechange = function() {
    if(ajaxReq.readyState == 4) {
      tElem.value = ajaxReq.responseText;
      }
    }
  }
```

First, you instantiate an object of type XMLHttpRequest. This works with Firefox, Chrome, Opera, and IE 9; I'm not sure whether it works with IE 7 and 8; and I know that it doesn't work with IE 6. That's why, to be on the safe side, I have added the code that instantiates the correct ActiveXObject in case the instantiation of XMLHttpRequest fails.

In any case, when ajaxReq "holds" an object of the correct type, you set up the HTML request method (e.g., GET) and the target URL (in this case, the JSP module time.jsp). At this point, you can send off the request.

■ **Tip** The caching of IE prevents Ajax from updating the date subsequent to the first clicking of the Update button. To avoid this problem, you can click on IE 9's toothed-wheel button, select Internet Options, click on the Settings button of the Browsing History section, and, under Check for newer versions of stored pages, select every time I visit the web page. This will disable browser caching and solve the problem. You could also disable caching of a particular page by adding one of the following elements to its head:

```
<meta http-equiv="Pragma" content="no-cache">
<meta http-equiv="Cache-Control" content="no-cache">
```

The control comes immediately back to JavaScript (the first letter of Ajax stands for *asynchronous*, remember?). In general, you don't want the browser to wait for the response, and you want your page to be able to do other things. This asynchronicity makes Ajax more useful than if its operations had to be done in sequence. When the state of the request changes, the browser executes the function ajaxReq.onreadystatechange. In that function you need to check that the request has been completed: in which case, you can then display the content of the response in the time field. Cool! In case you are curious to know the possible status codes, check out Table 7-3.

Table 7-3. List of ajaxReq.raeyState Codes

Code	Meaning
0	Uninitiated
1	Loading
2	Loaded
3	Interactive
4	Complete

I've taken a minimalist approach for this example. The idea is for your server to send back an XML document, which you can then parse on the client side. You can find the latest version of the Ajax standard at the following URL: http://www.w3.org/TR/XMLHttpRequest/.

One last thing: Listing 7-17 shows the deployment descriptor for this application.

Listing 7-17. web.xml

```
<?xml version="1.0" encoding="UTF-8"?>
<web-app xmlns="http://java.sun.com/xml/ns/javaee"
    xmlns:xsi="http://www.w3.org/2001/XMLSchema-instance"
    xsi:schemaLocation="http://java.sun.com/xml/ns/javaee ~CCC
http://java.sun.com/xml/ns/javaee/web-app_2_5.xsd"
    version="2.5">
  <display-name>Ajax example</display-name>
  <welcome-file-list>
    <welcome-file>index.xhtml</welcome-file>
    <welcome-file>index.html</welcome-file>
    </welcome-file-list>
</web-app>
```

As you can see, it is almost empty. I have only added a couple of welcome-file elements so that Tomcat tries index.html (which is the default) only if index.xhtml is not there.

Now that you know how Ajax works without JSF, let's see how to use f:ajax to achieve the same result.

f:ajax

Using f:ajax instead of the mechanism I described in the previous section has several advantages, the most important of which, in my opinion, is that you no longer need to write code in JavaScript, which adds another flavor of Java to the mix (and some people also disable this on their browser). Further, f:ajax is fully integrated with the other JSF libraries.

Figure 7-4 showed the six phases of the JSF life cycle. With f:ajax you can selectively *execute* components on the server by processing them through the first five phases, or *render* them, by passing them through the last phase. You *ajaxify* a component by enclosing it within the body of f:ajax or by passing to f:ajax the component id.

To convert the Ajax example of the previous section to JSF's Ajax, let's start from ajaxf.xhtml, shown in listing 7-18. The interesting bits are those highlighted in bold.

To test the application, copy the folder ajaxf from the software package for this chapter to Tomcat's webapps folder, and type http://localhost:8080/ajaxf in your web browser.

Listing 7-18. ajaxf.xhtml

```
<?xml version="1.0" encoding="UTF-8"?>
<!DOCTYPE html PUBLIC "-//W3C//DTD XHTML 1.0 Transitional//EN"
    "http://www.w3.org/TR/xhtml1/DTD/xhtml1-transitional.dtd"
    >
<html xmlns="http://www.w3.org/1999/xhtml"
    xmlns:f="http://java.sun.com/jsf/core"
    xmlns:h="http://java.sun.com/jsf/html"
    >
<h:head><title>Example of Ajax with JSF</title></h:head>
<h:body>
  <h:form>
    <h:outputText value="The time on the server is: "/>
    <h:outputText id="timeField" value="#{serverTimeBean.when}"/>
```

```
<h:outputText value=" "/>
<h:commandButton value="Update">
  <f:ajax render="timeField"/>
  </h:commandButton>
</h:form>
  </h:body>
</html>
```

The first highlighted line simply displays the value of the property when of the managed bean serverTimeBean. It is almost identical to the line

```
<h:outputText value="&quot;#{aStringBean.str}&quot; "/>
```

of second.jsp (Listing 7-2) that you encountered at the very beginning of this chapter.

But this time, I have added to h:outputText the setting of the id attribute. This is because we need to pass it to f:ajax, in the second group of highlighted lines.

The h:commandButton element, contrary to what you saw in previous examples, doesn't transfer control to another page. Its purpose is only to create an event that triggers f:ajax. Accordingly, the action attribute is not there and, if you look at the WEB-INF folder of the application, you will see that no faces-config.xml to handle navigation is present.

Every time the user clicks on the Update button, f:ajax sends a request to the server to obtain the value of serverTimeBean.when, which then the h:outputText element with id timeField displays. You don't need to write JavaScript because JSF automatically generates the little script that sends the Ajax request.

But you do need a Java bean like that shown in Listing 7-19.

Listing 7-19. ServerTime.java

```
import javax.faces.bean.ManagedBean;
import javax.faces.bean.SessionScoped;
import javax.faces.bean.ManagedProperty;
import java.util.GregorianCalendar;
@ManagedBean(name="serverTimeBean")
@SessionScoped
public class ServerTime {
  @ManagedProperty(value="#{ServerTime.when}")
  private String when;
  public ServerTime() { when = new GregorianCalendar().getTime().toString(); }
  public String getWhen() { return new GregorianCalendar().getTime().toString(); }
  public void setWhen(String w) { when = w; }
  }
```

The code is almost identical to that of AString.java (Listing 7-9), the major differences being that it has an initialization method and, obviously, generates a string with the current server time. In the software package you will also find the files that complete the application, index.jsp and web.xml, but they are very similar to the equivalent files you already encountered with other applications.

You will obtain the same result if you replace in ajaxf.html the content of the h:body with the code shown in Listing 7-20.

Listing 7-20. Alternate h:body for ajaxf.xhtml

```
<h:form>
  <f:ajax render="@form" event="click"/>
  <h:outputText value="The time on the server is: "/>
  <h:outputText value="#{serverTimeBean.when} "/>
  <h:commandButton value="Update"/>
</h:form>
```

With this settings, you ajaxify all components of the form. As a result, when you click on the Update button, JSF sends an Ajax request, as it did before, and because the render attribute is set to @form, serverTimeBean.when is updated, as before. Events applicable to whole forms are click, dblclick, keydown, keypress, keyup, mousedown, mousemove, mouseout, mouseover, and mouseup.

With input elements in the form, when the user changes the content in any of them, that also triggers an Ajax request. To test it, replace h:commandButton with an h:inputText element as shown in Listing 7-21.

Listing 7-21. Yet another h:body for ajaxf.xhtml

```
<h:form>
  <h:outputText value="The time on the server is: "/>
  <h:outputText id="timeField" value="#{serverTimeBean.when} "/>
  <h:inputText value="#{serverTimeBean.when}" size="30">
    <f:ajax render="@this timeField" event="blur"/>
  </h:inputText>
</h:form>
```

The resulting page is shown in Figure 7-7.

Figure 7-7. A modified ajaxf.xhtml

As long as you remain within the input field, nothing happens. When you hit enter or click outside it, Ajax sends a request to the server to update the property specified in h:inputText. In the example, it sends a request to set serverTimeBean.when to "Sun Jun 24 012". JSF does it in the Update Model Value phase. Then, during Render Response, Tomcat prepares the Javax response with two values obtained from serverTimeBean.when, one for h:outputText and one for h:inputText. As ServerTime.java always produces a fresh time string, that's what is returned to the browser, and what you typed in the input field remains unused in the bean's variable when.

Possible events for input fields are: blur, change, click, dblclick, focus, keydown, keypress, keyup, mousedown, mousemove, mouseout, mouseover, mouseup, select, and valueChange. The default is valueChange.

The value of the render attribute can be a single identifier, a space-delimited list of identifiers, or one of the special strings @all, @this, @form, and @none. One interesting thing, which I don't necessarily recommend, is that you can specify in a single f:ajax element the identifiers of components in more than one form. For example,

```
<f:ajax render=":form1:id3 id1 @this"/>
```

means that JSF fires a single Ajax request for the component id3 of the form with id set to form1, the component id1 of the form enclosing the f:ajax element, and the component enclosing the f:javax element.

Before we move on, I would like to show you another example of f:ajax. Check out Figure 7-8.

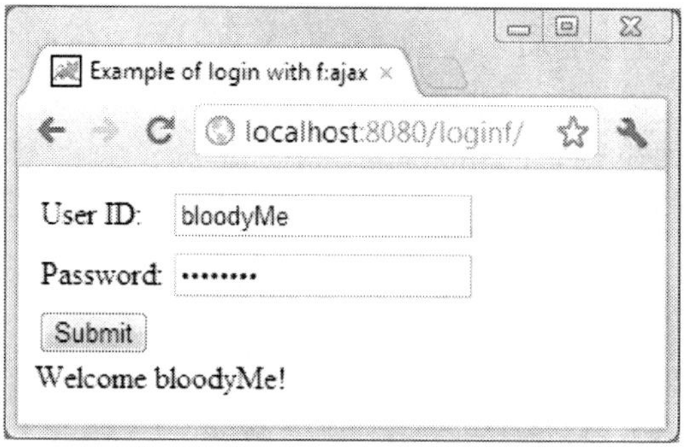

Figure 7-8. *The page produced with loginf*

You find the application in the loginf folder of the software package for this chapter. It is very similar to ajaxf. Listing 7-22 shows the managed bean and Listing 7-23 shows loginf.xhtml.

Listing 7-22. Login.java

```java
import javax.faces.bean.ManagedBean;
import javax.faces.bean.SessionScoped;
@ManagedBean(name="loginBean")
@SessionScoped
public class Login {
  private String user = "";
  public String getUser() { return user; }
  public void setUser(String u) { user = u; }

  private String pass = "";
  public String getPass() { return pass; }
  public void setPass(String p) { pass = p; }

  public String getMess() {
    String mess = "";
    if (user.length() * pass.length() > 0) {
      mess = "Welcome " + user + "!";
    }
    else if (pass.length() > 0) {
      if (user.length() == 0) mess = "Who the %@$# are you?";
    }
    else {
```

```
      if (user.length() > 0) mess = "No password " + user + "?";
      }
    return mess;
    }
  }
```

Nothing special here: a property to store the user ID, one for the password, and a read-only property to provide feedback to the user.

Listing 7-23. loginf.xhtml

```
<?xml version="1.0" encoding="UTF-8"?>
<!DOCTYPE html PUBLIC "-//W3C//DTD XHTML 1.0 Transitional//EN"
    "http://www.w3.org/TR/xhtml1/DTD/xhtml1-transitional.dtd"
    >
<html xmlns="http://www.w3.org/1999/xhtml"
    xmlns:f="http://java.sun.com/jsf/core"
    xmlns:h="http://java.sun.com/jsf/html"
    >
<h:head><title>Example of login with f:ajax</title></h:head>
<h:body>
  <h:form>
    <h:panelGrid columns="2">
      <h:outputText value="User ID:"/>
      <h:inputText id="user" value="#{loginBean.user}"/>
      <h:outputText value="Password:"/>
      <h:inputSecret id="pass" value="#{loginBean.pass}"/>
      </h:panelGrid>
    <h:commandButton value="Submit">
      <f:ajax execute="user pass" render="mess"/>
      </h:commandButton>
    <br/>
    <h:outputText id="mess" value="#{loginBean.mess}"/>
    </h:form>
  </h:body>
</html>
```

The two input components accept user ID and password from the user, and the last h:outputText displays the feedback. The interesting bit is the f:ajax element. You have already encountered the render attribute, but the execute attribute is new. This is how f:ajax sends data to be processed on the server. Most of what I explained about render applies to execute, including the availability of special @-values.

No more reloading of login pages.

The facelet Library

Facelets were originally developed as a view-handling technology in alternative to JSP. With release 2.0 of JSF, facelets have become its default view technology. But that doesn't mean that, with the necessary care, you cannot use them together with JSP and JSTL. What makes JSF's facelet library interesting is that it supports templating. That is, a mechanism that allows you to minimize duplication of code when developing pages with the same layout or common content.

While JSP with `jsp:include` provides an easy mechanism to re-use content, it doesn't provide any easy way to define the same layout for different pages. It is up to you to ensure that the pages look identical when viewed in a browser.

The JSF `facelet` library lets you form a page by defining a layout in an XHTML file and then filling it up with content defined in one or more other XHTMLs. I will show you an example shortly, but first, have a look at Table 7-4, which lists all tags of the `facelet` library. To help you make sense of the tags, I have flagged those that are part of the templating mechanism.

Table 7-4. *facelet Tags*

Tag Name	Description	Templating
`ui:component`	Creates a component	N
`ui:composition`	Creates a composition	Y
`ui:debug`	Creates a component to help you debug the page	N
`ui:decorate`	Defines a fragment containing a composition	Y
`ui:define`	Defines content to be inserted into a template	Y
`ui:fragment`	Defines a fragment containing a component	N
`ui:include`	Includes content from an XHTML file	N
`ui:insert`	Inserts content into a template	Y
`ui:param`	Defines a parameter for an included file or a template	Y
`ui:repeat`	An alternative to `h:dataTable` and `c:forEach`	N
`ui:remove`	Removes what is in its body	N

The templ Application

In this section, I will describe `templ`, an application that uses facelet templating.

To create it, I started from the example `simplefx` I explained in a previous section of this chapter. You will recall that it essentially consisted of two JSP documents that invoked each other: `first.jspx` asked you to type something into a text field, and `second.jspx` displayed what you had typed.

To make an example of templating, I added a third page almost identical to the second one, so that I could show you how to define a template for them. To get started, let's look at how the first two pages appear in a web browser (Figures 7-9 and 7-10).

Figure 7-9. templ first page

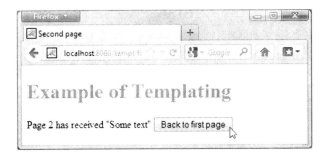

Figure 7-10. templ second page

Notice that the header of the second page is gray instead of black. The third page is identical to the second one, but its title is "Third page" and the text before the button starts with "Page 3". To try it out, copy the folder templ from the software package for this chapter to Tomcat's webapps folder, and then type in a browser http://localhost:8080/templ/.

The application consists of the following folders and files (the folders are in bold for easy reading):

templ
    first.xhtml
    index.jsp
    page2.xhtml
    page3.xhtml
    resources
        css
            styles.css
    templates
        defaults
            header.xhtml
        layout.xhtml
    WEB-INF
        classes
            AString.class
            AString.java
        faces-config.xml
        web.xml

Listing 7-24 shows the code of the first page.

Listing 7-24. *first.xhtml*

```
<?xml version="1.0" encoding="UTF-8"?>
<jsp:root
  xmlns:jsp="http://java.sun.com/JSP/Page"
  version="2.1"
  >
<jsp:directive.page
  language="java"
  contentType="application/xhtml+xml;charset=UTF-8"
  />
<jsp:output omit-xml-declaration="false"/>
<jsp:output
  doctype-root-element="html"
  doctype-public="-//W3C//DTD XHTML 1.0 Strict//EN"
  doctype-system="http://www.w3.org/TR/xhtml1/DTD/xhtml1-strict.dtd"
  />
<html xmlns="http://www.w3.org/1999/xhtml"
      xmlns:f="http://java.sun.com/jsf/core"
      xmlns:h="http://java.sun.com/jsf/html"
      xmlns:ui="http://java.sun.com/jsf/facelets"
      >
<h:head><title>First Page</title></h:head>
<h:body>
<f:view>
  <ui:include src="/templates/defaults/header.xhtml"/>
  <h:form>
    <h:outputText value="Type something here: "/>
    <h:inputText value="#{aStringBean.str}"/>
    <h:commandButton action="go2" value="Page 2"/>
    <h:commandButton action="go3" value="Page 3"/>
  </h:form>
</f:view>
</h:body>
</html>
</jsp:root>
```

First of all, notice that I renamed the file first.xhtml. This is because facelet elements (i.e., those with prefix ui) only work inside h:body. This means that you can no longer use the HTML body tag. As h:body requires the extension of the document to be xhtml, I had to ditch the extension jspx. Old Will Shakespeare said through Juliet's lips, "What's in a name? That which we call a rose by any other name would smell as sweet." The same applies to first.xhtml, which remains a valid JSP document despite the change of name.

Another difference from first.jspx is that I moved the namespace declarations for the core and HTML JSF libraries from jsp:root to the html tag, and then added to them the declaration for the JSF facelet library. As none of the JSF tags are used outside the html element, it makes sense to keep them there, which is where they normally are in XHTML documents.

Finally, notice that first.xhtml includes a standard header with ui:include.

So far so good. Nothing too exciting. You could have done the same with jsp:include, without need for facelets. But now let's look at page2.xhtml (Listing 7-25), and in particular to its h:body element.

Incidentally, I didn't have any technical reason for renaming second.jspx to page2.xhtml. I just found page2 and page3 more appealing than second and third.

Listing 7-25. page2.xhtml

```
<?xml version="1.0" encoding="UTF-8"?>
<jsp:root
  xmlns:jsp="http://java.sun.com/JSP/Page"
  version="2.1"
  >
<jsp:directive.page
  language="java"
  contentType="application/xhtml+xml;charset=UTF-8"
  />
<jsp:output omit-xml-declaration="false"/>
<jsp:output
  doctype-root-element="html"
  doctype-public="-//W3C//DTD XHTML 1.0 Strict//EN"
  doctype-system="http://www.w3.org/TR/xhtml1/DTD/xhtml1-strict.dtd"
  />
<html xmlns="http://www.w3.org/1999/xhtml"
      xmlns:f="http://java.sun.com/jsf/core"
      xmlns:h="http://java.sun.com/jsf/html"
      xmlns:ui="http://java.sun.com/jsf/facelets"
      >
<h:body>
  <ui:composition template="/templates/layout.xhtml">
    <ui:define name="title">Second page</ui:define>
    <ui:define name="pageNum">2</ui:define>
    </ui:composition>
</h:body>
</html>
</jsp:root>
```

Notice that there is no h:head element in page2.xhtml. This is because JSF, when it encounters a ui:composition element, it ignores everything other than the content of h:body. You got it right: JSF only looks at the lines I have highlighted in Listing 7-25.

But then, you might ask, why do we bother with all the stuff that precedes the h:body tag? The reason is that the file must be a valid XML document. But it is true that we can simplify it. That's why I dropped the h:head element (which JSF ignores anyway), without which the code remains valid XML. With a page that doesn't use JSP tags inside h:body, you can also get rid of the JSP elements. This is what I did with page3.xhtml, which you can see in Listing 7-26.

Listing 7-26. page3.xhtml

```
<?xml version="1.0" encoding="UTF-8"?>
<!DOCTYPE html PUBLIC "-//W3C//DTD XHTML 1.0 Transitional//EN"
    "http://www.w3.org/TR/xhtml1/DTD/xhtml1-transitional.dtd"
    >
<html xmlns="http://www.w3.org/1999/xhtml"
      xmlns:f="http://java.sun.com/jsf/core"
      xmlns:h="http://java.sun.com/jsf/html"
```

```
      xmlns:ui="http://java.sun.com/jsf/facelets"
      >
<h:body>
  <ui:composition template="/templates/layout.xhtml">
    <ui:define name="title">Third page</ui:define>
    <ui:define name="pageNum">3</ui:define>
    </ui:composition>
</h:body>
</html>
```

Obviously, you cannot remove the JSP header elements and jsp:root when you use JSP code inside h:body. But you can use JSTL and your own custom-tag libraries without declaring the jsp namespace, as long as you declare the appropriate namespaces in the html tag. What you certainly cannot use in any case, with or without JSP declaration, are JSP scripting and directive elements, because anything enclosed between <% and %> is not valid XML.

Let's go back to describing how JSF handles the pages that make use of templates.

The presence of the ui:composition element with a defined template attribute means that it is the template document that generates the page to be sent back to the user as a response, not the page that contains the ui:composition element.

Listing 7-27 shows the template for page*.xhtml.

Listing 7-27. layout.xhtml

```
<?xml version="1.0" encoding="UTF-8"?>
<!DOCTYPE html PUBLIC "-//W3C//DTD XHTML 1.0 Transitional//EN"
"http://www.w3.org/TR/xhtml1/DTD/xhtml1-transitional.dtd">
<html xmlns="http://www.w3.org/1999/xhtml"
      xmlns:f="http://java.sun.com/jsf/core"
      xmlns:h="http://java.sun.com/jsf/html"
      xmlns:ui="http://java.sun.com/jsf/facelets"
      >

<h:head>
  <title>
    <ui:insert name="title">Default Title</ui:insert>
    </title>
  <h:outputStylesheet name="styles.css" library="css"/>
</h:head>

<h:body>
<f:view>
  <ui:insert name="header">
    <ui:include src="/templates/defaults/header.xhtml"/>
    </ui:insert>
  <h:form>
    <h:outputText value="Page "/>
    <ui:insert name="pageNum"/>
    <h:outputText value=" has received &quot;#{aStringBean.str}&quot; "/>
    <h:commandButton action="goBack" value="Back to first page"/>
    </h:form>
</f:view>
</h:body>
```

```
</html>
```

The two highlighted lines identify two places where the template expects the "client" pages to insert content. If you go back to page2.xhtml and page3.xhtml (Listings 7-25 and 7-26), you will see that the two ui:defines inside ui:composition have the same name attributes as the two ui:inserts of the template.

When layout.xhtml is used to generate the response to a request sent to page2.xhtml, the element `<ui:insert name="title">Default Title</ui:insert>` is replaced with the string "Second page" and the element `<ui:insert name="pageNum"/>` is replaced with "2". For page3.xhtml, the string is "Third page" and the page number is "3". Notice that the body of ui:insert is the default value for that insert, to be used when the "client" page doesn't define any value.

Notice that both layout.xhtml and first.xhtml include a default header (shown in Listing 7-28).

Listing 7-28. header.xhtml

```
<?xml version="1.0" encoding="UTF-8"?>
<!DOCTYPE html PUBLIC "-//W3C//DTD XHTML 1.0 Transitional//EN"
    "http://www.w3.org/TR/xhtml1/DTD/xhtml1-transitional.dtd"
    >
<html xmlns="http://www.w3.org/1999/xhtml"
    xmlns:h="http://java.sun.com/jsf/html"
    xmlns:ui="http://java.sun.com/jsf/facelets"
    >
<h:body>
  <ui:composition>
    <h1>Example of Templating</h1>
    </ui:composition>
</h:body>
</html>
```

In header.xhtml, the element ui:composition doesn't define a template attribute. Its presence ensures that the rest of the page is ignored when header.xhtml is included with ui:include. Actually, the only line needed in header.xhtml is the one I have highlighted. But the advantage of having a well-formed XHTML page is that you can view it in a browser. With more complex pages, it is sometimes useful to be able to do so.

There is still something I need to clarify. Have you noticed that the header shown in the first page (see Figure 7-9) is black, while the header of the second page (see Figure 7-10) is gray?

This is because the template, with the element

```
<h:outputStylesheet name="styles.css" library="css"/>
```

loads a style sheet that defines the color of headers to be gray.

As first.xhtml doesn't use the template, the color of the headers remains the default black. Obviously, nothing prevents you from using the style sheet in first.xhtml by placing in its h:head the same element used in the template. Alternatively, you can also use the HTML element

```
<link rel="stylesheet" type="text/css" href="/templ/resources/css/styles.css"/>
```

Still on the subject of linking to the style sheet with h:outputStylesheet: notice that the name of the resources folder doesn't appear anywhere. This means that it is hardcoded within the component and that you are stuck with it. But the folder names templates and defaults are entirely my choice. Therefore, you can choose the names you like.

To complete the description of the templ application, I still need to show you web.xml (Listing 7-29), which is pretty obvious, and faces-config.xml (Listing 7-30), which is also self-explanatory.

Listing 7-29. web.xml

```xml
<?xml version="1.0" encoding="UTF-8"?>
<web-app version="2.5" xmlns="http://java.sun.com/xml/ns/javaee"
  xmlns:xsi="http://www.w3.org/2001/XMLSchema-instance"
  xsi:schemaLocation="http://java.sun.com/xml/ns/javaee http://java.sun.com/xml/ns/javaee/web-
app_2_5.xsd">
<servlet>
  <servlet-name>Faces Servlet</servlet-name>
  <servlet-class>javax.faces.webapp.FacesServlet</servlet-class>
  <load-on-startup>1</load-on-startup>
  </servlet>
<servlet-mapping>
  <servlet-name>Faces Servlet</servlet-name>
  <url-pattern>*.jsf</url-pattern>
  </servlet-mapping>
<context-param>
  <param-name>javax.faces.DEFAULT_SUFFIX</param-name>
  <param-value>.xhtml</param-value>
  </context-param>
</web-app>
```

Listing 7-30. faces-config.xml

```xml
<?xml version="1.0" encoding="UTF-8"?>
<faces-config xmlns="http://java.sun.com/xml/ns/javaee"
    xmlns:xi="http://www.w3.org/2001/XInclude"
    xmlns:xsi="http://www.w3.org/2001/XMLSchema-instance"
    xsi:schemaLocation="http://java.sun.com/xml/ns/javaee
http://java.sun.com/xml/ns/javaee/web-facesconfig_2_0.xsd"
    version="2.0"
    >
  <navigation-rule>
    <from-view-id>/first.xhtml</from-view-id>
    <navigation-case>
      <from-outcome>go2</from-outcome>
      <to-view-id>/page2.xhtml</to-view-id>
      </navigation-case>
    <navigation-case>
      <from-outcome>go3</from-outcome>
      <to-view-id>/page3.xhtml</to-view-id>
      </navigation-case>
    </navigation-rule>
  <navigation-rule>
    <from-view-id>/page2.xhtml</from-view-id>
    <navigation-case>
      <from-outcome>goBack</from-outcome>
      <to-view-id>/first.xhtml</to-view-id>
      </navigation-case>
```

```
      </navigation-rule>
    <navigation-rule>
      <from-view-id>/page3.xhtml</from-view-id>
      <navigation-case>
        <from-outcome>goBack</from-outcome>
        <to-view-id>/first.xhtml</to-view-id>
        </navigation-case>
      </navigation-rule>
    </faces-config>
```

Action Controllers and Action Listeners

So far, you have only seen examples in which the action attribute of h:commandButton is set to a fixed string. But you can also set it to the method of a bean. If you do so, when JSF reaches the Invoke Application phase while processing the request on the server, it executes that method and uses the value returned by that method to decide what page comes next. In this way, the destination page of an action is defined at execution time.

If this sounds too complicated, let's see whether an example clarifies the matter. We start by making a copy of the templ application and renaming it templa. I am talking about action controllers and listeners now because I have already shown to you the templ application we can work with.

I want to replace the two buttons Page 2 and Page 3 shown in Figure 7-9 with a single button that alternates between the two pages. To do this, I need to add the Java class shown in Listing 7-31.

Listing 7-31. Action.java

```
import javax.faces.bean.ManagedBean;
import javax.faces.bean.SessionScoped;
@ManagedBean(name="actionBean")
@SessionScoped
public class Action {
  int n = 3;
  public int getN() { return 5 - n; }
  public String goThere() {
    n = 5 - n;
    return "go" + n;
    }
  }
```

Notice that every time goThere is executed, n changes between the two values 2 and 3, so that the method returns alternatively "go2" and "go3". Also notice that getN returns 2 when n is 3 and 3 when n is 2.

The only other update I made to templ to change it into templa was to replace the following two lines of first.xhtml (Listing 7-24)

```
<h:commandButton action="go2" value="Page 2"/>
<h:commandButton action="go3" value="Page 3"/>
```

with

```
<h:commandButton action="#{actionBean.goThere}" value="Page #{actionBean.n}"/>
```

If you are thinking that this is a silly application, I fully agree with you. But the last thing I want is to give you examples in which the mechanism you should learn is buried in realistic but unnecessary complexities. Note that by moving the decision of what page comes next to the action-controller bean, you are effectively moving the business logic out of the View, thereby gaining in flexibility and maintainability.

That said, I am not yet happy about how this goThere method works. The problem I have is that the method does more than simply select the next page. It also has the side effect of modifying n. Side effects are dreaded by experienced programmers, because in a complex application they can cause bugs that are very difficult to trace. You want to write transparent programs in which nothing happens "behind your back."

The right way to do it is to move what is now a side effect to its own method. Check out Listing 7-32 for an improved version of Action.java.

Listing 7-32. Action.java (final)

```
import javax.faces.bean.ManagedBean;
import javax.faces.bean.SessionScoped;
import javax.faces.event.ActionEvent;
@ManagedBean(name="actionBean")
@SessionScoped
public class Action {
  int n = 3;
  public int getN() { return 5 - n; }
  public String goThere() { return "go" + n; }
  public void swapPages(ActionEvent event) { n = 5 - n; }
  }
```

Obviously, you also have to update first.xhtml. All you need to do is update the h:commandButton element as follows:

```
<h:commandButton action="#{actionBean.goThere}" value="Page #{actionBean.n}"
    actionListener="#{actionBean.swapPages}"
    />
```

During the Invoke Application phase, JSF executes first the action listener and then the action controller. The value of n is obtained from the bean during the Render Response phase. This works. Sometimes, though, you might like JSF to execute the action listener as soon as possible after receiving the request, before other things happen. In that case, you can add to the component with actionListener the attribute immediate="true", which forces the execution of the action listener already in the Apply Request Values phase.

In the next chapter, you will see how action control works in the JSF version of eshop, which is a more complex application.

The composite Library

JSF is based on user-interface components, but for a long time, it was difficult to create new components or combine existing components into a new one. JSF introduced the composite library with release 2.0 to make those tasks easier.

Table 7-5 lists the all the tags of the composite library. The two tags interface and implementation are special, in that they are containers for other tags.

Table 7-5. composite Tags

Tag Name	Description	Valid In
composite:implementation	Container of the XHTML code that implements the component	
composite:interface	Container of interface components	
composite:actionSource	Exposes components that generate action events	interface
composite:attribute	Declares attributes of components	interface
composite:editableValueHolder	Exposes components with editable values	interface
composite:extension	Inserts XML code in interface components	interface components
composite:facet	Declares a component's facet	interface
composite:insertChildren	Inserts XHTML code into component	implementation
composite:insertFacet	Inserts a facet	implementation
composite:renderFacet	Renders a facet	implementation
composite:valueHolder	Exposes components with non-editable values	interface

Conceptually, to define a new component, you need to go through the following steps:

- Define its namespace (i.e., where it is).
- Specify its functionality (i.e., what it does).
- Define how you use it (i.e., its interface).
- Design how you code it (i.e., its implementation).

Some Examples

To write the first example, let's go through the four points I listed at the end of the previous section.

- Define a namespace. I have chosen gz.
- Specify its functionality. The component should compose a greeting message with a parameterized addressee.

- Define how you use it. Just call it with an attribute to pass to it the addressee.

- Design how you code it. Simple. An h:outputText will do.

The code for the new component is shown in Listing 7-33. To test it, copy the folder composite from the software package for this chapter to Tomcat's webapps folder, and then type in the browser http://localhost:8080/composite.

Listing 7-33. hello.xhtml

```
<?xml version="1.0" encoding="UTF-8"?>
<!DOCTYPE html PUBLIC "-//W3C//DTD XHTML 1.0 Transitional//EN"
    "http://www.w3.org/TR/xhtml1/DTD/xhtml1-transitional.dtd"
    >
<html xmlns="http://www.w3.org/1999/xhtml"
      xmlns:h="http://java.sun.com/jsf/html"
      xmlns:composite="http://java.sun.com/jsf/composite"
      >
<h:head><title>Example of a composite component</title></h:head>
<h:body>
  <composite:interface>
    <composite:attribute name="x"/>
    </composite:interface>
  <composite:implementation>
    <h:outputText value="Hello, #{cc.attrs.x}!"/>
    </composite:implementation>
  </h:body>
</html>
```

Not surprisingly, for such a trivial component, the code is also trivial. But it tells you a lot about developing components with the composite library.

First of all, inside h:body, you find two elements, a composite:interface and a composite:implementation. Inside the former, you define the attribute named x, and inside the latter, you define the logic of the component.

To access the attribute from within the implementation, you use the expression #{cc.attrs.x}.

Listing 7-34 shows you how to use the new component, and Figure 7-11 is how the page appears in a browser.

Listing 7-34. comp.xhtml

```
<?xml version="1.0" encoding="UTF-8"?>
<!DOCTYPE html PUBLIC "-//W3C//DTD XHTML 1.0 Transitional//EN"
    "http://www.w3.org/TR/xhtml1/DTD/xhtml1-transitional.dtd"
    >
<html xmlns="http://www.w3.org/1999/xhtml"
      xmlns:h="http://java.sun.com/jsf/html"
      xmlns:gz="http://java.sun.com/jsf/composite/gz"
      >
<h:head><title>Example of a composite component</title></h:head>
<h:body>
  <gz:hello x="wherever you are"/>
  </h:body>
```

```
</html>
```

Figure 7-11. composite

Have you noticed anything unusual in `comp.xhtml`? Instead of separately declaring the namespaces of the JSF composite library and of your custom components, you declare a single namespace `composite/gz`. For this to work, you need to create in the root of your application a folder named `resources`; create a folder (in the example, named gz) inside `resources`; and place your custom components there. The name of the component (e.g., `hello`) is obtained from the name of the component file (e.g., `hello.xhtml`) by removing its extension.

It is an established practice to use the same string for the prefix and for naming the folder inside `resources`, and I recommend that you follow it, but the two strings can be different.

Note that if you place elements in an `interface` body, you need to define a corresponding `implementation`. But you can have code in `implementation` with an empty `interface`, like in:

```
<composite:interface/>
<composite:implementation>
  <h:outputText value="Hello, World!"/>
</composite:implementation>
```

It simply means that your new component will not have any attribute to set.

To include in a composite component an input component, do exactly what you did for an output component in `hello.xhtml`. In fact, if you replace in hello.xhtml the line

```
<h:outputText value="Hello, #{cc.attrs.x}!"/>
```

with

```
<h:inputText value="Hello, #{cc.attrs.x}!"/>
```

you will see the page shown in Figure 7-12, but be aware that this is not a working page. It's just to show you how to use `composite:attribute`.

Figure 7-12. composite with input element

You can also use composite:attribute to set the action attribute of h:commandButton and h:commandLink. For example, if you want to build a composite component called, say, flip around the h:commandButton you used in templa a couple of pages back, the body of flip.xhtml would look something like this:

```
<composite:interface>
  <composite:attribute name="act" targets="myB" method-signature="java.lang.String action()"/>
  </composite:interface>
<composite:implementation>
  <h:commandButton id="myB" action="#{cc.attrs.act}" value="Page #{actionBean.n}"
     actionListener="#{actionBean.swapPages}"
     />
  </composite:implementation>
```

Then, you would use the new composite component like this:

```
<gz:flip act="#{actionBean.goThere}"/>
```

As it was in the previous examples, you use the expression #{cc.attrs.act} to access from the implementation the value of the act attribute declared in interface. In addition, unlike what happened in the previous examples, you also need a reference in the opposite direction, from interface to implementation. This is because JSF must be able to wire the method set in gz:flip to the h:commandButton component for which the method is meant. In fact, if there were more components in implementation, you could wire the same method to several of them by writing their identifiers in the targets attribute separated by spaces (this is why the name of the attribute is targets, plural, instead of target).

The value of method-signature specifies that the value of act must evaluate to a method, and defines its signature. This means that <gz:flip act="go2"/> wouldn't work. You would have to replace:

```
method-signature="java.lang.String action()"
```

with

```
type="java.lang.String"
```

The two attributes are mutually exclusive, and if you leave out both of them, JSF assumes

```
type="java.lang.Object"
```

Now that you know how to make visible the action attribute of h:commandButton, you will perhaps be asking yourself how you expose its actionListener attribute as well. Here it is:

```
<composite:interface>
  <composite:attribute name="act" targets="myB" method-signature="java.lang.String action()"/>
  <composite:actionSource name="myB"/>
  </composite:interface>
<composite:implementation>
  <h:commandButton id="myB" action="#{cc.attrs.act}" value="Page #{actionBean.n}"/>
  </composite:implementation>
```

Then, you would use the new composite component like this:

```
<gz:flip act="#{actionBean.goThere}">
  <f:actionListener for="myB" binding="#{actionBean.swapPages}"/>
  </gz:flip>
```

The element composite:actionSource exposes the h:commandButton component, and f:actionListener wires to it the appropriate action listener. Notice that the attribute actionListener has disappeared from h:commandButton.

A few words about composite:facet and composite:renderFacet. Close to the beginning of the section about the core library, I mentioned that facets are a means to let components do something special with a block of code. Now, suppose that you want to include a special word in several places within the composite component you are developing and that the page that uses the component should be able to define that word. You could do it like this:

```
<composite:interface>
  <composite:facet name="aWord"/>
  </composite:interface>
<composite:implementation>
  <!-- ...some code... -->
  <composite:renderFacet name="aWord"/>    <!-- say it here -->
  <!-- ...some code... -->
  <composite:renderFacet name="aWord"/>    <!-- and here -->
  <!-- ...some code... -->
  <composite:renderFacet name="aWord"/>    <!-- and again here -->
  </composite:implementation>
```

And this is how you would use the component:

```
<gz:myFacetedComponent>
  <f:facet name="aWord"><h:outputText value="#@%!"/></f:facet>
  </gz:myFacetedComponent>
```

JSF will take the body of the facet element defined in the using page and insert it where you invoke composite:renderFacet. If you like to insert those components *as a facet*, you need to use composite:insertFacet instead.

Normally, JSF ignores what is inside the body of your custom component, like in

```
<gz:myComponent>
  <h:outputText value="#@%! "/>
  <h:inputText value="#{aBean.whatever}"/>
  </gz:myComponent>
```

If you want to include it in your composite component, you can do it with

```
<composite:insertChildren/>
```

Summary

In this chapter, we have covered a lot of ground. I gave you a first taste of JSF with the simplef, simplefx, and simpleh applications. Then, after describing the JSF life cycle, I went on to talk about all four JSF tag libraries html, core, facelet, and composite.

For each library, I listed their tags and showed you with simple examples how to use the most common or significant tags.

In the next chapter, we'll go back to eshop to see how we can convert it to a JSF application.

CHAPTER 8

JSF and eshop

In Chapter 3, I introduced the eshop project, followed in Chapter 6 by eshopx, functionally identical to eshop except that I replaced the JSP pages containing scripting elements with JSP documents in XML format.

In this chapter, I am going to describe eshopf, a version of eshopx based on JSF. You will find both the WAR file and the expanded project in the software package for this chapter.

eshopf

Figure 8-1 shows the welcome page of eshopf. Although it is identical to that of eshop and eshopx, I include it here so that you can refer to it without having to flip forth and back across several chapters. Instead of commenting the listings of the whole application, I will concentrate on some interesting fragments as they relate to JSF.

Figure 8-1. eshopf's home page

As a basis for developing eshopf, I used eshopx. If you look at the welcome pages of eshopx and eshopf, both named index.jspx, you will see at once that, in order to use JSF, I added the two namespace declarations for the core and html JSF tag libraries and the element f:view to enclose all JSF actions.

But there is another update that is less obvious. Check out Listing 8-1, which shows the body of the f:view element.

Listing 8-1. *eshopf: Body of f:view in index.jspx*

```
<h:form>
  <jsp:include page="TopMenu.jspx" flush="true"/>
  <jsp:include page="LeftMenu.jspx" flush="true"/>
  </h:form>
<div class="content">
  <h1>Welcome to e-Shop</h1>
  </div>
```

In index.jspx of eshopx, the two jsp:includes were not wrapped inside a form. The reason for this change is due to the fact that, inside the jsp:included documents, as you will see below, two HTML a elements are to be converted to h:commandLink components, which need to be inside h:form. It seemed reasonable to use a single form.

The Top Menu

Listing 8-2 shows TopMenu.jspx and its use of the h:panelGroup component.

Listing 8-2. *eshopf: TopMenu.jspx*

```
<?xml version="1.0" encoding="UTF-8"?>
<jsp:root
  xmlns:jsp="http://java.sun.com/JSP/Page"
  xmlns:c="http://java.sun.com/jsp/jstl/core"
  xmlns:f="http://java.sun.com/jsf/core"
  xmlns:h="http://java.sun.com/jsf/html"
  version="2.1"
  >
<jsp:directive.page
  language="java"
  contentType="application/xhtml+xml;charset=UTF-8"
  />
<f:subview id="viewcart">
  <h:panelGroup styleClass="header">
    <h:outputText styleClass="logo" value="e-Shopping Center"/>
    <h:commandLink action="showCart" immediate="true" styleClass="cart link2">
      <h:outputText value="Show Cart "/>
      <h:graphicImage url="/images/cart.gif"/>
      </h:commandLink>
    </h:panelGroup>
  </f:subview>
</jsp:root>
```

The purpose of TopMenu.jspx is to provide a standardized access to the shopping cart.

Notice that I used f:subview to enclose all actions. Also notice that f:subview exists precisely to contain actions when they are included via jsp:include or any custom actions like c:include. Its purpose is equivalent to that of a pair of braces in Java: it limits the scope of its content. For example, the component IDs defined in one subview can be identical to those defined in other subviews of the same page.

With TopMenu.jspx, you don't necessarily need to wrap everything inside a subview, because the content of that document doesn't conflict with what is inside LeftMenu.jspx or with index.jspx. Nevertheless, it's good practice to avoid possible side effects of included modules. Subviews are required to have an ID, which is why I defined id="viewcart", even though we don't actually have any use for it.

The attribute styleClass is the JSF-equivalent of the HTML attribute class. Refer to the file /css/eshopf.jspx to see the style definition for each class.

The function of h:panelGroup is grouping together UI components. In this case, it makes possible to apply the style class header to all elements it contains.

The JSF-equivalent of the HTML element img is h:graphicImage.

Notice that the immediate attribute of h:commandLink is set to true. You will recall from the previous chapter that by doing so, you force the execution of the action listener already in the Apply Request Values phase. This guarantees that, regardless of what page the user is viewing, perhaps with a partially and inconsistently filled in form, control goes directly to the page of the shopping cart.

The action attribute of h:commandLink sets the outcome to be showCart. You have already encountered this mechanism in several examples of the previous chapter (e.g., the value goOn in Listing 7-1).

The Left Menu (part 1)

Listing 8-3 shows the top-level structure of LeftMenu.jspx, with the h:panelGrid component.

Listing 8-3. eshopf: LeftMenu.jspx - structure

```
<?xml version="1.0" encoding="UTF-8"?>
<jsp:root
  xmlns:jsp="http://java.sun.com/JSP/Page"
  xmlns:c="http://java.sun.com/jsp/jstl/core"
  xmlns:f="http://java.sun.com/jsf/core"
  xmlns:h="http://java.sun.com/jsf/html"
  version="2.1"
  >
<jsp:directive.page
  language="java"
  contentType="application/xhtml+xml;charset=UTF-8"
  />
<f:subview id="leftMenu">
  <h:panelGrid styleClass="menu">
    Here goes the Search Box - See Listing 8-4
    Here goes the Category Selection Box - See Listing 8-6
    </h:panelGrid>
  </f:subview>
</jsp:root>
```

As I showed in the previous chapter (see Listing 7-12), the h:panelGrid component is rendered with an HTML table; each component it contains is rendered as an HTML td element; and the optional attribute columns determines the length of the rows.

In LeftMenu.jspx, you could have written columns="1", but I omitted it because 1 is the default. Here you need h:panelGrid instead of h:panelGroup, because otherwise the search and category selection boxes would have not been rendered one below the other. The rows are filled in from left to right with the components in the order in which they appeared inside h:panelGrid, from top to bottom. The search box shown in Listing 8-4 consists of some descriptive text, an input text field, and a button to submit the search.

Listing 8-4. eshopf: LeftMenu.jspx - Search Box

```
<h:panelGroup styleClass="box">
  <h:outputText styleClass="box_title" value="Quick Search"/>
  <h:outputText styleClass="box_p" value="Book Title/Author:"/>
  <h:inputText size="15"
      styleClass="box_searchTxt"
      binding="#{shopManager.searchTxt}"
      />
  <h:commandButton
      type="submit" value="Search"
      styleClass="box_searchBtn"
      action="#{shopManager.searchBooks}"
      immediate="true"
      />
</h:panelGroup>
```

Notice that the action attribute of h:commandButton is set to a method of a managed bean instead of to a string literal. You encountered this mechanism in the section of the last chapter about Action Controllers and Action Listeners.

The attribute binding="#{shopManager.searchTxt}" shows how you can wire the input field to a data object on the server. You can establish a similar link with the value attribute, as I explained in the previous chapter (e.g., see Listing 7-1).

The difference is that with binding, you establish a two-way link, which lets your backing bean modify the value of the field, while with value, the backing bean cannot modify the data entered by the user. The shopManager bean doesn't need to modify the search string entered in LeftMenu.jspx, but you still use binding for reasons that will become clear in a moment.

As with the shopping cart in TopMenu.jspx, the attribute immediate="true" tells JSF that the action should be executed during Apply Request Values, rather than during Invoke Application, which is the default for all actions. In this way, you can be sure that the user is always able to resume shopping from any page, even if it contains invalid input fields (e.g., from the checkout page with empty fields).

This immediate execution of the search action is why you need to use the binding attribute in the h:inputText component. With the value attribute, you could access the search string with the method getValue, but only during Invoke Application, after Process Validation and Update Model Value have done their job. This would have been too late, because, as I've just explained, the search action takes place during Apply Request Values. By using the binding attribute, you make available to the shop manager *the whole h:inputText component*. As a result, you can invoke the method getSubmittedValue (see line 120 of Listing 8-5) already during Apply Request Value, when the search action is executed.

The attribute required="true" tells JSF that it is invalid for the user to leave the field empty (although it accepts spaces), and requiredMessage defines the corresponding error message. If you omit the requiredMessage attribute, the default error message is something like this:

j_id_jsp_548875039_1:address: Validation Error: Value is required.

Before completing the study of LeftMenu.jspx, we should look at the ShopManager Java bean, which I have already mentioned a couple of times.

The Shop Manager

The shop manager is a managed bean defined in the session scope.

In the previous section, I said that the following two attributes realize the linking of user inputs and server entities:

```
binding="#{shopManager.searchTxt}"
action="#{shopManager.searchBooks}"
```

To understand exactly how this works, let's go through the relevant parts of ShopManager.java, as shown in Listing 8-5.

Listing 8-5. eshopf fragment: Searching for Books in ShopManager.java

```
014: private List<Book>      books;
...
023: private HtmlInputText searchTxt = new HtmlInputText();
...
103: public HtmlInputText getSearchTxt() {
104:   return searchTxt;
105:   }
...
118: public String searchBooks() {
119:   categoryName=null;
120:   String searchKeyword = (String)searchTxt.getSubmittedValue();
121:   books = dataManager.getSearchResults(searchKeyword);
122:   return "listBooks";
123:   }
...
147: public void setSearchTxt(HtmlInputText val) {
148:   searchTxt = val;
149:   }
```

The whole ShopManager.java is in the folder eshopf project\eshopf\WEB-INF\classes\eshop\beans of the software package for this chapter.

The binding attribute listed means that during Update Model Values, the JSF servlet saves the search string typed by the user in the attribute searchTxt, which is of type javax.faces.component.html.HtmlInputText. It does so by using the method setSearchTxt. Later in the life cycle, during Render Response, it uses the getSearchText method to get the value needed to prefill the input text field in HTML. The HtmlInputTxt class has a series of properties and methods that enable you, among other things, to make it a required input and to validate the value typed in by the user.

The action attribute of the Search button causes the JSF servlet to execute the method searchBooks during Invoke Application. As you can see in Listing 8-5, the method simply obtains the value of the search string, executes the dataManager method to obtain the list of books from the database, saves the list in the object books, and returns the string "listBooks".

If you now look at the following fragment of faces-config.xml, you'll see that by returning "listBooks", the searchBooks method forces JSF to switch from the current page to ListBooks.jspx:

```
<navigation-rule>
  <navigation-case>
    <from-outcome>listBooks</from-outcome>
    <to-view-id>/jsp/ListBooks.jspx</to-view-id>
```

```
    <redirect/>
  </navigation-case>
</navigation-rule>
```

The presence (or absence) of the redirect element determines how this switch is done. If redirect is present, as in the example, JSF will send a redirect response to the client that will cause the browser to request the new page. Without the redirect element, during Render Response, JSF will directly use the content of the books object to render in HTML the list of books found in the database. But in that case, the list will effectively be a new rendering of the page that the user launched the search from. As a result, the URL shown in the browser will remain unchanged (e.g., http://localhost:8080/eshopf/).

You also could have included this line in the navigation-case element to impose a more restrictive condition on when the page switch should take place:

```
<from-action>#{shopManager.searchBooks}</from-action>
```

However, this is clearly unnecessary in this case, because no other method returns "listBooks".

The Left Menu (part 2)

Now that you know how eshopf binds user inputs and actions to data objects and methods, we can complete the study of LeftMenu.jspx. Listing 8-6 shows the part where you select books by category.

Listing 8-6. eshopf: LeftMenu.jspx - Category Selection Box

```
01: <h:panelGroup styleClass="box" id="categBox">
02:   <h:outputText styleClass="box_title" value="Categories"/>
03:   <h:dataTable value="#{shopManager.categories}" var="category">
04:     <h:column>
05:       <h:commandLink
06:           action="#{shopManager.selectCategory}"
07:           value="#{category.name}"
08:           immediate="true"
09:         />
10:     </h:column>
11:   </h:dataTable>
12: </h:panelGroup>
```

JSF renders the h:dataTable component (line 3) with an HTML table element, in which every column is identified by an h:column component (line 4). In addition to the table functionality as you know it from HTML, JSF also provides an iteration mechanism similar to that of c:forEach and linked to the data model. The mechanism is based on two attributes: value, which contains an EL expression that returns a list of items, and var, which contains the name of a variable to which the items of the list are assigned one by one in sequence.

In this case, the EL expression #{shopManager.categories} executes the following method of shopManager:

```
068 public ListDataModel<Category> getCategories() {
069   categoriesDataModel.setWrappedData(dataManager.getCategories());
070   return categoriesDataModel;
071 }
```

with categoriesDataModel defined as follows:

```
017 private ListDataModel<Category> categoriesDataModel = new ListDataModel<Category>();
```

The result is that the List of categories obtained from the database via the dataManager.getCategories method is assigned to the value attribute of h:dataTable.

JSF implements an index that goes through all the items of the list, and the attribute var="category" defines the name of the variable that gives access to the current item. In practical terms, this means that when the JSF servlet renders the h:dataTable component during the Render Response phase, it renders the h:commandLink of lines 5–9 for each category found in the database.

The Checkout Page

The Checkout.jspx module of the eshopf application asks the user to provide the payment data (name, address, and credit-card information). Listing 8-7 shows the code associated with one of the input items.

Listing 8-7. eshopf: Checkout.jspx—Address Entry

```
<h:panelGrid columns="3" rendered="#{!shopManager.shoppingCartEmpty}"
    style="width:auto">
  ...
  <h:outputText value="Delivery Address"/>
  <h:inputText id="address" required="true"
      value="#{shopManager.customer.deliveryAddress}"
      requiredMessage="Value is required!"
      />
  <h:message for="address" styleClass="error"/>
  ...
</h:panelGrid>
```

The value of the h:inputText component is associated with the deliveryAddress attribute of the object customer, which is an instantiation of the class eshop.beans.Customer. Because the attribute required of h:inputText is set to true, if the user omits to fill in the field, the value of the attribute requiredMessage is displayed. If you define the the JSF element h:message, its location within the page and its style determine where the error message is displayed and how, as shown in Figure 8-2.

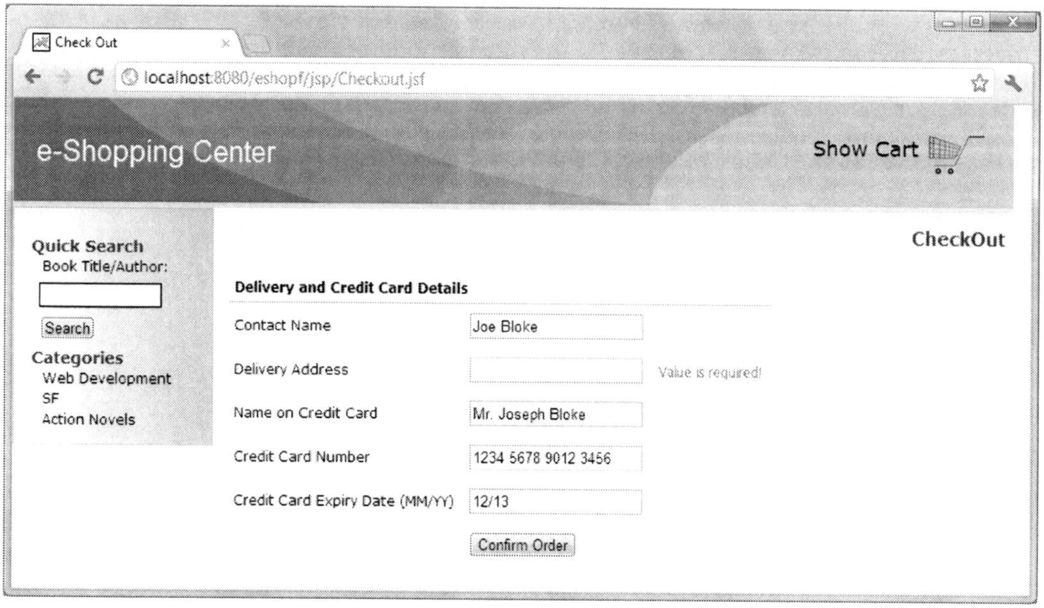

Figure 8-2. Incomplete input on Checkout.jspx

A potentially useful tag is `<f:verbatim>`. Its purpose is to let you insert HTML tags where a JSF component is expected. It isn't a practice that I encourage, but sometimes it can make your life much easier. For example, instead of using `h:panelGrid` to arrange components in a single column, you could insert `<f:verbatim><br/></f:verbatim>` between consecutive components.

web.xml

Listing 8-8 shows the file `WEB-INF\web.xml` for the application `eshopf`.

Listing 8-8. eshopf: web.xml

```
<?xml version="1.0" encoding="UTF-8"?>
<web-app version="2.5" xmlns="http://java.sun.com/xml/ns/javaee"
  xmlns:xsi="http://www.w3.org/2001/XMLSchema-instance"
  xsi:schemaLocation="http://java.sun.com/xml/ns/javaee ~CCC
http://java.sun.com/xml/ns/javaee/web-app_2_5.xsd">
  <display-name>eshop</display-name>
  <context-param>
    <param-name>javax.faces.DEFAULT_SUFFIX</param-name>
    <param-value>.jspx</param-value>
  </context-param>
  <servlet>
    <servlet-name>Faces Servlet</servlet-name>
    <servlet-class>javax.faces.webapp.FacesServlet</servlet-class>
    <load-on-startup>1</load-on-startup>
  </servlet>
```

```
  <servlet-mapping>
    <servlet-name>Faces Servlet</servlet-name>
    <url-pattern>*.jsf</url-pattern>
    </servlet-mapping>
  <login-config>
    <auth-method>BASIC</auth-method>
    </login-config>
  <resource-ref>
    <res-ref-name>jdbc/mysql</res-ref-name>
    <res-type>javax.sql.DataSource</res-type>
    <res-auth>Container</res-auth>
    </resource-ref>
</web-app>
```

Most of the tags should be familiar to you from previous examples.

The context-parameter element sets the file extension to be jspx, which is the extension of JSP documents, as those of eshopf. If you had left out this element, the extension would have been jsp, which is the extension of JSP pages.

The servlet element points to the class of the standard JSF servlet. By setting the element servlet-mapping to *.jsf, you specify that the JSP documents are to be accessed with that extension instead of their real extension, which is jspx. For example, when you select a book category in eshopf, the URL displayed in the browser is

```
http://localhost:8080/eshopf/jsp/ListBooks.jsf
```

while the JSP document is actually called ListBooks.jspx. This is called *extension mapping*.

The last element, resource-ref, states that the resource named jdbc/mysql is of type DataSource, and that Tomcat does its own authentication. Tomcat provides a Java Naming and Directory Interface (JNDI) InitialContext for each application. This means that once you've registered a resource in web.xml, you can provide in a separate context file all the information necessary to link it to your server environment. For eshopf, the information is shown in Listing 8-9.

Listing 8-9. context.xml

```
<?xml version="1.0" encoding="UTF-8"?>  <!-- MySQL database context -->
<!DOCTYPE Context [<!ELEMENT Context ANY> <!ATTLIST Context debug CDATA #IMPLIED
  reloadable CDATA #IMPLIED crossContext CDATA #IMPLIED>]>
<Context debug="5" reloadable="true" crossContext="true">
  <Resource
      name="jdbc/mysql"
      auth="Container"
      type="javax.sql.DataSource"
      username="root"
      password=""
      driverClassName="com.mysql.jdbc.Driver"
      url="jdbc:mysql://localhost:3306/shop"
      maxActive="8"
      maxIdle="4"
      />
  <Valve
      className="org.apache.catalina.valves.AccessLogValve"
      directory="logs"
      prefix="eshopf-access."
```

```
        suffix=".log"
        pattern="common"
        resolveHosts="false"
        />
</Context>
```

As you can see, the resource attributes url, username, and password specify the MySQL database used in all versions of E-shop application and how to access it. The context file must be named context.xml and placed in the META-INF folder of your application directory.

In eshop and eshopx, you defined the database parameters in web.xml with init-param elements and retrieved them in the eshop.ShopServlet.init method to make them available to the data manager (see Listings 3-9, 3-10, and 6-8).

In eshopf, as you have just seen, you define the same parameters (it actually is the same database) in context.xml and make them accessible to the application by defining a resource-ref element in web.xml.

Accordingly, you have to update the data manager's method getConnection. In practical terms, after removing all checks from the actual code for clarity, the line

```
conn = DriverManager.getConnection(getDbURL(), getDbUserName(), getDbPassword());
```

of eshop and eshopx is replaced in eshopf by the following four lines

```
Context ctx = new InitialContext();
Context envContext  = (Context)ctx.lookup("java:/comp/env");
DataSource ds = (DataSource)envContext.lookup("jdbc/mysql");
conn = ds.getConnection();
```

You find DataManager.java in the folder eshopf project\eshopf\WEB-INF\classes\eshop\model of the software package for this chapter.

The mechanism used in eshop and eshopx could not be used in eshopf because ShopServlet has been replaced by the JSF servlet. The mechanism relying on context.xml is in fact more flexible and elegant than the original one, but I think it was good for you to see both mechanisms.

Using and Creating Converters

As I said when describing the JSF life cycle, the JSF servlet executes the decode method of each component during Apply Request Values. The method saves the parameter values locally, but it first needs to convert the input strings to the corresponding types defined in the components, except when the components expect values of type String. JSF provides standard converters for the java.lang types Boolean, Byte, Character, Double, Enum, Float, Integer, Long, and Short, and for the java.math types BigDecimal and BigInteger.

The standard converters perform a series of checks that you can use to validate, at least in part, the user's input. To do so, you have to enable the reporting of converter messages.

For example, in the eshopf application, the user can update the number of copies of a book that is already in the shopping cart. Clearly, it doesn't make any sense to type a fractional number or a string that is not numeric. Therefore, you can write the input component in the ShoppingCart.jspx document as follows:

```
<h:inputText id="quantity" value="#{item.quantity}" size="2"
    required="true"
    requiredMessage="What? Nothing?"
    converterMessage="An integer, please!"
    />
```

Then, you only need to add this line to display the error messages of the standard Integer converter:

```
<h:message for="quantity" styleClass="error"/>
```

This is not yet a perfect solution, because the application still accepts negative integers. That is, you can type in -1, and the application will happily display negative prices! To see how to solve this problem, you'll have to wait for the section about validators.

Sometimes the standard converters are not sufficient. For example, you might like to save in a database a credit-card number without any dashes or spaces. To make a custom converter, you need to create an implementation of the javax.faces.Converter interface that overrides its methods getAsObject and getAsString. You must implement both directions of the converter. During Apply Request Values, JSF uses the getAsObject method to convert the input string to the data model object. During Render Response, JSF uses the getAsString method to do the conversion in the opposite direction, so that a string can be included in the HTML response. Once you complete the converter, you have to register it with the application.

To invoke the converter, you need to nest it as a property of f:converter or assign it to the converter attribute of the input component. Let's go through the three steps (i.e., develop, register, and invoke) one at a time. The converter will just clean up a credit-card number of any non-numeric character. Notice that it is the task of a validator to check that the credit-card number is valid. This normally takes place during Process Validation, while the conversions, as I just said, take place during phases Apply Request Values and Render Response.

Writing the Converter in Java

Listing 8-10 shows the full code of the converter used in eshopf to convert the credit-card number when checking out.

Listing 8-10. CCNumberConverter.java

```java
package eshop.converters;
import javax.faces.convert.Converter;
import javax.faces.context.FacesContext;
import javax.faces.component.UIComponent;
import javax.faces.convert.ConverterException;
public class CCNumberConverter implements Converter {
  //
  // getAsObject extracts from the input string all numeric characters
  public Object getAsObject(FacesContext ctx, UIComponent cmp,
      String val) {
    String convVal = null;
    if ( val != null ) {
      char[] chars = val.trim().toCharArray();
      convVal = "";
      for (int k = 0; k < chars.length; k++) {
        if (chars[k] >= '0' && chars[k] <= '9') {
          convVal += chars[k];
        }
      }
    }
/*
      System.out.println("CCNumberConverter.getAsObject: '"
          + val + "' -> '" + convVal + "'");
*/
```

```
        }
    return convVal;
    }
    //
    // getAsString inserts into the object string spaces to make it readable
    // default: nnnn nnnn nnnn nnnn, Amex: nnnn nnnnnn nnnnn
    public String getAsString(FacesContext ctx, UIComponent cmp, Object val)
        throws ConverterException {
      String convVal = null;
      if (val != null) {
        int[] spaces = {3, 7, 11, 99};
        int[] amex = {3, 9, 99};
        String sVal = null;
        try {
          sVal = (String)val; // The val object should be a String!
        }
        catch (ClassCastException e) {
          throw new ConverterException("CCNumberConverter: Conversion Error");
        }
        int kSpace = 0;
        char[] chars = sVal.toCharArray();
        if (chars.length == 15) spaces = amex;
        convVal = "";
        for (int k = 0; k < chars.length; k++) {
          convVal += chars[k];
          if (spaces[kSpace] == k) {
            convVal += ' ';
            kSpace++;
          }
        }
/*
        System.out.println("CCNumberConverter.getAsString: '"
            + sVal + "' -> '" + convVal + "'");
*/
      }
    return convVal;
    }
  }
```

The getAsObject method simply removes from the input string all the characters that are not decimal digits. The getAsString method inserts spaces to make the credit-card numbers more readable.

For example, if you during checkout type something such as 12-34. 56Abc78;90123--456, it will be reformatted to 1234 5678 9012 3456 as soon as you press the Check Out button. To verify that the object is correct, you can use the two println statements that you see commented out in the code. Here are a few examples taken from stdout_*yyyymmdd*.log in Tomcat's logs folder:

```
CCNumberConverter.getAsObject: 'abc1234 5678 1111x2222' -> '1234567811112222'
CCNumberConverter.getAsString: '1234567811112222' -> '1234 5678 1111 2222'
CCNumberConverter.getAsObject: '  1  23456789  012345' -> '123456789012345'
CCNumberConverter.getAsString: '123456789012345' -> '1234 567890 12345'
```

As you can see, the output of getAsObject, which is also the input of getAsString, is always stripped of non-digit characters, while the output of getAsString is always formatted with spaces. Once more, the checking of correctness is a task for the validator, not for the converter.

Registering the Converter with the Application

You can register the converter with the application by adding the following lines to the faces-config.xml file:

```
<converter>
  <converter-id>CCNumberConverter</converter-id>
  <converter-class>eshop.converters.CCNumberConverter</converter-class>
</converter>
```

You can choose any name you like inside the converter-id element, while the class in the converter-class element must match that of the converter that I described in the previous section.

Using the Converter

Here's how to write the input element for the credit-card number in the Checkout.jspx module:

```
<h:inputText id="ccnumber" required="true"
    value="#{shopManager.customer.ccNumber}"
    requiredMessage="Value is required!"
    converter="CCNumberConverter"
    />
```

As you can see, you only need to include the converter attribute and assign to it the converter-id you've registered in faces-config.xml. Alternatively, you could have nested an f:converter element inside the h:input component:

```
<f:converter converterId="CCNumberConverter"/>
```

The result would have been the same. This is a permissive converter, because it accepts almost everything without complaining. You could ask yourself whether a 30-character-long string that happens to include 16 digits is a valid credit-card number. I'll leave that up to you.

Using and Creating Validators

How do you ensure that the user of the eshopf application doesn't succeed in buying a negative number of books? Actually, the application should also reject any attempt of buying zero books. And what about checking the validity of a credit-card number? These are tasks for validators.

JSF features four types of validation mechanisms:

- Built-in validation components

- Application-level validation

- Custom validation components

- Validation methods in backing beans

Let's go through them one by one.

Built-In Validators

JSF provides the following validation components:

- f:validateBean: It delegates validation of the bean's local value to the Bean Validation API. You can download the documentation of the validation package from http://jcp.org/aboutJava/communityprocess/final/jsr303/.

- f:validateDoubleRange: It validates that a numeric input is within a given range. It is applicable to values that you can convert to a double.

- f:validateLength: It validates that the length of the input string is within a given range.

- f:validateLongRange: It validates that a numeric input is within a given range. It is applicable to values that you can convert to a long.

- f:validateRegex: It checks whether the String value of the component matches a given regular expression.

- f:validateRequired: It checks whether a value is present. It is equivalent to setting the required attribute to true.

To use these validation components, you simply nest them inside the h:input component you need to validate. For example, to check that only positive quantities can be entered in the eshopf shopping cart, you modify the h:inputText component in ShoppingCart.jspx as follows:

```
<h:inputText id="quantity" value="#{item.quantity}" size="2"
    required="true"
    requiredMessage="What? Nothing?"
    converterMessage="An integer, please!"
    validatorMessage="At least one copy!"
    >
  <f:validateLongRange minimum="1"/>
</h:inputText>
```

All three validators also accept the maximum attribute to set the upper limit of the range. For example, you can force the user to enter the correct number of credit-card digits by modifying the corresponding h:inputText in Checkout.jspx:

```
<h:inputText id="ccnumber" required="true"
    value="#{shopManager.customer.ccNumber}"
    converter="CCNumberConverter"
    requiredMessage="Value is required!"
    validatorMessage="Only 15 or 16 digits accepted!"
    >
  <f:validateLength minimum="15" maximum="16"/>
</h:inputText>
```

As the validation takes place after the conversion, the limits of 15 (for American Express) and 16 (for all other credit cards) are applied to the user's input after removing all nondigit characters.

Application-Level Validation

Application-level validation consists of performing checks inside the backing beans. This makes sense if you need to validate the business logic of your application, as opposed to validating formal correctness of individual fields. For example, before accepting an order, you might like to check that your bank has not blacklisted the credit-card number. Let's see how it works.

In eshopf, when the user clicks on the Check Out button after entering his or her name and credit-card data, the checkOut method of shopManager is executed, as shown in the following line taken from Checkout.jspx:

```
<h:commandButton value="Check Out" action="#{shopManager.checkOut}"/>
```

The method is as follows:

```
public String checkOut() {
  orderId = dataManager.insertOrder(customer, shoppingCart);
  if (orderId != 0) {
    customer = null;
    shoppingCart.clear();
  }
  return "orderConfirmation";
}
```

The dataManager.insertOrder method saves the order information in the database. If it fails, the dataManager will log a message to a Tomcat log file (i.e., logs\stdout_*yyyymmdd*.log) and return zero. If the database update succeeds, the value returned will be a unique orderId. In a real-world application, rather than 0, you would return error information to be passed on to the user.

The checkOut method returns an outcome that tells JSF what page should be displayed next.

If you want to do some application-level validation, you could insert its logic at the beginning of the checkOut method and make the database update and the method outcome dependent on the validation result. In case of validation failure, you could also send a message to the user, as shown in the following few lines:

```
FacesContext ctxt = FacesContext.getCurrentInstance();
FacesMessage mess = new FacesMessage();
mess.setSeverity(FacesMessage.SEVERITY_ERROR);
mess.setSummary("This is the summary text");
mess.setDetail("This is the detail text");
ctxt.addMessage(null, mess);
```

The message created in this way is a global message, not bound to any particular component, and you can display it with the following JSF component:

```
<h:messages globalOnly="true" styleClass="error"/>
```

If you want to create a message for a particular component, you need to replace the null argument of ctxt.addMessage with the clientId of the component. The clientId is a string containing all the IDs necessary to identify a particular component. For example, if you have <h:inputText id="it"...> inside <h:form id="fm"...>, the clientId of the input component is fm:it. I recommend that you don't use this option, because it forces you to hard-code the clientId in your Java method.

Custom Validators

In the section *Using and Creating Converters* of this chapter, I explained how to implement a custom converter. To implement a custom validator, you follow an almost identical process:

- Create an implementation of the interface `javax.faces.validator.Validator` that overrides the `validate` method.

- Register the validator in `faces-config.xml`.

- Within your JSF application, refer to the validator in an attribute or a component.

Suppose you want to ensure that the credit-card expiry date provided by the user during checkout is in the form MM/YY and that the card has not expired. Listing 8-11 shows the validator code.

Listing 8-11. CCExpiryValidator.java

```java
package eshop.validators;
import javax.faces.validator.Validator;
import javax.faces.context.FacesContext;
import javax.faces.component.UIComponent;
import javax.faces.application.FacesMessage;
import javax.faces.validator.ValidatorException;
import java.util.GregorianCalendar;
import java.util.Calendar;

public class CCExpiryValidator implements Validator {
  public CCExpiryValidator() {
  }
  public void validate(FacesContext cntx, UIComponent cmp, Object val) {
    String messS = null;
    String[] fields = ((String)val).split("/", 3);
    if (fields.length != 2) {
      messS = "Expected MM/YY!";
    }
    else {
      int month = 0;
      int year = 0;
      try {
        month = Integer.parseInt(fields[0]);
        year = Integer.parseInt(fields[1]);
      }
      catch (NumberFormatException e) {
      }
      if (month <= 0 || month > 12) {
        messS = "Month " + fields[0] + " not valid!";
      }
      else if (year < 0 || year > 99) {
        messS = "Year " + fields[1] + " not valid!";
      }
      else {
        GregorianCalendar cal = new GregorianCalendar();
        int thisMonth = cal.get(Calendar.MONTH) + 1;
```

```
      int thisYear = cal.get(Calendar.YEAR) - 2000;
      if (year < thisYear  ||  year == thisYear && month < thisMonth) {
        messS = "Credit card expired!";
        }
      }
    }
  if (messS != null) {
    FacesMessage mess = new FacesMessage(FacesMessage.SEVERITY_ERROR, messS, messS);
    throw new ValidatorException(mess);
    }
  }

}
```

To register the validator with the application, you only need to add the following lines to faces-config.xml—for example, immediately below the registration of the converter:

```
<validator>
  <validator-id>CCExpiryValidator</validator-id>
  <validator-class>eshop.validators.CCExpiryValidator</validator-class>
</validator>
```

Then, to validate the credit-card expiry date, you modify the h:inputText component used in Checkout.jspx as follows:

```
<h:inputText id="ccexpiry" required="true"
    value="#{shopManager.customer.ccExpiryDate}"
    requiredMessage="Value is required!"
    >
  <f:validator validatorId="CCExpiryValidator"/>
</h:inputText>
```

You'll be rewarded with error messages like those shown in Figure 8-3 (which I obtained by taking several screenshots and then putting them together with a graphics program).

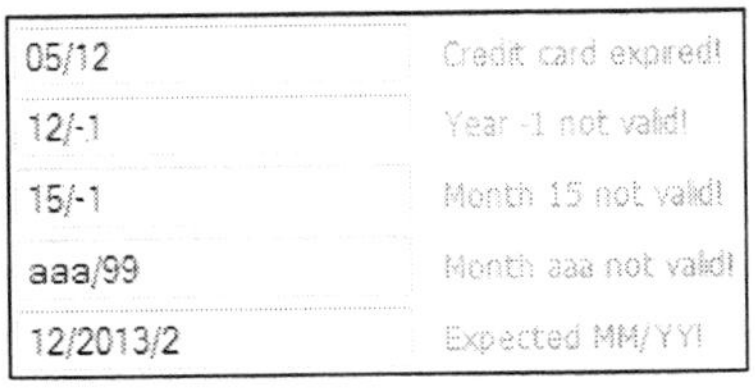

05/12	Credit card expired!
12/-1	Year -1 not valid!
15/-1	Month 15 not valid!
aaa/99	Month aaa not valid!
12/2013/2	Expected MM/YY!

Figure 8-3. Expiry-date validation in Checkout.jspx

Validation Methods in Backing Beans

Instead of creating a new class as described in the previous section, you can add a method to a backing bean. In this case, you could do the following:

- Copy the validate method from CCExpiryValidator.java to ShopManager.java, inside the class ShopManager, and rename it validateCCExpiry.

- Copy the imports of `FacesContext`, `UIComponent`, `FacesMessage`, `GregorianCalendar`, and `Calendar` from `CCExpiryValidator.java` to the beginning of `shopManager.java`.

- Replace in `validateCCExpiry` the line that throws the `ValidatorException` with `ctxt.addMessage(cmp.getClientId(ctxt), mess);`.

That's it! To use this validator instead of the previous one, modify the `h:inputText` in `Checkout.jspx` as follows:

```
<h:inputText id="ccexpiry" required="true"
    value="#{shopManager.customer.ccExpiryDate}"
    validator="#{shopManager.validateCCExpiry}"
    requiredMessage="Value is required!"
/>
```

The validator element in `faces-config.xml`, the element `f:validator` in `Checkout.jspx`, and the module `CCExpiryValidator.java` are then no longer needed.

■ **Tip** To modify the eshop* projects, use Eclipse instead of getting bogged down with classpaths when recompiling Java modules. Duplicate the project by selecting its icon in Eclipse's Project Explorer bar, and then copy and paste it. Eclipse will ask you to provide a new name for the duplicate project. In this way, it will be easier to go back to the original should you want to.

Creating Custom Components

The functionality of a component is centered on converting a user's inputs (i.e., the HTTP request parameters) to component values (via the decode method during Apply Request Values) and converting component values back to HTML (via the encode method during Render Response).

In the previous chapter, you saw how to create custom components with the facelets and composite JSF tag libraries. In this chapter, I want to give you an example of how to create a new JSF component without those tags. This will give you a better understanding of how JSF works. I am always a great defender of doing things "by hand" at least once!

When you design a JSF component, you can choose to move encoding and decoding to a separate renderer class. The advantage of this approach is that you can develop more than one renderer for the same component, each with a different representation in HTML. You will then have the same behavior associated with different ways of reading data from the request and writing it to the response.

In general, considering that JSF is open source, you might consider modifying an existing component instead of developing a new one; or, thanks to the separation of components and renderers, perhaps you can modify an existing renderer.

The root class of all JSF components is the abstract `javax.faces.component.UIComponent`, and the root class of all renderers is `javax.faces.render.Renderer`. To develop a component, though, you're *always* better off extending an existing component or, at the very least, the `UIComponentBase` class, which provides default implementations of all abstract methods of `UIComponent`. In this way, you only develop code for the methods you need to override. The same goes with the renderer.

To complete the picture of how to develop your custom component, you also need to create a custom tag that's useable with JSP. The root class of all tag classes is `javax.faces.webapp.UIComponentELTag`.

In summary, to develop a custom component, you need to follow these steps:

1. Create a component class that subclasses `UIComponent` by extending an existing component.

2. Register the component in `faces-config.xml`.

3. Create a renderer class that subclasses `Renderer` and overrides the methods for encoding and decoding.

4. Register the renderer in `faces-config.xml`.

5. Create a custom tag that subclasses `UIComponentELTag`.

6. Create a TLD for the custom tag.

One last word about components and renderers: unless you really think that you'll reuse the same component for different applications, it will be much easier to keep the renderer inside the component. I'll first show you what to do when they're separate, and then I'll tell you how to keep them together.

I'll show you how to develop a component that combines the functionality of all three standard components needed for accepting a user's input: a label explaining what is expected, the text field to accept the input, and a message to report input errors. In other words, I'll show you how to replace the following JSF code:

```
<h:outputText value="Contact Name"/>
  <h:inputText id="name" required="true"
      value="#{shopManager.customer.contactName}"
      requiredMessage="Value is required!"
      />
  <h:message for="name" styleClass="error"/>
```

with this custom component:

```
<eshop:inputEntry label="Contact Name" required="true"
    value="#{shopManager.contactName}"
    errorStyleClass="error" requiredMessage="Value is required!"
    />
```

I'll also show you how this new `eshop:inputEntry` component prints an asterisk beside the label if you set required to true.

Component

The component is actually the easiest part. Let's go through the methods one by one (see Listing 8-12).

Listing 8-12. InputEntryComponent.java

```
01: package eshop.components;
02: import javax.faces.component.UIInput;
03: import javax.faces.context.FacesContext;
04:
05: public class InputEntryComponent extends UIInput {
```

```
06:    private String label;
07:    public InputEntryComponent(){
08:       this.setRendererType("eshop.inputEntry");
09:       }
10:    public String getLabel() {
11:       return label;
12:       }
13:    public void setLabel(String label) {
14:       this.label = label;
15:       }
16:
17:    // Overridden methods
18:    public String getFamily() {
19:       return "eshop.inputEntry";
20:       }
21:    public void restoreState(FacesContext ctxt, Object state) {
22:       Object val[] = (Object[])state;
23:       super.restoreState(ctxt, val[0]);
24:       label = (String)val[1];
25:       }
26:    public Object saveState(FacesContext ctxt) {
27:       Object val[] = new Object[2];
28:       val[0] = super.saveState(ctxt);
29:       val[1] = label;
30:       return ((Object)val);
31:       }
32:    }
```

InputEntryComponent is the component initialization. Its only task is to register with the component the string that identifies the renderer. The only property of the component defined in InputEntryComponent.java is label. This is because you're extending UIInput, which takes care of defining everything that has to do with the input field.

The getter and setter methods of the label property are getLabel and setLabel. Nothing special there.

You use the getFamily method to find all the renderers associated with this component. We're going to create only one renderer, but it's still appropriate to define a family rather than inherit the family of UIInput, because you couldn't use UIInput's renderers with InputEntryComponent. By overriding the default getFamily, you ensure that only your renderer is visible.

The state of the component consists of the state of UIInput plus the label property. Therefore, you define its state as an array of two objects. The saveState method forms the array and returns it, so that JSF can save it. The restoreState method receives the state, unpacks it, and stores it locally. Notice how the operations that have to do with UIInput are always delegated to it.

Now that you have the component, you have to register it. You do this by inserting the following lines into faces-config.xml:

```
<component>
  <component-type>eshop.inputEntry</component-type>
  <component-class>eshop.components.InputEntryComponent</component-class>
  </component>
```

Renderer

The renderer is a bit trickier than the component. To implement it, you define a class that extends javax.faces.render.Renderer. Start by looking at the three methods that you need to override (see Listing 8-13).

Listing 8-13. InputEntryRenderer.java—Overridden Methods

```
59: public void decode(FacesContext ctxt, UIComponent cmp) {
60:    InputEntryComponent ieCmp = (InputEntryComponent)cmp;
61:    Map<String, String> requestMap =
62:        ctxt.getExternalContext().getRequestParameterMap();
63:    String clientId = cmp.getClientId(ctxt);
64:    String val = (String)requestMap.get(clientId);
65:    ((UIInput)ieCmp).setSubmittedValue(val);
66:    }
67:
68: public void encodeBegin(FacesContext ctxt, UIComponent cmp)
69:     throws IOException {
70:    InputEntryComponent ieCmp = (InputEntryComponent)cmp;
71:    ResponseWriter respWr = ctxt.getResponseWriter();
72:    encodeLabel(respWr, ieCmp);
73:    encodeInput(respWr, ieCmp);
74:    encodeMessage(ctxt, respWr, ieCmp);
75:    respWr.flush();
76:    }
77:
78: public Object getConvertedValue(FacesContext ctxt, UIComponent cmp,
79:     Object subVal) throws ConverterException {
80:    Object convVal = null;
81:    ValueExpression valExpr = cmp.getValueExpression("value");
82:    if (valExpr != null) {
83:      Class valType = valExpr.getType(ctxt.getELContext());
84:      if (valType != null) {
85:        convVal = subVal;
86:        if (!valType.equals(Object.class) && !valType.equals(String.class)) {
87:          Converter converter = ((UIInput)cmp).getConverter();
88:          converter =  ctxt.getApplication().createConverter(valType);
89:          if (converter != null ) {
90:            convVal = converter.getAsObject(ctxt, cmp, (String)subVal);
91:            }
92:          }
93:        }
94:      }
95:    return convVal;
96:    }
```

As I said before, the only property that you add to UIInput is label, which the user cannot modify. Therefore, not surprisingly, as you don't need to do anything concerning the label, you only need to decode the input field. In line 60, you typecast the component object to InputEntryComponent, so that you can work with it more comfortably. In line 61–62, you get the map of the input parameters, and in line 63, you get from the FacesContext the clientId of the component, so that in line 64, you can finally get the input string as typed by the user. After that, you only need to save the input string as a submitted value. Remember that this method is executed during Apply Request Values.

The encoding process requires more work than the decoding process, because you have to send to the HTTP response all three components that were combined to form InputEntryComponent. This takes place during Render response. In line 71 of the encodeBegin method, you get the response writer from the FacesContext. After executing the functions that write the three subcomponents, you flush the output, and you're done.

Listing 8-14 shows the method to encode the label. It opens the HTML label element with the startElement method, writes the label with a plain write method, writes an asterisk—but only if the component is required—and closes the label element with the endElement method. The result is something like <label>Contact Name*</label>.

Listing 8-14. InputEntryRenderer.java—EncodeLabel

```
31: private void encodeLabel(ResponseWriter respWr, InputEntryComponent cmp)
32:      throws IOException {
33:   respWr.startElement("label", cmp);
34:   respWr.write(cmp.getLabel());
35:   if (cmp.isRequired()) {
36:     respWr.write("*");
37:     }
38:   respWr.endElement("label");
39:   }
```

Listing 8-15 shows the method to encode the input field. It opens the HTML input element, adds the attributes with the writeAttribute method, and closes the element. The three parameters of writeAttribute are the name and value of the HTML attribute and the name of the component property. The result is something like the following element:

```
<input type="text" id="form:nameEntry" name="form:nameEntry" value=""/>
```

Listing 8-15. InputEntryRenderer.java—EncodeInput

```
18: private void encodeInput(ResponseWriter respWr, InputEntryComponent cmp)
19:      throws IOException {
20:   FacesContext ctxt = FacesContext.getCurrentInstance();
21:   respWr.startElement("input", cmp);
22:   respWr.writeAttribute("type", "text", "type");
23:   respWr.writeAttribute("id", cmp.getClientId(ctxt), "id");
24:   respWr.writeAttribute("name", cmp.getClientId(ctxt), "name");
25:   if(cmp.getValue() != null) {
26:     respWr.writeAttribute("value", cmp.getValue().toString(), "value");
27:     }
28:   respWr.endElement("input");
29:   }
```

Listing 8-16 shows the method to encode the error message. It gets the list of all messages queued for the component but only displays the first one. If you want to display them all, you just need to replace the if keyword with a while. To display the message, the method opens the HTML span element, adds the class attribute to show the message with the correct style, displays the message itself, and closes the element. The result is something like the following element:

```
<span class="error">Value is required!</span>
```

Listing 8-16. InputEntryRenderer.java—EncodeMessage

```
41: private void encodeMessage(FacesContext ctxt, ResponseWriter respWr,
42:     InputEntryComponent cmp) throws IOException {
43:   Iterator it = ctxt.getMessages(cmp.getClientId(ctxt));
44:   // Notice: an if instead of a while
45:   if (it.hasNext()){
46:     FacesMessage mess = (FacesMessage)it.next();
47:     if (!cmp.isValid()) {
48:       String errorStyleClass =
49:         (String)cmp.getAttributes().get("errorStyleClass");
50:       respWr.startElement("span", cmp);
51:       respWr.writeAttribute("class", errorStyleClass, "class");
52:       respWr.write(mess.getDetail());
53:       respWr.endElement("span");
54:     }
55:   }
56: }
```

To register the renderer, insert the following lines into `faces-config.xml`:

```
<render-kit>
  <renderer>
    <component-family>eshop.inputEntry</component-family>
    <renderer-type>eshop.inputEntry</renderer-type>
    <renderer-class>eshop.renderers.InputEntryRenderer</renderer-class>
  </renderer>
</render-kit>
```

Tag

The custom component is done, but to use it with JSP, you need to define a corresponding custom tag. I already explained how to define custom libraries in Chapter 4. Therefore, I won't spend too many words here on the overall process. Listing 8-17 shows the Java class that implements the tag handler.

Listing 8-17. InputEntryTag.java

```
package eshop.tags;
import javax.el.ValueExpression;
import javax.faces.component.UIComponent;
import javax.faces.webapp.UIComponentELTag;

public class InputEntryTag extends UIComponentELTag {
  private ValueExpression  errorStyleClass;
  private ValueExpression  label;
  private ValueExpression  required;
  private ValueExpression  requiredMessage;
  private ValueExpression  value;

  // Setters
  public void setErrorStyleClass(ValueExpression errorStyleClass) {
    this.errorStyleClass = errorStyleClass;
```

```
    }
    public void setLabel(ValueExpression label) {
      this.label = label;
    }
    public void setRequired(ValueExpression required) {
      this.required = required;
    }
    public void setRequiredMessage(ValueExpression requiredMessage) {
      this.requiredMessage = requiredMessage;
    }
    public void setValue(ValueExpression value) {
      this.value = value;
    }

    // Overridden methods
    public String getComponentType() {
      return "eshop.inputEntry";
    }
    public String getRendererType() {
      return "eshop.inputEntry";
    }
    protected void setProperties(UIComponent cmp) {
      super.setProperties(cmp);
      if (errorStyleClass != null) {
        cmp.setValueExpression("errorStyleClass", errorStyleClass);
      }
      if (label != null) {
        cmp.setValueExpression("label", label);
      }
      if (required != null) {
        cmp.setValueExpression("required", required);
      }
      if (requiredMessage != null) {
        cmp.setValueExpression("requiredMessage", requiredMessage);
      }
      if (value != null) {
        cmp.setValueExpression("value", value);
      }
    }
    public void release() {
      super.release();
      errorStyleClass = null;
      label = null;
      requiredMessage = null;
      value = null;
      required = null;
    }
}
```

As you can see, you define a property for each attribute supported by the tag, but not for the id attribute. The reason is that UIComponentELTag already defines it. Notice that you only have setter methods, without the corresponding getters. This is because you never need the get methods. The setProperties method copies the attribute values from the tag to the component, and the release method cleans up what is no longer needed.

Before you can use the custom tag in JSP, you still need to create a TLD to be placed in WEB-INF\tlds\. See Listing 8-18.

Listing 8-18. *eshop.tld*

```
01: <?xml version="1.0" encoding="UTF-8"?>
02: <taglib xmlns="http://java.sun.com/xml/ns/javaee"
03:     xmlns:xsi="http://www.w3.org/2001/XMLSchema-instance"
04:     xsi:schemaLocation="http://java.sun.com/xml/ns/javaee ➡
http://java.sun.com/xml/ns/j2ee/web-jsptaglibrary_2_1.xsd"
05:     version="2.1">
06:   <description>Eshopf Custom Tags</description>
07:   <tlib-version>1.0</tlib-version>
08:   <short-name>eshop</short-name>
09:   <tag>
10:     <display-name>inputEntry</display-name>
11:     <name>inputEntry</name>
12:     <tag-class>eshop.tags.InputEntryTag</tag-class>
13:     <body-content>empty</body-content>
14:     <attribute>
15:       <name>id</name>
16:       <required>false</required>
17:       <rtexprvalue>true</rtexprvalue>
18:     </attribute>
19:     <attribute>
20:       <name>value</name>
21:       <required>false</required>
22:       <deferred-value><type>java.lang.Object</type></deferred-value>
23:     </attribute>
24:     <attribute>
25:       <name>required</name>
26:       <required>false</required>
27:       <deferred-value><type>boolean</type></deferred-value>
28:     </attribute>
29:     <attribute>
30:       <name>label</name>
31:       <required>false</required>
32:       <deferred-value><type>java.lang.String</type></deferred-value>
33:     </attribute>
34:     <attribute>
35:       <name>errorStyleClass</name>
36:       <required>false</required>
37:       <deferred-value><type>java.lang.String</type></deferred-value>
38:     </attribute>
39:     <attribute>
40:       <name>requiredMessage</name>
41:       <required>false</required>
42:       <deferred-value><type>java.lang.String</type></deferred-value>
43:     </attribute>
```

```
44:      </tag>
45:   </taglib>
```

In lines 9, 12, and 13, you define the eshop:inputEntry tag and associate it with the tag handler. The eshop.tags.InputEntryTag string means that you have to place InputEntryTag.class in the folder WEB-INF\classes\eshop\tags\. In the rest of the TLD, you define all attributes and set them to accept the JSF expressions as values, with the exception of id.

With this, you're ready to use the new JSF UI component h:inputEntry. You only need to add the eshop namespace declaration to the jsp:root element at the beginning of the JSP document:

```
xmlns:eshop="urn:jsptld:/WEB-INF/tlds/eshop.tld"
```

The result will look like the field shown in Figure 8-4. The version of eshopf you find in the software package for this chapter already has everything in it. To see the field, you only need to remove the comments around the relevant lines of code in Checkout.jspx.

Figure 8-4. *Checkout.jspx—eshop:inputEntry*

The disadvantage of the new component compared to separate label, input, and message fields is that it isn't possible to align the input fields vertically. You could add an attribute to the tag to specify the space available for the label, but I'll leave that up to you.

Now that you're done, you might ask, "Why does eshop:inputEntry only support a handful of attributes, while h:inputText supports 40?" That's a good point. We could have added further attributes, such as the size of the input field, which h:inputText passes on to HTML transparently, but my purpose was to be able to replace with a single component the three fields as they are used in eshopf. More attributes than strictly necessary would have only used up space without adding anything to what you can learn from the example.

Inline Renderer

It's possible to include the rendering functionality inside the component class, so that the component effectively renders itself. As I mentioned before, unless you plan to use more than one renderer with the same component, you might choose not to bother with a separate renderer.

To make eshop:inputEntry self-rendering, you need to do the following:

1. Move the methods of InputEntryRenderer.java to InputEntryComponent.java. You'll need to make some cosmetic changes that I'll explain in a moment. After you have done the move, you can delete the renderer file.

2. Add the encodeEnd method to InputEntryComponent.java (more about this in a moment).

3. Return null in the getRendererType method of InputEntryTag.java.

4. Remove the registration of the renderer from faces-config.xml.

The UIInput class, which you extend to make the component, supports the three methods decode, encodeBegin, and getConvertedValue that you used in the separate renderer, but without the UIComponent parameter. It makes sense because the component object is directly accessible with the keyword this.

When you remove the cmp parameter from the three methods, you should also remove the line

```
InputEntryComponent ieCmp = (InputEntryComponent)cmp;
```

from decode and encodeBegin, because it has become useless. Then, make a global replace of ieCmp with this and replace the four occurrences of cmp in decode and getConvertedValue with this.

You need the encodeEnd method to override the method in UIComponentBase, which throws a NullPointerException. In fact, you don't need to do anything in encodeEnd; you can just write an empty method:

```
public void encodeEnd(FacesContext context) throws IOException { }
```

Note that you only need this method when a component renders itself, not when it uses a separate renderer class.

In InputEntryTag.java, the getRendererType method returns "eshop.inputEntry". If the method is to use its internal rendering methods, getRendererType has to return null. Finally, remove the seven lines of the render-kit element from faces-config.xml.

faces-config.xml

I've already explained all the elements of this file when I talked about the Shop Manager (<managed-bean> and <navigation-rule>) and when registering a converter (<converter>), a validator (<validator>), a component (<component>), and a renderer (<render-kit>). In this section, I only want to summarize with Table 8-1 the navigation rules of eshopf.

Table 8-1. *Eshopf Navigation Rules*

from-outcome	to-view-id	redirect
checkOut	/jsp/Checkout.jspx	Yes
listBooks	/jsp/ListBooks.jspx	Yes
orderConfirmation	/jsp/OrderConfirmation.jspx	No
showBook	/jsp/BookDetails.jspx	Yes
showCart	/jsp/ShoppingCart.jspx	Yes

Summary

In this chapter, I described how to use JSF to reimplement the user interface of eshopx, to create the application eshopf.

I showed how to work with the standard JSF components and then explained how to create your own converters, validators, and components. On the way, I also briefly described how to tie together the application with web.xml, faces-config.xml, and context.xml.

Based on the content of this chapter and the previous one, you should now be able to write your own application.

In the next chapter, I will talk about Tomcat.

■ ■ ■

CHAPTER 9

Tomcat

I've been using Tomcat in all the previous chapters to show you examples of servlets, JSP pages, and documents. Now it's time to talk about Tomcat itself.

Tomcat, an open-source Servlet/JSP server/container from Apache foundation, is essentially three things:

- A web server
- An application that executes Java servlets
- An application that converts JSP pages and documents into Java servlets

In this chapter, I'll describe the basics of Tomcat's architecture and its directory structure. I'll then show you examples of how to do a couple of useful things.

At the moment of writing this chapter, the latest release of Tomcat is 7.0.28, which runs on Java SE 6 (or later), implements the Servlet 3.0 and JSP 2.2 specifications, and supports EL 2.2.

Tomcat is a project of the Apache Software Foundation. Therefore, the authoritative source for obtaining further information on Tomcat is `http://tomcat.apache.org/`, which provides extensive documentation (`http://tomcat.apache.org/tomcat-7.0-doc/`).

Tomcat's Architecture and server.xml

Tomcat's architecture consists of a series of functional components that can be combined according to well-defined rules. The structure of each server installation is defined in the file `server.xml`, which is located in the `conf` subdirectory of Tomcat's installation folder.

In the rest of this section, I'll go through the components. Listing 9-1 shows the default `server.xml` (after removing the comments). I'll refer to it when describing the various components.

Listing 9-1. Default server.xml

```
01: <?xml version='1.0' encoding='utf-8'?>
02: <Server port="8005" shutdown="SHUTDOWN">
03:   <Listener className="org.apache.catalina.core.AprLifecycleListener" SSLEngine="on" />
04:   <Listener className="org.apache.catalina.core.JasperListener" />
05:   <Listener className="org.apache.catalina.core.JreMemoryLeakPreventionListener" />
06:   <Listener className="org.apache.catalina.mbeans.GlobalResourcesLifecycleListener" />
07:   <Listener className="org.apache.catalina.core.ThreadLocalLeakPreventionListener" />
08:   <GlobalNamingResources>
09:     <Resource name="UserDatabase" auth="Container"
```

```
10:             type="org.apache.catalina.UserDatabase"
11:             description="User database that can be updated and saved"
12:             factory="org.apache.catalina.users.MemoryUserDatabaseFactory"
13:             pathname="conf/tomcat-users.xml" />
14: </GlobalNamingResources>
15: <Service name="Catalina">
16:    <Connector port="8080" protocol="HTTP/1.1"
17:                connectionTimeout="20000"
18:                redirectPort="8443" />
19:    <Connector port="8009" protocol="AJP/1.3" redirectPort="8443" />
20:    <Engine name="Catalina" defaultHost="localhost">
21:      <Realm className="org.apache.catalina.realm.LockOutRealm">
22:        <Realm className="org.apache.catalina.realm.UserDatabaseRealm"
23:              resourceName="UserDatabase"/>
24:      </Realm>
25:      <Host name="localhost"  appBase="webapps"
26:           unpackWARs="true" autoDeploy="true">
27:        <Valve className="org.apache.catalina.valves.AccessLogValve" directory="logs"
28:              prefix="localhost_access_log." suffix=".txt"
29:              pattern="%h %l %u %t &quot;%r&quot; %s %b" />
30:      </Host>
31:    </Engine>
32:  </Service>
33: </Server>
```

Figure 9-1 shows how the major Tomcat components are organized in hierarchical fashion.

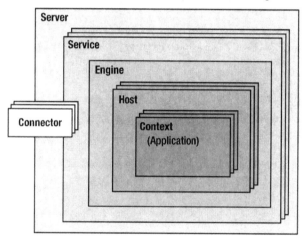

Figure 9-1. Tomcat's architecture

Context

A Context is the innermost element of a group of Tomcat components called *containers,* and it represents a single web application.

Tomcat automatically instantiates and configures a standard context upon loading your application. As part of the configuration, Tomcat also processes the properties defined in the \WEB-INF\web.xml file of your application folder and makes them available to the application. For example, the web.xml file for eshopf defines, among other properties, a context parameter and a resource reference (see Listing 8-8).

Connector

A Connector is a component associated with a TCP port that handles the communication between applications and clients (e.g., remote browsers). The default configuration of Tomcat includes a connector to handle HTTP communication. By default, this connector waits for requests coming through port 8080. This is why the URLs of our examples always start with http://localhost:8080/.

Later in this chapter, I'll show you how to change the port number from 8080 to 80, which is the default port for HTTP. Then, you'll be able to access the examples via http://localhost/.

The presence of an HTTP connector is what makes Tomcat a web server. Note that the requests for all applications go through a single instance of this connector. Each new request causes the instantiation of a new thread that remains alive within the connector for the duration of the request.

Articles about Tomcat often refer to this connector as "Coyote". Lines 16–18 of Listing 9-1 show how the HTTP connector is defined in server.xml. The connectionTimeout attribute set to 20,000 means that a session is terminated after 5 hours, 33 minutes, and 20 seconds of inactivity, while redirectPort="8443" means that incoming requests that require Secure Socket Layer (SSL) transport are redirected to port 8443. I'll show you later how you can enable SSL on Tomcat so that it can handle the HTTPS protocol.

By default, Tomcat defines another connector—Apache JServ Protocol (AJP)—which is used to communicate with a web server, such as the Apache HTTP server (see line 19 of Listing 9-1). This connector lets Tomcat only handle dynamic web pages and lets a pure HTML server (e.g., the Apache Web Server) handle the requests for static pages. This maximizes the efficiency with which the requests are handled. Nevertheless, you'll probably be better off keeping it simple and relying on Tomcat to handle all requests, especially if most of your pages are dynamic. Also, the efficiency of Tomcat has been improving with each release. If you don't plan on using a web server together with Tomcat, you can comment out this connector.

Host

A Host container represents a virtual host, which is the association of a name such as www.myDomain.com with the server. A host can contain any number of contexts (i.e., applications).

You can define several hosts on the same server. For example, if you have registered the domain myDomain.com, you can define host names such as w1.myDomain.com and w2.myDomain.com. Later in this chapter, I'll show you how to define a virtual host, but keep in mind that it will only be accessible from the Internet if a domain name server maps its name to the IP address of your computer. For this purpose, you should be able to use the DNS of the company you registered your domain with (i.e., your registrar), but only if you've obtained a fixed IP address from your ISP.

The default configuration of Tomcat includes the host named localhost (see lines 25–30 of Listing 9-1), which you've encountered in many examples. I just said that a host is reachable by name if it is mapped by a DNS to the IP address of your computer. It is obviously not possible to use such a mechanism that relies on external systems to map localhost, which is local by definition. The association between localhost and your computer is done instead by writing an entry in the file C:\Windows\System32\drivers\etc\hosts. I'll come back to this file when I will explain how to define a virtual host.

The Host attribute appBase defines the application directory within the Tomcat installation folder. Each application is then identified by its path within that directory. The only exception is the path ROOT, which is mapped to the empty string. The application base directory for localhost is webapps. This means that the application in the following directory:

`C:\Program Files\Apache Software Foundation\Tomcat 6.0\webapps\ROOT\`

is identified by the empty string. Therefore, its URL is http://localhost:8080/.

For other applications, which reside in directories other than ROOT, as in

`C:\Program Files\Apache Software Foundation\Tomcat 6.0\webapps\appl-dir\`

the URL is like http://localhost:8080/appl-dir/.

You can also assign an absolute directory to appBase.

The attribute unpackWARs="true" means that if you drop a WAR file in the appBase directory, Tomcat will automatically expand it into a normal folder. If you set this attribute to false, the application will run directly from the WAR file. This obviously means a slower execution of the application, because Tomcat needs to unzip the WAR file at execution time.

The attribute autoDeploy="true" means that if you drop an application in the appBase directory while Tomcat is running, it will be deployed automatically. Actually, this definition is redundant because the default for autoDeploy is true.

Engine

The Engine is the highest level of container. It can contain several hosts, but it cannot be contained by any other container component.

An engine must contain one or more hosts, one of which is designated as the default host. The default Tomcat configuration includes the engine Catalina (see line 20 of Listing 9-1), which contains the host localhost (obviously designated to be the default host because it is the only one).

The Catalina engine handles all incoming requests received via the HTTP connector and sends back the corresponding responses. It forwards each request to the correct host and context on the basis of the information contained in the request header.

This Catalina engine is the servlet engine that I mentioned in Chapter 1 (see Figure 1-8).

Service

The purpose of the Service component is to associate one or more connectors to a particular engine.

Tomcat's default configuration includes the service Catalina (see line 15 of Listing 9-1, and yes, it is named like the engine), which associates the HTTP and AJP connectors to the Catalina engine. Accordingly, Connector and Engine are subelements of the Service element.

Server

The Server is the top component, which represents an instance of Tomcat. It can contain one or more services, each with its own engine and connectors.

You might find this hierarchy of components more complicated than necessary, but it provides a flexible structure. In any case, it is unlikely that you'll need more than one instance of Tomcat and more than the default Catalina service and engine.

Listener

A Listener is a Java object that, by implementing the org.apache.catalina.LifecycleListener interface, is able to respond to specific events. The default server.xml, as you can see in lines 3-7 of Listing 9-1, defines five listeners inside the Server component.

The first listener enables the Apache Portable Runtime (APR) library. This library provides functionality that integrates what is made available by the operating system (in our case, Microsoft Windows). Its purpose is to increase portability across OSs. One of the functions of the package is to support OpenSSL if the SSLEngine attribute is on (which is the default).

The second listener enables Jasper, which is the JSP engine. This listener is what makes it possible to recompile JSP documents that have been updated.

The third and fifth listeners deal with different known situations that can cause memory leaks.

The fourth listener is responsible for instantiating the managed beans associated with global Java Naming and Directory Interface (JNDI).

The bottom line is that these listeners improve or provide some of Tomcat's functionality and should remain untouched.

Global Naming Resources

The GlobalNamingResources element can only be defined inside the Server component. It defines JNDI resources that are accessible throughout the server.

The only resource defined in the default server.xml is a user and password memory-based database defined via the file conf/tomcat-users.xml (see lines 9–13 of Listing 9-1). In Chapter 2, you saw an example of user authentication that relies on this element.

Realm

The Realm component can appear inside any container component (Engine, Host, and Context). It represents a database of users, passwords, and user roles. Its purpose is to support container-based authentication. In other words, you can specify an authentication database for each application, host, or engine.

The only realm defined in the default server.xml is in the Catalina engine (see lines 21–24 of Listing 9-1). It refers to the user database defined as a JNDI global resource.

Beside UserDatabaseRealm, the following realm classes are available: JDBCRealm (to connect to a relational database via its JDBC driver), DataSourceRealm (to connect to a JDBC data source named via JNDI), JNDIRealm (to connect to a Lightweight Directory Access Protocol directory), and MemoryRealm (to load an XML file in memory).

Cluster

Tomcat supports server clustering by providing the following three functions:

- **Replication of sessions across the clustered servers**: This ensures that a session opened on one server is valid on all other servers.

- **Replication of context attributes**: This makes it possible for you to access the attributes on all servers.

- **Cluster-wide deployment via WAR files**: This ensures that the same application executes on all servers of a cluster.

You can place a `Cluster` element inside an `Engine` or a `Host` container.

Valve

A `Valve` is an element that, when inserted in a `Container` (Context, Host, or Engine), intercepts all the incoming HTTP requests before they reach the application. This gives you the ability to preprocess the requests directed to a particular application, to the applications running in a virtual host, or to all the applications running within an engine.

The valve you see in lines 27–29 of Listing 9-1 logs all requests received by `localhost`. I will talk about it in one of the following sections.

One of the valves you might like to use is the *access log valve*, which lets you customize request log entries in a file of your choice. Later in this chapter, I'll show you an example of how to do it.

The *remote address filter* valve lets you selectively block requests on the basis of their source IP address. It supports two attributes—allow and deny—which accept regular expressions as values (for a brief description of regular expressions, see the "Regular Expressions" sidebar in Chapter 5). For example, the following valve allows all requests originated from any of the IP addresses 192.168.*.* and rejects all the others:

```
<Valve className="org.apache.catalina.valves.RemoteAddrValve" allow="192\.168.*"/>
```

On the other hand, by replacing the `allow` attribute with deny=`"84.74.97.75"`, you would have allowed all requests with the exception of those coming from the IP address 84.74.97.75.

The *remote host filter* valve operates like remote address filter but on client host names instead of client IP addresses. For example, the following valve only allows requests from hosts belonging to the domain `myweb.com`:

```
<Valve className="org.apache.catalina.valves.RemoteHostValve" allow=".*myweb\.com"/>
```

The *request dumper valve* logs details of the incoming requests and therefore is useful for debugging purposes. Here's how you define it:

```
<Valve className="org.apache.catalina.valves.RequestDumperValve"/>
```

The *single sign on* valve, when included in a `Host` container, has the effect of requiring only one authentication for all the applications of that host. Without this valve, the user would have to enter his ID and password before using each separate application. Here's how you use it:

```
<Valve className="org.apache.catalina.valves.SingleSignOn"/>
```

Loader and Manager

By defining a `Loader` element inside a `Context` element, you can replace the standard class-loading mechanism in an application with your own. I see no reason for you to do so, as the default `Loader` works just fine.

You define a `Manager` if you want to replace the default session management. As I said concerning the `Loader` element, it isn't likely that you'll ever need to do so.

Directory Structure

If you've installed Tomcat as I explained in Chapter 1, Tomcat will be in the following directory:

```
C:\Program Files\Apache Software Foundation\Tomcat\
```

The Tomcat folder contains the following subdirectories: bin, conf, lib, logs, temp, webapps, and work, as shown in Figure 9-2. Two of them are pretty obvious: bin is where the Tomcat executable resides, and temp is a working directory for temporary files.

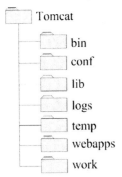

Figure 9-2. Tomcat's top directories

conf

The conf directory contains the configuration files that apply to all applications. The server.xml file, which I described earlier in this chapter, is one of them. Besides two property files and one policy file used internally by Tomcat, you'll also see context.xml, tomcat-users.xml, and web.xml, which define defaults for all the applications of the server, and two property-definition files.

In Chapter 8, I showed you how to use a context.xml file containing a Context element to make the information concerning a MySQL database accessible to eshopf (see Listing 8-9). On that occasion, context.xml was in the META-INF application subfolder. The same file placed in the conf folder would make the same database data accessible to all applications. In Chapter 2, you saw an example of how to use tomcat-users.xml to implement user authentication.

This conf folder also includes a subfolder for each engine. By default, only a folder named Catalina exists. Inside the engine folder is a folder for each host, containing host-specific context information. By default, only a folder named localhost exists. We'll come back to this later in this chapter, when I will tell you how to create virtual hosts.

lib

All the JAR files are kept in the lib directory. If you look into it after doing all the installations I described in the previous chapters, you should see the following libraries or some newer versions of them: annotations-api.jar, catalina.jar, catalina-ant.jar, catalina-ha.jar, catalina-tribes.jar, commons-lang3-3.1.jar, ecj-3.7.1.jar, el-api.jar, jasper.jar, jasper-el.jar, javax.faces-2.1.7.jar, javax.servlet.jsp.jstl-1.2.1.jar, javax.servlet.jsp.jstl-api-1.2.1.jar, jsp-api.jar, mysql-connector-java-5.1.18-bin.jar, servlet-api.jar, tomcat-api.jar, tomcat-coyote.jar, tomcat-dbcp.jar, tomcat-i18n-es.jar, tomcat-i18n-fr.jar, tomcat-i18n-ja.jar, tomcat-jdbc.jar, tomcat-util.jar, xercesImpl.jar, and xml-apis.jar.

Your Tomcat release might have slightly different JARs. And you might see internationalization JARs named like tomcat-i18n-fr.jar but with different language codes.

logs

Tomcat keeps its log files in the logs directory. On any given day of operation, you'll see the following files: catalina.*yyyy-mm-dd*.log, commons-daemon.*yyyy-mm-dd*.log, host-manager.*yyyy-mm-dd*.log, localhost.*yyyy-mm-dd*.log, localhost_access_log.*yyyy-mm-dd*.txt, manager.*yyyy-mm-dd*.log, tomcat7-stderr.*yyyy-mm-dd*, and tomcat7-stdout.*yyyy-mm-dd*.log.

If you have tested eshopf, you will also see eshopf-access.*yyyy-mm-dd*.log.

If you want to write something to the stdout log from JSP, you can simply write to System.out. For example, the following code writes a line containing "bla bla bla" in the file stdout_*yyyy-mm-dd*.log:

```
<% System.out.println("bla bla bla"); %>
```

The output of System.err also goes to stdout. Therefore, you won't be able to write to stderr. Later in this chapter, I'll show you how you can log the requests received by your applications.

webapps

The webapps directory is the application base directory of localhost. The content of any subdirectory of webapps is accessible by browsers. For example, if you create the folder aaa inside webapps and copy into it the file bbb.jsp, you'll be able to execute it by typing this in your browser:

```
http://localhost:8080/aaa/bbb.jsp
```

You can also drop into webapps a WAR file at any time and Tomcat will automatically expand it.

work

Tomcat keeps the translation of JSP into Java in the work directory. For example, if you create inside webapps\ROOT\ folder the the file lineout.jsp containing the following two lines:

```
<%@page language="java" contentType="text/html"%>
<html><body><% out.println("jsp out"); %></body></html>
```

and execute it by typing this in a browser:

```
http://localhost:8080/lineout.jsp
```

Tomcat will translate it into lineout_jsp.java and compile it into lineout_jsp.class. The two files will be in work\Catalina\localhost_\org\apache\jsp\, where Catalina is the engine name, localhost is the host name, and the underscore indicates that it is the default application of the host.

The Java listing is 77 lines long. Therefore, I won't show it here. However, you should look at least once at how Tomcat converts a JSP page into a servlet. The actual JSP code becomes:

```
out.write("\r\n");
out.write("<html><body>ok");
out.println("jsp out");
out.write("</body></html>\r\n");
```

The characters "\r\n" after the closing HTML tag are there because I hit the Enter key after typing the second line of lineout.jsp. The initial empty line is due to the fact that the start HTML tag is not immediately after the JSP page directive.

Logging the Requests

To log the incoming requests directed to all applications present on a particular host, you need to include an access log valve in the corresponding Host element of server.xml. By default, Tomcat logs all the requests sent to localhost in a file named localhost-access.*yyyy-mm-dd*.txt. This is achived with the following valve (see lines 27–28 of Listing 9-1).

```
<Valve className="org.apache.catalina.valves.AccessLogValve" directory="logs"
       prefix="localhost_access_log." suffix=".txt"
       pattern="%h %l %u %t &quot;%r&quot; %s %b" />
<Valve className="org.apache.catalina.valves.AccessLogValve"
    directory="logs" prefix="localhost-access." suffix=".log"
    pattern="common" resolveHosts="false"/>
```

Listing 9-2 shows some examples of log entries.

Listing 9-2. localhost-access.2012-07-05.log

```
01: 127.0.0.1 - - [05/Jul/2012:17:50:51 +1000] "GET / HTTP/1.1" 200 11535
02: 127.0.0.1 - - [05/Jul/2012:17:50:51 +1000] "GET /tomcat.css HTTP/1.1" 200 5926
03: 127.0.0.1 - - [05/Jul/2012:17:50:51 +1000] "GET /tomcat.png HTTP/1.1" 200 5103
04: 127.0.0.1 - - [05/Jul/2012:17:50:52 +1000] "GET /bg-upper.png HTTP/1.1" 200 3103
05: 127.0.0.1 - - [05/Jul/2012:17:50:52 +1000] "GET /bg-nav.png HTTP/1.1" 200 1401
06: 127.0.0.1 - - [05/Jul/2012:17:50:52 +1000] "GET /bg-button.png HTTP/1.1" 200 713
07: 127.0.0.1 - - [05/Jul/2012:17:50:52 +1000] "GET /asf-logo.png HTTP/1.1" 200 17811
08: 127.0.0.1 - - [05/Jul/2012:17:50:52 +1000] "GET /bg-middle.png HTTP/1.1" 200 1918
09: 127.0.0.1 - - [05/Jul/2012:17:56:00 +1000] "GET /tomcat-docs HTTP/1.1" 404 988
10: 127.0.0.1 - - [05/Jul/2012:17:56:08 +1000] "GET /docs HTTP/1.1" 302 -
11: 127.0.0.1 - - [05/Jul/2012:17:56:08 +1000] "GET /docs/ HTTP/1.1" 200 14939
12: 127.0.0.1 - - [05/Jul/2012:17:56:08 +1000] "GET /docs/images/tomcat.gif HTTP/1.1" 200 2066
13: 127.0.0.1 - - [05/Jul/2012:17:56:08 +1000] "GET /docs/images/asf-logo.gif HTTP/1.1" 200 7279
```

Tomcat logged lines 1–8 when I requested the page http://localhost:8080/, line 9 when I requested http://localhost/tomcat-docs (which doesn't exist), and lines 10–13 when I requested http://localhost/docs/ (which does exist).

Each log entry begins with the IP address of localhost (127.0.0.1), followed by the date and time of the request. The next field is a quoted string (e.g., "GET /docs/ HTTP/1.1"), which contains the type of request (GET), the relative URL of the page (/docs/), and the protocol used (HTTP/1.1). The last two fields are the HTTP status code and the request size in bytes.

The status codes are defined in the standard RFC 2616 (see http://www.w3.org/Protocols/rfc2616/rfc2616-sec10.html). For example, 200 means OK, while 404 means Not Found. There are no codes below 100, and the codes between 100 and 299 indicate that everything is OK. The user doesn't see them. The codes between 300 and 399 indicate that the client (i.e., the browser) needs to take additional actions (e.g., the server reports a redirection). Usually, the user is not aware of them. What the user always see are the codes between 400 and 499, which indicate client errors (e.g., 404 when the requested URL doesn't exist), and the codes between 500 and 599, which indicate server errors (e.g., 500, which often indicates that your JSP page contains an error). There are no codes above 599.

Note how the request for the images contained in the page follows the request of the page itself. Also, after requesting the nonexistent page (but before requesting the existing documentation page), I redisplayed Tomcat's home page. Nevertheless, Tomcat made no entry in the log. This is because the browser had cached the page when I requested it the first time and didn't actually send any request to the server. You have to keep this issue of caching in mind if you want to make sense of the access logs, especially since caching can occur not only in the client's browser but also in proxy servers between the client and the server.

When I reloaded the page, according to the log, the browser sent a new request to the server. But it was interesting to note that Tomcat didn't reply with the OK code 200, but with code 304, which means that the page had not changed since the previous request. This allowed the browser to respond more quickly, because the server had only sent a short response instead of a response containing the page.

If you want to log only the requests directed to a particular application, you can include the valve in a Context element, as in the following example:

```
<Context debug="5" reloadable="true" crossContext="true">
  <Valve className="org.apache.catalina.valves.AccessLogValve"
    directory="logs" prefix="eshop-access." suffix=".log" pattern="common"
    resolveHosts="false"/>
</Context>
```

and place it in the META-INF\context.xml file of the application folder.

The directory attribute specifies where Tomcat creates the log file. In this case, I decided to use the relative path logs, which is where Tomcat keeps all the other logs. The prefix and suffix attributes define the strings to be placed around the log date to form the daily file names. The resolveHosts attribute specifies whether Tomcat should try to resolve the originating IP address into a host name. I strongly recommend that you leave out the attribute or set it to false, because the name resolution would significantly slow down the logging process.

The pattern attribute defines the format of the log entries. You can form your own pattern by concatenating some of the identifiers listed in Table 9-1 (adapted from the Tomcat documentation).

Table 9-1. Pattern Identifiers

ID	Function
%a	Remote IP address
%A	Local IP address
%b	Bytes sent, excluding HTTP headers, or - if zero
%B	Bytes sent, excluding HTTP headers
%h	Remote host name (or IP address if resolveHosts is false)
%H	Request protocol
%I	Request thread name (can compare later with stacktraces)
%l	Remote logical username from identd (always returns -)

ID	Function
%m	Request method (GET, POST)
%p	Local port on which this request was received
%q	Query string (prepended with a ? if it exists)
%r	First line of the request (method and request URI)
%s	HTTP status code of the response
%S	User session ID
%t	Date and time, in Common Log Format
%u	Remote user who was authenticated (if any), else -
%U	Requested URL path
%v	Local server name
%D	Time taken to process the request, in milliseconds
%T	Time taken to process the request, in seconds

pattern="common" tells Tomcat to use the standard log entry format and is equivalent to the pattern %h %l %u %t "%r" %s %b. You can also use the predefined pattern combined, which is like common with the addition of the referer (i.e., the page that made the request) and the user-agent (e.g., Firefox).

Tomcat on Port 80

The standard HTTP port is 80, while Tomcat by default waits for incoming requests on port 8080. You might like to change the port number to the standard 80, so that no port needs to be specified in the URLs.

All you need to do is update the HTTP connector defined in server.xml. Change the value assigned to the port attribute from 8080 to 80, restart Tomcat, and you're done.

But, as I remarked in Chapter 1 concerning the default ports when I explained how to install Tomcat, you should check beforehand that port 80 is not being used by other applications.

Creating a Virtual Host

Suppose that you register the domain name jsp-jsf.com (not registered at the time of writing) and would like to point it to your server. Normally, you should have a fixed IP address to be able to do it. Unfortunately, unless you ask your ISP to have a fixed address and pay for it, you just get a dynamic IP address from the ISP. In that case, you can still point a domain name to your computer by using the dynamic DNS service offered online by several providers.

In any case, once requests sent to jsp-jsf.com reach your computer, Tomcat must be able to recognize them and send them to the right applications. For that to happen, you have to create a Host element in server.xml and a couple of directories.

Place the following element inside the Catalina Engine element of server.xml, for example, immediately before the engine end tag:

```
<Host name="www.jsp-jsf.com"  appBase="webapps/www.jsp-jsf.com"
    unpackWARs="true" autoDeploy="true"
    xmlValidation="false" xmlNamespaceAware="false">
  <Alias>jsp-jsf.com</Alias>
  <Valve className="org.apache.catalina.valves.AccessLogValve"
    directory="logs" prefix="www.jsp-jsf.com_access." suffix=".log"
    pattern="common" resolveHosts="false"/>
</Host>
```

Notice that I've defined an Alias, so that the "naked" domain name jsp-jsf.com becomes an alternate name for the host name, which is www.jsp-jsf.com. There is no need to have a www host, but it is what almost everybody expects. Obviously, you could choose any other name. Also, notice that the application base directory has the same name as the host. Any other name would have been perfectly acceptable, but if the base directory has the same name as the host, then you'll never get the directories mixed up, regardless of the number of virtual hosts you create.

Now create a folder named www.jsp-jsf.com inside conf\Catalina, a second folder also named www.jsp-jsf.com inside webapps, and a third folder named ROOT inside the newly created webapps\www.jsp-jsf.com (all paths relative to the Tomcat folder).

Restart Tomcat, and you're ready to access your host—but only, as I said, if you have a DNS mapping the name jsp-jsf.com to your IP address.

To test your new website without any DNS entry, open the file C:\Windows\System32\drivers\etc\hosts and add the following lines to the end:

```
127.0.0.1     www.jsp-jsf.com
127.0.0.1     jsp-jsf.com
```

This maps your domain and host names to the local system. As the communication software checks the file host before asking external DNSs to look up a host name, you'll be able to test your virtual hosts without DNSs, and test an application on any computer before deploying it to its final destination.

Finally, place the following index.html file inside ROOT:

```
<html><head></head><body>Welcome to www.jsp-jsf.com!</body></html>
```

and type http://www.jsp-jsf.com or http://jsp-jsf.com in a browser.

You will see your welcome page. Stop Tomcat to force it to save the logs to their corresponding files and open logs\www.jsp-jsf.com_access.2012-07-05.log. You will see the following entries:

```
127.0.0.1 - - [05/Jul/2012:18:42:07 +1000] "GET / HTTP/1.1" 200 49
127.0.0.1 - - [05/Jul/2012:18:42:07 +1000] "GET /favicon.ico HTTP/1.1" 404 988
127.0.0.1 - - [05/Jul/2012:18:42:07 +1000] "GET /favicon.ico HTTP/1.1" 404 988
```

The first entry is clear: it's your home page in the ROOT directory of your new website. But what is the favicon.ico file that Tomcat looks for and cannot find?

favicon.ico is the file containing the little icon that appears in the address field of the browsers when they access websites. If you do an Internet search, you will find several free tools that let you convert an image into a favicon.ico file.

All browsers look for the little file in the ROOT directory of your website. There are other mechanisms to supply the icon, but they are not completely standardized.

HTTPS

In this section, I'll explain how to create a secure web site for the virtual host www.jsp-jsf.com I created in the previous section.

With the HTTPS protocol, the traffic between browser and server is encrypted. This is achieved by sticking the HTTP protocol on top of the protocol layers that actually manage the encryption, Secure Socket Layer (SSL) and Transport Layer Security (TLS).

When you request a page via HTTPS, before sending the response, the server communicates the identity of its service by sending to the browser an encrypted certificate. This means that you need to install a certificate in Tomcat before you can access www.jsp-jsf.com via HTTPS.

Note that you can create a certificate for services (e.g., catalina), but not for virtual hosts (e.g., localhost and www.jsp-jsf.com), because you need a connector for each protocol (e.g., HTTP and HTTPS), and you can only associate connectors with services. The reason is simple: SSL must be tied to a unique combination of IP address and port, but all virtual servers share the same combination.

Obviously, if you create your own certificates, their existence doesn't prove at all that your websites are where they claim to be. For that, a Certification Authority (CA) of proven respectability must sign your certificates to confirm their validity.

That said, in the remainder of this section, I am precisely going to tell you how to create and sign your own certificates. Once you know how things work, you can always contact a CA and get a "real" certificate from them. They don't necessarily come cheap, though. Alternatively, you can obtain a certificate via CAcert (http://cacert.org), an "open source" organization that is gaining acceptance worldwide.

The first step is to install the program that lets you create your own certificates. OpenSSL (http://openssl.org) is the logical choice, but they only distribute the sources. To download an installer for Windows, go to http://gnuwin32.sourceforge.net/packages/openssl.htm and click on the Setup link beside "Complete package, except sources".

Launch the installer (openssl-0.9.8h-1-setup.exe) and keep clicking on the Next button until you reach the Select Components dialog. Untick the boxes beside Documentation and Developer files before clicking Next. I recommend that you don't install documentation and developer files (i.e., things like C header files) because they cause error messages during installation. I know, it is a bit unsettling, but you can download the documentation directly from the OpenSSL website.

To create the certificate, start by creating a working folder (I created a folder named SSL on the desktop) and copy to it the file shown in Listing 9.3, which you will find in the software package for this chapter.

Listing 9-3. openssl.cfg

```
dir = .

[ req ]
default_bits = 2048
default_keyfile = tomcatkey.pem
distinguished_name = req_distinguished_name

[ req_distinguished_name ]
0.organizationName = Giulio Zambon
countryName= AU
```

271

```
countryName_min= 2
countryName_max = 2
stateOrProvinceName= Australia
localityName = Canberra
organizationalUnitName = n.a.
commonName = www.jsp-jsf.com
commonName_max = 64
emailAddress = giulio@giuliozambon.org
emailAddress_max = 40

O.organizationName_default = Giulio Zambon
localityName_default = Canberra
stateOrProvinceName_default = Australia
countryName_default = AU
commonNameDefault = www.jsp-jsf.com
```

```
[ v3_ca ]
basicConstraints = CA:TRUE
subjectKeyIdentifier = hash
```

As you can see, it consists of a series of assignments with some square-bracketed headers. To explain everything would take too long. You can read a description of the configuration file in http://www.openssl.org/docs/apps/config.html. If you go to http://www.openssl.org/docs/apps/, you will also find the raw list of many documents that don't appear to be reachable from links in the OpenSSL website.

In any case, it should be clear that most of the fields refer to the identity of the organization that requests the certificate. Notice that I set the commonName field to www.jsp-jsf.com. It will become clear in a moment. Obviously, you should update the fields to reflect your identity and not mine.

To create the certificate for Tomcat, open a command-line window by navigating to Accessories ➤ Command Prompt, change the directory to the working folder, and launch the OpenSSL application with the command (including the quotes):

```
"C:\Program Files\GnuWin32\bin\openssl"
```

At the prompt, type the OpenSSL command:

```
req -new -x509 -out tomcatcert.pem -days 365 -config openssl.cfg
```

X.509 is the ITU-T standard for public-key cryptography that defines the type of certificate you need, and the parameter days lets you set the validity of the certificate. Listing 9-4 shows what you are going to see when you hit Enter.

Listing 9-4. Capture of Creating a Certificate

```
OpenSSL> req -new -x509 -out tomcatcert.pem -days 365 -config openssl.cfg
Loading 'screen' into random state - done
Generating a 2048 bit RSA private key
...........................................................+++
.........................................................................
.....................+++
writing new private key to 'tomcatkey.pem'
Enter PEM pass phrase:
Verifying - Enter PEM pass phrase:
```

```
-----
You are about to be asked to enter information that will be incorporated
into your certificate request.
What you are about to enter is what is called a Distinguished Name or a DN.
There are quite a few fields but you can leave some blank
For some fields there will be a default value,
If you enter '.', the field will be left blank.
-----
Giulio Zambon [Giulio Zambon]:
AU [AU]:
Australia [Australia]:
Canberra [Canberra]:
n.a. []:
www.jsp-jsf.com [www.jsp-jsf.com]:
giulio@giuliozambon.org []:
OpenSSL>
```

I have highlighted the lines where you need to provide an input. PEM stands for Privacy Enhanced Mail, the format used for encoding certificates. The program asks for a pass phrase, which can consist of several words, used to protect the generated certificate. As a pass phrase for this example, I used the word whatever. In real life you should use something less predictable.

The lower block of questions gives you the possibility of modifying the configuration stored in openssl.cfg. As you can see from Listing 9-4, I didn't type anything before hitting Enter after each question, which means that I didn't change anything.

You will find that your working directory now contains two additional files: tomcatkey.pem and tomcatcert.pem. You should move or copy them to a place where Tomcat can find them. I moved mine to the Tomcat folder.

Now that you have in place a certificate, to be able to use HTTPS, you need to "open" the corresponding connector in the Catalina service defined in server.xml. A connector definition for this purpose is already there, but you cannot use it as it is. To explain why, I need to take a small digression.

Tomcat supports two different implementations of SSL: JSSE and APR. JSSE stands for Java Secure Socket Extension and is provided as part of the Java Runtime. APR means Apache Portable Runtime and is the provided as part of Tomcat itself.

Do you remember that in Chapter 1 I recommended to install Tomcat with native libraries for better performance? One of the effects of that choice is that Tomcat uses the APR implementation of SSL, while the connector already defined (but commented out) in server.xml is for JSSE. That's why you cannot simply uncomment the HTTPS connector in server.xml.

No big deal. It took more to explain the whole story than to modify the existing connector as needed. Here it is:

```
<Connector port="443" protocol="HTTP/1.1" SSLEnabled="true"
    maxThreads="150" scheme="https" secure="true"
    SSLCertificateFile="/Program Files/Apache Software Foundation/Tomcat/tomcatcert.pem"
    SSLCertificateKeyFile="/Program Files/Apache Software Foundation/Tomcat/tomcatkey.pem"
    SSLPassword="whatever"
    clientAuth="false" sslProtocol="TLS"
/>
```

The only difference is that I inserted the three attributes that start with SSL. As I had changed the HTTP port from 8080 to 80, I also changed the HTTPS port from 8443 to 443, which is the standard one for that protocol. Finally, to make server.xml self-consistent, I removed the redirectPort="8443" attribute from the HTTP connector.

After restarting Tomcat, open a browser window and type `https://www.jsp-jsf.com/`. The browser will open a dialog like that shown in Figure 9-3 (screenshot taken with IE).

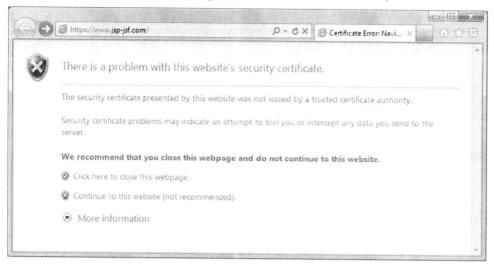

Figure 9-3. Unknown authority (Internet Explorer)

You see this dialog because the certificate was issued by you insteayd of by a recognized CA. If you click on `Continue to this website` and then on the little red shield that will appear in the address bar, you will see the dialog shown in Figure 8-4.

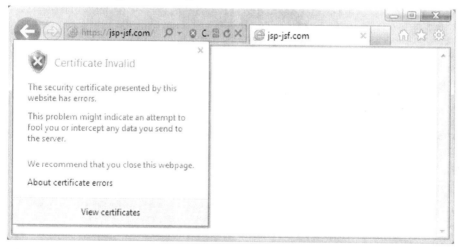

Figure 9-4. Security report (Internet Explorer)

If you click on `View certificates`, you will see the certificate shown in Figure 9-5.

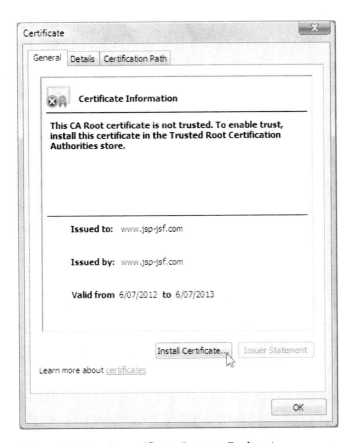

Figure 9-5. Security certificate (Internet Explorer)

What causes the warning is the fact that Issued by doesn't name a trusted CA. The browser will keep asking for confirmation before displaying every page of the web site https://www.jsp-jsf.com unless you install the web site certificate in the browser. Note that every browser displays equivalent warnings, although in different formats.

If the Issued To name on the certificate doesn't match the host name, instead of getting the dialog displayed in Figure 9-3, you get the one shown in Figure 9-6.

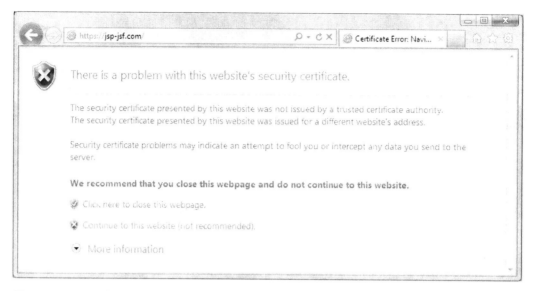

Figure 9-6. Domain name mismatch (Internet Explorer)

At first sight, the two dialogs seem identical, but there is a difference: in the dialog of Figure 9-6, there are two lines of warnings instead of one. The certificate's common name is `www.jsp-jsf.com`, but to cause the dialog in Figure 9-6 to appear I displayed `https://jsp-jsf.com`, without `www`. Something to keep in mind when you publish a secure website.

Application Deployment

The simplest way to deploy an application with Tomcat is to create an application folder and place it inside the application base directory of the host (`webapps` by default).

For example, if you go to the Source Code/Download area of the Apress web site (`http://www.apress.com`) and download the software package containing the examples I developed for this manual, you'll find that the folder with the examples for Chapter 3 contains a folder named `eshop` `folder` that contains a folder named `eshop`. Copy the folder `eshop` to the directory

`C:\Program Files\Apache Software Foundation\Tomcat 6.0\webapps\www.jsp-jsf.com`

and you'll be able to launch the application with the following URL:

`http://www.jsp-jsf.com/eshop/shop`

If you copy the folder `eshop` to `webapps` rather than to `webapps\www.jsp-jsf.com`, the URL will be:

`http://localhost/eshop/shop`

Another way of deploying an application is to create a WAR file (as I described in Chapter 3), and place it in the application base directory of the host. Tomcat will then expand it into the application folder. For example, copy the `eshop.war` file you find in the `eshop` `folder` I mentioned above to the directory

`C:\Program Files\Apache Software Foundation\Tomcat 6.0\webapps\www.jsp-jsf.com`

and wait a few seconds while Tomcat expands it.

You can deploy an application without having to restart Tomcat, because the definitions of localhost and www.jsp-jsf.com contained in server.xml include the attributes unpackWARs="true" and autoDeploy="true".

You might decide to define hosts that don't support automatic deployment. This would improve security, but it would also force you to restart Tomcat in order to deploy or redeploy applications. To resolve this issue, Tomcat's developers have created a manager application that lets you deploy your applications without having to restart Tomcat.

To be able to use the manager application, edit the server.xml file and insert the following element into the element that defines the host you want to manage:

```
<Context path="/manager" privileged="true" docBase="manager">
  <Valve className="org.apache.catalina.valves.RemoteAddrValve" allow="127.0.0.1"/>
  </Context>
```

The Valve element prevents you from using it remotely. Remove the Valve element if you want to be able to use it from a system other than the one you have installed Tomcat on. As an added measure of security, the manager application requires you to log in with a user ID that has manager capabilities. You defined such a user ID when you installed Tomcat. If you've forgotten the ID or its associated password, look inside the tomcat-users.xml file, which is located in the same conf directory as server.xml. There, you'll find the following element:

```
<user username="userID" password="pass" roles="admin-gui,manager-gui" />
```

Now, if you type the URL http://localhost/manager/html in a browser, you will be requested to enter user ID and password of an admin/manager user, as shown in Figure 9-7.

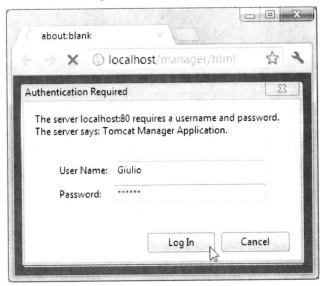

Figure 9-7. Logging in to manage the server

After logging in, you'll see a page with the list of the deployed applications and additional information. Figure 9-8 shows the top of the page, including the first application, which is the ROOT application of localhost.

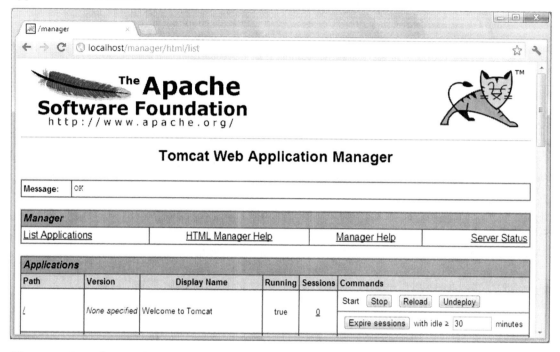

Figure 9-8. Top of Tomcat's Web Application Manager page

Notice that you can undeploy (i.e., remove) the application, reload it, and stop it. You can also change the session idle timeout, which is currently set to the default value of 30 minutes.

If you scroll down, you will find a part of the page that lets you deploy new applications. Figure 9-9 shows the bottom of the page beginning from the entry of the last deployed application. There is no point in showing you the entries of all my applications.

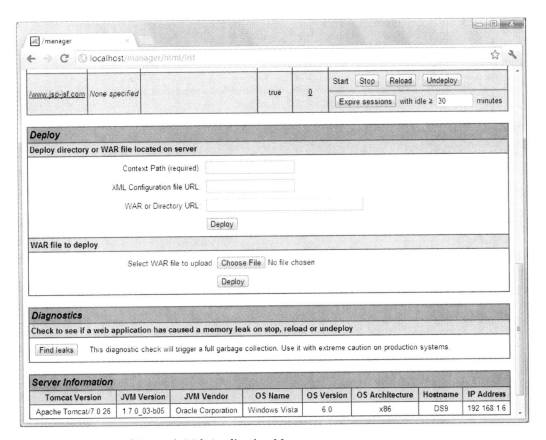

Figure 9-9. Bottom of Tomcat's Web Application Manager page

Cool!

Notice the versions of Tomcat and of the Java Virtual Machine. If you want to know more about your server, you only need to click on the Server Status tab you see in Figure 9-8. If you do so, you will see that the tab changes to Complete Server Status. Click on it again and you will get detailed information on all the applications.

Summary

In this chapter, I provided a very brief introduction to a complex package. Nevertheless, Tomcat's default configuration already covers all the functionality that most people are ever going to need.

I started by describing the components that make up Tomcat. Then, I continued my introduction to Tomcat by explaining how its directories are organized. Finally, I showed some examples of how to modify Tomcat's default configuration. In particular, I explained how to log incoming requests, how to use the standard HTTP ports, and how to create a virtual host, including the handling of encrypted pages.

In the next chapter I'll complete the description of the eshop, eshopx, and eshopf applications I have used in several chapters as a source of examples.

CHAPTER 10

eshop*

In several chapters of this book, I've used examples taken from three different versions of an online bookshop application: eshop (see Chapter 3), eshopx (introduced in Chapter 6), and eshopf (the subject of Chapter 8). In this chapter, I'll complete the description of those applications so that you can use them as models for your own.

All three versions have the same functionality and generate almost identical HTML pages. Their differences are in their implementation. The main difference between the first two versions, eshop and eshopx, is that the JSP code in eshop is in standard JSP syntax, while the code in eshopx is in XML syntax. The third version of the application, eshopf, is quite different from the first two, because I implemented it with JSF. This required me to replace the original servlet with the JSF servlet. Although I used eshopx as a base for developing eshopf, I obviously had to rewrite the user interface almost from scratch.

For your convenience, I have included the code of all three applications in the software package for this chapter. The three folders are identical to those you have already encountered in Chapters 3, 6, and 8.

The eshop Application

In Chapter 3, where I introduced eshop, I described the objects this application deals with (product categories, books, shopping cart, and orders) and the operations the user can perform on those objects. I then described the MVC architecture of eshop. In particular, I listed the methods of the DataManager class (Table 3-1), described the initialization of the servlet (Listing 3-9 and Table 3-2), summarized how the servlet handles incoming requests, and listed the JSP pages (Table 3-3). I also took you through a typical user session.

In Chapter 6, I described the SQL scripts shop_create.sql (Listing 6-1), shop_populate.sql (Listing 6-3) and shop_orders.sql (Listing 6-7), which create the shop database containing categories, books, and orders. I also showed you the code of Category.java (Listing 6-6). Then, I devoted the whole "DB Access in eshop" section to describing how the data manager updates the database via the *peer* methods (Figure 6-5 and Listings 6-10 to 6-13).

In this chapter, I'll start by listing all the subfolders and files in the eshop application folder (see Listing 10-1, where the folder names are in bold).

Listing 10-1. The eshop Files

```
css
    eshop.css
images
    1.gif, 2.gif, 3.gif, 4.gif, 5.gif, 6.gif
    bg_header.gif
```

```
        bg_menu.gif
        cart.gif
jsp
        BookDetails.jsp
        Checkout.jsp
        LeftMenu.jsp
        OrderConfirmation.jsp
        SearchOutcome.jsp
        SelectCatalog.jsp
        ShoppingCart.jsp
        TopMenu.jsp
META-INF
        MANIFEST.MF
WEB-INF
        web.xml
        classes
            eshop
                ShopServlet.class
                ShopServlet.java
                beans
                    Book.class, Book.java
                    CartItem.class, CartItem.java
                    Category.class, Category.java
                    Customer.class, Customer.java
                model
                    BookPeer.class, BookPeer.java
                    CategoryPeer.class, CategoryPeer.java
                    DataManager.class, DataManager.java
                    OrderDetailsPeer.class, OrderDetailsPeer.java
                    OrderPeer.class, OrderPeer.java
                    shop.sql
```

To complete the description of the ShopServlet class, I need to show you how it selects the appropriate JSP page on the basis of the request, thereby fulfilling its role as a controller. Listing 10-2 shows the code of the doPost method (as I mentioned already in Chapter 3, doGet simply executes doPost).

Listing 10-2. ShopServlet.java - doPost Method

```
protected void doPost(HttpServletRequest request,
    HttpServletResponse response) throws ServletException, IOException {
  String base = "/jsp/";
  String url = base + "index.jsp";
  String action = request.getParameter("action");
  if (action != null) {
      switch (action) {
      case "search":
        url = base + "SearchOutcome.jsp";
        break;
      case "selectCatalog":
        url = base + "SelectCatalog.jsp";
        break;
```

```
      case "bookDetails":
        url = base + "BookDetails.jsp";
        break;
      case "checkOut":
        url = base + "Checkout.jsp";
        break;
      case "orderConfirmation":
        url = base + "OrderConfirmation.jsp";
        break;
      default:
        if (action.matches("(showCart|(add|update|delete)Item)"))
          url = base + "ShoppingCart.jsp";
        break;
    }
  }
  RequestDispatcher requestDispatcher =
    getServletContext().getRequestDispatcher(url);
  requestDispatcher.forward(request, response);
}
```

As you can see, doPost obtains the request parameter named action and then uses it to form the correct URL of the JSP page. It then uses the request dispatcher obtained from the servlet context to forward control to the page. If no action parameter exists or if it doesn't match any of the expected strings, the servlet will execute the default page (/jsp/index.jsp).

To cover the eshop functionality in detail, I'll show you what happens in a typical user session, as I already did in Chapter 3. This time, though, instead of showing it from the point of view of the user, I'll look at the behavior of the application on the server. The architecture of eshop is consistent with the general MVC architecture shown in Figure 3-2.

What Happens When the Application Starts

The user starts the application by typing http://localhost:8080/eshop/shop/ in his or her browser. The doGet method of ShopServlet is executed, and that simply executes doPost. The doPost method, as I just explained, doesn't find a request parameter named action, so it forwards the request to index.jsp.

The index.jsp page, like all other pages of eshop, displays a header with a link to the shopping cart and a menu on the left-hand side with search and selection controls (see Figure 10-1). It does so by including two separate modules, as follows:

```
<jsp:include page="TopMenu.jsp" flush="true"/>
<jsp:include page="LeftMenu.jsp" flush="true"/>
```

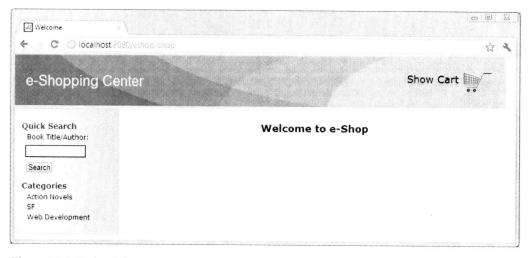

Figure 10-1. *E-shop's home page*

The central area of the page only displays the text welcome to e-Shop.
The TopMenu.jsp module is trivial. Essentially, it consists of the following element:

```
<a class="link2" href="<%=base%>?action=showCart">Show Cart
  <img src="<%=imageURL%>/cart.gif" border="0"/></a>
```

where the two variables are obtained from the application scope

```
String base = (String)application.getAttribute("base");
String imageURL = (String)application.getAttribute("imageURL");
```

The action parameter set to showCart causes ShopServlet to forward the request to
/jsp/ShoppingCart.jsp.

The LeftMenu.jsp module has to do more. It displays a search field and a list of selectable book
categories. The code to accept a search request is as follows:

```
<p>Book Title/Author:</p>
  <form style="border: 0px solid; padding: 0; margin: 0;">
    <input type="hidden" name="action" value="search"/>
    <input id="text" type="text" name="keyword" size="15"/>
    <input id="submit" type="submit" value="Search"/>
  </form>
```

Notice the presence of the hidden parameter named action with the value "search", which causes
ShopServlet to forward the request to /jsp/SearchOutcome.jsp when the user clicks on the Search button
to perform a book search.

Here's the code that lists the book categories:

```
<%
    Hashtable<String, String> categories = dataManager.getCategories();
    Enumeration<String> categoryIds = categories.keys();
    while (categoryIds.hasMoreElements()) {
      Object categoryId = categoryIds.nextElement();
```

```
    out.println("<p><a href=" + base + "?action=selectCatalog&id="
      + categoryId.toString() + ">" + categories.get(categoryId) + "</a></p>"
      );
    }
%>
```

The DataManager method getCategories only executes another method of the data model

```
public Hashtable<String, String> getCategories() {
  return CategoryPeer.getAllCategories(this);
  }
```

that interrogates the database to obtain identifiers and names of the available categories (see Listing 10-3).

Listing 10-3. CategoryPeer.java—getAllCategories Method

```
public static Hashtable<String, String>
    getAllCategories(DataManager dataManager) {
  Hashtable<String, String> categories = new Hashtable<String, String>();
  Connection connection = dataManager.getConnection();
  if (connection != null) {
    try {
      Statement s = connection.createStatement();
      String sql = "select category_id, category_name from categories";
      try {
        ResultSet rs = s.executeQuery(sql);
        try {
          while (rs.next()) {
            categories.put(rs.getString(1), rs.getString(2));
            }
          }
        finally { rs.close(); }
        }
      finally {s.close(); }
      }
    catch (SQLException e) {
      System.out.println("Could not get categories: " + e.getMessage());
      }
    finally {
      dataManager.putConnection(connection);
      }
    }
  return categories;
  }
```

I've highlighted the lines that do all the work: first, the database query is performed, and then the result is saved in a hash table in which the key is the category ID and the value is the category name.

LeftMenu.jsp uses the content of the hash table to generate one link for each category with the statement:

```
out.println("<p><a href=" + base + "?action=selectCatalog&id="
  + categoryId.toString() + ">" + categories.get(categoryId) + "</a></p>"
  );
```

as shown in the following example for action novels:

```
<p><a href=/eshop/shop?action=selectCatalog&id=3>Action Novels</a></p>
```

Notice that the `action` parameter is set to `selectCatalog`. This is done for all categories and causes `ShopServlet` to forward the request to `/jsp/SelectCatalog.jsp` when the user clicks on a category name.

As you can see from the code of `CategoryPeer.java`, I took great care to ensure that the database connection is closed before the method returns. Also notice that I logged a message to the standard output (mapped by Tomcat to the file `stdout_yyyymmdd.log`) if the database access fails. In a real-world application, you should throw an exception with an error message that you can then display to the user.

Handling Requests for Book Selection and Book Search

As you saw in the previous section, when the user selects a book category or performs a search, the pages displayed are `SelectCatalog.jsp` and `SearchOutcome.jsp`, respectively. Both pages display a list of books and are similar to each other. Actually, they are so alike that I merged them into a single page in the JSF version of the application, eshopf, as you'll see later in this chapter. Figure 10-2 shows the list you will see when you search for the letter F (or f, as the searches are case insensitive), while Figure 10-3 shows the list of books in the category `Action Novels`.

			Search results
Title	**Author**	**Price**	**Details**
Foundation	Isaac ASimov	8.95	Details
Term Limits	Vince Flynn	6.99	Details

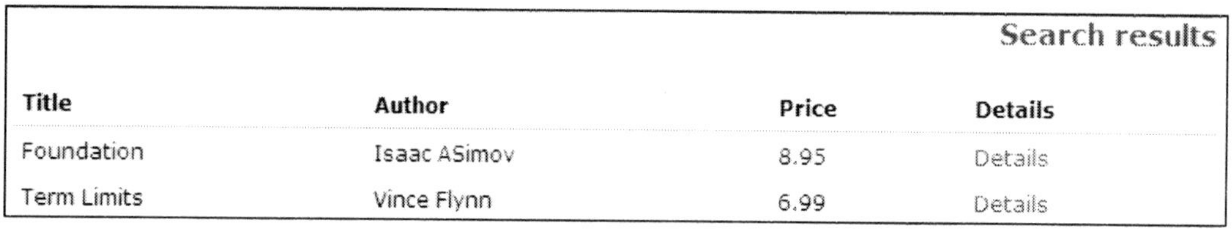

Figure 10-2. Titles and author names containing an F

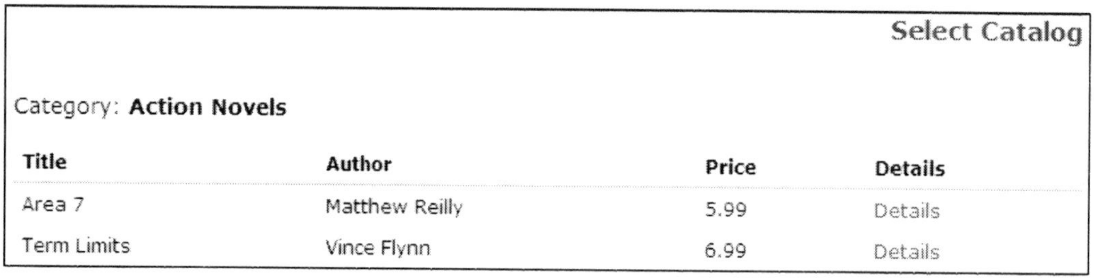

			Select Catalog
Category: **Action Novels**			
Title	**Author**	**Price**	**Details**
Area 7	Matthew Reilly	5.99	Details
Term Limits	Vince Flynn	6.99	Details

Figure 10-3. Action Novels

In `SelectCatalog.jsp`, the requested category is specified by the `id` parameter. To obtain the category name, you execute the `DataManager` method `getCategoryName`

```
public String getCategoryName(String categoryID) {
  Category category = CategoryPeer.getCategoryById(this, categoryID);
  return (category == null) ? null : category.getName();
  }
```

and this loads the category record from the database via the corresponding peer method.

In `SearchOutcome.jsp`, the search string is in the `keyword` parameter.

To obtain the list of books, `SelectCatalog.jsp` executes the following statement in a scriptlet:

```
ArrayList books = dataManager.getBooksInCategory(categoryId);
```

while SearchOutcome.jsp executes the statement:

```
ArrayList books = dataManager.getSearchResults(keyword);
```

For each book in the list, both pages generate a link such as the following one:

```
<a class="link1" href="/eshop/shop?action=bookDetails&bookId=3">Details</a>
```

With the action parameter set to bookDetails, ShopServlet forwards the request to BookDetails.jsp.

Displaying the Book Details

By now, the mechanism should be pretty clear: each JSP page passes its key request parameter to a DataManager method that encapsulates the business logic. This is how the *view* and the *model* of the MVC architecture are kept separate, making it possible for the web-page designers and the software developers to work independently. One creates visually appealing and clear pages, and the other handles the databases. The signatures of the data model methods are the only interface needed between page designers and software developers.

BookDetails.jsp passes the bookId request parameter to the DataManager method getBookDetails:

```
public Book getBookDetails(String bookID) {
   return BookPeer.getBookById(this, bookID);
   }
```

and the BookPeer method getBookById gets the corresponding book record from the database.

To buy the book (see Figure 10-4), the user then clicks on a link that looks like this in HTML:

```
<a class="link1" ="/eshop/shop?action=addItem&bookId=4">Add To Cart</a>
```

With the action parameter set to addItem, ShopServlet forwards the request to ShoppingCart.jsp.

Figure 10-4. Buying a book

Managing the Shopping Cart

The application displays the shopping cart (see Figure 10.5) not only when the user clicks on the Add to Cart link while viewing the book details but also when the user clicks on the shopping cart link in the header of any page. The difference is that in the first case, the action parameter passed to ShoppingCart.jsp has the value addItem, while in the second case the value is showCart.

Title	Author	Price	Quantity		Subtotal	Delete
Web Standards	Leslie Sikos	44.99	2	Update	89.98	Delete
Getting Started with CSS	David Powers	24.99	1	Update	24.99	Delete

Shopping Cart

Total: 114.97

Check Out

Figure 10-5. The shopping cart

The shopping cart itself is an object of type Hashtable<String, String> stored as a session attribute. Note that the scope of the attribute must be session, because the shopping cart must be available across multiple HTTP requests. The hashtable key is the book ID, while the value is an object of type CartItem. The CartItem class has no methods except the getters and setters for the author, title, price, bookID, and quantity properties.

It's appropriate to save the book price in the shopping cart, because the user should pay the price shown in the book details when he or she clicks on Add to Cart, even if the book price stored in the database is then changed before the order is completed.

For each shopping cart item, ShoppingCart.jsp displays the quantity of books in an input field and adds the Update and Delete buttons enclosed in separate forms. This makes it possible for the user to modify the number of copies ordered or to remove an item altogether. Here's an example of an update form:

```
<form>
    <input type="hidden" name="action" value="updateItem"/>
    <input type="hidden" name="bookId" value="4"/>
    <input type="text" size="2" name="quantity" value="1"/>
    <input type="submit" value="Update"/>
    </form>
```

and here's an example a delete form:

```
<form>
  <input type="hidden" name="action" value="deleteItem"/>
  <input type="hidden" name="bookId" value="4"/>
  <input type="submit" value="Delete"/>
  </form>
```

When the user clicks on one of the buttons, ShopServlet forwards the request back to ShoppingCart.jsp.

Before displaying the content of the cart, ShoppingCart.jsp needs to do some work that depends on the value of the action parameter (see Table 10-1).

Table 10-1. ShoppingCart.jsp—Action Parameter

Action Value	Additional Parameters	Previous Page
showCart	None	Any
addItem	bookId	BookDetails.jsp
updateItem	bookId, quantity	ShoppingCart.jsp
deleteItem	bookId	ShoppingCart.jsp

To handle addItem, ShoppingCart.jsp obtains the book details from the data manager via the getBookDetails method and creates a new CartItem object, which it then adds to the cart. To handle updateItem, ShoppingCart.jsp uses the setQuantity method to update the quantity in the cart item identified by bookId. To handle deleteItem, ShoppingCart.jsp simply removes the cart item identified by bookId from the cart.

After listing the cart content, ShoppingCart.jsp displays this link:

```
<a class="link1" href="<%=base%>?action=checkOut">Check Out</a>
```

With the action parameter set to checkOut, ShopServlet forwards the request to Checkout.jsp.

Accepting an Order

Checkout.jsp asks the user to provide his or her personal and financial data (see Figure 10-6).

Figure 10-6. Checking out

When the user clicks on the Confirm Order button, the hidden action parameter is set to orderConfirmation, which causes ShopServlet to forward the request to OrderConfirmation.jsp. In real life, you should implement validation on as many fields as possible.

To perform validation of the user's inputs, you have to decide what fields to validate, whether the validation should take place on the client or on the server (or on both), whether to check the fields one by one or all together, and what technique to use.

There are some fields that you cannot really validate (e.g., the contact name). Others might not be critical enough to warrant the effort you would need to spend in order to implement validation. For example, to check the delivery address provided via a simple form like that of Figure 10-6, you could parse the field, extract the country, if present, the ZIP/post code, and check whether they are consistent. To minimize the risk of input errors, it would make more sense to break down the address into several fields and give a multiple choice of countries and, depending on the chosen country, on ZIP codes. This would involve quite a bit of work, and the lists would have to be kept up to date, for example, by downloading them from an online service. All in all, you might decide to forego such complex checks. That said, it is not uncommon for web sites to check that the *format* of the ZIP code is consistent with the country.

In general, how far you go with validation is something you need to decide on a case-by-case basis.

Concerning the question of whether to validate on the server or on the client, my advice is to *always* validate on the server. This is mainly because a user could manage to work around validation done on the client with unknown consequences. The fact that validation on the client provides immediate feedback to the user might encourage you to do both types of validation. On the other hand, in order to do so, you effectively duplicate the same checks in JavaScript on the client and in your application on the server.

Ajax, which you learned in Chapter 7, relies on checks done on the server; but because it relies on transferring a minimum amount of data in both directions, Ajax also provides a quick turnaround.

With the check-out form of Figure 10-6, I would make sure the user has typed something in all fields and that the values of the credit-card number and expiry date are plausible. The best time to do checks on an individual field is when the value of the corresponding HTML element changes: that is, when the user modifies the value of a field and then clicks outside it.

As a warm-up exercise, let's see how you can easily check that the user has typed something into all fields of the form when he or she clicks on Confirm Order. For this check, you can use a straight JavaScript function, like that shown in Listing 10-4.

Listing 10-4. nonemptyForm.js

```
function validateForm() {
  var f = document.getElementById("frm");
  var k = -1;
  for (var i = 1; i < f.length && k < 0; i++) {
    if(f.elements[i].value.length == 0) k = i;
    }
  if (k >= 0) alert("Field " + f.elements[k].name + " empty");
  return (k < 0);
  }
```

As you can see, it is pretty straightforward: you check in a loop all fields of the form named frm and display an alert with the name of the first element you find to be empty. You will find nonemptyForm.js in the folder eshop project of the software package for this chapter. To use it, you need to copy it to the folder eshop\jsp\ and change the file eshop\jsp\Checkout.jsp in two places.

The first change is necessary to load the JavaScript file. All you need to do is insert the line

```
<script type="text/javascript" src="/eshop/jsp/nonemptyForm.js"></script>
```

immediately before the form element.

The second change links the validation function to the form's submit button. You do it by adding the two attributes id and onsubmit to the form element, as in:

```
<form action="" id="frm" onsubmit="return validateForm()">
```

Figure 10-7 shows what happens when you leave a field empty and hit the Confirm Order button.

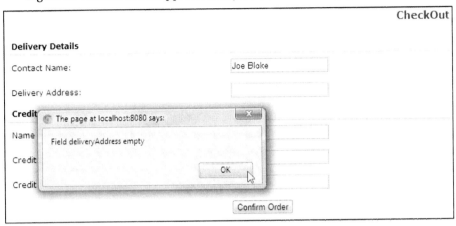

Figure 10-7. *Empty-form check with JavaScript*

To validate all fields individually, you need to associate a checking function to each input field in Checkout.jsp you want to validate. Let's do it entirely on the client side first. Listing 10-5 shows the modified Checkout.jsp, with the added or updated lines in bold. You will find the file immediately inside the eshop project folder. Later, we will move validation to the server using Ajax.

Listing 10-5. *Checkout.jsp (modified for client-side validation)*

```
<%@page language="java" contentType="text/html"%>
<%@page import="java.util.Hashtable"%>
<%@page import="eshop.beans.CartItem"%>
<html>
<head>
  <meta http-equiv="Content-Type" content="text/html; charset=UTF-8"/>
  <title>Check Out (with client validation)</title>
  <link rel="stylesheet" href="/eshop/css/eshop.css" type="text/css"/>
  </head>
<body>
<jsp:include page="TopMenu.jsp" flush="true"/>
<jsp:include page="LeftMenu.jsp" flush="true"/>
<div class="content">
  <h2>CheckOut (with client validation)</h2>
<%
  @SuppressWarnings("unchecked")
  Hashtable<String, CartItem> shoppingCart =
      (Hashtable<String, CartItem>)session.getAttribute("shoppingCart");
  if (shoppingCart != null && !shoppingCart.isEmpty()) {
```

```
%>
<script type="text/javascript" src="/eshop/jsp/validForm.js"></script>
  <form action="" id="frm" onsubmit="return validateForm()">
      <input type="hidden" name="action" value="orderConfirmation"/>
      <table class="checkout">
        <tr>
          <th colspan="2">Delivery Details</th>
          </tr>
        <tr>
          <td>Contact Name:</td>
          <td><input type="text" name="contactName"/></td>
          </tr>
        <tr>
          <td>Delivery Address:</td>
          <td><input type="text" name="deliveryAddress"/></td>
          </tr>
        <tr>
          <th colspan="2">Credit Card Details</th>
          </tr>
        <tr>
          <td>Name on Credit Card:</td>
          <td><input type="text" name="ccName"/></td>
          </tr>
        <tr>
          <td>Credit Card Number:</td>
          <td><input type="text" name="ccNumber"
                     onchange="valNumber(this.value)"
                     /></td>
          </tr>
        <tr>
          <td>Credit Card Expiry Date:</td>
          <td><input type="text" name="ccExpiryDate"
                     onchange="valExpiry(this.value)"
                     /></td>
          </tr>
        <tr>
          <td> </td>
          <td><input type="submit" value="Confirm Order"/></td>
          </tr>
        </table>
      </form>
<%
    }
  else {
    %><p class="error">ERROR: You can't check out an empty shopping cart!</p><%
    }
  %>
  </div>
</body>
</html>
```

What could be simpler than that? Let's look together at validForm.js (Listing 10-6).

Listing 10-6. validForm.js

```
var numberOk = true;
var expiryOk = true;

function valNumber(val){
  numberOk = true;
  val += "";
  if (val != "undefined" && val != "null" && val != "") {
    var nnn = "";
    for (var k = 0; k < val.length && numberOk == true; k++) {
      var c = val.charAt(k);
      if (c >= '0' && c <= '9') {
        nnn += c;
        }
      else if (c != ' ') {
        numberOk = false;
        alert("Invalid characters in the credit card number");
        }
      }
    if (numberOk && nnn.length != 15 && nnn.length != 16) {
      alert("Credit card numbers can only have 15 or 16 digits");
      numberOk = false;
      }
    }
  }

function valExpiry(val){
  expiryOk = true;
  val += "";
  if (val != "undefined" && val != "null" && val != "") {
    var nnn = "";
    for (var k = 0; k < val.length && numberOk == true; k++) {
      var c = val.charAt(k);
      if (c != ' ') nnn += c;
      }
    if (nnn.length != 5 || nnn.charAt(2) != "/") {
      expiryOk = false;
      alert("The format of the expiry date must be MM/YY");
      }
    else {
      var month = (nnn.charAt(0) - '0') * 10 + (nnn.charAt(1) - '0');
      if (month < 1 || month > 12) {
        expiryOk = false;
        alert("Invalid expiry month");
        }
      else {
        var year = (nnn.charAt(3) - '0') * 10 + (nnn.charAt(4) - '0');
        var now = new Date();
        var thisYear = now.getFullYear() - 2000;
        var thisMonth = now.getMonth() + 1;
```

```
            if (year * 12 + month < thisYear * 12 + thisMonth) {
              expiryOk = false;
              alert("The credit card has expired");
              }
            }
          }
        }
      }

    function validateForm() {
      if (numberOk != true) {
        alert("Invalid credit card number");
        return false;                                          //-->
        }
      if (expiryOk != true) {
        alert("Invalid credit card expiry date");
        return false;                                          //-->
        }
      var f = document.getElementById("frm");
      var k = -1;
      for (var i = 1; i < f.length && k < 0; i++) {
        if(f.elements[i].value.length == 0) k = i;
        }
      if (k >= 0) alert("Field " + f.elements[k].name + " empty");
      return (k < 0);
      }
```

The function validateForm is an extension of the function with the same name defined in nonemptyForm.js (Listing 10-4). The only difference is that before ensuring all fields contain something, it checks whether the two flags numberOk and expiryOk are true. If not, it reports an error and returns false, so that the form is not submitted.

The two flags are set respectively in the two functions valNumber and valExpiry. The function valNumber accepts as valid credit-card numbers all strings that contain either 15 or 16 numeric digits plus any number of spaces. valExpiry only accepts as valid expiry dates strings in the format MM/YY plus, again, any number of spaces.

To try out the validation, replace the version of Checkout.jsp originally in the eshop\jsp\ folder with the modified one, and copy validForm.js to the same eshop\jsp\ folder. Figure 10-8 shows an example of an invalid expiry date.

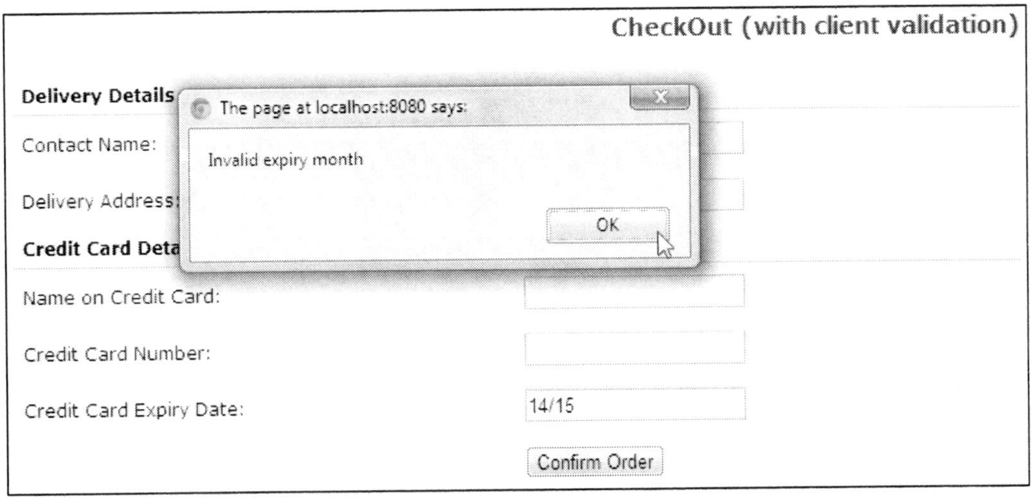

Figure 10-8. Individual field validation with JavaScript

Before we move the validation of credit-card number and expiry date to the server, we need to take a few things into consideration.

The first 'A' of Ajax stands for "Asynchronous." Although you can actually use it in synchronous mode, if you do so, your page might hang while waiting for the server to respond. However, if you use it asynchronously, it is possible the user could attempt to submit the form before the validation responses from the server arrive. This should be avoided because what's the point of asking for validation if you don't wait for the reply? It would result in the server receiving non-validated (and therefore possibly invalid) field values.

The simplest way to wait for Ajax to complete its dialogs with the server is to block the submit button until all validations have been completed and let the user know why he or she cannot submit the page. You could also keep the submit button disabled (i.e., grayed out) until Ajax has done its job. You could also add disabled check boxes beside the fields being validated, which your JavaScript code ticks when the corresponding validation has been done successfully. I favor the minimalist approach: unless you are forced to address the user, you keep quiet. This makes for cleaner pages and simpler coding. In most cases, by the time the user clicks on the submit button, Ajax will have done its job, and the user will remain unaware of what has been going on behind the scene.

If you look at validForm.js (Listing 10-6), you will see that we can use for this purpose the two variables numberOk and expiryOk. All we need to do is set them to a special value while the client is waiting for the server to respond. Then we can extend the check of the two flags in validateForm, so that if necessary we can ask the user to wait.

To avoid confusion, I made a copy of validForm.js, which I then renamed validFormAjax.js. To use it, after copying it to eshop\jsp\, you will only need to change in Checkout.jsp the script element to load validFormAjax.js instead of validForm.js. During my tests, I also changed the title of Checkout.jsp, from "Check Out (with client validation)" to "Check Out (with server validation)," but it is not necessary for you to do so. To have validation with Ajax working, you will also need to copy to the eshop\jsp\ folder the two files ccNumber.jsp and ccExpiry.jsp, which perform the validation on the server. More about that later.

Listing 10-7 shows validFormAjax.js.

Listing 10-7. validFormAjax.js

```javascript
var numberOk = "";
var expiryOk = "";

function valNumber(val){
  numberOk = "waiting";
  var ajaxReq;
  try { // Firefox, Opera, IE 9, Chrome
    ajaxReq = new XMLHttpRequest();
    }
  catch (e) { // older IEs
    try{
      ajaxReq = new ActiveXObject("Msxml2.XMLHTTP");
      }
    catch (e) {
      try{ // still older IEs
        ajaxReq = new ActiveXObject("Microsoft.XMLHTTP");
        }
      catch (e) {
        alert("Your browser does not support Ajax!");
        return false;
        }
      }
    }
  ajaxReq.open("GET", "/eshop/jsp/ccNumber.jsp?v="+val);
  ajaxReq.send(null);
  ajaxReq.onreadystatechange = function() {
    if(ajaxReq.readyState == 4) {
      numberOk = ajaxReq.responseText;
      if (numberOk.length > 0) alert(numberOk);
      }
    }
  }

function valExpiry(val){
  expiryOk = "waiting";
  var ajaxReq;
  try { // Firefox, Opera, IE 9, Chrome
    ajaxReq = new XMLHttpRequest();
    }
  catch (e) { // older IEs
    try{
      ajaxReq = new ActiveXObject("Msxml2.XMLHTTP");
      }
    catch (e) {
      try{ // still older IEs
        ajaxReq = new ActiveXObject("Microsoft.XMLHTTP");
        }
      catch (e) {
        alert("Your browser does not support Ajax!");
```

```
              return false;
            }
         }
     }
   ajaxReq.open("GET", "/eshop/jsp/ccExpiry.jsp?v="+val);
   ajaxReq.send(null);
   ajaxReq.onreadystatechange = function() {
     if(ajaxReq.readyState == 4) {
       expiryOk = ajaxReq.responseText;
       if (expiryOk.length > 0) alert(expiryOk);
       }
     }
   }

function validateForm() {
   if (numberOk.length > 0) {
     if (numberOk == "waiting") {
       alert(   "Waiting for the server to validate the credit"
               + " card number.\nTry again in a second or two."
               );
       }
     else {
       alert(numberOk);
       }
     return false;                                      //-->
     }
   if (expiryOk.length > 0) {
     if (expiryOk == "waiting") {
       alert(   "Waiting for the server to validate the credit"
               + " card expiry date.\nTry again in a second or two."
               );
       }
     else {
       alert(expiryOk);
       }
     return false;                                      //-->
     }
   var f = document.getElementById("frm");
   var k = -1;
   for (var i = 1; i < f.length && k < 0; i++) {
     if(f.elements[i].value.length == 0) k = i;
     }
   if (k >= 0) alert("Field " + f.elements[k].name + " empty");
   return (k < 0);
   }
```

As you can see, the two functions valNumber and valExpiry no longer contain any check of the input fields. Instead, they have become very similar to the function ajaxFun contained in the file ajax.js of Chapter 7 (Listing 7-16).

If you look at the handling of the credit-card number, you will see that numberOk is now initialized to an empty string and set to "waiting" immediately inside the valNumber function. valNumber uses Ajax to execute the JSP page ccNumber.jsp, which accepts the value entered by the user as the input parameter named v. The response received from the server is stored directly into numberOk.

As you will see in a moment, the validating page ccNumber.jsp returns an empty response when the validation is successful, or an error message describing the error.

valExpiry is almost identical to valNumber, and validateForm is pretty self-explanatory.

The two validating JSP pages are shown in Listings 10-8 and 10-9. They contain the Java implementation of the checks that used to be in the JavaScript functions valNumber and valExpiry when they didn't use Ajax.

Listing 10-8. ccExpiry.jsp

```
<%@page language="java" contentType="text/html"
%><%
  String val = request.getParameter("v");
  String res = "";
  if (val != null && val != "") {
    String nnn = "";
    for (int k = 0; k < val.length() && res.length() == 0; k++) {
      char c = val.charAt(k);
      if (c >= '0' && c <= '9') {
        nnn += c;
      }
      else if (c != ' ') {
        res = "Invalid characters in the credit card number";
      }
    }
    if (res.length() == 0 && nnn.length() != 15 && nnn.length() != 16) {
      res = "Credit card numbers can only have 15 or 16 digits";
    }
  }
  out.print(res);
%>
```

Listing 10-9. ccNumber.jsp

```
<%@page language="java" contentType="text/html"
%><%@page import="java.util.Calendar,java.util.GregorianCalendar"
%><%
  String val = request.getParameter("v");
  String res = "";
  if (val != null && val != "") {
    String nnn = "";
    for (int k = 0; k < val.length() && res.length() == 0; k++) {
      char c = val.charAt(k);
      if (c != ' ') nnn += c;
    }
    if (nnn.length() != 5 || nnn.charAt(2) != '/') {
      res = "The format of the expiry date must be MM/YY";
    }
    else {
      int month = (nnn.charAt(0) - '0') * 10 + (nnn.charAt(1) - '0');
      if (month < 1 || month > 12) {
```

```
      res = "Invalid expiry month";
      }
    else {
      int year = (nnn.charAt(3) - '0') * 10 + (nnn.charAt(4) - '0');
      GregorianCalendar now = new GregorianCalendar();
      int thisYear = now.get(Calendar.YEAR) - 2000;
      int thisMonth = now.get(Calendar.MONTH) + 1;
      if (year * 12 + month < thisYear * 12 + thisMonth) {
        res = "The credit card has expired";
        }
      }
    }
  }
out.print(res);
%>
```

Figure 10-9 shows an example of eshop with the validation done on the server.

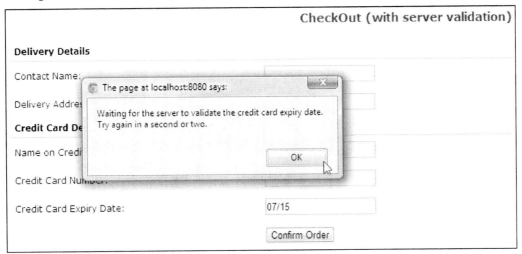

Figure 10-9. *Waiting for the server to respond*

To see the "waiting" alert, "touch" ccExpiry.jsp (e.g., insert a space anywhere, remove it, and save the file) and then, after typing something in the expiry-date field, click on Confirm Order before doing anything else. The little time needed by Tomcat to recompile the JSP page will be enough to make validFormAjax.js display the alert.

Providing the Payment Details

In this skeleton implementation of eshop, OrderConfirmation.jsp only saves the order in the database. In a real-world situation, it should perform a series of checks, including verifying with a bank that the credit card is valid and not blocked.

All the work to store the order in the database is done in the DataManager method insertOrder, which I've already discussed in Chapter 6.

The eshopx Application

After completing eshop, I showed you how to create the eshopx application by replacing the JSP pages with JSP documents (i.e., modules in XML syntax). This required us to move scriptlet code to JSP custom tags.

Listing 10-10 shows the annotated list of files and folders that constitute eshopx.

Listing 10-10. *The Eshopx Files*

```
css
    eshop.jspx  (replaces eshop.css)
images  (content unchanged)
jsp  (all pages rewritten as XML documents)
    BookDetails.jspx
    Checkout.jspx
    LeftMenu.jspx
    OrderConfirmation.jspx
    SearchOutcome.jspx
    SelectCatalog.jspx
    ShoppingCart.jspx
    TopMenu.jspx
META-INF   (content unchanged)
WEB-INF
    web.xml   (minor update)
    classes
        eshop  (ShopServlet unchanged)
            beans   (content unchanged)
            model   (content unchanged)
            tags   (new folder)
                AddBookTag.class, AddBookTag.java
                BookDetailsTag.class, BookDetailsTag.java
                BooksInCartTag.class, BooksInCartTag.java
                BooksInCategoryTag.class, BooksInCategoryTag.java
                CategoryNameTag.class, CategoryNameTag.java
                DeleteBookTag.class, DeleteBookTag.java
                InsertOrderTag.class, InsertOrderTag.java
                RoundToCentTag.class, RoundToCentTag.java
                SearchResultsTag.class, SearchResultsTag.java
                UpdateBookTag.class, UpdateBookTag.java
    tlds  (new folder)
        eshop.tld
```

As you can see, I only changed the *view* part of the application (i.e., the JSP modules), while I didn't need to touch the *controller* and the *model* (i.e., the servlet, the beans, the peer classes, and the data manager). This confirms the advantage of implementing an MVC architecture.

As I already mentioned, the views of eshop and eshopx differ in the implementation but are functionally identical.

Style Sheet

I replaced the shop.css file used in eshop with shop.jspx. Listing 10-11 shows the differences between the two files.

Listing 10-11. shop.jspx

```xml
<?xml version="1.0" encoding="UTF-8"?>
<jsp:root
  xmlns:jsp="http://java.sun.com/JSP/Page"
  xmlns:c="http://java.sun.com/jsp/jstl/core"
  version="2.1"
  >
<jsp:directive.page
  language="java"
  contentType="text/css; charset=UTF-8"
  pageEncoding="UTF-8"
  />
<c:url var="imgUrl" value="/images"/>
<jsp:text>
  ----------  shop.css lines 1 - 42  ----------
  background: url(${imgUrl}/bg_header.gif) no-repeat top left;
  ----------  shop.css lines 44 - 82  ----------
  background: url(${imgUrl}/bg_menu.gif) repeat-y top left;
  ----------  shop.css lines 84 - 105  ----------
  background: url(${imgUrl}/menubar.gif) repeat-x bottom left;
  ----------  shop.css lines 107 - 206 (the last one)  ----------
</jsp:text>
</jsp:root>
```

As you can see, I only wrapped shop.css inside a jsp:text element and changed three lines. If you look at the original lines, it should become clear why I did it:

```css
background: url(/eshop/images/bg_header.gif) no-repeat top left;
background: url(/eshop/images/bg_menu.gif) repeat-y top left;
background: url(/eshop/images/menubar.gif) repeat-x bottom left;
```

The string "/eshop/images" of shop.css has become "${imgUrl}" in shop.jspx, and if you look at the beginning of shop.jspx, you'll notice that the variable imgUrl is set as follows:

```xml
<c:url var="imgUrl" value="/images"/>
```

The advantage of doing it with the EL expression is that c:url takes care of adding the application folder (i.e., /eshop) before the relative URL /images. This makes it possible to deploy the application in any folder. You should try to avoid hard-coding paths.

Obviously, you need to change the way in which the style sheet is loaded in the JSP modules. In eshop, with shop.css, you needed to include the following line in the <head> element:

```html
<link rel="stylesheet" href="/eshop/css/eshop.css" type="text/css"/>
```

In eshopx, with shop.jspx, you need to write the line

```xml
<c:url var="cssUrl" value="/css/eshop.jspx"/>
```

and then include the following line in the <head>:

```
<link rel="stylesheet" href="${cssUrl}" type="text/css"/>
```

By doing so, you remove the hard-coded /eshop path from all JSP modules, which is a good thing to do.

web.xml

When moving from eshop to eshopx, I needed to modify in web.xml the definitions of two parameters: base and imageURL. The definition of base changed from /eshop/shop to /shop, because in eshop, I used base as follows:

```
<a class="link1" href="<%=base%>?action=checkOut">Check Out</a>
```

while in eshopx, I first define the page attribute myURL as

```
<c:url value="${base}" var="myURL">
  <c:param name="action" value="checkOut"/>
  </c:url>
```

and then use the attribute to make the link, as follows:

```
<a class="link1" href="${myURL}">Check Out</a>
```

As I said when talking about the style sheet, c:url accepts in the value attribute URLs relative to the application folder and then completes them to make them relative to the server root. Within eshop, you had to include the application folder in base, because you didn't form the URL with c:url.

The definition of imageURL changed from /eshop/images/ to /images/ because I used imageURL in eshop as follows:

```
<img src="<%=imageURL%>cart.gif" border="0"/>
```

while in eshopx, I first define the page attribute imgURL:

```
<c:url value="${imageURL}" var="imgURL"/>
```

and then use the attribute in the img element:

```
<img src="${imgURL}cart.gif" border="0"/>
```

Thanks to these two changes, I could remove all hard-coded references to the application directory in eshopx.

But these small changes in the handling of the images cause a problem in the welcome page of the application.

Perhaps you will recall that in Chapter 4, when talking about c:url, I mentioned that Tomcat attaches a jsessionid string to a URL before sending it to the client in the response.

Tomcat does it when it opens a new session, to handle clients that don't accept cookies. When Tomcat receives subsequent requests from the same client and they contain the session cookie, it stops appending the session ID string to the URLs, because it knows that it is unnecessary.

Now, the welcome page (index.jspx) includes TopMenu.jspx, which contains the two lines

```
<c:url value="${imageURL}" var="imgURL"/>
...
<img src="${imgURL}cart.gif" border="0"/>
```

to display the image of the shopping cart.

When you view `http://localhost:8080/eshopx/shop` the first time, Tomcat creates a session and then systematically attaches the `jsessionid` string to all URLs. This means that the value of the `src` attribute of the `img` tag becomes something like this:

`"/eshopx/images/;jsessionid=AC559D1E83F5714252E310897A65A3D3cart.gif"`

As a result, when the client browser requests the image of the cart, Tomcat cannot find it, and the shopping cart cannot be displayed. At best, with some browsers, you get a "broken image" icon. All subsequent pages, including a reloaded welcome page, unless you disable the cookies in your browser, are OK.

Fortunately, Servlet 3.0 lets you switch off the appending of the session ID. All you need to do is add in the body of `web-app` the following element:

```
<session-config>
  <tracking-mode>COOKIE</tracking-mode>
</session-config>
```

It tells Tomcat to use the cookie (and nothing else) to track the session. By default, the `session-config` element contains both the `COOKIE` and the `URL` tracking modes.

With this change, everything works fine, although it makes the acceptance of cookies compulsory for the users.

At the time of writing, Eclipse doesn't recognize the `tracking-mode` element and reports an error, as shown in Figures 10-10 and 10-11. This doesn't affect the normal working of the application.

Figure 10-10. Eclipse reports an error in web.xml

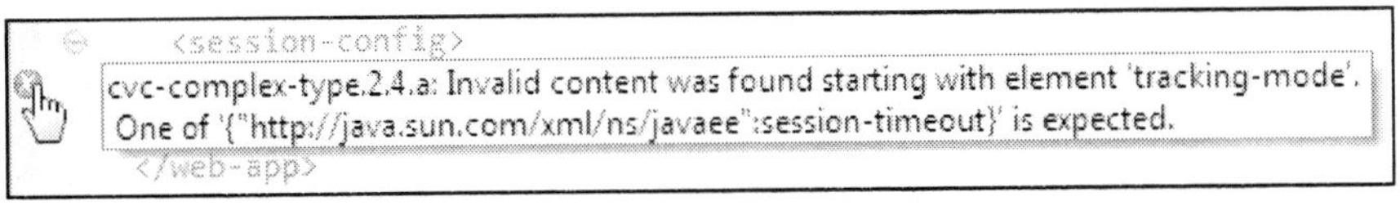

Figure 10-11. Eclipse's description of the web.xml error

JSP Documents

To explain how I converted the JSP pages of eshop (with extension `jsp`) to the corresponding JSP documents of eshopx (with extension `jspx`), I'll go through one example in detail.

Listing 10-12 shows `OrderConfirmation.jsp`. I choose it because it is one of the simplest modules.

Listing 10-12. OrderConfirmation.jsp

```
01: <%@page language="java" contentType="text/html"%>
02: <%@page import="java.util.Hashtable"%>
03: <%@page import="eshop.beans.CartItem"%>
04: <jsp:useBean id="dataManager" scope="application"
05:   class="eshop.model.DataManager"/>
06: <html>
07: <head>
```

```
08:    <meta http-equiv="Content-Type" content="text/html; charset=UTF-8"/>
09:    <title>Order</title>
10:    <link rel="stylesheet" href="/eshop/css/eshop.css" type="text/css"/>
11:    </head>
12: <body>
13: <jsp:include page="TopMenu.jsp" flush="true"/>
14: <jsp:include page="LeftMenu.jsp" flush="true"/>
15: <div class="content">
16:    <h2>Order</h2>
17:    <jsp:useBean id="customer" class="eshop.beans.Customer"/>
18:    <jsp:setProperty property="*" name="customer"/>
19: <%
20:        @SuppressWarnings("unchecked")
21:        Hashtable<String, CartItem> cart =
22:            (Hashtable<String, CartItem>)session.getAttribute("shoppingCart");
23:        long orderId = dataManager.insertOrder(customer, cart);
24:        if (orderId > 0L) {
25:            session.invalidate();
26:    %>
27:        <p class="info">
28:            Thank you for your purchase.<br/>
29:            Your Order Number is: <%=orderId%>
30:        </p>
31: <%
32:        }
33:        else {
34:        %><p class="error">Unexpected error processing the order!</p><%
35:        }
36:    %>
37:    </div>
38: </body>
39: </html>
```

When converting to the XML syntax, you first need to replace the first 11 lines of the JSP page with those shown in Listing 10-13.

Listing 10-13. *Top Portion of OrderConfirmation.jspx*

```
01: <?xml version="1.0" encoding="UTF-8"?>
02: <jsp:root
03:    xmlns:jsp="http://java.sun.com/JSP/Page"
04:    xmlns:c="http://java.sun.com/jsp/jstl/core"
05:    xmlns:eshop="urn:jsptld:/WEB-INF/tlds/eshop.tld"
06:    version="2.1"
07:    >
08: <jsp:directive.page
09:    language="java"
10:    contentType="application/xhtml+xml;charset=UTF-8"
11:    />
12: <jsp:output omit-xml-declaration="false"/>
13: <jsp:output
14:    doctype-root-element="html"
```

```
15:    doctype-public="-//W3C//DTD XHTML 1.0 Strict//EN"
16:    doctype-system="http://www.w3.org/TR/xhtml1/DTD/xhtml1-strict.dtd"
17:    />
18: <c:url var="cssUrl" value="/css/eshop.jspx"/>
19: <html xmlns="http://www.w3.org/1999/xhtml">
20: <head>
21:    <title>Order</title>
22:    <link rel="stylesheet" href="${cssUrl}" type="text/css"/>
23:    </head>
```

In XML format, you no longer need to declare the Java classes, but you need to declare the namespaces of JSP, the JSTL core, and the custom library. The page directive becomes a jsp:directive.page element. Also, notice that the style sheet is loaded as I explained in a previous section.

Lines 12–18 of OrderConfirmation.jsp remain practically the same, the only difference being that now the two modules have the extension jspx. The last three lines (37–39) also remain the same. You only have to append the end tag of jsp:root.

The major changes take place in lines 19–36. They are replaced by the code shown in Listing 10-14.

Listing 10-14. Central Portion of OrderConfirmation.jspx

```
31: <eshop:insertOrder var="orderID" customer="${customer}"/>
32: <c:choose>
33:    <c:when test="${orderID > 0}">
34:      <p class="info">
35:        Thank you for your purchase.<br/>
36:        Your Order Number is: <c:out value="${orderID}"/>
37:      </p>
38:    </c:when>
39:    <c:otherwise>
40:      <p class="error">Unexpected error processing the order!</p>
41:    </c:otherwise>
42: </c:choose>
```

Line 31 of OrderConfirmation.jspx is the XML equivalent of lines 20–25 plus line 32 of OrderConfirmation.jsp. Notice that in eshop, the order ID is returned by the insertOrder method and stored in the scripting variable orderID, while in eshopx, the order ID is stored into the EL variable orderID directly by the custom tag eshop:insertOrder.

The if/else of lines 24 and 33 in the JSP code is replaced in the JSPX code by the elements c:choose/c:when/c:otherwise of lines 32–33 and 39. As I said on other occasions, you cannot use c:if because a c:else doesn't exist.

To complete the picture, let's look at Listing 10-15, which shows the doEndTag method of InsertOrderTag.java.

Listing 10-15. InsertOrderTag.java—doEndTag Method

```
public int doEndTag() {
  ServletContext context = pageContext.getServletContext();
  DataManager dataManager =(DataManager)context.getAttribute("dataManager");
  HttpSession session = pageContext.getSession();
  @SuppressWarnings("unchecked")
  Hashtable<String, CartItem> cart =
```

```
    (Hashtable<String, CartItem>)session.getAttribute("shoppingCart");
  long orderID = dataManager.insertOrder(customer, cart);
  if (orderID > 0L) session.invalidate();
  pageContext.setAttribute(var, new Long(orderID).toString());
  return EVAL_PAGE;
  }
```

Not surprisingly, here you find (highlighted in bold) the code originally in lines 20–25 of OrderConfirmation.jsp that executes the dataManager method insertOrder and terminates the user session if the insertion succeeds.

On the basis of this example, you should now be able to figure out how to convert the other modules. In the next section, you'll find additional information concerning the eshop custom tag library.

Custom Tags and TLD

EL expressions can include bean properties. This means that they can invoke "getter" methods. What they cannot do is invoke methods that require input parameters. You can work around that difficulty by setting an attribute with c:set and picking it up in a bean method.

For example, in SelectCatalog.jspx, the request parameter id specifies a book category, and you need to know the category name. This operation requires a database search, which you can implement with the following custom tag:

```
<eshop:categoryName var="cat" catID="${param.id}"/>
```

It accepts the ID as an input and sets the variable cat to the category name. The doEndTag method of CategoryNameTag.java is simple:

```
public int doEndTag() {
  ServletContext context = pageContext.getServletContext();
  DataManager dataManager =(DataManager)context.getAttribute("dataManager");
  pageContext.setAttribute(var, dataManager.getCategoryName(catID));
  return EVAL_PAGE;
  }
```

The getCategoryName method of the data manager (invoked exclusively by the doEntTag method of CategoryNameTag.java) is even simpler:

```
public String getCategoryName(String categoryID) {
  Category category = CategoryPeer.getCategoryById(this, categoryID);
  return (category == null) ? null : category.getName();
  }
```

Instead of defining the custom tag, you could add the categoryID property to the data manager

```
private String categoryID = "0";
public void setCategoryID(String categoryID) {
  this.categoryID = categoryID;
  }
```

and remove its input parameter from the getCategoryName method.

Then, in SelectCatalog.jspx, you could replace the eshop:categoryName element with jsp:setProperty to set the categoryID in the data manager and c:setVar to invoke the getCategoryName method:

```
<jsp:setProperty name="dataManager" property="categoryID"
    value="${param.id}"/>
<c:set var="cat" value="${dataManager.categoryName}"/>
```

The result would be the same. I didn't do it in that way because it makes the code less "transparent," but it is ultimately a matter of taste. I just want to make the point that you can replace the input parameters of bean methods by setting bean properties with jsp:setProperty. Then, you only need to name the getter methods appropriately (e.g., getWhatever), and you'll be able to execute them with an expression such as ${myBean.whatever}.

In any case, I introduced a total of ten tags, as listed in Table 10-2.

Table 10-2. eshop Custom Tag Library

Name	Attributes	Where Used
bookDetails	var, bookID	BookDetails.jspx
insertOrder	var, customer	OrderConfirmation.jspx
searchResults	var, keyword	SearchOutcome.jspx
categoryName	var, catID	SelectCatalog.jspx
booksInCategory	var, catID	SelectCatalog.jspx
addBook	bookID	ShoppingCart.jspx
updateBook	bookID, quantity	ShoppingCart.jspx
deleteBook	bookID	ShoppingCart.jspx
booksInCart	items	ShoppingCart.jspx
roundToCent	var, value	ShoppingCart.jspx

Listing 10-16 shows an example of a TLD tag element.

Listing 10-16. A TLD Tag element

```
<tag>
  <description>Insert an order into storage</description>
  <display-name>insertOrder</display-name>
  <name>insertOrder</name>
  <tag-class>eshop.tags.InsertOrderTag</tag-class>
  <body-content>empty</body-content>
  <attribute>
    <name>var</name>
    <type>java.lang.String</type>
    <rtexprvalue>true</rtexprvalue>
```

```
        </attribute>
      <attribute>
        <name>customer</name>
        <type>eshop.beans.Customer</type>
        <rtexprvalue>true</rtexprvalue>
        </attribute>
      </tag>
```

The eshopf Application

Although I used eshopx as a basis for the JSF version of the application, its architecture is quite different from that of the first two versions. This is partly due to the fact that I had to replace ShopServlet with the standard FacesServlet class. In the process, I also removed the custom tags I had introduced in eshopx. In this section, I'll refer to the eshopf application as described in Chapter 8 after the addition of a custom converter, a custom validator, and a custom component with a separate renderer.

Listing 10-17 shows the annotated list of files and folders that constitute eshopf. The folders marked "= eshopx" have the same content as the corresponding folders of eshopx (not of the original eshop); the modules marked "rewritten" are completely different from the previous versions; and those marked "~ eshop" are those obtained by updating the corresponding modules in eshop.

Listing 10-17. The Eshopf Files

```
css
    eshopf.jspx  (updated version of eshop.jspx)
images  (content = eshopx)
jsp
    BookDetails.jspx  (~ eshop)
    Checkout.jspx  (~ eshop)
    LeftMenu.jspx  (~ eshop)
    ListBooks.jspx  (update of SelectCatalog.jspx + SearchOutcome.jspx)
    OrderConfirmation.jspx  (~ eshop)
    ShoppingCart.jspx  (~ eshop)
    TopMenu.jspx  (~ eshop)
META-INF
    MANIFEST.MF  (= eshopx)
    context.xml  (new file)
WEB-INF
    faces-config.xml  (new file)
    web.xml  (rewritten)
    classes
        eshop  (ShopServlet removed)
            beans
                Book.class, Book.java  (= eshopx)
                CartItem.class, CartItem.java  (~ eshop)
                Category.class, Category.java  (= eshopx)
                Customer.class, Customer.java  (= eshopx)
                ShopManager.class, ShopManager.java  (new file)
            components  (new folder)
                InputEntryComponent.class, InputEntryComponent.java
            converters  (new folder)
                CCNumberConverter.class, CCNumberConverter.java
```

model
    BookPeer.class, BookPeer.java (= eshopx)
    CategoryPeer.class, CategoryPeer.java (~ eshop)
    DataManager.class, DataManager.java (~ eshop)
    OrderDetailsPeer.class, OrderDetailsPeer.java (= eshopx)
    OrderPeer.class, OrderPeer.java (= eshopx)
    shop.sql (= eshopx)
renderers (new folder)
    InputEntryRenderer.class, InputEntryRenderer.java
tags (removed all the custom tags of eshopx)
    InputEntryTag.class, InputEntryTag.java (new file)
validators (new folder)
    CCExpiryValidator.class, CCExpiryValidator.java
tlds
    eshop.tld (rewritten)

In fact, I described almost everything in Chapter 8. In this chapter, I'll systematically go through the changes I made to eshopx to transform it into eshopf.

web.xml and context.xml

In eshopx, I defined ShopServlet.java to implement the controller part of the MVC architecture. In eshopf, this function is performed by the standard FacesServlet. As a result, I had to rewrite most of web.xml. In particular, I replaced the servlet element used in the web.xml version of eshopx

```
<display-name>ShopServlet</display-name>
<servlet-name>ShopServlet</servlet-name>
<servlet-class>eshop.ShopServlet</servlet-class>
```

with this:

```
<servlet-name>Faces Servlet</servlet-name>
<servlet-class>javax.faces.webapp.FacesServlet</servlet-class>
<load-on-startup>1</load-on-startup>
```

I also changed the body of servlet-mapping from this:

```
<servlet-name>ShopServlet</servlet-name>
<url-pattern>/shop/*</url-pattern>
```

to this:

```
<servlet-name>Faces Servlet</servlet-name>
<url-pattern>*.jsf</url-pattern>
```

In eshopx, to access the database containing books, book categories, and orders, I defined the initialization parameters jdbcDriver, dbURL, dbUserName, and dbPassword. They were used in ShopServlet to set up an object of type DataManager, which implemented the model part of the MVC architecture and interfaced to the database. The replacement of ShopServlet with FacesServlet forced me to implement a different mechanism in eshopf for passing the database parameters to the data manager.

I defined the database as a resource external to the application by creating the context.xml file in the META-INF folder with the following content:

```
<Context debug="5" reloadable="true" crossContext="true">
  <Resource
      name="jdbc/mysql"
      auth="Container"
      type="javax.sql.DataSource"
      username="root"
      password=""
      driverClassName="com.mysql.jdbc.Driver"
      url="jdbc:mysql://localhost:3306/shop"
      maxActive="8"
      maxIdle="4"
      />
  <Valve
      className="org.apache.catalina.valves.AccessLogValve"
      directory="logs"
      prefix="eshopf-access."
      suffix=".log"
      pattern="common"
      resolveHosts="false"
      />
</Context>
```

I then registered the resource in the web.xml file as follows:

```
<resource-ref>
  <res-ref-name>jdbc/mysql</res-ref-name>
  <res-type>javax.sql.DataSource</res-type>
  <res-auth>Container</res-auth>
</resource-ref>
```

Note that with this mechanism, you effectively pool the connections to the database, thereby achieving a more efficient use of resources. I leave up to you to retrofit eshopx with this mechanism. To complete the conversion from eshopx to eshopf, I also removed the definition of the initialization parameters base and imageURL from web.xml, because they were no longer needed, and I added the element to direct Tomcat to perform the basic authentication needed to access the database resource. Listing 8-8 shows the full web.xml file of eshopf.

Style Sheet

CSS lets you define new styles by adding attributes to already defined styles. This "cascading" mechanism is a form of inheritance, and therefore it requires an underlying hierarchical structure. CSS uses the structure provided by HTML documents instead of creating its own. This is fine as long as you write the HTML code yourself or generate it with JSP. When you use JSF, though, the control you have on the generated HTML is reduced. As a result, you have to pay greater attention when designing the style sheets.

When converting eshopx to eshopf, I encountered this issue in several places and had to modify the style-sheet file accordingly.

For example, in eshopx\css\eshop.jspx, I first defined .box (lines 130–133)

```
.box {
  padding: 0px 0px 10px 0px;
  margin: 0px;
```

```
}
```

and then extended it to define .box p (lines 134–139)

```
.box p {
  font-size: 12px;
  padding: .2em 1em .2em 1em;
  margin: 0px;
  border: 0px;
  }
```

I know, I didn't need to repeat margin:0px, but these things happen when you cut and paste!

In any case, LeftMenu.jspx uses the two styles as follows:

```
<div class="box">
  ...
  <p>Book Title/Author:</p>
  ...
  </div>
```

In eshopf, I replaced the HTML p element with a h:outputText component, which generates an HTML span element, not a p. Therefore, if I had left the style sheet unchanged, the .box p style wouldn't have had any effect, and the search box would have been rendered as shown in Figure 10-12.

Figure 10-12. *Wrong style in the search box*

Not nice.

To resolve the issue, I defined in eshopf\css\eshopf.jspx the new style .box_p as follows (lines 153–159):

```
.box_p {
  font-size: 12px;
  padding: .2em 1em .2em 1em;
  margin: 0px;
  border: 0px;
  display: block;
  }
```

By writing in eshopf\jsp\LeftMenu.jspx the code

```
<h:panelGroup styleClass="box">
  ...
  <h:outputText styleClass="box_p" value="Book Title/Author:"/>
  ...
  </h:panelGroup>
```

I could generate the following HTML output:

```
<span class="box">
  ...
  <span class="box_p">Book Title/Author:</span>
</span>
```
and this resulted in the correct formatting of the search box, as shown in Figure 10-13.

Figure 10-13. *Correctly styled search box*

In case you are wondering, the effect of display:block is to insert a new line before and after and take up the full width available. You will find that I applied it a few times in the style sheet for eshopf to ensure that the generated page looked as similar as possible to the corresponding page of eshopx (and eshop).

As a last remark about styles, I would like to point out that I could have "salvaged" the inheritance from h:panelGroup to h:outputText by renaming the .box p style of eshopx.jspx to .box .p, and then writing the h:outputText component as follows:

```
<h:outputText styleClass="p" value="Book Title/Author:"/>
```

This would have worked because the span element it generates is enclosed inside the span element generated by h:panelGroup. I would have still needed to add the display:block style, however. There are often several ways to achieve the same result, and sometimes it is just a matter of what comes to mind first.

This issue concerning style sheets is a disadvantage of using JSF, but it becomes less and less important as you become familiar with the HTML code that JSF generates. Furthermore, you'll normally start developing directly with JSF. When converting eshopx into eshopf, I was dealing with an existing user interface that I wanted to alter as little as possible.

JSP Documents

I had to modify all JSP documents. This shouldn't be a surprise, considering that the JSP documents generate the HTML pages that the user sees in his or her web browser. In Chapter 8, I described all the JSF components you need for eshopf. Therefore, it wouldn't make much sense to do it again here. In this section, I'll only tell you how JSF allows you to merge two separate JSP documents of eshopx (SelectCatalog.jspx and SearchOutcome.jspx) into a single document of eshopf (ListBooks.jspx).

The two modules were already very similar in eshopx. Without considering page titles, text headers, and error messages, the differences boiled down to less than a handful of lines. In SearchOutcome.jspx, I was using the custom tag eshop:searchResults, while in SelectCatalog.jspx, I was first obtaining the category name with eshop:categoryName and then the list of books with eshop:booksInCategory.

After converting the two modules to use JSF, the list of books in both cases was obtained from a property of shopManager: when the user performed a search via the search field of LeftMenu.jspx, the method that filled in the list of books in shopManager was searchBooks, and when the user selected a category, the method was selectCategory.

The only difference left between the two modules was in a couple of messages. To make the merging possible, I added the categoryName property to shopManager and reset it to null within the searchBooks method. In this way, I could use the name of the category as a flag, because it would be null after a search and non-null after a category selection.

Perhaps I could have also merged the JSP documents in eshopx, but it would have required some "awkward" coding, while it works out quite naturally with JSF.

Java Modules

One major change I made was to replace the custom tags defined in eshopx with the eshop.beans.ShopManager class. I did this to take advantage of JSF.

For example, to update the number of copies of a book in eshopx, you use the custom tag UpdateBook. Listing 10-18 shows the code to implement the tag.

Listing 10-18. Eshopx—UpdateBookTag.java

```
package eshop.tags;

import java.util.Hashtable;
import javax.servlet.jsp.tagext.TagSupport;
import javax.servlet.http.HttpSession;
import eshop.beans.CartItem;

public class UpdateBookTag extends TagSupport {
  static final long serialVersionUID = 1L;
  private String bookID;
  private String quantity;

  public void setBookID(String bookID) {
    this.bookID = bookID;
    }

  public void setQuantity(String quantity) {
    this.quantity = quantity;
    }

  public int doEndTag() {
    HttpSession session = pageContext.getSession();
    @SuppressWarnings("unchecked")
    Hashtable<String, CartItem> shoppingCart =
        (Hashtable<String, CartItem>)session.getAttribute("shoppingCart");
    CartItem item = (CartItem)shoppingCart.get(bookID);
    if (item != null) {
      item.setQuantity(quantity);
      }
    return EVAL_PAGE;
    }
}
```

In eshopf, the following JSF component of ShoppingCart.jspx takes care of updating the number of copies:

```
<h:inputText id="quantity" value="#{item.quantity}" size="2"
    required="true"
    requiredMessage="What? Nothing?"
    converterMessage="An integer, please!"
    validatorMessage="At least one copy!"
    >
  <f:validateLongRange minimum="1"/>
  </h:inputText>
```

As a result, when you trigger an update by pressing the corresponding button

```
<h:commandButton action="#{shopManager.updateItem}" value="Update"/>
```

there's nothing left for the updateItem method of the shop manager to do:

```
public String updateItem() {
  return null;
}
```

Another example is the RoundToCent tag, which rounds amounts in dollars to two decimal places in eshopx. This is necessary because sometimes the result of multiplying the price of a book by the ordered quantity results in a sequence of '9's after the decimal point. Here is an example of its usage taken from ShoppingCart.jspx:

```
<eshop:roundToCent var="itemPrice" value="${item.quantity * item.price}"/>
```

In eshopf, I introduced the subtotal attribute to the CartItem bean and added the functionality to recalculate it and round it to two decimals after every shopping cart update. This is the only update I made to the four eshop.beans modules.

Of the eshop.model modules, I only needed to modify CategoryPeer.java and DataManager.java. In CategoryPeer.java, I changed the getAllCategories method to return a list of categories instead of an object of type java.util.Hashtable. I then changed the getCategories methods in DataManager.java and ShopManager.java accordingly. This allowed me to display the list of categories in LeftMenu.jspx with the following JSF element without having to do any type conversion:

```
<h:dataTable value="#{shopManager.categories}" var="category">
```

In DataManager, besides the change to the getCategories method that I've already discussed and the removal of the getCatIDs method that was no longer needed, I only updated the algorithm used in the getConnection method to open a database connection. This was necessary because I had replaced the database initialization parameters of eshopx with a JNDI resource.

In eshopx, DataManager opened a database connection by invoking the static getConnection method of the java.sql.DriverManager class:

```
conn = DriverManager.getConnection(getDbURL(), getDbUserName(), getDbPassword());
```

The dbURL, dbUserName, and dbPassword attributes were set by ShopServlet using the servlet initialization parameters. In eshopf, the code to obtain a database connection is as follows:

```
Context ctx = new InitialContext();
if (ctx != null){
  Context envContext  = (Context)ctx.lookup("java:/comp/env");
  if (envContext != null) {
    DataSource ds = (DataSource)envContext.lookup("jdbc/mysql");
    if (ds != null) {
      conn = ds.getConnection();
```

```
      }
    }
  }
}
```

Finally, I added Java modules to implement a custom JSF component, a converter, a renderer, and a validator. Please refer to the corresponding sections of Chapter 8 for their description.

Summary

In this chapter, I completed the description of the various versions of the online bookshop example and explained what I had to do in order to convert standard JSP syntax to XML syntax and then to use JSF.

This chapter completes the main body of the book. After the first introductory chapter, I took you through five chapters about JSP, application architectures, JSP actions, XML, and databases, followed by two chapters about JSF and one about Tomcat.

Next, two appendixes will help you in two areas that, although not part of the core technologies explained in this book, are essential to develop web applications. Appendix A will talk about HTML and its associated technologies, like JavaScript and CSS, while Appendix B will provide a quick reference of SQL. The third appendix will list all the abbreviations you have encountered in the book.

What more is there to say?

I hope that you'll find this book useful. Perhaps, in a few areas I could have gone a bit deeper or provided additional examples, but a lot of ground had to be covered in a limited space.

I wish you all the best. Happy programming!

The Web Page

This appendix is mainly aimed at those of you who have little experience in web development and feel a bit lost among the myriad of web pages you get when searching the Web for "HTML" and "HTTP". But I have also included some information that experienced web developers could find interesting.

You can find on the Internet several web sites that describe HTML, CSS, and JavaScript in detail. Therefore, instead of attempting to cover everything there is to know about them, I will introduce a few key concepts of networking and then describe some useful techniques.

Hopefully, after seeing how the different components work together to deliver web pages, you will find it easier to fill the gaps.

The WWW Network

For your browser to render a web page correctly, it must be able to communicate with the server, or servers, where the page content is stored. This means that the browser must support the necessary communication protocols, be configured correctly, and use the proper addressing.

So far, I have concentrated on what happens when a web server receives a HTTP request and replies with a HTTP response. In this section, I will talk about requests and responses while they cross the network that connects browsers and servers.

A data-communication protocol is a standardized set of rules that computers must follow to be able to communicate with each other. The protocol rules define the format of the *data packets* being transferred and the way in which the exchange takes place.

To make this complex process more manageable, the functionality necessary to move data across networks is broken down into layers organized into *protocol stacks*, or *protocol suites*. Higher layers can perform more general and complex tasks by relying on the services of the lower layers. Computers communicate across the Internet by means of the Internet protocol stack, which consists of five layers. Starting from the top, these layers are *application*, *transport*, *network*, and *network interface*.

To get an idea of the complexity of the whole Internet protocol suite, consider that the list of Internet standards has become a standard itself: Request for Comments (RFC) 5000, with title *Internet Official Protocol Standards* (http://tools.ietf.org/html/rfc5000). It lists more than 5200 RFCs that specify 68 Standard Protocols (STDs) and 135 Best Current Practices (BCPs), and, yes, it lists itself in the top spot.

The operating system of every computer connected to the Internet includes an implementation of the Internet protocol stack. However, this chapter focuses on web applications, so I'm not going to discuss the two lowest layers (physical and link), which are local to your setup (for example, Ethernet and wireless local area network).

The first layer—from the bottom—of interest to us is the network layer (the Internet Protocol layer, or simply IP), which is the lowest one operating end to end. Each computer directly connected to the Internet is identified via its IP address, which is assigned by the ISP. To find out the IP address of your

PC, open a command-line window and type ipconfig. You'll get several lines of information, including one that shows your IP address as a string of four numbers separated by dots—something like 84.74.96.111.

Each one of the four numbers is between 0 and 255 (well, except the first one), because it is stored in eight unsigned bits. If you have a home network and connect to the ISP via a router, the router will "keep" the address assigned by the ISP for itself and assign to each one of your home computers a private address, which will probably be like 192.168.x.x, although it could also be 172.16.x.x or 10.x.x.x. Note that a transition from the current Internet Protocol with 32-bit addresses to an addressing scheme based on 128 bits is taking place. There are dozens of standard documents (RFCs) that specify all aspects of the new Internet Protocol (IP version 6, or IPv6). The general specification document is RFC 2460 (http://www.ietf.org/rfc/rfc2460.txt). A general resource is the wiki of the American Registry for Internet Numbers (ARIN) at http://www.getipv6.info/.

To get the IP address of a server, type the command nslookup. When you get a greater-than sign as a prompt, type the name of the server and hit Enter. For example, if you type google.com, you'll get a dozen IP addresses like 74.125.237.x, which are the IP addresses of Google's clustered servers. If you then open a browser and type one of Google's IP addresses where you'd normally type a URL, you'll see Google's home page.

The next layer up, the transport layer, uses the Transmission Control Protocol (TCP) to ensure that information packets reach their destination reliably. TCP associates so-called ports with the applications running on a computer, thereby ensuring separate and concurrent data communication for, say, your e-mail and your Skype calls. You might have heard of the User Datagram Protocol (UDP). Like TCP, UDP belongs to the transport layer and assigns ports to applications, but unlike TCP, it doesn't guarantee reliable delivery of packets. It isn't relevant to us in this book.

The top layer is the application layer. Each application running on one computer *attaches* itself to its TCP/UDP port or ports. The protocol for web pages is HTTP, or HTTPS for encrypted pages. The web server can be attached to several ports. For example, Tomcat by default expects to receive HTTP requests via port 8080 and HTTPS requests via port 8443.

By default, the web browsers send to port 80 the requests for URLs that begin with http://, and to port 443 those for URLs that begin with https://. For ftp://, the browsers use ports 20 and 21. Note that the browser will use additional ports if necessary. For example, a video stream in Windows Media format will go through port 1755. This is important to know if a firewall exists between client and server to block communication through ports you don't use. The Internet Assigned Numbers Authority (IANA) is in charge of keeping official port assignments. You'll find the list at http://www.iana.org/assignments/port-numbers (warning: it takes a while to load it).

A URL like http://localhost:8080/ebookshop/ that you saw in the previous chapters specifies that on the host side, the port number for HTTP is 8080 (IANA identifies it as *HTTP Alternate*) instead of 80, which is the standard port for HTTP. This is because Tomcat expects and routes HTTP traffic through port 8080. This is appropriate if you intend to use Tomcat to handle requests for JSP pages and place it behind a server (typically, the Apache web server) that handles static HTTP/HTTPS. But if you intend to use Tomcat to handle HTTP/HTTPS as well, you should change its default ports 8080 and 8443 to 80 and 443 respectively. In Chapter 9 you saw how you can change Tomcat's ports.

Figure A-1 shows you what happens when you send a request from your PC to a web server.

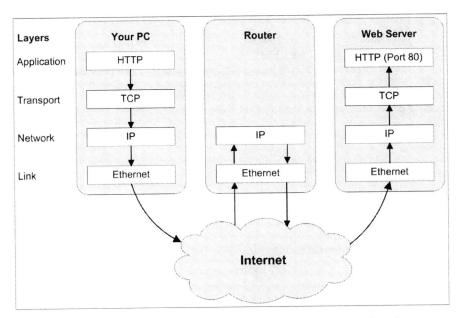

Figure A-1. *Following an HTTP request through the Internet protocol stacks*

Note how a router operates at the Network layer. The router in Figure A-1 represents one of the many routers your IP packets will go through before reaching their final destination. You can check this out with the command cacert, which traces the packet routes. If you open a command window and type cacert apress.com, you will probably be surprised to see how many routers separate your PC from the web site belonging to this book's publisher.

When you request a web page, the web browser sends the request to the Internet protocol stack that is implemented on your PC. Each of the layers attaches information to your request in the form of a header, so that the same layer on the server knows what to do with the packet. The packet grows as it descends the protocol stack, and it often ends up fragmented into several parts before reaching the bottom.

The IP header contains, among other fields, the source IP address (i.e., your IP address) and the destination IP address (i.e., the address of the server, which you can obtain from the name server of your ISP with the command nslookup). Instead of Ethernet, you might have a wireless LAN layer, but ultimately your request will end up encapsulated in data packets traveling through the Internet. On their way to the server, the data packets encounter routers that forward them toward the server on the basis of the destination IP address. Depending on your location relative to that of the server, the packets might "hop" on a dozen or more routers. Finally, your packets reach the server. The process that occurred on your PC is reversed, and your request is put back together. The destination port tells the protocol stack what application handles it (i.e., a web server such as the Apache web server or the Apache Tomcat Java web server). The response follows a similar logical path in the reverse direction.

If you have a home network, you are connected to your router by a direct Ethernet connection or a wireless LAN. Before forwarding your packets to the Internet, toward their destination, your home router translates the private IP addresses that appear as a source address in your outgoing packets (i.e., the address you see with ipconfig), so that when they go through the Internet, the packets of all your computers appear to be coming from a single computer having as source address the address assigned to you by your ISP.

URLs, Hosts, and Paths

URLs tell your browser where to find web pages, files, File Transfer Protocol (FTP) sites, and more. To be precise, a URL doesn't really tell where a resource is; it only provides the information necessary to be able to address the resource locally or across a network and establish communication with it. That is, I'm not talking about physical locations here.

A URL consists of several parts. For example, `http://localhost:8080/ebookshop/` can be broken down as follows:

- `http` is the protocol.

- `localhost` is the host name.

- `8080` is the port number on the host.

- `/ebookshop/` is the path.

In fact, although everybody speaks of URLs, the more general term is Uniform Resource Identifier (URI), which lets you define even a *fragment* within a resource. The Internet Society (ISOC) defines the URI format in the document RFC 3986.

Let's break down this fictitious URI:

`http://localhost:8080/first/second_one/page.html?answer=no#exactly_here`

- `http` is the protocol (the standard name for this part of the URI is *scheme*).

- `//` is called the *hier-part* and determines what format is acceptable for the part of the URI that follows it.

- `localhost:8080` is referred to as the *authority*.

- `/first/second_one/page.html` is the path.

- `answer=no` is the query string, which can include several parameters.

- `exactly_here` is the fragment.

The purpose of the RFC 3986 standard is to define a method of identification for all possible resources and to include particular cases already in common use. However, we're only concerned with HTTP and web pages in this chapter, so I won't spend any more time on the most general formats.

There is just one more scheme that you might find useful in your web pages: `mailto`. By including a link to the URI `mailto:John.Doe@nowhere.com` within a web page, you can allow the viewer to start his or her e-mail program and create a new e-mail with the correct address already set. However, you might not like to do that, because many programs are capable of scanning web pages and extracting e-mail addresses from them for the sole purpose of sending junk mail. For a while, it was safe to display email addresses like `John.Doe(at)nowhere.com`, and create a JavaScript that converted the `(at)` into @ before returning the link. Unfortunately the programs that extract email addresses from web pages have become more sophisticated in their searches and can deal with masked addresses. Linking a JavaScript to a clickable image of your address might still be safe.

Host names are case-insensitive, meaning that you can write `WwW.GOOgle.cOM` if you prefer. You'll still land on the same web site. Incidentally, the same applies to e-mail addresses. It's irrelevant whether you capitalize names, such as in `John.Doe@nowhere.com`.

The same is not true for the paths. Even though you're running Tomcat under Windows, which has case-insensitive file and folder names, if you type `http://localhost:8080/Ebookshop/`, with the path capitalized, you'll get an error page like that shown in Figure A-2.

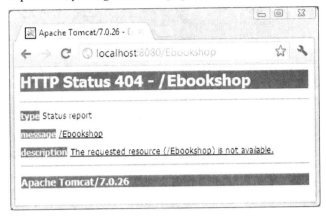

Figure A-2. Resource not available

Originally, domain and host names could only be made out of the 26 letters of the English alphabet, the 10 decimal digits, and dashes. In July 2003, it became possible to register .jp domains containing Japanese characters, and in March 2004, .de domains with diacritical characters, such as in Lösung and Müller, sprung up. Today, you can even use languages that are written from right to left.

The situation is different for paths and queries. They can include any character of the ISO 8859-1 (ISO Latin1) character set, which is a superset of the well-known ASCII standard. But of the 256 ISO Latin1 characters, all the non-ASCII characters, the non-printing ASCII characters, and even some of the printing ASCII characters need to be encoded in hexadecimal format.

For example, the path `/my preferred physicists/Erwin Schrödinger.html` must be encoded as follows:

`/my%20preferred%20phycisists/Erwin%20Schr%F6dinger.html`

where %20 is ISO Latin1-32 (the space) and %F6 is ISO Latin1-246 (the o-umlaut ö).

In some cases, it is necessary to encode characters to prevent the browser from interpreting them as URL separator characters. For example, suppose you want to execute a JSP page with a parameter set to the ampersand. If you type this URL:

`http://myServer.com/myPage.jsp?myPar=&`

your browser will send to the server a request with the parameter myPar set to the empty string. This is because the ampersand is normally used to indicate that another parameter follows, and the browser doesn't complain about the trailing ampersand because it is legal not to write any further parameter after it. As a result, the browser behaves exactly as if you had ended the URL at the equal sign. To send the correct query, you have to replace the ampersand with %26.

Although ampersands cause problems in queries because they are used as separators, they are OK within the file and folder names that form paths. Conversely, some characters, such as colons and question marks, are OK in the query but not in the path.

All in all, be careful when using special characters. You can download tables of Unicode characters and their hex representations from `http://unicode.org/charts/`.

XHTML vs HTML

Throughout this book, I have mostly showed you markup code conforming to the XHTML standard, rather than HTML. The current WorldWide Web Consortium (W3C) standards for the two languages are HTML 4.01 (`http://www.w3.org/TR/1999/REC-html401-19991224/`) and XHTML 1.1 (`http://www.w3.org/TR/xhtml11/`).

Except for the *ruby* collection of elements (`http://www.w3.org/TR/2001/REC-ruby-20010531/`), which provides a mechanism to write annotations, and the replacement of the name attribute of the elements a and map with the id attribute, tags and attributes defined in the two standards are the same.

In essence, the differences between HTML and XHTML are as follows:

- **All XHTML elements must be properly nested**: For example, in HTML, you can write `<b><i>whatever</b></i>`. In XHTML, you must write `<b><i>whatever</i></b>`.

- **All XHTML elements must be closed**: For example, in HTML, you can write `<p>` without a corresponding `</p>`, and you can write `<hr>` and `<br>` without a slash before the closing bracket. In XHTML, you must match each `<p>` with a `</p>` and write `<hr/>` and `<br/>`.

- **All XHTML elements must be in lowercase**: XHTML doesn't allow you to write elements in uppercase, such as `<HTML>` and `<BODY>`.

- **All XHTML elements must be nested inside the `<html>` element**: This is not enforced in HTML.

Both standards have deprecated some elements that were widely used in past versions of HTML. Just in case you see them in some non-conforming documents, I have listed them in Table A-1.

Table A-1. Deprecated HTML Elements

Element	Purpose	Use this instead
applet	Embed an applet	object element
basefont	Set default font color and size	CSS
center	Center-align text	CSS
dir	Format directory list	CSS
font	Set text font, color, and size	CSS
menu	Format a menu list	CSS
s / strike	Display strikethrough text	del element
u	Display underlined text	CSS
xmp	Defines preformatted text	pre element

As you can see, you can replace most of the deprecated elements by defining styles.

To do strict validation of XHTML code against the latest standard, you write at the top of your documents the following two special elements:

```
<?xml version='1.0' encoding='utf-8'?>
<!DOCTYPE html PUBLIC "-//W3C//DTD XHTML 1.1//EN" ➡
    "http://www.w3.org/TR/xhtml11/DTD/xhtml11.dtd">
```

With HTML, you write instead:

```
<!DOCTYPE HTML PUBLIC "-//W3C//DTD HTML 4.01//EN" ➡
    "http://www.w3.org/TR/html4/strict.dtd">
```

You can also decide *not* to apply strict validation, in which case the two document-type elements become respectively

```
<!DOCTYPE html PUBLIC "-//W3C//DTD XHTML 1.0 Transitional//EN" ➡
    "http://www.w3.org/TR/xhtml1/DTD/xhtml1-transitional.dtd">
```

and

```
<!DOCTYPE HTML PUBLIC "-//W3C//DTD HTML 4.01 Transitional//EN" ➡
    "http://www.w3.org/TR/html4/loose.dtd">
```

If you do so, you can use the deprecated elements listed in Table A-1.

If you want to use HTML frames within your XHTML page, you have to use the following doctype:

```
<!DOCTYPE html PUBLIC "-//W3C//DTD XHTML 1.0 Frameset//EN" ➡
    "http://www.w3.org/TR/xhtml1/DTD/xhtml1-frameset.dtd">
```

This performs the exact same validation as the transitional DOCTYPE, but it also accepts <frameset>, which can replace <body>. In other words, the pages with frames aren't strictly validated, although obviously this doesn't prevent you from conforming to the strict validation rules when using frames. Before deciding to use frames, keep in mind that their use is somewhat controversial. Some people don't like them and simply disable them in their browsers. Others might use audio browsers and simply be unable to access frames. If you want to reach the widest audience, you should develop a second version of your pages without frames. Actually, to be sure that everything will work, you should design frameless pages first and only add the frames later. You might wonder why you should develop framed versions at all, and you'd be right. Follow my advice: forget the frames and apply strict XHTML validation. The time will certainly come when you'll be happy to have made these choices.

In any case, to complete the subject, here is the DOCTYPE element for HTML 4.01 that allows you to use frames:

```
<!DOCTYPE HTML PUBLIC "-//W3C//DTD HTML 4.01 Frameset//EN" ➡
    "http://www.w3.org/TR/html4/frameset.dtd">
```

Before moving on, I will still mention the XHTML 2.0 standard (http://www.w3.org/TR/xhtml2/). In my opinion, it is not likely to see wide adoption. Its main problem is that it is not back compatible with HTML4 and XHTML1.

XHTML/HTML Elements

Table A-2 summarizes all valid HTML elements according to the standards HTML 4.01 and XHTML 1.0 when strictly applied. A slash after a tag name indicates that the element is always bodyless.

Table A-2. *HTML Elements*

Element	Purpose
`<!-- -->`	Comment tags
`a`	An anchor
`abbr`	An abbreviation
`acronym`	An acronym
`address`	Contact information
`area/`	An area inside an image-map
`b`	Bold text
`base/`	Base URL for all relative URLs in the document
`bdo`	Overrides the current text direction
`big`	Big text
`blockquote`	A long quotation
`body`	The document's body
`br/`	A single line break
`button`	A clickable button
`caption`	A table caption
`cite`	A citation
`code`	A piece of computer code
`col/`	Attribute values for one or more columns in a table

Element	Purpose
colgroup	A group of one or more columns in a table
dd	Description of an item in a definition list
del	Deleted text
dfn	A definition
div	A document section
dl	A definition list
dt	An item in a definition list
em	Emphasized text
fieldset	Groups related elements in a form
form	An HTML input form
h1–h6	HTML headings
head	Document information
hr/	A horizontal line
html	Root of the HTML document
i	Italic text
img/	An image
input/	An input control
ins	Inserted text
kbd	Keyboard input
label	A label for an input element
legend	A caption for a fieldset element
li	A list item

Element	Purpose
link/	Links in an external resource
map	A client-side image-map
meta/	Defines metadata about the HTML document
noscript	Alternate content for users that don't accept client-side scripts
object	An embedded object
ol	An ordered list
optgroup	A group of related options in a drop-down list
option	An option in a drop-down list
p	A paragraph
param/	An object parameter
pre	Preformatted text
q	A short quotation
samp	The sample output from a program
script	A client-side script
select	A drop-down list
small	Small text
span	A section in the document
strong	Strong text
style	Style information for the HTML document
sub	Subscripted text
sup	Superscripted text
table	A table

Element	Purpose
tbody	Groups table content
td	A table cell
textarea	An input control with multiple lines of text
tfoot	Groups content of a table footer
th	A header cell in a table
thead	Groups content of a table header
title	The document title
tr	A table row
tt	Teletype text
ul	An unordered list
var	A variable

HTML5

HTML5 is a specification originally created by the Web Hypertext Application Technology Working Group (WHATWG, http://www.whatwg.org), a group founded by people from Apple, the Mozilla Foundation, and Opera Software that now includes many other organizations. HTML5's main purpose is to provide a comfortable language to develop cross-platforms mobile applications.

Steve Jobs welcomed HTML5 as an alternative to Flash to embed rich content in web pages and Adobe announced that, for mobile devices, they will move from Flash to HTML5. W3C is working on adopting it as a standard (http://www.w3.org/TR/2012/WD-html5-20120329/) but it has not happened just yet.

HTML5 has removed some HTML4 elements (acronym, big, and tt), redefined or modified some others (a, address, hr, i, legend, and u), and resurrected a few elements that had been deprecated in HTML4 (iframe, menu, and s). The most important aspect of HTML5, though, is the introduction of elements that support a structuring of web pages and the easy embedding of rich content. I have listed the new elements in Table A-3, but I am not going to describe them in detail, because it would be beyond the scope of this book.

Table A-3. The New Elements of HTML5

Element	Description
article	An article
aside	Content aside from the page content
audio	Sound content
bdi	Text that might be formatted in a different direction
canvas	To draw graphics dynamically with JavaScript
command	A command button
datalist	A list of pre-defined options for input controls
details	Additional viewable details
embed	A container for a plug-in
figcaption	A figure caption
figure	A figure
footer	A footer for a document or a section
header	A header for a document or a section
hgroup	Groups heading
keygen	A generator of key-pair to be used in forms
mark	Highlighted text
meter	A scalar value within a given range
nav	A navigation link
output	The result of a calculation
progress	Progress of a task
rp	What to show in browsers that don't support ruby annotations

Element	Description
rt	An explanation of characters
ruby	A ruby annotation
section	A section in a document
source	Defines multiple resources for video and audio elements
summary	A heading for a details element
time	Date/time
track	Text tracks for video and audio elements
video	Video content
wbr	A possible line-break

HTML Documents

HTML documents are organized as a hierarchy of elements that normally consist of content enclosed between a pair of start and end tags. For example, the tags `<html>` and `</html>` delimit the whole HTML document.

The start tag can include element attributes, such as id in `<map id="mymap">`. Some elements are empty, in which case you can usually replace the end tag with a slash immediately before the closing bracket of the start tag, as in `<img src="mypict.gif"/>`. Unfortunately, this isn't always possible, as the form `<script ... />` isn't valid, and you have to keep both `<script>` and `</script>` tags even when there is nothing between them.

You can nest HTML elements inside each other and, in fact, without nesting, no HTML page would be possible.

Listing A-1 shows the simplest possible HTML page you can write while still applying strict XHTML validation.

Listing A-1. basic.html

```
<!DOCTYPE html PUBLIC "-//W3C//DTD XHTML 1.0 Strict//EN"
  "http://www.w3.org/TR/xhtml1/DTD/xhtml1-strict.dtd">
<html xmlns="http//www.w3.org/1999/xhtml">
<head><title>Page title</title></head>
<p>This shouldn't be displayed, but it is!</p>
<body>
Here is where you put your page content.<br/>
Of the following 11 spaces >            < only one is displayed.
</body>
</html>
```

Figure A-3 shows the outcome of Listing A-1.

Figure A-3. A basic HTML page

Place your content between <body> and </body> to have it displayed in the main browser window. The browser also displays the page title, but most of the rest of Listing A-1 remains hidden. Furthermore, any sequence of spaces, tabs, and newlines is normally rendered as a single space, and in several cases, even that single remaining space is omitted—for example, when it immediately follows the start paragraph tag (<p>) or the break tag (<br/>). This gives you plenty of flexibility to format the page source as you like, and you should use it to make the code more maintainable through proper indentation and spacing.

Notice that the paragraph

```
<p>This shouldn't be displayed, but it is!</p>
```

shouldn't be displayed in the browser because it is outside the body element. And yet, as you can see in Figure A-3, it is. All browsers I have tested (IE, Chrome, Firefox, and Opera) do it. I recommend that you include all the content elements of your pages inside the body, where they should be, because you never know what will happen in the future.

Essentially, an HTML document consists of text, images, audio and video clips, active components such as scripts and executables, and hyperlinks. A browser then interprets and renders the components in sequence, mostly without inserting any empty space or newline between them.

A browser renders every component according to a series of defaults specified in the HTML/XHTML standard. You can change the defaults regarding fonts and font sizes of normal text by setting the appropriate browser options. In general, and more importantly, you can override the defaults when writing your HTML pages by defining the corresponding attributes of the enclosing tags or by defining a style. For example, you can underline text:

```
<p style="text-decoration: underline">this is underlined</p>
```

or you can choose a background color for your page:

```
<body style="background-color: yellow">
```

■ **Tip** To shrink an image, reduce the original image on the server rather than change its height and width with the corresponding attributes of the <img> element. Your page will load faster.

You can use the `<object>` element to include any component. For example, this code shows how to display a short video clip in Flash format:

```
<object type="application/x-shockwave-flash"
    data="myClip.swf" width="400" height="300">
  <param name="movie" value="myClip.swf"/>
  <p>This is a Flashy movie</p>
  </object>
```

The following code lets you download an MPEG movie file:

```
<object type="video/mpeg"
    data=myClip.mpeg height="120" width="180">
  <p>Click <a href=MyMovie.mpeg>here</a> to download</p>
  </object>
```

And this code lets you display a JPEG image:

```
<object type="image/jpeg"
    data="myImage.jpg"
    style="border-style: solid; border-width: 1px"/>
```

In any case, you might prefer to use the `<img>` element for images, because it allows you to define the short description text that appears when you hover with your mouse over the image:

```
<img src="myImage.jpg" alt="whatever it is"/>
```

Caution The example showing how to embed Flash only works for short video clips. To show long Flash movies or Flash streams, you have to do something more complicated; otherwise, it won't work with Internet Explorer. For more information, go for example to http://helpx.adobe.com/flash/kb/object-tag-syntax-flash-professional.html.

Standard Attributes

Most HTML elements support a standard set of attributes, which are classified in core, language, and keyboard attributes.

Core Attributes

The core attributes are valid in all elements except `base`, `head`, `html`, `meta`, `param`, `script`, `style`, and `title`.

class

The `class` attribute accepts as a value the name of a class to which the element belongs. Use it as a CSS selector. For example, you can define the style of the class `warning_text` as follows:

```
<style> p.warning_text {color:red} </style>
```

and then use the class name in the appropriate element:

```
<p class="warning_text" id="warn1">This text is displayed in red</p>
```

id

The id attribute associates an element with a unique identifier within the document. Use it whenever you need to identify a particular element. For example, if you write `<a id="point1"/>` somewhere within a long web page stored in, say, `mypage.html`, you'll be able to jump directly to that position by clicking on a hyperlink created with this code:

```
<a href="http://mysite.com/mypage.html#point1">go to my page point 1</a>
```

To jump there from within the same page, you don't need to include the full URI, but only the locator part, as in

```
<a href="#point1">go to point 1</a>
```

style

The style attribute identifies an inline style definition. It's good to be able to define simple one-off styles within the HTML page, but if you use the same styles in several elements, you should define them by placing a style element inside the head element of the document. If you define styles to be used in more than one document, you should write a separate style sheet and load it by placing a link element inside the head.

The following is a simple example of a style definition using the style attribute:

```
<table style="font-weight:bold; background-color:#C0C0C0">
```

title

The title attribute displays tooltip text when the cursor is held over the element.

Language Attributes

Language attributes are *not* valid in base, br, frame, frameset, hr, iframe, param, and script. A good reference for these attributes is in http://www.w3.org/TR/html4/struct/dirlang.html.

dir

You use the dir attribute to set the text direction. It can have the values ltr (left-to-right) and rtl (right-to-left).

lang

The lang attribute sets the language of the element and accepts a language code as a value. The valid language codes are listed in the ISO standard ISO 639-1:2002. Unfortunately, it is only available for 140 Swiss Francs. If you search the Internet, you will find several web sites that list the codes like, for example, `http://xml.coverpages.org/iso639a.html` and `http://www.mathguide.de/info/tools/languagecode.html`. Even if they might refer to the previous version of the ISO standard, ISO 639:1988, they will still be to a large extent correct. Alternatively, you can also look at the half a dozen Wikipedia pages on ISO 639 (`http://en.wikipedia.org/wiki/ISO_639`).

Examples of valid language codes are `en` for English, `he` for Hebrew, `en-US` for American English, and `x-klingon` for Star Trek's Klingon language. The setting of a language can assist search engines, speech synthesizers, and spell and grammar checkers, to name a few. It can also help render language-specific features such as hyphenation.

Keyboard Attributes

You're probably never going to use keyboard attributes, but I'll list them just to be thorough.

accesskey

The `accesskey` attribute assigns a keyboard key to an element. By pressing that key when the page is displayed in a browser, the user shifts the focus to that element. This was meant as a way of helping people with some disabilities, but it doesn't work well, and not all keys are possible with all browsers. Also, you're supposed to press the Alt key while pressing the `accesskey`, so you run into trouble with IE because Alt is used to give all sorts of commands. Good luck!

tabindex

The `tabindex` attribute lets you specify the sequence of fields in a form when you tab through them. Again, I couldn't get it to work consistently (or at all).

Event Attributes

The purpose of most of these attributes is to link scripts (typically, JavaScript code) to particular actions that the user performs on HTML elements. They are called event attributes because they generate events that trigger the execution of scripts. There are five types of event attributes: object, form, image, keyboard, and mouse.

The general format is as follows:

```
<element event_attribute="script to be executed">
```

For example:

```
<input type="submit" onmouseover="show_mess()"/>
```

executes the function `show_mess` when the cursor passes across the submit button of a form.

Object Event Attributes

There are four attributes in this group: `onload`, `onunload`, `onresize`, and `onabort`.

`onload`, which is available for the elements `body`, `frame`, `frameset`, `iframe`, `img`, `input` with the attribute `type="image"`, `link`, `script`, and `style`, executes a script when the element is loaded. For example,

```
<body onload="initFun()">
```

causes the JavaScript function named initFun to run when the page is loaded.

onunload, which is only valid with body and frameset, causes a script to be executed when the page unloads.

onresize is available for most elements. It triggers the execution of a script when the size of an element changes.

oabort triggers an event when the loading of an image is stopped before completion.

Form Event Attributes

Table A-4 describes the events in this group.

Table A-4. Form Event Attributes

Attribute	Event
onblur	An element loses focus
onchange	An element changes value
onfocus	An element gets focus
onreset	A form is reset
onselect	An element is selected
onsubmit	A form is submitted

While onreset, onsubmit, and onselect specifically apply to form elements, the other attributes apply to most HTML elements.

Keyboard Event Attributes

There are only three attributes in this group: onkeydown, onkeyup, and onkeypressed. They trigger an event for the element that is currently on focus. The attribute onkeypressed is activated when the user presses a key down and then releases it. These attributes apply to most HTML elements.

Mouse Event Attributes

Table A-5 describes the events in this group. These attributes apply to most HTML elements.

Table A-5. Mouse Event Attributes

Attribute	Event
onclick	A mouse click
ondblclick	A mouse double-click
onmousedown	A mouse button is pressed
onmousemove	The cursor moves
onmouseout	The cursor moves out of an element
onmouseover	The cursor moves over an element
onmouseup	A mouse button is released

Tables

A table consists of rows and columns, with cells containing text, images, and other components. In almost every chapter of this book, you'll find examples of tables. Tables are an easy way to present components in an organized fashion.

Listing A-2 shows the code that generates the simple table of Figure A-4.

Listing A-2. HTML Code for a Table

```
<table border="1"><tr style="background-color: #c0c0c0"><th>abc</th><th
align="center" colspan="2">a 2-column span</th></tr><tr><td>a1</td><td>
a2</td><td>a3</td></tr><tr><td rowspan="2">2-row<br/>span</td><td>b2
</td><td>b3</td></tr><tr><td>c2</td><td>c3</td></tr></table>
```

Figure A-4. An HTML-generated table

I've purposely packed the code to show you how difficult it is to interpret it without proper indentation. You should find Listing A-3 more readable.

Listing A-3. table.html

```
<!DOCTYPE html PUBLIC "-//W3C//DTD XHTML 1.0 Strict//EN"
    "http//www.w3.org/TR/xhtml1/DTD/xhtml1-strict.dtd">
<html xmlns="http//www.w3.org/1999/xhtml" xmllang="en" lang="en">
<head><title>Table</title></head>
<body>
<table border="1">
  <tr style="background-color: #c0c0c0">
    <th>abc</th>
    <th align="center" colspan="2">a 2-column span</th>
    <!-- item merged into item on the left -->
    </tr>
  <tr>
    <td>a1</td>
    <td>a2</td>
    <td>a3</td>
    </tr>
  <tr>
    <td rowspan="2">2-row<br/>span</td>
    <td>b2</td>
    <td>b3</td>
    </tr>
  <tr>
    <!-- item merged into item above -->
    <td>c2</td>
    <td>c3</td>
    </tr>
  </table>
</body>
</html>
```

This code should be pretty self-explanatory. Notice how the browser sets the size of the different cells to the minimum necessary. You can change that by defining styles to set cell dimensions.

Table Structure

You use the element table to define a table. Inside table, immediately after the start tag, you can place a single caption element to identify a string that the browsers display immediately above the table.

Use the tr element to define rows within the table, and use td to define cells (i.e., columns) within the rows. If you want, you can use th for the table header instead of tr. The browsers will highlight it in bold.

To facilitate scrolling and printing of long tables, you can flag some rows at the top and/or at the bottom of the table as having particular significance. To do so, place the header rows inside the thead element, the footer rows inside the element tfoot, and the rest of the rows inside the tbody element.

You can also define attributes of columns before defining the rows that contain the actual table cells. You do this with the col element, which is not as useless as it might appear at first, because tables are defined one cell at a time. Therefore, without col, you would have to define the cell attributes for each individual cell. With col, you can define those attributes only once for all the cells belonging to one column. It potentially avoids a lot of repetitions and makes the code more readable.

Table Width

To define the width of the whole table, you use the width attribute. You can express it either in pixels or as a percentage of the enclosing window. For example, <table width="100%"> defines a table as wide as the whole window. Please note that the browsers tend to have a lot of initiative when it comes to rendering tables. You cannot really rely on this attribute. Trial and error using different browsers is advisable.

Table Borders

You can define the thickness in pixels of the border enclosing the whole table with the border attribute. The default is border="0", and with any border greater than zero, each individual cell is highlighted by a thin border.

Once you've defined a border of nonzero thickness, you can use the frame attribute to define which sides of the border surrounding the whole table are to be visible. Table A-6 shows the possible values. The default (i.e., when you omit the frame attribute) is "border".

Table A-6. Possible Values of the frame Attribute

Value	Meaning
void	No border at all
above	Top side
below	Bottom side
hsides	Horizontal side (top and bottom)
lhs	Left-hand side
rhs	Right-hand side

Value	Meaning
vsides	Vertical sides (left-hand side and right-hand side)
box	All four sides
border	All four sides (same as box)

The rules attribute defines the horizontal and vertical divider lines between rows and columns. It can have the following values: none, groups, rows, cols, and all. The rules are single lines, not the thin cell borders that are shown when the rules attribute is missing. With rules="groups", the lines are only drawn between the groups of columns defined with colgroup. Figure A-5 shows some examples of tables with different combinations of frames and rules viewed with Firefox. Unfortunately, the major browsers don't agree on how these borders, frames, and rules should be displayed. Figures A-6 to A-8 show how Chrome, Opera, and IE9 render the same document table_frame.html used for Figure A-5.

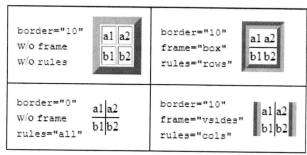

Figure A-5. *Rendering of table frames and rules - Firefox*

Figure A-6. *Rendering of table frames and rules - Chrome*

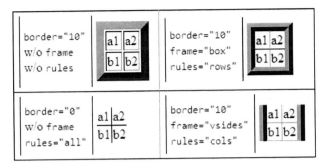

Figure A-7. Rendering of table frames and rules - Opera

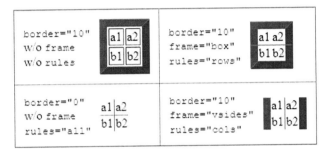

Figure A-8. Rendering of table frames and rules – IE9

The differences between the browsers mean that, when using table formatting, you need to check your pages with all major browsers and choose the best combination of attributes.

Row and Cell Alignment

All three elements tr, which defines rows; td, which define cells within rows; and th, which defines header cells; accept the four alignment attributes align, valign, char, and charoff. Additionally, td and th also accept the attributes abbr, axis, colspan, headers, rowspan, and scope.

Caution Cell elements are contained inside row elements. That's why it makes sense to talk about cells rather than columns. It's your responsibility to ensure that each row element includes the correct number of cell elements.

---

align, char, and charoff

The align attribute defines the horizontal alignment of the content in a table cell, or in all cells of a row when applied to tr. It can have the following values: left, right, center, justify, and char.

In particular, align="char" means that the text is aligned with respect to one particular character. The default for this character is the period, so that numbers with decimal digits are displayed with the periods aligned vertically. To change the character used for alignment, use the attribute char, as in char="; ", which would align the values on a semicolon instead of on the default period. You also have the possibility of introducing an offset in the alignment with the attribute charoff. For example, charoff="10%" shifts the alignment to the right by 1/10 of the cell size, while charoff="10" shifts it to the right by 10 pixels. Shifts to the left are obtained with negative values. It sounds cool, doesn't it? Well, forget it, because none of the major browsers supports either char or charoff. Same story with align="justify". There goes our beloved conformance to standards! I'm keeping this description in this book because the problem might be fixed in the future. Also, I don't want you to waste the time I invested in testing those features.

valign

The valign attribute defines the vertical alignment of the content in a table cell. It can have the values top, middle, bottom, and baseline. Baseline means that the characters are aligned on the same line of text regardless of their size. Figure A-9 clearly shows the differences when the four possible values of valign are applied to the cells with the small joy. The document I used to generate the figure is table_valign.html.

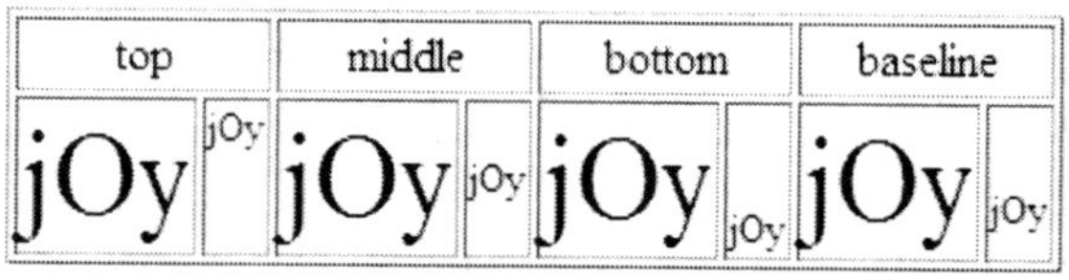

Figure A-9. The four possible values of the valign attribute

abbr and axis

The abbr attribute specifies an abbreviated version of the cell content. The axis attribute provides a way of categorizing cells. Its value is a string identifying the category.

Neither attribute has any effect on normal browsers, but they can be useful for screen readers.

colspan and rowspan

colspan and rowspan let you expand a cell over several columns and rows. For example, let's say you want to generate the table you see in Figure A-10.

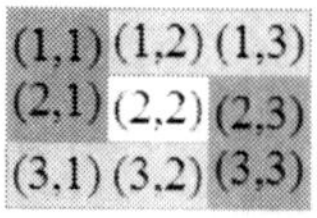

Figure A-10. Grouping of table columns and rows with colspan and rowspan

To create such a table, you can use the code shown in Listing A-4.

Listing A-4. cr_span.html

```
<!DOCTYPE html PUBLIC "-//W3C//DTD XHTML 1.0 Strict//EN"
  "http//www.w3.org/TR/xhtml1/DTD/xhtml1-strict.dtd">
<html xmlns="http//www.w3.org/1999/xhtml" xmllang="en" lang="en">
<head>
  <title>Example of colspan and rowspan</title>
  <style type="text/css">body {font-size:16pt}</style>
  <style type="text/css">.g1 {background-color: #c0c0c0}</style>
  <style type="text/css">.g2 {background-color: #808080}</style>
  </head>
<body>
<table cellpadding="2" border="1" rules="all">
  <tr>
    <td rowspan="2" class="g2">(1,1)<br/>(2,1)</td>
    <td colspan="2" class="g1">(1,2) (1,3)</td>
    </tr>
  <tr>
    <!-- (2,1) was defined one row up -->
    <td>(2,2)</td>
    <td rowspan="2" class="g2")>(2,3)<br/>(3,3)</td>
    </tr>
  <tr>
    <td colspan="2" class="g1">(3,1) (3,2)</td>
    <!-- (3,3) was defined one row up -->
    </tr>
  </table>
</body>
</html>
```

Be very systematic when using these attributes, because you can easily mess up the table!

headers

The headers attribute is a space-separated list of cell IDs that supplies header information for the cells.
Its purpose is to allow text-only browsers to render the header information. Listing A-5 shows how to
use it.

Listing A-5. td_headers.html

```
<!DOCTYPE html PUBLIC "-//W3C//Dtd XHTML 1.0 Strict//EN"
  "http//www.w3.org/TR/xhtml1/Dtd/xhtml1-strict.dtd">
<html xmlns="http//www.w3.org/1999/xhtml" xmllang="en" lang="en">
<head><title>Test of td headers attribute</title></head>
<body>
<table border="1">
  <caption>Average Height</caption>
  <tr>
    <th id="c">Country</th>
    <th id="m">Males</th><th id="f">Females</th>
```

```
    </tr>
  <tr>
    <td id="au" headers="c">Australia</td>
    <td headers="m au">5 ft 10.2</td><td headers="f au">5 ft 4.5</td>
    </tr>
  <tr>
    <td id="us" headers="c">U.S.A.</td>
    <td headers="m us">5 ft 9.4</td><td headers="f us">5 ft 4</td>
    </tr>
  </table>
</body>
</html>
```

Note that headers has no effect on how the table is rendered on normal browsers.

scope

The scope attribute identifies a cell that provides header information for the row that contains it (scope="row"), the column (scope="col"), the row group (scope="rowgroup"), or the column group (scope="colgroup"). A row group consists of the rows identified by one of the elements thead, tbody, or tfoot). For an explanation of column groups, see below.

scope, like headers, abbr, and axis, is only useful for non-visual browsers.

Columns

As I said in the "Table Structure" section, you can define attributes for all the cells in a column by means of the col element. In the table of Figure A-11, I used col to give a gray background to the second column and a right alignment to the third one. The code is shown in Listing A-6.

first	second	third
column	column	column
only defaults	in gray	right aligned

Figure A-11. Example of col

Listing A-6. table_col.html

```
<!DOCTYPE html PUBLIC "-//W3C//Dtd XHTML 1.0 Strict//EN"
  "http//www.w3.org/TR/xhtml1/Dtd/xhtml1-strict.dtd">
<html xmlns="http//www.w3.org/1999/xhtml" xmllang="en" lang="en">
<head><title>Test of table col element</title></head>
<body>
<table border="1">
  <col/>
  <col style="background-color:#C0C0C0"/>
  <col align="right"/>
  <tr><th>first</th><th>second</th><th>third</th></tr>
  <tr><td>column</td><td>column</td><td>column</td></tr>
  <tr><td>only defaults</td><td>in gray</td><td>right aligned</td></tr>
```

```
  </table>
</body>
</html>
```

As you can see from Listing A-6, there are three col elements that apply to the three columns of the table, from left to right. It isn't necessary to have all the col elements before the tr elements or to have as many col elements as the number of columns actually present in the table. You can freely mix col and tr. What counts is only the order in which you write the col elements.

Unfortunately, so far, the only one of the major browsers that completely supports col is Opera. If you view table_col.html with Firefox, IE9, or Chrome, the second column has a gray background, but the third column is not right-aligned. And yet, all three browsers correctly render align="right" when it is placed inside individual cells rather than in the col element.

Column Groups

You can identify groups of contiguous columns with the table element colgroup. In addition to the attributes align, char, charoff, valign, and width, colgroup also accepts span, which defines how many columns from left to right are to be grouped. In connection with the table attribute rules, you can use column groups to decide when to show column separators. For example, see Figure A-12 and the corresponding code in Listing A-7.

```
(1,1)(1,2)(1,3)(1,4)
(2,1)(2,2)(2,3)(2,4)
(3,1)(3,2)(3,3)(3,4)
```

Figure A-12. Example of colgroup

Listing A-7. table_colgroup.html

```
<!DOCTYPE html PUBLIC "-//W3C//Dtd XHTML 1.0 Strict//EN"
  "http//www.w3.org/TR/xhtml1/Dtd/xhtml1-strict.dtd">
<html xmlns="http//www.w3.org/1999/xhtml" xmllang="en" lang="en">
<head>
  <title>Test of table colgroup element</title>
  <style type="text/css">body {font-size:16pt}</style>
  </head>
<body>
<table border="1" cellpadding="2" rules="groups">
  <colgroup span="1"/>
  <colgroup span="2" style="background-color:#C0C0C0"/>
  <colgroup span="1"/>
  <tr><td>(1,1)</td><td>(1,2)</td><td>(1,3)</td><td>(1,4)</td></tr>
  <tr><td>(2,1)</td><td>(2,2)</td><td>(2,3)</td><td>(2,4)</td></tr>
  <tr><td>(3,1)</td><td>(3,2)</td><td>(3,3)</td><td>(3,4)</td></tr>
  </table>
</body>
</html>
```

Notice how you can use the style attribute of colgroup to define styles shared by all the columns of the groups. As this works with all four major browsers (while, as we have just seen, col does not), you can use colgroup with span="1" where you would normally use col.

I encourage you to check the rendering of your pages with all major browsers before deploying them, because you shouldn't take anything for granted. For example, in table_colgroup.html, you shouldn't need to define the third colgroup. It doesn't serve any purpose. But if you remove it, IE9 and Opera will *not* render the rule on the right-hand side of the second group, which separates the third group of columns from the second one.

Table Header, Body, and Footer

With the table elements thead, tbody, and tfoot, you can split all the rows of a table into three groups: header, body, and footer. This allows browsers to perform a more intelligent scrolling of long tables. In practice, you can use them to separate cells horizontally, as shown in Figure A-13.

(1,1)	(1,2)	(1,3)
(2,1)	(2,2)	(2,3)
(3,1)	(3,2)	(3,3)
(4,1)	(4,2)	(4,3)
(5,1)	(5,2)	(5,3)
(6,1)	(6,2)	(6,3)

Figure A-13. Example of thead, tbody, and tfoot

Listing A-8 shows you how to create the table of Figure A-13.

Listing A-8. table_rowgroup.html

```
<!DOCTYPE html PUBLIC "-//W3C//Dtd XHTML 1.0 Strict//EN"
  "http//www.w3.org/TR/xhtml1/Dtd/xhtml1-strict.dtd">
<html xmlns="http//www.w3.org/1999/xhtml" xmllang="en" lang="en">
<head>
  <title>Test of table row grouping</title>
  <style type="text/css">body {font-size:16pt}</style>
  </head>
<body>
<table border="1" cellpadding="2" rules="groups">
  <colgroup span="1"/>
  <thead style="font-weight:bold; background-color:#C0C0C0">
    <tr><td>(1,1)</td><td>(1,2)</td><td>(1,3)</td></tr>
    </thead>
  <tr><td>(2,1)</td><td>(2,2)</td><td>(2,3)</td></tr>
  <tr><td>(3,1)</td><td>(3,2)</td><td>(3,3)</td></tr>
  <tr><td>(4,1)</td><td>(4,2)</td><td>(4,3)</td></tr>
  <tfoot style="font-weight:bold">
    <tr><td>(5,1)</td><td>(5,2)</td><td>(5,3)</td></tr>
    <tr><td>(6,1)</td><td>(6,2)</td><td>(6,3)</td></tr>
    </tfoot>
  </table>
</body>
</html>
```

Notice that I've only defined a header and a footer. It would be better programming to define the body as well. But I wanted to show you that it is not essential.

Input Forms

To turn your web pages into an interactive experience, you have to give users the ability to make choices and type or upload information. To achieve this, you use the form element, which accepts data from the user and sends it to the server.

This book is full of examples of input forms. But a summary of all possible input elements as shown in Figure A-14 might be useful as a reference. The browser was Chrome.

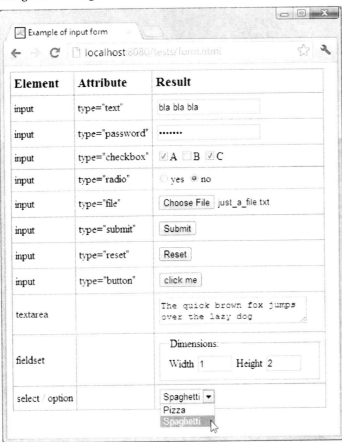

Figure A-14. An HTML form with examples of all input elements

The various types of the input element let the user enter a string of text or a password, check one or more check boxes, choose one of several radio buttons, upload a file, submit a form, reset a form's fields, or trigger a JavaScript action by clicking a button. The textarea element lets the user enter several lines of text, while the fieldset element lets you group several input fields under one or more headings. To present multiple choices, you use the select element, which contains one option element for each alternative. Listing A-9 shows the source code of Figure A-14.

Listing A-9. form.html

```
<!DOCTYPE html PUBLIC "-//W3C//DTD XHTML 1.0 Strict//EN"
  "http//www.w3.org/TR/xhtml1/DTD/xhtml1-strict.dtd">
<html xmlns="http//www.w3.org/1999/xhtml" xmllang="en" lang="en">
<head>
  <title>Example of input form</title>
  <style type="text/css">
    td.h {font-size: 120%; font-weight: bold}
  </style>
</head>
<body>
<form action="">
  <input type="hidden" name="agent" value="007"/>
  <table  cellpadding="5" border="1" rules="all">
    <tr>
      <td class="h">Element</td><td class="h">Attribute</td>
      <td class="h">Result</td></tr>
    <tr>
      <td>input</td><td>type="text"</td>
      <td><input type="text" name="t"/></td>
      </tr>
    <tr>
      <td>input</td><td>type="password"</td>
      <td><input type="password" name="p"/></td>
      </tr>
    <tr>
      <td>input</td><td>type="checkbox"</td>
      <td>
        <input type="checkbox" value="a" name="abc">A</input>
        <input type="checkbox" value="b" name="abc">B</input>
        <input type="checkbox" value="c" name="abc">C</input>
        </td>
      </tr>
    <tr>
      <td>input</td><td>type="radio"</td>
      <td>
        <input type="radio" name="yn" value="y">yes</input>
        <input type="radio" name="yn" value="n">no</input>
        </td>
      </tr>
    <tr>
      <td>input</td><td>type="file"</td>
      <td><input type="file" name="f"/></td>
      </tr>
    <tr>
      <td>input</td><td>type="submit"</td>
      <td><input type="submit"/></td>
      </tr>
```

```
<tr>
  <td>input</td><td>type="reset"</td>
  <td><input type="reset"/></td>
  </tr>
<tr>
  <td>input</td><td>type="button"</td>
  <td><input type="button" value="click me" name="b"/></td>
  </tr>
<tr>
  <td>textarea</td><td></td>
  <td><textarea name="ta">Default text</textarea></td>
  </tr>
<tr>
  <td>fieldset</td><td></td>
  <td><fieldset>
    <legend>Dimensions:</legend>
    Width <input type="text" size="3" name="w"/>
    Height <input type="text" size="3" name="h"/>
    </fieldset></td>
  </tr>
<tr>
  <td>select / option</td><td></td>
  <td><select name="food">
    <option value="pizza">Pizza</option>
    <option value="spaghetti" selected>Spaghetti</option>
    </select></td>
  </tr>
</table>
</form>
</body>
</html>
```

I've highlighted two lines. The first line, which contains the form element, shows that the action attribute is set to the empty string. The action attribute defines the URL of the page that must handle the request form. An empty string means that the same page displaying the form will also handle it. The second highlighted line shows how you can use the input element to set parameters without the user being aware of it (unless he or she peeks at the source, that is).

If you fill in the form as shown in Figure A-14 and click on the Submit button (or hit the Enter key), you'll see in the address field of your browser that the following string appears at the end of the URL (I've inserted newlines for readability):

```
?agent=007
&t=bla+bla+bla
&p=a++b++c
&abc=a
&abc=c
&yn=n
&f=just_a_file.txt
&ta=The+quick+brown+fox+jumps+over+the+lazy+dog
&w=1
&h=2
&food=spaghetti
```

The browser has translated each input element into a string *parameter-name=parameter-value*. Notice that each space in the text fields has been replaced by a plus sign, including the spaces within the password. Also notice that the parameter abc appears twice, because I checked two of the three available check boxes. To avoid seeing all the parameters in the browser, add to the form element the attribute method="post".

Buttons and Images

You can define a button in several ways, as shown in Figure A-15. All allow the disable attribute. The document to generate Figure A-15 is form_buttons.html (Listing A-10), available in the folder form buttons of the software package for this appendix. To view the page you can just double-click the HTML file.

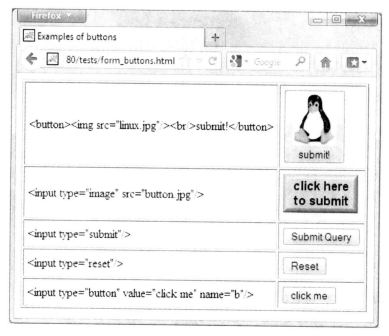

Figure A-15. HTML elements to render buttons

Listing A-10. form_buttons.html

```
<!DOCTYPE html PUBLIC "-//W3C//DTD XHTML 1.0 Strict//EN"
  "http//www.w3.org/TR/xhtml1/DTD/xhtml1-strict.dtd">
<html xmlns="http//www.w3.org/1999/xhtml" xmllang="en" lang="en">
<head><title>Examples of buttons</title></head>
<body>
<form action="">
  <table  cellpadding="5" border="1">
    <tr>
      <td>&lt;button>&lt;img src="linux.jpg"/>&lt;br/>submit!&lt;/button></td>
```

```
          <td><button><img src="linux.jpg"/><br/>submit!</button></td>
        </tr>
      <tr>
        <td>&lt;input type="image" src="button.jpg"/></td>
        <td><input type="image" src="button.jpg"/></td>
        </tr>
      <tr>
        <td>&lt;input type="submit"/></td>
        <td><input type="submit"/></td>
        </tr>
      <tr>
        <td>&lt;input type="reset"/></td>
        <td><input type="reset"/></td>
        </tr>
      <tr>
        <td>&lt;input type="button" value="click me" name="b"/></td>
        <td><input type="button" value="click me" name="b"/></td>
        </tr>
      </table>
    </form>
  </body>
</html>
```

Note how I used the HTML entity < to replace the open angle-bracket. This was necessary to prevent the browser from interpreting the code fragments I wanted to display in clear.

Perhaps the most obvious way of defining a button is with the button element. As you can see from Figure A-15, you can then use images and text to make your button interesting. You can also define the attribute type="submit" (the default), type="reset", or type="button". A "reset" button returns all the form's input fields to the values they had before any user input. You can use a button of type "button" to execute a JavaScript on the client side, and you can assign to it a default value with the value attribute. You can also use the name attribute.

<input type="submit"/>, <input type="reset"/>, and <input type="button"/> let you define standard buttons. You can specify the text to be displayed inside the button with the value attribute. Note that the name attribute is allowed with type="button", but not with type="submit" and type="reset".

<input type="image" src="image-file"/> is yet another way to create submit buttons. However, the behavior is slightly different: when you use an image to create a submit button and click on it to submit the form, the browser sends to the server two additional parameters named x and y and representing the position of the cursor within the image, with 0,0 indicating the top-left corner of the image, x increasing from left to right, and y increasing from the top down. Furthermore, if you add to the element the attribute name="whatever", the browser names the parameters whatever.x and whatever.y, instead of simply x and y.

If you define the name attribute and also define the attribute value="val", the browser will send the whatever=val parameter in addition to the coordinates. Finally, with image buttons, you can define the alt attribute to specify text associated with the image. A nice feature of all major browsers is that they display the *hand cursor* on image buttons (while they display the *arrow cursor* on the other types of buttons).

With an appropriate server-side script, you can use the coordinate parameters to create an image map, but then the script would have to do all the analysis to determine what region was clicked and then forward the request to the appropriate page. You will find a section about image maps later on in this appendix.

Lists

Together with tables, lists are the workhorses of web development. There are three types of lists: definition lists, ordered lists, and unordered lists. Figures A-16 to A-18 show the three types of lists. The HTML documents that generate the three figures are respectively `list_definition.html`, `list_ordered.html`, and `list_unordered.html`.

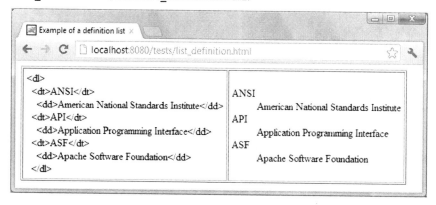

Figure A-16. *A definition list*

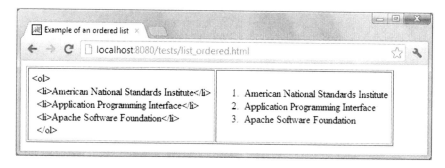

Figure A-17. *An ordered list*

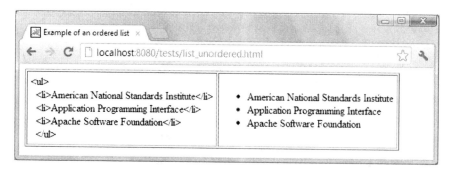

Figure A-18. *An unordered list*

Before the latest HTML releases, it was possible to use some attributes to personalize the lists, but they have been deprecated. Use styles instead.

Image Maps

A useful thing to be able to do when developing web sites is to link areas of an image to different URLs. There are three ways of doing it, but two of them do not always work. On the Web, you will find a lot of discussions about this issue. That's why it is worthwhile to talk about it in a clear and straightforward way. I will start with the easiest method.

Splitting an Image with a Table

For this example, I will use the well-known GNU/Linux image of a penguin[1] (Figure A-19).

Figure A-19. The GNU/Linux penguin

Suppose you want to divide the penguin image into four separately clickable areas, as shown in Figure A-20.

---

[1] Tux, the penguin logo, was created by Larry Ewing (lewing@isc.tamu.edu) using the General Image Manipulation Program (http://www.isc.tamu.edu/~lewing/gimp/)

Figure A-20. *The GNU/Linux penguin*

The trivial solution is that you split the image into four pieces that you can place in a 2x2 table, one piece per cell, as shown in Listing A-11. To try the code, copy the penguin folder from the software package for this chapter to the usual test folder (i.e., webapps\ROOT\tests in the Tomcat folder) and view http://localhost:8080/tests/penguin/penguin_tbl.html. You can also view it without Tomcat, by double-clicking penguin_tbl.html. I haven't included any of the four pages the image is linked to, but you don't need them to see how the mechanism works.

Listing A-11. *penguin_tbl.html*

```
<?xml version='1.0' encoding='utf-8'?>
<!DOCTYPE html PUBLIC "-//W3C//DTD XHTML 1.1//EN"
    "http://www.w3.org/TR/xhtml11/DTD/xhtml11.dtd">
<html xmlns="http//www.w3.org/1999/xhtml">
<head>
  <title>Penguin</title>
  <style type="text/css">img {border-width: 0px}</style>
  </head>
<body>
<table border="1" rules="none" cellpadding="0" cellspacing="0">
  <tr>
    <td><a href="top_left.html"><img src="penguin_tl.gif"/></a></td>
    <td><a href="top_right.html"><img src="penguin_tr.gif"/></a></td>
    </tr>
  <tr>
    <td><a href="bottom_left.html"><img src="penguin_bl.gif"/></a></td>
    <td><a href="bottom_right.html"><img src="penguin_br.gif"/></a></td>
    </tr>
  </table>
</body>
</html>
```

As you can see, this code defines a table with two rows and two columns, where each cell contains a hyperlinked image. I've styled the images to be rendered without borders, and I've defined the table to show no cell padding or spacing. The intention is to have the browser compose a large image by placing the four partial images adjacent to each other. Unfortunately, it doesn't work, as shown in Figure A-21.

Figure A-21. The GNU/Linux penguin sawed in half

Notice that the name of the link correctly matches the position of the cursor.

The same problem is shown consistently with all four major browsers (it actually used to work as expected with older versions of IE). Funnily enough, the gaps disappear if you change the document type from strict 1.1 to transitional 1.0 (although with Opera you also need to set table's border attribute to 0).

Using an Image Map with a Table or a List

I'll tell you upfront that this method is also unusable, because it only works with Firefox and Opera but not with Chrome or IE9. I describe it here because you should be aware of it, and I can also use it to explain some things you need to know anyway. Somewhere on the Web you might find people who tell you that you can make it work if you limit the validation of XHTML 1.0 / HTML 4.01 to be transitional. That is not true.

For this example, I will use an image as shown in Figures A-22 and A-23.

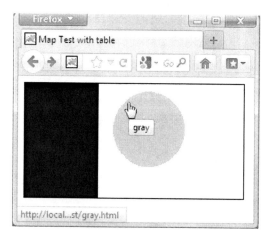

Figure A-22. *Status bar and screen tip pointing to gray in a map test*

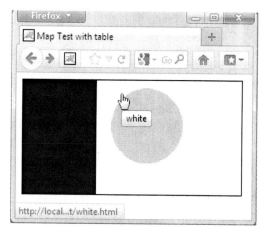

Figure A-23. *Status bar and screen tip pointing to white in a map test*

This method doesn't require you to cut the image into pieces. You only need to define the portions of the image associated with the links. The idea is that you associate to the image a map consisting of a series of clickable shapes, as shown in Listing A-12. To try it out, copy the folder maptest from the software package for this chapter to the usual test folder and view `http://localhost:8080/tests/maptest/maptest_tbl.html`. Note that you can view this HTML file, like others that don't contain JSP, by double-clicking its icon in Windows Explorer. I always suggest that you view all pages in Tomcat; I'm sure everything will always work if you do so.

Listing A-12. maptest_tbl.html

```
<?xml version='1.0' encoding='utf-8'?>
<!DOCTYPE html PUBLIC "-//W3C//DTD XHTML 1.1//EN"
    "http://www.w3.org/TR/xhtml11/DTD/xhtml11.dtd">
```

```
<html xmlns="http//www.w3.org/1999/xhtml">
<head><title>Map Test with Table</title></head>
<body>
<img src="maptest.gif" usemap="#mymap" width="300" height="150"
    style="border-width:1px;border-style:solid;border-color:black;"
    />
<map id="mymap"><table><tr>
  <td><a href="black.html" shape="rect" coords="0,0,100,150"
    title="black"/></td>
  <td><a href="gray.html" shape="circ" coords="170,60,50"
    title="gray"/></td>
  <td><a href="white.html" shape="rect" coords="100,0,300,150"
    title="white"/></td>
  </tr></table></map>
</body>
</html>
```

As you can see, you associate a map to the image by setting img's usemap attribute to the URI of the map element. Notice how the shape and coords attributes are set to identify the three clickable areas. The shapes are rendered from the bottom up, as it is obvious considering that if that were not the case, the white rectangle would hide the gray circle in Figures A-22 and A-23.

The shape attribute can have the values rect, rectangle, circ, circle, poly, and polygon. The coordinates are defined in coords as a comma-separated list of numeric values. Obviously, you have to match the coordinates you define in coords with those of the areas of the image you want to make clickable.

Table A-7 shows the meaning of the numeric values associated with each shape. The x coordinate is measured horizontally from left to right, and the y coordinate is measured vertically from top to bottom. Therefore, the top-left corner of the map always represents the origin of the coordinates, with x=0, y=0. In the example, the bottom-right corner of the map has the coordinates x=300 and y=150.

Table A-7. Meaning of the coords attribute

shape	coords
rect/rectangle	x,y of the top-left corner, and x,y of the bottom-right corner. For example, the white rectangle in Figure A-22 has coords set to "100,0,300,150".
circ/circle	x,y of the center, and radius. For example, the gray circle in Figure A-22 has coords set to "170,60,50", 170,60 being the coordinates of the center and 50 the length of the radius.
poly/polygon	x,y of each vertex. For example, coords="0,0,50,0,0,30" defines a rectangular triangle with the corners in 0,0, 50,0, and 0,30. A side of length 50 is parallel to the x-axis, a side of length 30 is parallel to the y-axis, and the right angle is in the top-left corner of the map.

Clearly, with enough points, a polygon can approximate the contours of any shape you like, especially when you combine it with several partially overlapping circles of different radii.

Listing A-13 shows a variant of this technique, with an object element replacing img and an unnumbered list replacing the table. You will find maptest_list.html in the same folder of maptest_tbl.html.

Listing A-13. maptest_list.html

```
<?xml version='1.0' encoding='utf-8'?>
<!DOCTYPE html PUBLIC "-//W3C//DTD XHTML 1.1//EN"
    "http://www.w3.org/TR/xhtml11/DTD/xhtml11.dtd">
<html xmlns="http//www.w3.org/1999/xhtml">
<head><title>Map Test</title></head>
<body>
<object data="maptest.gif" usemap="#mymap" type="image/gif"
    width="300" height="150"
    style="border-width:1px;border-style:solid;border-color:black;"
    >
  <map id="mymap">
    <ul>
      <li><a href="black.html" shape="rect" coords="0,0,100,150"
            title="black"/></li>
      <li><a href="gray.html" shape="circ" coords="170,60,50"
            title="gray"/></li>
      <li><a href="white.html" shape="rect" coords="100,0,300,150"
            title="white"/></li>
    </ul>
  </map>
  </object>
</body>
</html>
```

Unfortunately, as I said at the beginning of this section, neither variant will work with Chrome or IE9. But the explanation of how to use a map has not been a waste of time, because the next method tells you how to make an image map work with all browsers.

Using an Image Map with Areas

Listing A-14 shows you how to make an image map work. I have added a gray square to the bottom-right corner of the image to show you how to define "dead" areas.

Listing A-14. maptest_area.html

```
<?xml version='1.0' encoding='utf-8'?>
<!DOCTYPE html PUBLIC "-//W3C//DTD XHTML 1.1//EN"
    "http://www.w3.org/TR/xhtml11/DTD/xhtml11.dtd">
<html xmlns="http//www.w3.org/1999/xhtml">
<head><title>Map Test with areas</title></head>
<body>
<img src="maptest_area.gif" usemap="#mymap" width="300" height="150"
    style="border-width:1px;border-style:solid;border-color:black;"
    />
<map name="mymap" id="mymap">
  <area nohref shape="rect" coords="280,130,300,150" title="nothing"/>
```

```
    <area href="black.html" shape="rect" coords="0,0,100,150" title="black"/>
    <area href="gray.html" shape="circ" coords="170,60,50" title="gray"/>
    <area href="white.html" shape="rect" coords="100,0,300,150" title="white"/>
    </map>
</body>
</html>
```

Notice that I have added the definition of the `name` attribute to the `map` element. It is needed for Chrome. With the three other browsers, the `id` attribute is sufficient. Figure A-24 shows the final result.

Figure A-24. *Screen tip pointing to a disabled area of an image map*

The Bottom Line

I have tested all methods described in the previous sections with the four most widely used browsers, and validating against XHTML 1.1, XHTML 1.0 strict, XHTML transitional, HTML 4.01 strict, and HTML 4.01 transitional. The only method that works in all situations is the one based on the `area` element. It is also the most flexible method and doesn't require you to split the image.

For simple maps, you can use the simple method of placing rectangular sections of the image in the cells of a table, as long as you validate against transitional standards of either XHTML 1.0 or HTML 4.01. But I recommend that you stick to the area-based method.

Cascading Style Sheets

According to Wikipedia, *Cascading Style Sheets (CSS) is a [...] language used for describing [...] the look and formatting [...] of a document written in a markup language. Its most common application is to style web pages written in HTML and XHTML.*

I reproduced the core of Wikipedia's definition because I couldn't have said it better.

Some time ago, I found somewhere on the W3C web site the following description, which is also worth reproducing: *CSS2 supports media-specific style sheets so that authors may tailor the presentation of their documents to visual browsers, aural devices, printers, braille devices, handheld devices, etc. This specification also supports content positioning, downloadable fonts, table layout, features for internationalization, automatic counters and numbering, and some properties related to user interface.*

The CSS standard (see `http://www.w3.org/Style/CSS/current-work.en.html` for the latest developments) doesn't have versions, but levels, with each level adding features and refining the definition of the previous one. The latest CSS specification is CSS2.1 (`http://www.w3.org/TR/CSS21/`).

Style Syntax

Here is a valid CSS style definition (also called a CSS rule):

```
h1, h2, h3 {
  font-family: "sans serif";
  color: red
  }
```

Each rule consists of one or more comma-separated selectors (e.g., h1) followed by semicolon-separated declarations enclosed in braces. Each declaration consists of a property name (e.g., color) and a property value (e.g., red).You can freely insert spaces and newlines to make the styles more readable.

Listing A-15 shows how you can define several paragraph styles and use them separately or together.

Listing A-15. p_styles.html

```
<!DOCTYPE html PUBLIC "-//W3C//DTD XHTML 1.0 Strict//EN"
  "http://www.w3.org/TR/xhtml1/DTD/xhtml1-strict.dtd">
<html xmlns="http//www.w3.org/1999/xhtml">
<head>
  <title>Styled paragraphs</title>
  <style type="text/css">
    p {font-size: 130%}
    p.bold {font-weight: bold}
    p.italic {font-style: italic}
    p.p123 {font-size: 100%; font-weight: normal; font-style: normal}
    </style>
  </head>
<body>
<p>This is a default paragraph</p>
<p class="bold">This is a bold paragraph</p>
<p class="bold italic">This is a bold italic paragraph</p>
<p class="bold p123 italic">This is a normal paragraph</p>
</body>
</html>
```

Notice that to assign a paragraph (or any element) to more than one style class, you only need to use the names of the classes separated by spaces. Also, notice how you can use the class p.p123 to override the font size, weight, and style as defined in the preceding styles. The class p.p123 takes precedence over all others, because you defined it last within the style element in head. The order in which the class names appear in the class attribute of the paragraphs is irrelevant. Figure A-25 shows the output of p_styles.html.

Figure A-25. Styled paragraphs

If you omit the element name when defining a class, the style will apply to all the elements. For example, you can use this class with all elements rendering text:

```
.bold {font-weight: bold}
```

■ **Caution** Class names must start with a letter.

The file `eshop project\eshop\css\eshop.css` that you find in the software pacakage for Chapter 3 provides several examples of style rules.

Now that you know the syntax of a style rule and have seen a couple of examples, you shouldn't have any problem using other properties. They're clearly described in the standard, and several web sites provide extensive descriptions.

Placing Styles

You can define styles in three places: inline (as attributes within element start tags), internally (in the `style` element inside the head), and externally (in separate style sheet files). Note that inline styles override internal styles, and internal styles override external styles.

You can define inline styles in most elements, as the following example shows:

```
<p style="color: red; font-weight: bold">bold and red</p>
```

This is appropriate when you want to use a style only once or for testing purposes. It wouldn't make sense to repeat the same style over and over again in several elements.

Styles defined in the head of an HTML document by means of the `style` element, as I showed you in Listing A-15, apply to the whole document. This makes sense for styles that you want to use exclusively in a single document. However, if you intend to reuse the styles in more than one document, you should define them in a separate file.

By defining styles in a CSS file, you maximize maintainability of complex applications. You have seen examples of this technique when I described the eshop, eshopx, and eshopf applications. You normally include a CSS file in an HTML document by writing in the document's head element an element like this:

```
<link rel="stylesheet" type="text/css" href="filename.css"/>
```

Note that the browser loads all style definitions one after the other in the order in which it encounters them. Therefore, if you include more than one file and/or if you mix in the head element file inclusions and style elements, you can easily end up with conflicting styles rules.

You can use the optional attribute media of the style element to specify the destination of the style information. See Table A-8 for a list of valid media values.

Table A-8. *Values Valid for the media Attribute*

Value	Purpose
all	For all devices (default)
braille	For braille tactile-feedback devices
embossed	For paged braille printers
handheld	For handheld devices with small screens and limited bandwidth
print	For paged media and for documents viewed on screen in print-preview mode
projection	For projectors
screen	For nonpaged computer screens
speech	Intended for speech synthesizers but not yet defined
tty	For media using a fixed-pitch character grid, such as teletypes
tv	For TV-type devices with low resolution and limited scroll ability

HTML Elements div and span

You can use both div and span to apply styles to groups of elements, as in the following example:

```
<div style="color:red">
  <p>a red paragraph</p>
  <p>a red paragraph <span style="color:green">with green</span> in it</p>
</div>
```

While div can contain paragraphs, <span> cannot. This is because div identifies a block and can therefore contain other block-level elements (such as p and table), while span can only contain inline-level elements (such as a and img). So far, so good. However, the standards don't clearly distinguish between block-level and inline-level elements. Moreover, some elements are sometimes considered to be block-level and sometimes inline-level. Usually, the browsers display a new line before rendering a block-level element, but this also is not always true. The elements that are certainly block-level (and *cannot* therefore appear inside span, are address, blockquote, dl, fieldset, form, h1 to h6, hr, noframes, noscript, ol, p, pre, table, and ul. The elements that are certainly inline-level (and can therefore appear inside span), are a, abbr, acronym, b, bdo, big, br, cite, code, dfn, em, i, img, input, kbd, label, q, samp, select, small, strong, sub, sup, textarea, tt, and var. For all the others, I cannot give you a clear indication.

I recommend using div when you need to apply styles to sections of documents and span only to style individual strings. To apply styles to a single element (e.g., a table), you should define the style attribute directly in the start tag of the element itself. In fact, if you use several styles, defining the corresponding classes in a separate style-sheet file would make your code more maintainable.

Caution To use a feature that is not identically rendered by the major browsers, you might decide to rely on the user-agent information available via JSP to determine what browser issued the request, and then adjust your HTML output accordingly. But I think you will be happier in the long run if you just forget that particular feature.

Using a Style Sheet to Implement Tabs

Web sites often use tabs like those shown in Figure A-26 to let the users select different subjects. In this section, I'll show you how to use style sheets to implement such tabs in a simple and elegant way.

Figure A-26. Tabs

Listing A-16 shows the JSP document used to generate Figure A-26. To view it, copy the folder named tabs to the usual test folder webapps\ROOT\tests\ and type in the browser the URL http://localhost:8080/tests/tabs/tabs.jsp.

Listing A-16. tabs.jsp

```
<%@page language="java" contentType="text/html"%>
<%
  final char HOME = 'H', TEST = 'T', NUM = '1';
  String    s = request.getParameter("t");
  char      p = (s != null && s.length() > 0) ? s.charAt(0) : HOME;
%>
<html>
<head>
  <title>Tabs with CSS</title>
  <link rel="stylesheet" type="text/css" href="tabs.css"/>
```

```
      </head>
<body>
<p>This appears above the tabs</p>
<div class="tabs">
  <ul>
    <li <% if (p == HOME) out.print("id=\"on\""); %>>
      <a href="tabs.jsp?t=<%=HOME%>"><span>Home</span></a>
      </li>
    <li <% if (p == TEST) out.print("id=\"on\""); %>>
      <a href="tabs.jsp?t=<%=TEST%>"><span>Test</span></a>
      </li>
    <li <% if (p == NUM) out.print("id=\"on\""); %>>
      <a href="tabs.jsp?t=<%=NUM%>"><span>123456789 abcdef</span></a>
      </li>
    </ul>
  </div>
<p>
   <br/>
  This appears below the tabs
  </p>
</body>
</html>
```

The first section in bold is a scriptlet that sets the character variable p to the first character found in the input parameter t. If the input parameter is missing or empty, the scriptlet sets p to 'H'.

Each tab is implemented as an item of an unnumbered list. I've highlighted the item corresponding to the Test tab. This scriptlet writes id="on" to the output when the first character of the input parameter matches the character designated to identify the Test tab:

```
<% if (p == TEST) out.print("id=\"on\""); %>
```

You will see that the presence of the "on" identifier causes the tag to be displayed with a different style. Notice that in Figure A-26, the tab is indeed *on*.

The content of the unnumbered item is:

```
<a href="tabs.jsp?t=<%=TEST%>"><span>Test</span></a>
```

The hyperlink points to the URI tabs.jsp?t=T, which the browser loads when the user clicks on the tab. In Figure A-26, the cursor hovers on the Home tab. Accordingly, the link shown at the bottom of the figure is http://localhost:8080/tests/tabs/tabs.jsp?t=H. Listing A-17 shows the style sheet.

Listing A-17. tabs.css

```
div.tabs {
  float                 : left;
  width                 : 100%;
  background            : white url(tab_pixel.gif) repeat-x bottom;
  }
div.tabs ul {
  list-style            : none;
  margin                : 0px;
  padding               : 0px;
  }
```

```
div.tabs li {
  display            : inline;
  margin             : 0px;
  padding            : 0px;
  }
div.tabs a {
  float              : left;
  background         : url(tab_right.gif) no-repeat right top;
  border-bottom      : 1px solid black;
  font-family        : Arial, Helvetica, sans-serif;
  font-size          : 12px;
  font-weight        : bold;
  text-decoration    : none;
  }
div.tabs li#on a {
  background         : url(tab_right_on.gif) no-repeat right top;
  border-bottom      : 1px solid white;
  }
div.tabs a:link, div.tabs a:active, div.tabs a:visited {
  color              : black;
  }
div.tabs a:hover {
  color              : #808080;
  }
div.tabs span {
  float              : left;
  background         : url(tab_left.gif) no-repeat left top;
  padding            : 5px;
  white-space        : nowrap;
  }
```

All entries refer to div.tabs, which means that the styles are only to be applied to elements enclosed between <div class="tabs"> and </div>. In this way, you can define the properties that apply to all the tab elements by default. In particular, you can specify that the tabs are to build up from left to right as you defined them in the JSP page. It also helps you define the gray line at the bottom of the line of tabs by repeating a single gray pixel (tab_pixel.gif) to span horizontally across the whole window.

You use list-style:none to specify that the unnumbered lists (element ul) should not be displayed with bullets. You need this style, because you want to display the items as tabs, and the default bullets would get in the way. Similarly, you need display:inline for the list item elements (li) to ensure that no line breaks are displayed before or after each item.

Next, you define how hyperlinks (element a) are to be rendered. First, you specify how you want to have the tab labels written and state that the image tab_right.gif (see Figure A-27) is to be used as a background image aligned top-right. When you use it as a tab background top-right justified, its width is adjusted to match the width needed to display the tab name. The longer the text inside the tab, the more the image will be stretched horizontally, ensuring that the shading is applied to the whole tab. Its height is appropriate for the font size I've chosen. If you want to use larger fonts, you will need to adjust the height of both tab_right.gif and tab_left.gif.

Figure A-27. tab_right.gif

When the id attribute of a li element is set to "on", the style

```
div.tabs li#on a {
    background          : url(tab_right_on.gif) no-repeat right top;
    border-bottom       : 1px solid white;
    }
```

replaces tab_right.gif with tab_right_on.gif and the bottom black line with a white one.
Now, let's take a look at the second-to-last style:

```
div.tabs a:hover {
    color               : #808080;
    }
```

This style has the effect of graying out the text of a tab when the cursor hovers over it, as shown in Figure A-26.

To complete the tabs, you only need to display the left border of the tabs, and you can do this by attaching tab_left.gif as a left-justified, non-repeating background image to the span element.

In conclusion, as you have just seen, CSS is a powerful tool that can do much more than just set a font size or a background color.

JavaScript

JavaScript is the most widely used client-side scripting language on the Web. By adding it to your web pages, you can make your pages *do things*, such as prevalidate forms or immediately react to a user's actions. As you have seen in Chapter 7, JavaScript is also the basis for Ajax.

The syntax of JavaScript was modeled on that of Java. Therefore, if you know Java, you should find JavaScript easy to learn. One noteworthy difference from Java is that you can omit variable declarations in the top-level code. Moreover, JavaScript lacks Java's static typing and strong type checking. This gives you more freedom, but it comes with the risk of messing things up in a big way. JavaScript relies on built-in objects, but it doesn't support classes or inheritance. It's an interpreted language, and object binding is done at runtime.

At the end of 1995, Netscape introduced JavaScript in its Netscape Navigator web browser. Microsoft reverse-engineered JavaScript, added its own extensions (as Microsoft always does), and renamed it JScript. Some years later, Ecma International merged the two languages into the standard ECMA-262 (http://www.ecma-international.org/publications/standards/Ecma-262.htm) and named the scripting language ECMAScript. Today, all major browsers conform to the ECMA-262 standard, which has been adopted as the ISO/IEC standard 16262. If you go to the ISO/IEC web site, you will see that you need to pay 238 Swiss Francs if you want to download the standard in PDF format. I can't imagine why anyone would pay for it when the same standard is free to download from the ECMA web site. In any case, as everybody keeps referring to JavaScript (although they should really be saying "ECMAScript"), I will use JavaScript as well.

Placing JavaScript Inside a Web Page

Before showing an example of what you can do with JavaScript, let's see how you can include it in your web pages. You have two possibilities: you can either keep the script inside your HTML document:

```
<script type="text/javascript">
  /* Place your script here */
  </script>.
```

or save it in a separate file and include it with a script element:

```
<script type="text/javascript" src="myScript.js"></script>
```

Caution In both cases, you have to keep the end tag `</script>`, because the form `<script ... />` is invalid.

In either case, you can decide to place your script in the head element or within the body element. If you want the script to execute in response to some event (e.g., when you pass your cursor over a button), place it in head. If you place it in body, the browser will execute it upon loading the page.

Responding to Events

You can place the onload and onunload events, which are associated with the whole window, in the body element (or in frameset, but I recommend that you forget that one). For example, you can execute a JavaScript function when your page is loaded as follows:

```
<body onload="functionName()">
```

You can include in most tags a series of events, which are generated directly by a keyboard or a mouse. They are onclick, ondblclick, onkeydown, onkeypress, onkeyup, onmousedown, onmousemove, onmouseout, onmouseover, and onmouseup. In particular, onmouseover allows you to change the appearance of an element when you pass the cursor over it without clicking. There are tags like head, html, script, style, and others that are excluded, because it doesn't make any sense to associate events to those elements.

Finally, some events are associated with the status of form-related elements and are therefore only valid within forms. These events are onblur, onchange, onfocus, onreset, onselect, and onsubmit. The events onsubmit and onreset refer to the whole form, while the others refer to individual elements. In particular, onfocus is triggered when an element is clicked on or tabbed to and therefore becomes ready to accept input, while onblur is triggered when an element loses focus. You can check the form input by using either onchange to trigger a testing function specifically designed for an element or onsubmit to perform several checks bundled inside a single function. You should ensure that input errors are detected as soon as possible. You don't want your user to keep typing only to be told upon submitting the form that he or she did something wrong at the very beginning. In general, a combination of checks on individual elements plus a consistency check when the form is submitted is a good way to go.

Checking and Correcting Dates

As I already said, checking user inputs with JavaScript before the data leaves the browser makes for a quicker response, but it doesn't necessarily reduce the checks you have to do on the server side, because you cannot entirely depend on what happens on the client side. The user might have disabled JavaScript or maliciously altered your page to bypass the checks.

Nevertheless, security issues aside, client-side checks make for a better user experience. In this section, I'll give you an example of how to prevent a user from entering incorrectly formatted dates and how to work with dates. I'll use JSP instead of straight HTML, because it's much easier to use a JSP loop to prepare a select on days and months, rather than type them all by hand in plain HTML. Figure A-28 shows you what you want to achieve. To view it, copy the folder dates from the software package for this appendix to the usual test folder and type `http://localhost:8080/tests/dates/dates.jsp`.

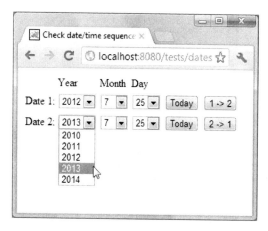

Figure A-28. Setting and copying dates

You want to be able to set any valid date within a certain number of years, set a date to today, or copy a date at the press of a button. In particular, you need to ensure that when you select a month, the number of days changes automatically. Listing A-18 shows the JSP page, where I've highlighted the JavaScript code in bold. Study this code first before passing to the file that contains the JavaScript functions.

Listing A-18. dates.jsp

```
01:  <%@page language="java" contentType="text/html"%>
02:  <html>
03:  <head>
04:    <title>Check date/time sequence in form</title>
05:    <script type="text/javascript">
06:      var now = new Date();
07:      var thisDay    = now.getDate() - 1;
08:      var thisMonth = now.getMonth();
09:      var thisYear  = now.getYear();
10:      if (thisYear < 2000) thisYear += 1900; //for some browsers
11:      var firstYear = thisYear - 2;
12:      var lastYear = thisYear + 2;
13:    </script>
14:    <script type="text/javascript" src="dates.js"></script>
15:  </head>
16:  <body>
17:  <form name="f" action="">
18:    <table border="0">
19:      <tr><td> </td>
20:        <td>Year</td><td>Month</td><td>Day</td>
21:        <td> </td>
22:      </tr>
23:  <%  for (int k = 1, kMax = 2; k <= kMax; k++) { %>
24:  <%    String upd = "updateMonthDays('f', '"+k+"')"; %>
25:      <tr>
```

```
26:            <td>Date <%=k%>:</td>
27:            <td>
28:              <select name="yy<%=k%>" onchange="<%=upd%>">
29:                <script type="text/javascript">
30:                  for (var jy = firstYear; jy <= lastYear; jy++) {
31:                    document.writeln("<option>" + jy + "</option>");
32:                  }
33:                </script>
34:              </select>
35:            </td>
36:            <td>
37:              <select name="mm<%=k%>" onchange="<%=upd%>">
38:    <%          for (int jm = 1; jm <= 12; jm++) { %>
39:                  <option><%=jm%></option>
40:    <%          } %>
41:              </select>
42:            </td>
43:            <td>
44:              <select name="dd<%=k%>">
45:    <%          for (int jd = 1; jd <= 31; jd++) { %>
46:                  <option><%=jd%></option>
47:    <%          } %>
48:              </select>
49:            </td>
50:            <td>
51:              <input type="button" name="today<%=k%>"
52:                value="Today" onclick="selectToday('f', '<%=k%>')"/>
53:    <%        int k1 = k; int k2 = k + 1; if (k2 > kMax) k2 = 1; %>
54:              <input type="button" name="same_day"
55:                value="<%=k1%> -> <%=k2%>"
56:                onclick="copyDay('f', '<%=k1%>', '<%=k2%>')"/>
57:            </td>
58:          </tr>
59:          <script type="text/javascript">
60:            selectToday('f', '<%=k%>')
61:          </script>
62:    <%    } /* for (int k.. */ %>
63:        </table>
64:      </form>
65:    </body>
66:  </html>
```

Lines 5–12 set up some JavaScript variables that you'll use in several places. You could have used the Calendar class in JSP, but it would have provided the time of the server, not of the client. You cannot assume that the viewers of your web site are all located within your time zone. You might be wondering why you subtract 1 when calculating thisDay, while you don't subtract anything when calculating thisMonth. This is because getDate returns the day of the month (i.e., 1, 2, and so on), while getMonth returns 0 for January, 1 for February, and so on. I prefer to have all indices starting with the same value.

Lines 11 and 12 reflect my decision of making available two years in the past and two years in the future. In the real world, this decision will depend on your application. You use the year limits to define the options for the year selection in lines 29 and 30. Notice that you use JavaScript to write the option elements to the web page.

Line 60 shows a call to the function selectToday, which is a script that you insert directly into the page. It means that after rendering one row of the table of dates, the browser will set the date to today (the user's today, not the server's today).

Other bits of JavaScript are linked to the event onclick of each button and to the event onchange of the year and month selectors.

The onclick attributes in line 52

```
onclick="selectToday('f', '<%=k%>')"
```

and in line 56

```
onclick="copyDay('f', '<%=k1%>', '<%=k2%>')"
```

have the effect of executing the respective functions selectToday and copyDay with the argument list ('f', '1') if you click on a button of the first date, and with the argument list ('f', '2') if you click on a button of the second date.

I'll explain the functions when we look at the JavaScript file dates.js in Listing A-19, but you can already see that you always pass the name of the form element as the first argument of the call. You do this because hard coding the form name inside a separate file would be bad practice.

The onchange="<%=upd%>" attribute, which you see in line 37, is expanded by JSP to onchange="updateMonthDays('f', '1')" for the first date and to onchange="updateMonthDays('f', '2')" for the second date. Its purpose is to ensure that when the user changes the month selection, the number of days changes accordingly. Remember that this happens on the client side and doesn't involve the server. The identical attribute also appears in line 28, to take into account that the user could select a leap year. In this case, you need to ensure that you display February with 29 days.

Now you can see why it's better to use JSP instead of plain HTML: you only need to write the code for one date, and the big loop between lines 23 and 62 repeats it for you for as many dates as you like. You only need to increase kMax to see more than two dates.

Listing A-19 shows the JavaScript functions hidden in dates.js. I've highlighted the function headers.

Listing A-19. dates.js

```
01:  /*
02:  **   Determine the number of days in the given month of the given year
03:  */
04:  function daysInMonth(m, y) {
05:     var daysInMonth = 31;
06:     if (m == 4  ||  m == 6  ||  m == 9  ||  m == 11) daysInMonth = 30;
07:     if (m == 2) {
08:        daysInMonth = ((y%4) == 0)
09:                          ? (((y%100) == 0)
10:                                ? (((y%400) == 0) ? 29 : 28)
11:                                : 29
12:                             )
13:                          :28
14:                          ;
15:     }
16:     return daysInMonth;
17:    }
18:  /*
19:  **   Adjust the days to the requested month and year
20:  */
```

```
21:   function updateMonthDays(formName, kDate) {
22:     var ddObj = eval("document." + formName + ".dd" + kDate);
23:     var mmObj = eval("document." + formName + ".mm" + kDate);
24:     var yyObj = eval("document." + formName + ".yy" + kDate);
25:     var mm = mmObj[mmObj.selectedIndex].text;
26:     var yy = yyObj[yyObj.selectedIndex].text;
27:     var wantedDays  = daysInMonth(mm, yy);
28:     var currentDays = ddObj.length;
29:     /*
30:      *  REMOVE days from the end if we have too many
31:      */
32:     while (wantedDays < currentDays) {
33:       ddObj.options[ddObj.length - 1] = null;
34:       currentDays--;
35:       }
36:     /*
37:      *  ADD days at the end if we are missing some
38:      */
39:     while (wantedDays > currentDays) {
40:       currentDays++;
41:       ddObj.appendChild(new Option(currentDays));
42:       }
43:     //
44:     if (ddObj.selectedIndex < 0) ddObj.selectedIndex = 0;
45:     }
46:   /*
47:   **  Select today
48:   */
49:   function selectToday(formName, kDate) {
50:     var ddObj = eval("document." + formName + ".dd" + kDate);
51:     var mmObj = eval("document." + formName + ".mm" + kDate);
52:     var yyObj = eval("document." + formName + ".yy" + kDate);
53:     yyObj[thisYear - firstYear].selected = true;
54:     mmObj[thisMonth].selected = true;
55:     updateMonthDays(formName, kDate);
56:     ddObj[thisDay].selected = true;
57:     }
58:   /*
59:   **  Copy a day to another
60:   */
61:   function copyDay(formName, kFrom, kTo) {
62:     var ddFromObj = eval("document." + formName + ".dd" + kFrom);
63:     var mmFromObj = eval("document." + formName + ".mm" + kFrom);
64:     var yyFromObj = eval("document." + formName + ".yy" + kFrom);
65:     var ddToObj = eval("document." + formName + ".dd" + kTo);
66:     var mmToObj = eval("document." + formName + ".mm" + kTo);
67:     var yyToObj = eval("document." + formName + ".yy" + kTo);
68:     yyToObj[yyFromObj.selectedIndex].selected = true;
69:     mmToObj[mmFromObj.selectedIndex].selected = true;
70:     updateMonthDays(formName, kTo);
71:     ddToObj[ddFromObj.selectedIndex].selected = true;
72:     }
```

The function daysInMonth is pretty straightforward. It accepts the month and year as arguments and returns the number of days in that month. Lines 8–14 express the fact that the leap years are divisible by 4, but not if they're also divisible by 100, but yes if they're also divisible by 400. That's why the year 2000 was a leap year, but the year 1900 was not, and the year 2100 will not be.

Remember that updateMonthDays ensures that you display the correct number of days for each month. Also keep in mind that the days are option elements within a select control element. In lines 23–27, you extract the selected text from the select elements for month and year and use daysInMonth to obtain the number of days you need. In line 28, you obtain the number of days displayed before changing either the year or month. The length of the select element is nothing else than the length of the array of option elements, which the select element contains. Therefore, you can use ddObj.length instead of ddObj.options.length. Each iteration of the while loop in lines 32–35 deletes the last option (i.e., the last day) by setting it to null and decreases the number of current days accordingly:

```
while (wantedDays < currentDays) {
  ddObj.options[ddObj.length - 1] = null;
  currentDays--;
}
```

The iterations continue until the number of current days has been reduced to the number of days you need for the current month. Similarly, each iteration of the while loop in lines 39–42 increases the number of current days, creates a new option with the increased number, and appends it to the select element:

```
while (wantedDays > currentDays) {
  currentDays++;
  ddObj.appendChild(new Option(currentDays));
}
```

The iterations continue until the number of current days has been increased to the number of days you need for the current month. The last line of updateMonthDays (line 44) is necessary in case the previously selected day has been removed. For example, if you selected March 31st and then changed the month to April, the day is set to the 1st because the 31st is no longer there.

The client's current day is set with selectToday. All the work is done in lines 54–56. Line 54 selects the month, line 55 adjusts the number of days of the month, and line 56 selects the day.

You use copyDay to copy the day, month, and year from one date to another. All the work is done in the lines 68–71. Line 68 selects in the destination year the same index selected in the source year, line 69 does the same for the month, line 70 adjusts the number of days of the month, and line 71 selects in the destination day the same index selected in the source day.

Animation: Ticker Tape

In principle, the idea is simple: you write a message in a text field, and then, at regular intervals, you remove the first character of the message and stick it to the end. The message appears to scroll from right to left (see Figure A-29). Nevertheless, to do a good ticker tape, there is more than meets the eye.

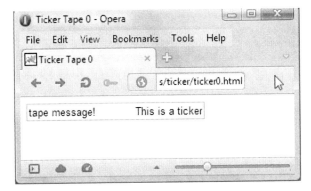

Figure A-29. *The simplest possible ticker tape*

Listing A-20 shows you how to create a simple ticker tape.

Listing A-20. ticker0.html

```
<!DOCTYPE html PUBLIC "-//W3C//DTD XHTML 1.0 Strict//EN"
  "http://www.w3.org/TR/xhtml1/DTD/xhtml1-strict.dtd">
<html xmlns="http//www.w3.org/1999/xhtml">
<head>
  <title>Ticker Tape 0</title>
  <script type="text/javascript">
    var msg = " This is a ticker tape message!               ";
    function tick_it() {
      msg = msg.substring(1) + msg.charAt(0);
      document.f.t.value = msg;
      window.setTimeout("tick_it()", 150);
      }
  </script>
</head>
<body>
  <form name="f"><input name="t" size="30" value=""/></form>
  <script type="text/javascript">tick_it();</script>
</body>
</html>
```

The function tick_it calls itself recursively every 150 ms. Every time it executes, it moves the first character of msg to the end, thereby creating the effect of a message scrolling to the left.

ticker0.html may look straightforward, but it's not necessarily that simple. Notice that the message I defined in the example, including an initial space, is 31 characters long. And yet I've still appended a dozen spaces to display it in a text element of size 30. This is because the size attribute of a text element doesn't really reflect the correct number of characters it can contain. Without the extra spaces, a portion of the text field would have remained blank. In other words, the scrolling text would have not scrolled through the whole text field. Ugly. You can usually resolve this issue by appending a large number of spaces or copies of the message itself to the end of the message. This solution is effective, but it would be nice to have a more elegant solution.

The crux of the problem lies in the fact that the length of a string depends on its font type and size. Developing software for the Macintosh, already decades ago, it was easily possible to determine the number of pixels needed to display a string. Java lets you do it now with the Graphics and FontMetrics classes. However, in HTML, it is not *officially* possible to know how long a piece of string is (pun intended). In other words, the W3C hasn't standardized a way of obtaining the size of an element in pixels. However, Microsoft did it in IE, and then all major browsers adopted the Microsoft extension to the standard. As a result, there is an *unofficial* way of getting the length of a string in pixels. Have a look at Listing A-21.

Listing A-21. ticker.html

```
01:  <!DOCTYPE html PUBLIC "-//W3C//DTD XHTML 1.0 Strict//EN"
02:    "http://www.w3.org/TR/xhtml1/DTD/xhtml1-strict.dtd">
03:  <html xmlns="http//www.w3.org/1999/xhtml">
04:  <head>
05:    <title>Ticker Tape</title>
06:    <script type="text/javascript">
07:      var msg = " This is a ticker tape message!";
08:      var TAPE_SIZE = 300; // in pixels
09:      function start_ticker() {
10:        document.f.t.style.width = TAPE_SIZE + "px";
11:        var xx = document.getElementById("x");
12:        var space_size = xx.offsetWidth - 1;
13:        xx.innerHTML = msg;
14:        var msg_size = xx.offsetWidth;
15:        var nSpaces = Math.ceil((TAPE_SIZE - msg_size) / space_size);
16:        for (var k = nSpaces; k > 0; k--) msg += " ";
18:        document.f.t.value = msg;
19:        tick_it();
20:      }
21:      function tick_it() {
22:        msg = msg.substring(1) + msg.charAt(0);
23:        document.f.t.value = msg;
24:        window.setTimeout("tick_it()", 150);
25:      }
26:    </script>
27:  </head>
28:  <body>
29:    <span id="x" style="visibility:hidden"> </span>
30:    <form name="f"><input name="t" value=""/></form>
31:    <script type="text/javascript">start_ticker();</script>
32:  </body>
33:  </html>
```

I've highlighted the differences between this version and ticker0.html, shown in Listing A-18. Note that in line 7, I removed the dozen trailing spaces from the message. I did this because the script will automatically extend the message with enough spaces to bring its length to match that of the text element. Also note that ticker.html uses HTML's Document Object Model to identify the x element and manipulate its content.

All the work is done in the start_ticker function. In line 10, you set the size of the text element in pixels, rather than use the size attribute expressed in characters. In line 29, you define an invisible span element containing a single space, and in line 12, you determine the size of the element (i.e., the pixels occupied by the space in the horizontal direction) via the read-only property offsetWidth. This is one of the properties originally introduced by Microsoft and not included in any W3C specification.

In line 13, you replace the content of span with the message using innerHTML, another Microsoft-originated property that has been implemented in all browsers. This lets you obtain the length of the message string in pixels with offsetWidth (see line 14).

You now have all the information you need to calculate the number of spaces you need to append to your message in order to fill the whole text field. Everything works just fine, even when the message without any additional spaces already takes up more space than what is available in the text field. In that case, nSpace becomes negative, and the for loop in line 16 terminates without adding any space. Incidentally, this is one of the reasons for adding a hard-coded space at the beginning of any message: you want to be sure that you display at least one empty space between repetitions of the message. It's better to insert the space at the beginning, because it makes the initial display of the message more readable.

Opera, Firefox, and Chrome report that the length of the string is 177 pixels, while Internet Explorer counts 189 pixels, which confirms once more that Microsoft tends to do things differently. Odd, but inconsequential. If you want to check it for yourself, you can insert the following line toward the end of start_ticker:

```
alert("space: " + space_size + "; msg: " + msg_size);
```

Animation: Bouncing Balls

You can use JavaScript to animate your pages. Figure A-30 shows you a page with a text field containing a couple of numbers, a button, and a square full of dots. This isn't so interesting, but that's only because it's a snapshot of a window. In reality, the dots bounce around within the square in all possible directions and at different speeds. To view the page, copy the folder named balls to the usual test folder and view http://localhost:8080/tests/balls/balls.html.

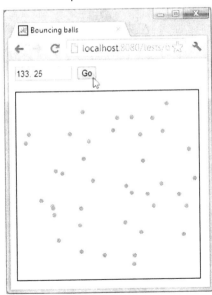

Figure A-30. A square full of bouncing balls

Let's go through the HTML code, shown in Listing A-22 after removing from the file the JavaScript code.

Listing A-22. balls_no_js.html

```
<!DOCTYPE html PUBLIC "-//W3C//DTD XHTML 1.0 Strict//EN"
  "http://www.w3.org/TR/xhtml1/DTD/xhtml1-strict.dtd">
<html xmlns="http//www.w3.org/1999/xhtml">
<head>
  <title>Bouncing balls</title>
  <style>
    #square {
      position: absolute;
      border: thin solid;
      }
    div.ball img {
      position: absolute;
      }
    </style>
</head>
<body>
  <form name="f">
    <input type="text" name="t" size="10"/>
    <input type=button id="stop_go" onclick="stop()" value="Stop"/>
    </form>
  <div id="square"></div>
  <div id="ball" class="ball"><img src="ball.gif" alt=""/></div>
  </body>
</html>
```

The first style defines an object with a thin, solid border identified as square, and the second style only states that all images within a division of class ball have absolute coordinates.

The body element includes a small form with the text field, the button, and two divisions: one identified as square and one of class ball. Figure A-31 shows how a browser renders such a page.

Figure A-31. No square and one ball at rest (balls_no_js.html)

Boring. Listing A-23 shows the full code of the page after you add the JavaScript part. I've highlighted the JavaScript variable definitions and the function names.

Listing A-23. balls.html

```
01:   <!DOCTYPE html PUBLIC "-//W3C//DTD XHTML 1.0 Strict//EN"
02:     "http://www.w3.org/TR/xhtml1/DTD/xhtml1-strict.dtd">
```

```
03:  <html xmlns="http//www.w3.org/1999/xhtml">
04:  <head>
05:    <title>Bouncing balls</title>
06:    <style>
07:      #square {
08:        position: absolute;
09:        border: thin solid;
10:        }
11:      div.ball img {
12:        position: absolute;
13:        }
14:      </style>
15:  <script type="text/javascript">
16:  var MIN_X = 10;
17:  var MIN_Y = 50;
18:  var MAX_X = 310;
19:  var MAX_Y = 350;
20:  var DIAM = 7;
21:  var balls = [];
22:  var timer = null;
23:  //-----------------------------
24:  function speed() {
25:    return DIAM*(0.5+1.5*Math.random())*((Math.random()>0.5)?1:-1);
26:    }
27:  function initBall(ball, xx, yy) {
28:    ball.xx = xx;
29:    ball.yy = yy;
30:    ball.sX = speed();
31:    ball.sY = speed();
32:    }
33:  function mouseDown(e) {
34:    var xx = e.clientX;
35:    var yy = e.clientY;
36:    document.f.t.value = xx + ", " + yy;
37:    if (xx > MIN_X && xx < MAX_X && yy > MIN_Y && yy < MAX_Y) {
38:      document.getElementById("ball").appendChild(balls[0].cloneNode(true));
39:      initBall(balls[balls.length-1], xx, yy);
40:      }
41:    }
42:  function moveBall(b) {
43:    b.xx += b.sX;
44:    b.yy += b.sY;
45:    b.style.left = b.xx + "px";
46:    b.style.top = b.yy + "px";
47:    if ((b.xx + b.sX + DIAM >= MAX_X) || (b.xx + b.sX <= MIN_X)) b.sX *= -1;
48:    if ((b.yy + b.sY + DIAM >= MAX_Y) || (b.yy + b.sY <= MIN_Y)) b.sY *= -1;
49:    }
50:  function moveBalls() {
51:    for (var k = 0; k < balls.length; k++) {
52:      moveBall(balls[k]);
53:      }
54:    }
```

```
55:  function go() {
56:     if (!timer) timer = setInterval(moveBalls, 20);
57:     var but = document.getElementById("stop_go");
58:     but.onclick = stop;
59:     but.value = "Stop";
60:     }
61:  function stop() {
62:     if (timer) {
63:       clearInterval(timer);
64:       timer = null;
65:       var but = document.getElementById("stop_go");
66:       but.onclick = go;
67:       but.value = "Go";
68:       }
69:     }
70:  function init() {
71:     var field = document.getElementById("square");
72:     field.style.left = MIN_X + "px";
73:     field.style.top = MIN_Y + "px";
74:     field.style.width = MAX_X - MIN_X + "px";
75:     field.style.height = MAX_Y - MIN_Y + "px";
76:     balls = document.getElementById("ball").getElementsByTagName("img");
77:     initBall(
78:       balls[0],
79:       (MAX_X - MIN_X)*Math.random(),
80:       (MAX_Y - MIN_Y)*Math.random()
81:       );
82:     balls[0].style.width = DIAM + "px";
83:     balls[0].style.height = DIAM + "px";
84:     document.onmousedown = mouseDown;
85:     go();
86:     }
87:  window.onload = init;
88:  </script>
89:  </head>
90:  <body>
91:     <form name="f">
92:       <input type="text" name="t" size="10"/>
93:       <input type=button id="stop_go" onclick="stop()" value="Stop"/>
94:       </form>
95:     <div id="square"></div>
96:     <div id="ball" class="ball"><img src="ball.gif" alt=""/></div>
97:     </body>
98:  </html>
```

(MIN_X, MIN_Y) and (MAX_X, MAX_Y) define the coordinates of the top-left and bottom-right corners of the rectangular area within which you want the balls to bounce. DIAM is the diameter of the balls. All dimensions are measured in pixels.

Line 87 directs the browser to execute the function init upon loading the HTML page. init uses MIN_X, MIN_Y, MAX_X, and MAX_Y to set the position and dimensions of the div element with id square (in lines 71–75). Instead of doing this, you could have simply added the following four lines to the #square style (defined in lines 7–10):

```
left: 10px;
top: 50px;
width: 300px;
height: 300px;
```

However, it's never good practice to duplicate definitions, because sooner or later they will diverge and cause problems. It would have been worse if the style sheet had been in a separate file, but even in this case, we want to do it right, don't we?

After defining the square to be used as the field for the bouncing balls, init points the variable balls (which is defined as an array) to the list of img elements inside the div element with id ball (in line 76). As the HTML page contains a single image within the division ball (see line 96), that image is then accessible as balls[0]. To set the initial coordinates and the speed of the ball, init executes the function initBall. Then init calculates the initial coordinates as a random point within the square (see lines 79–80), while initBall calculates the horizontal and vertical components of the speed (in lines 30–31) by means of the function speed (lines 24–26). The speed along each axis is the number of pixels covered by a ball in a given period of time (a 50th of a second, as you'll see in a moment). Notice how simply JavaScript lets you define new element attributes. The variable ball used inside initBall, like balls[0], points to an object that is the img element defined in line 96; when you write ball.xx = xx, JavaScript creates an attribute of ball named xx and assigns to it the value of the xx parameter.

Once initBall returns, init sets the dimensions of the ball image by updating its style (in lines 82–83) and assigns the JavaScript function mouseDown to the event document.mousedown (in line 84). This means that the function mouseDown will be executed every time the user presses a mouse button. I intend to create a new bouncing ball whenever this happens. The last action of init is to execute the function go, which starts the animation.

First of all, go (in line 56) starts a time interval of 20ms (the 50th of a second I already mentioned), which causes the browser to execute the function moveBalls every 20ms. Notice that you only do this if no timer is already running. This is a safety measure that isn't really necessary, because immediately after dealing with the timer, go sets the button but to execute the function stop (in lines 57–59). Therefore, there is theoretically no way to execute go more than once. However, as you've learned, some defensive code usually results in more stable programs without significantly penalizing performance.

After go has completed, the name of the button is Stop, as shown in Figure A-31. When the user clicks on it, the function stop removes the timer (in lines 63–64), thereby halting the animation. It then associates the button back to the function go and renames it as Go (in lines 65–67).

When the animation is running, every 20ms the browser executes moveBalls, which just executes moveBall for each element in the array balls[]. moveBall increments the coordinates by their corresponding speed components (in lines 43–44) and updates the position stored in the style (in lines 45–46), which is what actually causes the image on the screen to move. After moving a ball, moveBall checks whether the ball has reached one of the sides of the rectangular field. If it has, moveBall inverts the corresponding speed component, so that when it executes the next time, the ball will "bounce off" the wall. By doing that, you don't really ensure that the ball bounces when it touches the border rather than when it overlaps with it or when it is one pixel away from it. It all depends on using the appropriate operations (<, <=, >=, and >) and adding or not adding a +1 when calculating the differences between coordinates. However, I don't think this is worth spending time on. I leave it up to you to ensure that the ball bounces back when it touches one side—not one pixel before and not one pixel after!

When you press the mouse button anywhere within the main browser window, the function mouseDown is executed. The first two lines (34 and 35) have the purpose of saving in two variables the horizontal and vertical coordinates of the cursor (incidentally, the e stands for *event*). This makes the code shorter and more readable. Line 36 writes the coordinates in the text field, as shown in Figure A-30. I did this to show you how to do it, although it's irrelevant for bouncing the balls. Notice how you use the names to identify the form and its text element, as opposed to defining an ID and using getElementById as you do elsewhere. The two important lines are 38 and 39, which are executed only when you click the mouse inside the rectangular field. By doing so, you cause the creation of a new bouncing ball that starts with random speed from the position where you click the mouse.

The purpose of line 38 is to display a new ball in the web page. If you study the code carefully, you'll see that line 38 is equivalent to the following three lines:

```
var ballDivObject = document.getElementById("ball");
var newBallObject = balls[0].cloneNode(true);
ballDivObject.appendChild(newBallObject);
```

The first line gets a pointer to the div element with the identifier set to ball. The second line makes a copy of the first ball. Remember that you defined it when the page was loaded. Therefore, when you click with the mouse, balls[0] certainly exists and points to a properly initialized ball—that is, to an img element with the additional attributes xx, yy, sX, and sY. The third line takes the new ball and attaches it to the ball div as a new child.

As a result, it is as if you had added an image to the div defined in line 96:

```
<div id="ball" class="ball">
  <img src="ball.gif" alt=""/>
  <img src="ball.gif" alt=""/>
</div>
```

Now, however, the images also have the coordinate and speed attributes, which aren't part of the initial HTML code.

Being a clone of the first ball, the new ball has the same coordinates and speed that the first ball has when you click the mouse. With line 39, you tell initBall to set the coordinates of the new ball to those of the mouse event (i.e., xx and yy). initBall also replaces the speed components of the new ball with two new random values. Notice that after executing line 38, as you had set the array balls to point to the list of img objects within the ball div, the last element of balls points to the new ball you've just created by cloning.

■ **Caution** Remember that the identifiers are supposed to be unique within the document. Make sure this is so!

An interesting extension would be to have the balls bounce against each other, but this would require a bit of math. At each wake-up, you'd have to check each ball against all the others to identify the pairs that come into contact. Then, for each one of those pairs, you'd have to calculate the total momentum, find the components of the two velocities perpendicular to the direction of the momentum, and invert those components. The assumption that all the balls have the same mass would reduce the problem to be purely geometrical, but probably not trivial for many. Anyhow, for those interested in physics, with several balls and after enough cycles, the exchange of momentum between the balls would model a *gas* of balls regardless of the initial conditions.

SQL Practical Introduction

Structured Query Language (SQL) is the most widely used language to interact with DBMSs. The purpose of this appendix is not to provide a comprehensive manual of SQL but rather to list and explain the most common concepts, terms, and statements. Most DBMSs don't support the whole SQL standard. Moreover, vendors sometimes add nonstandard elements that, in practice, prevent full portability across DBMSs. In this appendix, I'll limit myself to standard elements. To help you identify nonstandard keywords, I have included Table B-12 at the end of this appendix, which lists the standard keywords that should work with most implementations.

Note Unless otherwise specified, all the SQL statements you will find in this appendix refer to and have been tested with MySQL's implementation of SQL.

SQL Terminology

Data is organized in *tables* consisting of *rows* and *columns*. This is a natural way of organizing data, and you're probably familiar with it through the use of spreadsheets. Nevertheless, although there are some similarities, a database table is *not* an Excel worksheet. For example, in a spreadsheet, you can assign data types to individual cells, while in a database, all the cells of a column have the same data type. The column definitions, each with their name and the type of data permitted, are the core of the table structure.

For example, a table of employees would probably include columns named FirstName, LastName, and SocialSecurityNumber containing strings of text; columns named EmployeeNumber and YearSalary would contain numbers; and columns named DateOfBirth and EmployedSince would contain dates. The data associated with each employee would then all be stored into a row.

A *field* is an individual data item within a table, corresponding to the intersection of a row and a column. This would be a cell in a spreadsheet.

One or more columns can be specified as *unique keys*, used to identify each individual employee. For this purpose, you could use either one of the columns mentioned previously (e.g., EmployeeNumber), or the combination of first and last name. The unique key used in preference over the others is called the *primary key* of a table.

An additional type of key is the *foreign key*. In this case, the column is defined as a reference to a unique key of another table. Besides avoiding duplication of data, this type of constraint increases the consistency of the database. For example, a table containing customer contracts could include a column referring to the column of employee numbers defined in the employee table. This would ensure that each contract would be associated with an existing salesperson.

The DBMS can build an *index* for each key, so that the data can be retrieved more quickly. This will obviously slow down insertion and deletion of rows (i.e., of new records), because the DBMS will have to spend time updating the indexes, but most databases are more frequently interrogated than modified. Therefore, it usually pays to define indexes, at least those that can speed up the most common queries. Here you have a hint of another difference from Excel: in a database table, the data items are not moved around once they're inserted; if you want to access them in a particular order, you must either sort them every time or create an index. You will learn about indexing later in this appendix.

Sometimes it's useful to present only some columns and rows, as if they were a table in their own right. Such virtual tables are called *views*. Under certain circumstances (I'll discuss this further when I describe individual statements, later in this chapter), you can also use views to collect columns from different tables and handle them as if they belonged to a single table.

Transactions

Transactions deserve a little more attention, because they represent a key concept in DBMSs. A *transaction* indicates a series of database operations that have to be performed without interruption—that is, without any other operation "sneaking in" between them. To make sense of this, you have to think in terms of concurrent access to the same tables.

For example, imagine the following scenario, in which two money transfers involve three bank accounts:

1.   Transfer $100 from account A to account B

2.   Transfer $200 from account B to account C

Conceptually, each transfer consists of the following operations:

- Read the balance of the source account.

- Reduce it by the amount of the transfer.

- Write it back.

- Read the balance of the destination account.

- Increase it by the amount of the transfer.

- Write it back.

Now, imagine that transfer number 2 starts while transfer number 1 is not yet completely done, as illustrated in the sequence of elementary operations listed in Table B-1.

Table B-1. Sequence of Elementary Operations

Op #	Transfer	Operation Description
1.	1:	Read the balance of account A.
2.	1:	Reduce the balance of account A by $100.

Op #	Transfer	Operation Description
3.	1:	Write back the balance of account A.
4.	1:	Read the balance of account B.
5.	1:	Increase the balance of account B by $100.
6.	**2:**	**Read the balance of account B.**
7.	2:	Reduce the balance of account B by $200.
8.	2:	Write back the balance of account B.
9.	2:	Read the balance of account C.
10.	2:	Increase the balance of account C by $200.
11.	**1:**	**Write back the balance of account B.**
12.	2:	Write back the balance of account C.

The owner of account B is going to be very happy, because she will end up with $200 more than what she actually owns. The problem is that the two steps numbered 6 and 11 should have *not* been executed in that order. Let's say that account B initially held $500. At the end, it should hold $500 + $100 - $200 = $400, but this is not what happened. Just before the end of the first transfer, when the balance of $600 was about to be written back, the second transfer started. The balance of account B stored in the database was changed as a result of the second transfer, but when the first transfer resumed and completed, the balance of $600 was written back to account B. The effect of the second transfer was "forgotten." As far as account B was concerned, it was as if the second transfer hadn't happened!

You can solve this problem by handling each transfer as a transaction. The second transfer won't start until the first one is completed, and by then, the balance of account B will have been updated to reflect the first transfer.

A transaction is characterized by four properties—atomicity, consistency, isolation, and durability (ACID):

- **Atomicity**: It guarantees that either all the individual steps of an operation are performed or none at all. You must not be able to perform partial transactions.

- **Consistency**: It refers to the fact that a transaction is not supposed to violate the integrity of a database. For example, it shouldn't be able to store a negative value in a numeric field that is supposed to be positive. When it comes to distributed systems, it also means that all the nodes will have consistent values.

- **Isolation**: It means that concurrent operations cannot see intermediate values of a transaction. Lack of isolation is what caused the example of Table B-1 to fail, when the balance of account B could be read even though the transaction that was modifying it was not yet complete. Unfortunately, the serialization of the transactions (i.e., performing them one after the other) has an impact on performance precisely when there is a high workload. Lack of isolation is a problem in the example, but this is not always the case. For example, it might not matter that searches on a list of products take place while products are being added or removed. Given the potential impact on performance, you might decide in some cases to ignore the existence of concurrent transactions.

- **Durability:** It refers to the capacity of a DBMS to guarantee that a transaction, once completed, is never going to be "forgotten," even after a system failure.

Conventions

I'll use the following conventions to describe SQL statements:

- SQL keywords that you must enter exactly as shown are in uppercase (e.g., CREATE). Note that most keywords can actually be in lowercase.

- Variable values are in lowercase (e.g., db_name).

- Elements that you can omit are enclosed in square brackets (e.g., [WITH]).

- References to further definitions are enclosed in angle brackets (e.g., <create_spec>).

- The ellipsis immediately preceding a closing square bracket means that you can repeat the element enclosed between the brackets (e.g., [<create_spec> ...]). That is, you can omit the element, enter it once, or enter it more than once.

- Mutually exclusive alternatives are enclosed in curly brackets and separated by vertical bars (e.g., {DATABASE | SCHEMA}). You must enter one (and only one) of them.

- I close every statement with a semicolon, although, strictly speaking, it is not part of the official syntax. I do so because it makes for easier reading and reminds you that you must type the semicolon when including the statement in scripts.

For example, Listing B-1 shows part of the SQL statement used to create a database. It begins with the CREATE keyword followed by either DATABASE or SCHEMA and a database name. It is then possible (but not mandatory) to add one or more <create_spec> elements, the meaning of which is defined separately.

Listing B-1. *Syntax of an SQL Statement*

```
CREATE {DATABASE | SCHEMA} db_name [<create_spec> ...];
```

Statements

In general, regardless of whether we're talking about database organization, table structure, or actual data, you'll need to perform four basic operations: create, retrieve, update, and delete (CRUD). The corresponding SQL statements begin with a keyword that identifies the operation (e.g., INSERT, SELECT, UPDATE, or DELETE), followed when necessary by a keyword specifying on what type of entity the operation is to be performed (e.g., DATABASE, TABLE, or INDEX) and by additional elements. You use the SELECT statement for retrieving information.

You can create databases, tables, and indexes with the CREATE statement, update them with ALTER, and delete them with DROP. Similarly, you can create and delete views with CREATE and DROP, but you cannot update them once you've created them. You use INSERT to create new rows within a table, and you use DELETE to delete them. The UPDATE statement lets you modify entire rows or one or more individual fields within them.

The statements that let you modify the structures are collectively referred to as Data Definition Language (DDL), while those that let you modify the content are called Data Manipulation Language (DML).

That said, you won't find anything about ALTER DATABASE and ALTER INDEX in this appendix, because there is very little you can update in a database or an index definition once you've created them, and there is no agreement among DBMS vendors about what you can do. Table B-2 shows a summary of the possible combinations of keywords. In the following sections, I will explain how to use them going through Table B-2 by columns. This will tell you how to create new structures and new data, how to modify them, and how to remove them.

Table B-2. SQL Keywords to Create, Update, and Delete

Entity	Create	Update	Delete
DATABASE	CREATE	~n/a	DROP
TABLE	CREATE	ALTER	DROP
INDEX	CREATE	~n/a	DROP
VIEW	CREATE	n/a	DROP
Row	INSERT	UPDATE	DELETE

In many applications, the structure of databases, tables, indexes, and views, once initially defined, remains unchanged. Therefore, you'll often need within your applications only the statements operating on rows and fields. In any case, you'll certainly need SELECT, which you use to interrogate databases both in terms of their structure and the data they contain. Finally, to complete the list of statements you're likely to need when developing applications, I'll also describe START TRANSACTION, COMMIT, and ROLLBACK, which you need to use transactions.

SQL interprets all text enclosed between /* and */ as comments and ignores it.

■ **Note** In all statements, you can always use the column position within the table instead of the column name. Column numbering in SQL starts with 1. In some particular cases, this can be useful, but use it sparingly, because it leads to errors and code that's difficult to maintain.

The WHERE Condition

When you want to retrieve, update, or delete rows, you obviously have to identify them. You do this with the WHERE keyword followed by a <where_condition>. Listing B-2 shows you the format of this condition. I explain WHERE before discussing individual statements, because you'll need it for several of them.

Listing B-2. The WHERE Condition

```
<where_condition> = {
      col_name {= | < | > | <= | >= | !< | !> | <> | !=} <val>
    | col_name [NOT] BETWEEN <val> AND <val>
    | col_name [NOT] LIKE <val> [ESCAPE <val>]
    | col_name [NOT] IN (<val> [, <val> ...])
    | col_name IS [NOT] NULL
    | col_name [NOT] CONTAINING <val>
    | col_name [NOT] STARTING [WITH] <val>
    | NOT <search_condition>
    | <where_condition> OR <where_condition>
    | <where_condition> AND <where_condition>
    | (<where_condition>)
}
<val> = A valid SQL expression that results in a single value
```

Note that the WHERE condition is more powerful (and complex) than what I explain here. You could actually include complete query statements within a condition and use the result of a first search to delimit the scope of the following one. However, to explain such techniques involving subqueries would go beyond the scope of this manual.

I'll describe the listed possibilities by simply showing and explaining valid examples of WHERE selections on a hypothetical employee table:

- lastname = 'Smith' selects all employees with the family name Smith.

- startdate < '2000-01-01' selects all employees who joined the company before the beginning of the century.

- startdate BETWEEN '2010-01-01' AND '2010-12-31' selects all employees who joined the company in 2010, while startdate NOT BETWEEN '2010-01-01' AND '2010-12-31' selects those who didn't.

- lastname LIKE 'S%' selects all employees whose family name starts with S. In other words, the percent sign is the SQL equivalent of the asterisk you use when listing a directory from the command line. You can use more than one percent sign in a condition. For example, lastname LIKE 'S%z%a' selects all names that start with S, end with a, and have a z somewhere in between. While the percent sign stands for any number of characters (including none), the underscore stands for exactly one character, like the question mark when listing directories. For example, lastname NOT LIKE '_' selects all names that contain at least two characters (or none, if you allow it when designing the database). The ESCAPE keyword lets you search for strings containing one of the escape characters. For example, lastname LIKE '%!%%' ESCAPE '!' selects all names that contain a percent sign in any position.

- `firstname IN ('John', 'Jack')` selects all employees who have either John or Jack as their first name.

- `middlename IS NULL` selects all employees who have no middle name.

- `lastname CONTAINING 'qu'` selects all employees who have the string "qu" in their family name. This is identical to `lastname LIKE '%qu%'`.

- `lastname STARTING WITH 'Sm'` selects all employees whose family name starts with "Sm". This is identical to `lastname LIKE 'Sm%'`.

- You can use the logical operators `NOT`, `AND`, and `OR` to build complex conditions. For example, `startdate >= '2010-01-01' AND startdate <= '2010-12-31'` is equivalent to `startdate BETWEEN '2010-01-01' AND '2010-12-31'`. To avoid ambiguities, use the parentheses to set the order of execution. For example, `lastname CONTAINING 's' OR (lastname CONTAINING 'q' AND lastname NOT CONTAINING 'qu')` selects all employees whose family names contain an 's' or a 'q', but only if the 'q' is not followed by a 'u'. The statement `(lastname CONTAINING 's' OR lastname CONTAINING 'q') AND lastname NOT CONTAINING 'qu'` would not select names containing both 's' and "qu". A name such as "quasi" would be selected by the first condition but not by the second one.

Data Types

When designing your database, you have to decide what type of data you need to store in the columns of your tables. SQL supports different data types to store numbers, text, date/time, and unspecified data (called LOB, for large object), as summarized in Listing B-3.

Listing B-3. The SQL Data Types

```
<data_type> = {<num_dt> | <datime_dt> | <text_dt> | <lob_dt>}
```

Numbers

The space reserved in memory for the numeric data types determines their precision—that is, the number of digits they can have. Java and JSP specify the space allocated for each data type, so that they are the same regardless of operating systems and virtual machines. Unfortunately, the same cannot be said of SQL, where the precision of the data types, like so many other things, is vendor-dependent. Therefore, you always have to refer to the manual of your DBMS if you want to be sure that your applications will work correctly. Listing B-4 shows how you specify a numeric data type.

Listing B-4. The SQL Data Types for Numbers

```
<num_dt> = {
     {DECIMAL | DEC | NUMERIC} [(precision [, scale])]
   | {SMALLINT | INTEGER | INT | BIGINT | REAL | FLOAT | DOUBLE PRECISION}
   }
```

The types `DECIMAL` (which can be abbreviated to `DEC`) and `NUMERIC` require you to specify the total number of digits and the number of decimal places. For example, you specify numbers of the type xxxx as (4), numbers of the type xxx.y as (4,1), and numbers of the type 0.yyy as (3,3). The scale must never exceed the precision. As different DBMS vendors set different defaults, you should always at least specify the precision. When doing so, keep in mind that 18 decimal digits require 64 bits. Therefore, larger precisions might not be accepted by all DBMSs.

The difference between DECIMAL and NUMERIC is that with DECIMAL, the DBMS is free to allocate more space than the minimum required in order to optimize access speed, while with NUMERIC, the number of digits allocated is exactly what you specify as precision.

The other types are easier to use but require some attention, because, again, different DBMS vendors allocate different numbers of bytes for the different data types. If you don't pay attention, you'll risk writing code that won't be portable.

SMALLINT, INTEGER or INT, and BIGINT refer to integer types of different sizes, while the remaining three types refer to numbers with a decimal point. Table B-3 shows the ranges possible with different numbers of bits, and their corresponding data types in Java.

Some versions of MySQL also support the numeric data types BIT and TINYINT, but they are not always supported by other SQL implementations or by all versions of MySQL. I suggest that you stick to the standard types.

Table B-3. *Space Occupied by Numeric Java Types*

Bits	Minimum	Maximum	Java Type
16	-32,768	32,767	short
32	-2,147,483,648	2,147,483,647	int
64	-9,223,372,036,854,775,808	9,223,372,036,854,775,807	long
32	1.175×10^{-38}	3.402×10^{38}	~float
64	2.225×10^{-308}	1.797×10^{308}	~double

Table B-4 lists the number of bits allocated by some vendors to the different SQL data types. I include this information here to help you in case you need to port your code to SQL implementations other than MySQL.

Table B-4. *Vendor-Specific Numeric Data Types*

Vendor	SMALLINT	INTEGER	BIGINT	REAL	FLOAT	DOUBLE PRECISION
MySQL	16	32	64	32	32	64
PostgreSQL	16	32	64	32		64
FirebirdSQL	16	32			32	64
Microsoft SQL Server	16	32	64	32	64	
Oracle		38			126	

FirebirdSQL supports 64-bit integers, but it doesn't recognize the type BIGINT. You have to use INT64. Microsoft SQL Server and Oracle aren't open source DBMSs, but given their large customer bases, I thought you might be interested to know.

Date and Time

Listing B-5 shows how dates and times are defined in SQL, but its simplicity is somewhat misleading, because the DBMSs of different vendors, by now certainly unsurprisingly, behave differently.

Listing B-5. The SQL Data Types for Date and Time

```
<datime_dt> = {DATE | TIME | TIMESTAMP}
```

One area where the vendors don't agree is the range of dates. MySQL accepts dates between the year 1000 CE and the year 9999 CE, PostgreSQL between 4713 BCE and 5874897 CE, and FirebirdSQL between 100 CE and February 32767 CE. The bottom line is that any date within our lifetimes should be accepted by every DBMS!

You can use DATE when you're not interested in the time of the day. It occupies 4 bytes. TIME stores the time of the day in milliseconds and occupies 8 bytes. TIMESTAMP manages to fit both the date and the time of the day in milliseconds into 8 bytes.

You can set date and time values in different formats, but I recommend that you conform to the ISO 8601 standard and set dates as 'YYYY-MM-DD', times as 'HH:MM', 'HH:MM:SS', or 'HH:MM:SS.mmm', and timestamps as a standard date followed by a space and a standard time, as in 'YYYY-MM-DD HH:MM:SS.mmm'. In particular, pay attention to years specified with only two digits, because the different DBMSs interpret the dates differently. MySQL has defined the DATETIME type, but I see no reason for you do adopt it, because MySQL also accepts the standard TIMESTAMP. I mention it here only because you'll probably encounter it sooner or later.

Text

Listing B-6 shows how you specify strings of characters.

Listing B-6. The SQL Data Types for Text

```
<text_dt> = {CHAR | CHARACTER | VARCHAR | CHARACTER VARYING} [(int)]
```

There are only two data types for text: CHARACTER and VARCHAR. CHAR is a synonym of CHARACTER, and CHARACTER VARYING is a synonym of VARCHAR. Use CHARACTER or CHAR to store strings of fixed length, and VARCHAR or CHARACTER VARYING for strings of variable length.

For example, a field of type CHARACTER (16) always occupies 16 bytes. If you use it to store a string of only 6 characters, it will be left-justified and right-padded with 10 spaces. If you attempt to store a string of 19 characters, you'll only succeed if the last 3 characters are spaces, in which case the DBMS will remove them. Different DBMSs set different limits to the maximum number of characters you can store into a CHARACTER data type, but they will all accept 255 characters. If you need more than that, check the user manual of the DBMS you're using.

The practical difference between VARCHAR and CHARACTER is that with VARCHAR, the DBMS stores the strings as they are, without padding. Also, with VARCHAR, you should be able to store up to 32,767 characters with all DBMSs.

Large Objects

LOBs let you store large amount of data, including binary data. This is an alternative to saving data in files and then storing their URIs into the database. In general, I am reluctant to store in a database large blocks of data that can be stored in the file system outside the database: like images, video clips, documents, and executable code. By storing data outside the database, you can easily access it with other tools, but by doing so, you also risk compromising the integrity of the data and leave references in the database that point to nonexisting files.

Note A URI is a generalization of a URL. Strictly speaking, the name location of a code fragment (i.e., the #whatever that you sometimes see in your browser's address field) is part of the URI but not of the URL, which only refers to the whole resource. Unfortunately, the definition of URI came when the term URL had already become universally known. That's why most people, including many specialists, keep referring to URLs when they should really be talking about URIs.

We have to distinguish between binary large objects (BLOBs) and character large objects (CLOBs). Unfortunately, once more, the major DBMS vendors haven't agreed. See Listing B-7 for the generalized definition of LOBs.

Listing B-7. The SQL Data Types for Large Objects

```
<lob_dt> = {<blob_dt> | <clob_dt>}
<blob_dt> = {
      BLOB(maxlen)      /* MySQL */
    | BYTEA             /* PostgreSQL */
    | BLOB(maxlen, 0)   /* FirebirdSQL */
    }
<clob_dt> = {
      TEXT              /* MySQL */
    | TEXT              /* PostgreSQL */
    | BLOB(maxlen, 1)   /* FirebirdSQL */
    }
```

LOBs can store up to 64KB of data. MEDIUMBLOBs can store up to 16MB and LONGBLOBs up to 4GB. Once more, check the user manual of your DBMS if you are not sure.

Caution MySQL only supports limited indexing of LOBs.

SELECT

SELECT retrieves data from one or more tables and views. See Listing B-8 for a description of its format.

Listing B-8. *The SQL Statement SELECT*

```
SELECT [ALL | DISTINCT ]
    {* | <select_list> [[<select_list>] {COUNT (*) | <function>}]
    [FROM <table_references> [WHERE <where_condition>]
      [GROUP BY col_name [ASC | DESC], ... [WITH ROLLUP]
        [HAVING <where_condition>]
        ]
      ]
    [ORDER BY <order_list>]
    [LIMIT {[offset,] row_count | row_count OFFSET offset}]
    ;
<select_list> = col_name [, <select_list>]
<table_references> = one or more table and/or view names separated by commas
<order_list> = col_name [ASC | DESC] [, <order_list> ...]
<function> = {AVG | MAX | MIN | SUM | COUNT} ([{ALL | DISTINCT}] <val>)
```

In part, the complication of SELECT is due to the fact that you can use it in two ways: to retrieve actual data or to obtain the result of applying a function to the data. To make it worse, some of the elements only apply to one of the two ways of using SELECT. To explain how SELECT works, I'll split the two modes of operation.

SELECT to Obtain Data

Listing B-9 shows how you use SELECT to obtain data.

Listing B-9. *SELECT to Obtain Data*

```
SELECT [ALL | DISTINCT ] {* | <select_list>}
    [FROM <table_references> [WHERE <where_condition>]]
    [ORDER BY <order_list>]
    [LIMIT {[offset,] row_count | row_count OFFSET offset}]
    ;
<select_list> = col_name [, <select_list>]
<table_references> = one or more table and/or view names separated by commas
<order_list> = col_name [ASC | DESC] [, <order_list> ...]
```

Conceptually, it is simple: SELECT one, some, or all columns FROM one or more tables or views WHERE certain conditions are satisfied; then present the rows ORDERed as specified. Some examples will clarify the details:

- SELECT * is the simplest possible SELECT, but you'll probably never use it. It returns everything you have in your database.

- SELECT * FROM table is the simplest practical form of SELECT. It returns all the data in the table you specify. The DBMS returns the rows in the order it finds most convenient, which is basically meaningless to you and me. Instead of a single table, you can specify a mix of tables and views separated by commas.

- `SELECT a_col_name, another_col_name FROM table` still returns all the rows of a table, but for each row, it returns only the values in the columns you specify. Use the keyword `DISTINCT` to tell the DBMS that it should *not* return any duplicate row. The default is `ALL`. You can also use column positions instead of column names.

- `SELECT * FROM table WHERE condition` only returns the rows for which the condition you specify is satisfied. Most `SELECT`s include a `WHERE` condition. Often only a single row is selected—for example, when the condition requires a unique key to have a particular value.

- `SELECT * FROM table ORDER BY col_name` returns all the rows of a table ordered on the basis of a column you specify. Note that you can provide more than one ordering. For example, `SELECT * FROM employee_tbl ORDER BY last_name, first_name` returns a list of all employees in alphabetical order. With the keyword `DESD`, you specify descending orderings.

- `SELECT * FROM table LIMIT first, count` returns count rows starting from `first`. You can obtain the same result with `SELECT * FROM table LIMIT count OFFSET first`. Be warned that not all DBMSs support both formats. I discourage you to use this element, because it doesn't deliver entirely predictable results. I only include it here because you could find it useful to debug some database problem.

SELECT to Apply a Function

Sometimes you need to obtain some global information on your data and are not interested in the details. This is where the second format of `SELECT` comes to the rescue. Listing B-10 shows how you use `SELECT` to apply a function.

Listing B-10. SELECT to Apply a Function

```
SELECT [ALL | DISTINCT ] [<select_list>] {COUNT (*) | <function>}
    [FROM <table_references>
        [GROUP BY col_name [ASC | DESC], ... [WITH ROLLUP]
          [HAVING <where_condition>]
          ]
        ]
    ;
<select_list> = col_name [, <select_list>]
<table_references> = one or more table and/or view names separated by commas
<function> = {AVG | MAX | MIN | SUM | COUNT} ([{ALL | DISTINCT}] <val>)
```

Here are some examples of how you apply a function with `SELECT`:

- `SELECT COUNT (*) FROM employee_tbl` counts the number of rows in the employee table.

- `SELECT department, citizenship, gender COUNT(employee_id) FROM employee_tbl GROUP BY department, citizenship, gender` provides counts of employees for each possible department, citizenship, and gender combination. If you append `WITH ROLLUP` to the statement, you'll also obtain partial totals, as shown in the example presented in Table B-5.

- `SELECT last_name COUNT(first_name) FROM employee_tbl GROUP BY first_name HAVING COUNT(first_name) > 1` counts the number of first names for each family name but only reports the family names that appear with more than one first name. `HAVING` has the same function for the aggregated values produced by `GROUP BY` that `WHERE` had for data selection.

Table B-5. Employees per Department, Citizenship, and Gender

Department	Citizenship	Gender	Count
Dev	India	Male	1
Dev	India	NULL	1
Dev	USA	Female	2
Dev	USA	Male	3
Dev	USA	NULL	5
Dev	NULL	NULL	6
Ops	Canada	Male	2
Ops	Canada	NULL	2
Ops	USA	Female	4
Ops	USA	Male	3
Ops	USA	NULL	7
Ops	NULL	NULL	9
Sales	USA	Female	7
Sales	USA	Male	5
Sales	USA	NULL	12
Sales	NULL	NULL	12
NULL	NULL	NULL	27

JOINs

When describing SQL terminology, I said that a foreign key is a reference to a unique key of another table. This means that information associated with each unique value of that key can be in either table or in both tables. For example, in a database representing a bookstore, you could imagine having one table with book authors and one with books. The name of the author would be a unique key in the authors' table and would appear as a foreign key in the books' table. Table B-6 shows an example of the authors' table.

Caution You should only use as foreign keys columns that are not expected to change. The use of columns that have a real-life meaning (like the author's name in the examples that follow) is often risky.

Table B-6. Authors' Table

Name	City
Isaac Asimov	New York (NY)
David Baldacci	Alexandria (VA)
Matthew Reilly	Sydney (Australia)

Table B-7 shows the books' table.

Table B-7. Books' Table

Title	Author
I, Robot	Isaac Asimov
Foundation	Isaac Asimov
Contest	Matthew Reilly
Scarecrow	Matthew Reilly
BlaBlaBla	NULL

If you perform the query SELECT * FROM books, authors;, the DBMS will return 15 combined rows, the first 7 of which are shown in Table B-8.

Table B-8. Disjoined Query on Books and Authors

Title	Author	Name	City
I, Robot	Isaac Asimov	Isaac Asimov	New York (NY)
Foundation	Isaac Asimov	Isaac Asimov	New York (NY)
Contest	Matthew Reilly	Isaac Asimov	New York (NY)
Scarecrow	Matthew Reilly	Isaac Asimov	New York (NY)
BlaBlaBla	NULL	Isaac Asimov	New York (NY)
I, Robot	Isaac Asimov	David Baldacci	Alexandria (VA)
Foundation	Isaac Asimov	David Baldacci	Alexandria (VA)

In other words, all books would be paired with all authors. This doesn't look very useful. You can get a more useful result when you perform the following query:

```
SELECT * FROM books, authors WHERE author = name;
```

Table B-9 shows its result.

Table B-9. Traditional Joined Query on Books and Authors

Title	Author	Name	City
I, Robot	Isaac Asimov	Isaac Asimov	New York (NY)
Foundation	Isaac Asimov	Isaac Asimov	New York (NY)
Contest	Matthew Reilly	Matthew Reilly	Sydney (Australia)
Scarecrow	Matthew Reilly	Matthew Reilly	Sydney (Australia)

You can achieve the same result with the JOIN keyword:

```
SELECT * FROM books [INNER] JOIN authors ON (author = name);
```

The result is the same, but conceptually, the JOIN syntax is clearer, because it states explicitly that you want to join two tables matching the values in two columns.

There is another type of JOIN, called OUTER JOIN, which also selects rows that appear in one of the two tables. For example, the following two SELECTs return the results shown respectively in Tables B-10 and B-11:

```
SELECT * FROM books LEFT [OUTER] JOIN authors ON (author = name);
```

while this line of code returns the result shown in Table B-11:

```
SELECT * FROM books RIGHT [OUTER] JOIN authors ON (author = name);
```

Table B-10. *LEFT JOIN Query*

Title	Author	Name	City
I, Robot	Isaac Asimov	Isaac Asimov	New York (NY)
Foundation	Isaac Asimov	Isaac Asimov	New York (NY)
Contest	Matthew Reilly	Matthew Reilly	Sydney (Australia)
Scarecrow	Matthew Reilly	Matthew Reilly	Sydney (Australia)
BlaBlaBla	NULL	NULL	NULL

Table B-11. *RIGHT JOIN Query*

Title	Author	Name	City
I, Robot	Isaac Asimov	Isaac Asimov	New York (NY)
Foundation	Isaac Asimov	Isaac Asimov	New York (NY)
Contest	Matthew Reilly	Matthew Reilly	Sydney (Australia)
Scarecrow	Matthew Reilly	Matthew Reilly	Sydney (Australia)
NULL	NULL	David Baldacci	Alexandria (VA)

To decide of which table you want to include all rows, choose LEFT or RIGHT depending on whether the table name precedes or follows the JOIN keyword in the SELECT statement.

You'd probably like to obtain a list with the names of all authors, regardless of whether they appear only in the first table, only in the second table, or in both tables. Can you have a JOIN that is both LEFT and RIGHT at the same time? The answer is that the SQL standard defines a FULL JOIN, which does exactly what you want, but MySQL doesn't support it.

CREATE DATABASE

CREATE DATABASE creates a new, empty database. See Listing B-11 for a description of its format.

Listing B-11. *The SQL Statement CREATE DATABASE*

```
CREATE {DATABASE | SCHEMA} db_name [<create_spec> ...];
<create_spec> = {
    [DEFAULT] CHARACTER SET charset_name
```

```
|   [DEFAULT] COLLATION collation_name
}
```

The DATABASE and SCHEMA keywords are equivalent, and the DEFAULT keyword is only descriptive. The default character set determines how strings are stored in the database, while the collation defines the rules used to compare strings (i.e., precedence among characters).

When using SQL with Java and JSP, you need to specify the Unicode character set, in which each character is stored in a variable number of bytes. With a minimal database creation statement such as CREATE DATABASE 'db_name', you risk getting the US-ASCII character set, which is incompatible with Java. Therefore, always specify Unicode, as in the following statement:

```
CREATE DATABASE 'db_name' CHARACTER SET utf8;
```

In fact, there are several Unicode character sets, but utf8 is the most widely used and also the most similar to ASCII. As such, it is the best choice for English speakers. You don't need to bother with specifying any collation. The default will be fine.

CREATE TABLE

CREATE TABLE creates a new table, together with its columns and integrity constraints, in an existing database. See Listing B-12 for a description of its format.

Listing B-12. The SQL Statement CREATE TABLE

```
CREATE TABLE tbl_name (<col_def> [, <col_def> | <tbl_constr> ...]);
<col_def> = col_name <data_type> [DEFAULT {value | NULL}] [NOT NULL] [<col_constr>]
<col_constr> = [CONSTRAINT constr_name] {
      UNIQUE
    | PRIMARY KEY
    | REFERENCES another_tbl [(col_name [, col_name ...])]
        [ON {DELETE | UPDATE} { NO ACTION | SET NULL | SET DEFAULT | CASCADE }]
    | CHECK (<where_condition>)
    }
<tbl_constr> = [CONSTRAINT constr_name] {
      {PRIMARY KEY | UNIQUE} (col_name [, col_name ...])
    | FOREIGN KEY (col_name [, col_name ...]) REFERENCES another_tbl
        [ON {DELETE | UPDATE} {NO ACTION | SET NULL | SET DEFAULT | CASCADE}]
    | CHECK (<where_condition>)
    }
```

To understand how CREATE TABLE works, concentrate on the first line of Listing B-12. It says that a table definition consists of a table name followed by the definition of one or more columns and possibly some table constraints. In turn, each column definition consists of a column name followed by the definition of a data type, a dimension, a default, and possibly some column constraints.

The following examples and comments should make it clear:

- CREATE TABLE employee_tbl (employee_id INTEGER) creates a table with a single column of type INTEGER and without any constraint. If you want to ensure that the employee ID cannot have duplicates, append the UNIQUE constraint to the column definition: CREATE TABLE employee_tbl (employee_id INTEGER UNIQUE).

- With DEFAULT, you can set the value to be stored in a field when you insert a new row. For example, the column definition employee_dept VARCHAR(64) DEFAULT '' sets the department to an empty string (without the DEFAULT element, the field is set to NULL). The distinction between an empty string and NULL is important when working with Java and JSP, because you can rest assured that a variable containing an unforeseen NULL will sooner or later cause a runtime exception. To avoid setting a field to NULL by mistake, append NOT NULL to a column definition. This will ensure that you get an error when you insert the row and not later when you hit the unexpected NULL. It will make debugging your code easier.

- The column constraints UNIQUE and PRIMARY KEY ensure that the values stored in that column are unique within the table. You can specify the PRIMARY KEY constraint only for one column of each table, while you can specify UNIQUE even for all columns of a table, if that is what you need.

- Use the column constraint REFERENCES to force consistency checks between tables. For example, if you store the list of departments in the table department_tbl, which includes the column dept_name, you could use REFERENCES to ensure that all new employee records will refer to existing departments. To achieve this result, when you create the employee table, define the employee's department column as follows: employee_dept VARCHAR(64) REFERENCES department_tbl (dept_name). This will make it impossible for the creator of the employee record to enter the name of a nonexisting department. Note that you must have defined the referenced columns with the UNIQUE or PRIMARY KEY constraints, because this constraint actually creates foreign keys. It wouldn't make sense to reference a column that allows duplicate values, because then you wouldn't know which row you would actually be referring to.

- The ON DELETE and ON UPDATE elements, which you can append to the REFERENCES column constraint, tell the DBMS what you want to happen when the referenced column (or columns) are deleted or updated. For example, if the department named 'new_product' is merged into 'development' or renamed to 'design', what should happen with the records of employees currently working in 'new_product'? You have four possibilities to choose from. With NO ACTION, you direct the DBMS to leave the employee record as it is. With SET NULL and SET DEFAULT, you choose to replace the name of the updated or deleted department with NULL or the default value, respectively. With CASCADE, you tell the DBMS to repeat for the referencing employee record what has happened with the referenced department record. That is, if the employee_dept column of the employee table has the ON UPDATE CASCADE constraint, you can change the department name in the department table and automatically get the same change in the employee table. Great stuff, but if you have the constraint ON DELETE CASCADE and remove a department from the department table, all the employee records of the employee table referencing that department will disappear. This is not necessarily what you want to happen. Therefore, you should be careful when applying these constraints.

- The CHECK column constraint only lets you create columns that satisfy the specified check condition. For example, to ensure that a bank account can only be opened with a minimum balance of $100, you could define a column named initial_balance with the following constraint: CHECK (initial_balance >= '100.00').

- The table constraints are similar to the column constraints, both in meaning and in syntax. However, there is one case in which you must use the table constraints: when you want to apply the UNIQUE or PRIMARY KEY constraints to a combination of columns rather than to a single one. For example, you might need to require that the combination of first and last name be unique within an employee table. You could achieve this result with the following constraint on the employee table: UNIQUE (last_name, first_name).

- The purpose of CONSTRAINT constraint_name is only to associate a unique name to a constraint. This then allows you to remove the constraint by updating the table with the DROP constraint_name element. As you never know whether you'll need to remove a constraint in the future, you should play it safe and name the constraints you apply. Otherwise, in order to remove the unnamed constraint, you would have to re-create the table (without the constraint) and then transfer the data from the original constrained table.

Caution Constraints are good to help maintain database integrity, but they reduce flexibility. What you initially considered unacceptable values might turn out to be just unlikely but perfectly valid. Therefore, only create the constraints that you're really sure about. With increasing experience, you'll develop a feel for what's best.

CREATE INDEX

CREATE INDEX creates an index for one or more columns in a table. You can use it to improve the speed of data access, in particular when the indexed columns appear in WHERE conditions. See Listing B-13 for a description of its format.

Listing B-13. *The SQL Statement CREATE INDEX*

```
CREATE [UNIQUE] [{ASC[ENDING] | DESC[ENDING]}] INDEX index_name
    ON tbl_name (col_name [, col_name ...])
    ;
```

For example, CREATE UNIQUE INDEX empl_x ON employee_tbl (last_name, first_name) creates an index in which each entry refers to a combination of two field values. Attempts to create employee records with an existing combination of first and last name will fail.

CREATE VIEW

CREATE VIEW lets you access data belonging to different tables as if each data item were part of a single table. Only a description of the view is stored in the database, so that no data is physically duplicated or moved. See Listing B-14 for a description of its format.

Listing B-14. The SQL Statement CREATE VIEW

```
CREATE VIEW view_name [(view_col_name [, view_col_name ...])]
    AS <select> [WITH CHECK OPTION];
    ;
<select> = A SELECT statement without ORDER BY elements
```

Here are some examples of CREATE VIEW:

- CREATE VIEW female_employees AS SELECT * FROM employee_tbl WHERE gender = 'female' creates a view with all female employees. The column names of the view are matched one by one with the column names of the table.

- CREATE VIEW female_names (last, first) AS SELECT last_name, first_name FROM employee_tbl WHERE gender = 'female' creates a similar view but only containing the name columns of the employee table rather than its full rows.

- CREATE VIEW phone_list AS SELECT last_name, first_name, dept_telephone, phone_extension FROM employee_tbl, department_tbl WHERE department = dept_no creates a view with columns from both the employee and the department tables. The columns of the view are named like the original columns, but it would have been possible to rename them by specifying a list of columns enclosed in parentheses after the view name. The WHERE condition is used to match the department numbers in the two tables so that the department telephone number can be included in the view. Note that views that join tables are read-only.

- When a view only refers to a single table, you can update the table by operating on the view rather than on the actual table. The WITH CHECK OPTION element prevents you from modifying the table in such a way that you could then no longer retrieve the modified rows. For example, if you create a view WITH CHECK OPTION containing all female employees, it won't allow you to use the view to enter a male employee or to change the gender of an employee. Obviously, you would still be able to do those operations by updating the employee table directly.

INSERT

INSERT stores one or more rows in an existing table or view. See Listing B-15 for a description of its format.

Listing B-15. The SQL Statement INSERT

```
INSERT INTO {tbl_name | view_name} [(col_name [, col_name ...])]
    {VALUES (<val> [, <val> ...]) | <select>};
    ;
<select> = A SELECT returning the values to be inserted into the new rows
```

You can use INSERT to create one row in a table (or a single-table view) from scratch or to create one or more rows by copying data from other tables, as shown in the following examples.

- INSERT INTO employee_tbl (employee_id, first_name, last_name) VALUES ('999', 'Joe', 'Bloke') creates a new row for the employee Joe Bloke. All the columns not listed after the table name are filled with their respective default values. You could omit the list of column names, but the values would be stored beginning from first column in the order in which the columns were created. Be sure that you get the correct order.

- INSERT INTO foreigners SELECT * from employee_tbl WHERE citizenship != 'USA' copies the full records of all employees who are not U.S. citizens to the table foreigners. Note that this is different from creating a view of foreign employees, because the records are actually duplicated and stored in a different table. With a view, you would only specify a different way of accessing the same data. Be extremely cautious when INTO and SELECT refer to the same table. You could create an endless insertion loop. It's best if you simply refrain from inserting rows by copying the data from rows that are in the same table.

DROP

DROP is the statement you use when you want to remove a database, a table, an index, or a view. See Listing B-16 for a description of their format.

Listing B-16. *The SQL DROP Statements*

```
DROP DATABASE;
DROP TABLE tbl_name;
DROP INDEX index_name;
DROP VIEW view_name;
```

DROP DATABASE removes the database you're connected to. The rest are pretty self-explanatory. Just one point: with DROP INDEX, you cannot eliminate the indexes that the DBMS automatically creates when you specify the UNIQUE, PRIMARY KEY, or FOREIGN KEY attribute for a column.

DELETE

DELETE removes one or more rows from an existing table or a view that is not read-only. See Listing B-17 for a description of its format.

Listing B-17. *The SQL Statement DELETE*

```
DELETE FROM {tbl_name | view_name} [WHERE <where_condition>];
```

ALTER TABLE

ALTER TABLE modifies the structure of an existing table. See Listing B-18 for a generalized description of its format.

Listing B-18. The SQL Statement ALTER TABLE

```
ALTER TABLE tbl_name <alter_tbl_op> [, <alter_tbl_op> ...];
<alter_tbl_op> = {
        ADD <col_def>
    |   ADD <tbl_constr>
    |   DROP col_name
    |   DROP CONSTRAINT constr_name
    |   <alter_col_def>
    }
<alter_col_def> = {
        ALTER [COLUMN] col_name SET DEFAULT <val>        /* MySQL, postgreSQL */
    |   ALTER [COLUMN] col_name DROP DEFAULT             /* MySQL, postgreSQL */
    |   CHANGE [COLUMN] col_name <col_def>               /* MySQL */
    |   MODIFY [COLUMN] <col_def>                        /* MySQL */
    |   ALTER [COLUMN] col_name { SET | DROP } NOT NULL  /* PostgreSQL */
    |   RENAME [COLUMN] col_name TO new_col_name         /* PostgreSQL */
    |   ALTER [COLUMN] col_name TO new_col_name          /* FirebirdSQL */
    |   ALTER [COLUMN] TYPE new_col_type                 /* FirebirdSQL */
    }
```

As you can see from Listing B-18, the DBMS vendors once more cannot agree on how you can modify columns.

The addition or removal of columns and table constraints is pretty straightforward. Refer to CREATE TABLE for a description of <col_def> and <tbl_constr>.

What you can do in terms of changing the definition of an existing column depends on which DBMS you've chosen for your application. Only MySQL gives you full flexibility in redefining the column with ALTER TABLE tbl_name CHANGE col_name <col_def>. Note that <col_def> must be complete, including a column name. If you don't want to change the name of a column, you can use its current name within <col_def>. In fact, besides being compatible with Oracle, the only reason for having MODIFY is that you don't need to type the same column name twice.

UPDATE

UPDATE modifies the content of one or more existing rows in a table (or single-table view). See Listing B-19 for a description of its format.

Listing B-19. The SQL Statement UPDATE

```
UPDATE {tbl_name | view_name} SET col_name = <val> [, col_name = <val> ...]
    [WHERE <where_condition>]
    ;
```

For example, use the statement UPDATE employee_tbl SET first_name = 'John' WHERE first_name = 'Jihn' to correct a typing error. Nothing could be simpler.

SET TRANSACTION and START TRANSACTION

The purpose of a transaction is to ensure that nobody else can "sneak in" and modify rows after you've read them but before you've updated them in the database. The DBMS can achieve this by locking the rows you read within a transaction until you commit your updates. As with other statements, different DBMSs behave differently. Listing B-20 shows what you need to do with MySQL and PostgreSQL, while Listing B-21 shows an example valid for FirebirdSQL.

Listing B-20. Start a Transaction with MySQL and PostgreSQL

```
SET TRANSACTION ISOLATION LEVEL READ COMMITTED;
START TRANSACTION;
```

Listing B-21. Start a Transaction with FirebirdSQL

```
SET TRANSACTION ISOLATION LEVEL READ COMMITTED;
```

As you can see, to start a transaction with MySQL and PostgreSQL, you have to execute a SET TRANSACTION and a START, while you only need to execute SET TRANSACTION without START when starting a transaction with FirebirdSQL. Note that all three DBMSs provide additional options, but I'm only showing a mode of operation that is common to them all.

You need to specify the ISOLATION LEVEL if you want to write portable code, because the three DBMSs have different defaults.

COMMIT and ROLLBACK

COMMIT confirms the updates you've performed since starting the current transaction and terminates it. ROLLBACK discards the updates and returns the database to its condition prior to the current transaction. Their syntax couldn't be simpler: COMMIT; and ROLLBACK;.

Reserved SQL Keywords

Table B-12. Reserved SQL Keywords

ABC	Keywords	
A	ADD	ALL
	ALLOCATE	ALTER
	AND	ANY
	ARE	ARRAY
	AS	ASENSITIVE
	ASYMMETRIC	AT
	ATOMIC	AUTHORIZATION
B	BEGIN	BETWEEN
	BIGINT	BINARY
	BLOB	BOOLEAN
	BOTH	BY

ABC Keywords

C	CALL	CALLED
	CASCADED	CASE
	CAST	CHAR
	CHARACTER	CHECK
	CLOB	CLOSE
	COLLATE	COLUMN
	COMMIT	CONNECT
	CONSTRAINT	CONTINUE
	CORRESPONDING	CREATE
	CROSS	CUBE
	CURRENT	CURRENT_DATE
	CURRENT_DEFAULT_TRANSFORM_GROUP	CURRENT_PATH
	CURRENT_ROLE	CURRENT_TIME
	CURRENT_TIMESTAMP	CURRENT_TRANSFORM_GROUP_FOR_TYPE
	CURRENT_USER	CURSOR
	CYCLE	
D	DATE	DAY
	DEALLOCATE	DEC
	DECIMAL	DECLARE
	DEFAULT	DELETE
	DEREF	DESCRIBE
	DETERMINISTIC	DISCONNECT
	DISTINCT	DOUBLE
	DROP	DYNAMIC
E	EACH	ELEMENT
	ELSE	END
	END-EXEC	ESCAPE
	EXCEPT	EXEC
	EXECUTE	EXISTS
	EXTERNAL	
F	FALSE	FETCH
	FILTER	FLOAT
	FOR	FOREIGN
	FREE	FROM
	FULL	FUNCTION
G	GET	GLOBAL
	GRANT	GROUP
	GROUPING	
H	HAVING	HOLD
	HOUR	

ABC Keywords

I	IDENTITY	IMMEDIATE
	IN	INDICATOR
	INNER	INOUT
	INPUT	INSENSITIVE
	INSERT	INT
	INTEGER	INTERSECT
	INTERVAL	INTO
	IS	ISOLATION
J	JOIN	
L	LANGUAGE	LARGE
	LATERAL	LEADING
	LEFT	LIKE
	LOCAL	LOCALTIME
	LOCALTIMESTAMP	
M	MATCH	MEMBER
	MERGE	METHOD
	MINUTE	MODIFIES
	MODULE	MONTH
	MULTISET	
N	NATIONAL	NATURAL
	NCHAR	NCLOB
	NEW	NO
	NONE	NOT
	NULL	NUMERIC
O	OF	OLD
	ON	ONLY
	OPEN	OR
	ORDER	OUT
	OUTER	OUTPUT
	OVER	OVERLAPS
P	PARAMETER	PARTITION
	PRECISION	PREPARE
	PRIMARY	PROCEDURE
R	RANGE	READS
	REAL	RECURSIVE
	REF	REFERENCES
	REFERENCING	RELEASE
	RETURN	RETURNS
	REVOKE	RIGHT
	ROLLBACK	ROLLUP
	ROW	ROWS

ABC	Keywords	
S	SAVEPOINT	SCROLL
	SEARCH	SECOND
	SELECT	SENSITIVE
	SESSION_USER	SET
	SIMILAR	SMALLINT
	SOME	SPECIFIC
	SPECIFICTYPE	SQL
	SQLEXCEPTION	SQLSTATE
	SQLWARNING	START
	STATIC	SUBMULTISET
	SYMMETRIC	SYSTEM
	SYSTEM_USER	
T	TABLE	THEN
	TIME	TIMESTAMP
	TIMEZONE_HOUR	TIMEZONE_MINUTE
	TO	TRAILING
	TRANSLATION	TREAT
	TRIGGER	TRUE
U	UNION	UNIQUE
	UNKNOWN	UNNEST
	UPDATE	USER
	USING	
V	VALUE	VALUES
	VARCHAR	VARYING
W	WHEN	WHENEVER
	WHERE	WINDOW
	WITH	WITHIN
	WITHOUT	
Y	YEAR	

APPENDIX C

Abbreviations and Acronyms

Here you'll find all the abbreviations and acronyms used in this book, even if some are pretty obvious!

ACID	Atomicity, Consistency, Isolation, Durability, the properties of SQL transactions
AD	Anno Domini, the year of the Lord
Ajax	Asynchronous JavaScript and XML
AJP	Apache JServ Protocol
AMD	Advanced Micro Devices, a semiconductor manufacturer
ANSI	American National Standards Institute
API	Application Programming Interface
APR	Apache Portable Runtime
ARIN	American Registry for Internet Numbers
ASF	Apache Software Foundation
BC	Before Christ
BCE	Before Common Era, equivalent to BC but non-religious
BCP	Best Current Practice, an Internet specification
BLOB	Binary LOB
CA	Certification Authority
CE	Common Era, equivalent to AD but non-religious
CLI	Command-Line Interface, interaction via the keyboard
CLOB	Character LOB
CRUD	Create, Retrieve, Update, and Delete, the operations supported by a DBMS
CSS	Cascading Style Sheets
DAO	Data Access Object, a J2EE pattern
DBMS	DataBase Management System

DCL	Data Control Language, SQL grant, revoke, ...
DDL	Data Definition Language, SQL create, alter, drop, rename, ...
DML	Data Manipulation Language, SQL select, insert, update, delete, ...
DNS	Domain Name System / Domain Name Server
DOM	Document Object Model
DOS	Disk Operating System, a relic from when hard disks were a novelty
DTD	Document Type Definition
DVD	Digital Versatile Disk, originally meaning Digital Video Disk
EE	Enterprise Edition
EL	The JSP Expression Language
FTP	File Transfer Protocol
GB	GigaBytes = 1 073 741 824 bytes of computer memory or one billion bytes of computer storage
GHz	GigaHertz = one million cycles per second, a measure of frequency
GNU	GNU is Not Unix, the bulk of Linux (which should be called GNU/Linux)
GUI	Graphical User Interface, interaction via mouse, graphic tablet, or touch screen
HTML	HyperText Markup Language, the language used to write web pages
HTTP	Hypertext Transfer Protocol, the protocol to request and communicate web pages
HTTPS	HTTP Secure
IANA	Internet Assigned Numbers Authority
IDE	Integrated Development Environment
IEC	International Electrotechnical Commission
IP	Internet Protocol
IPv6	IP version 6, with 128-bit addressing
ISO	International Organization for Standardization
ISOC	Internet SOCiety
ISP	Internet Service Provider
ITU-T	International Telecommunication Union - Telecommunication Standardization Sector
J2EE	Java 2 Enterprise Edition, now superseded by release 6
JAR	Java ARchive
JAXP	Java API for XML Processing
JCP	Java Community Process
JDBC	Java DataBase Connector, to access a database from Java

JDK	Java Development Kit, software package necessary to develop Java code
JEE	Java Enterprise Edition
JNDI	Java Naming and Directory Interface
JRE	Java Runtime Environment, software package necessary to execute Java bytecode
JSE	Java Standard Edition
JSF	JavaServer Faces
JSP	JavaServer Pages
JSR	Java Specification Request
JSSE	Java Secure Socket Extension
JSTL	JSP Standard Tag Library
JVM	Java Virtual Machine
LDAP	Lightweight Directory Access Protocol
LOB	Large OBject, an SQL data type to store blocks of data
MB	MegaBytes = 1 048 576 bytes of computer memory or one million bytes of computer storage
MS	Microsoft
MSI	Microsoft Windows Installer
MVC	Model-View-Controller application architecture
ODBC	Open DataBase Connectivity
OO	Object Oriented
OS	Operating System, software pre-installed on a computer to make available its functions
PC	Personal Computer, a desktop or laptop running a version of the MS Windows OS
PDF	Portable Document Format, the de-facto standard for posting documents onto the Web
PEM	Privacy Enhanced Mail, the file extension for X.509 certificates
PHP	Hypertext PreProcessor
POM	Project Object Model
RFC	Request For Comments, an Internet technical specification document
RI	Reference Implementation
SAX	Simple API for XML
SGML	Standard Generalized Markup Language
SP	Service Pack, a set of several software updates released as a single package
SQL	Structured Query Language, to work with databases. Sometimes pronounced as "Sequel".
SSL	Secure Socket Layer

STD	STandarD protocol, an Internet technical specification
TCL	Transaction Control, SQL commit, rollback, ...
TCP	Transmission Control Protocol
TLD	Tag Library Descriptor
TLS	Transport Layer Security
UAC	User Account Control, a protection mechanism of files
UCS	Universal Character Set
UDP	User Datagram Protocol
UEL	Unified Expression Language, unified across JSP and JSF
UI	User Interface
URI	Uniform Resource Identifier, a string to identify a resource, more general than URL
URL	Uniform Resource Locator, a string to reference an Internet resource
UTF-8	UCS Transformation Format – 8 bits
W3C	WorldWide Web Consortium, the organization that standardizes HTML
WAR	Web ARchive
WHATWG	Web Hypertext Application Technology Working Group (the WHAT Working Group)
XHTML	HTML compliant with the XML standard
XML	Extensible Markup Language
xmlns	XML namespace
XSD	XML Schema Definition
XSL	Etensible Stylesheet Language
XSLT	Extensible Stylesheet Language Transformations
XNI	Xerces Native Interface

Index

CPSIA information can be obtained at www.ICGtesting.com
Printed in the USA
LVOW111705231012

304104LV00003B/3/P